Central Europe on the Threshold of the 21st Century

CGS Studies

Edited by

Ralph Schattkowsky and Miloš Řeznik

Volume 1

Central Europe on the Threshold of the 21st Century: Interdisciplinary Perspectives on Challenges in Politics and Society

Edited by

Lucyna Czechowska and Krzysztof Olszewski

CAMBRIDGE SCHOLARS PUBLISHING

Central Europe on the Threshold of the 21st Century:
Interdisciplinary Perspectives on Challenges in Politics and Society,
Edited by Lucyna Czechowska and Krzysztof Olszewski

Reviewed by:
Prof. Dr. Jaroslav Miller
Prof. Dr. Miloš Řeznik

This book first published 2012

Cambridge Scholars Publishing

12 Back Chapman Street, Newcastle upon Tyne, NE6 2XX, UK

British Library Cataloguing in Publication Data
A catalogue record for this book is available from the British Library

ISBN (10): 1-4438-4254-0, ISBN (13): 978-1-4438-4254-9

The publication has been financially supported by the
Visegrad Fund, City of Toruń and the Nicolaus Copernicus University in Toruń.

TABLE OF CONTENTS

INTRODUCTION

LUCYNA CZECHOWSKA AND KRZYSZTOF OLSZEWSKI

Significant changes have taken place in Central Europe since the end of the Cold War. The political, economic and social transformations of the countries freed from Soviet domination have changed them almost entirely. Since 1989, new countries have emerged on the map of the region; Lithuania, Estonia and Latvia, as well as Belarus and Ukraine. The German Democratic Republic ceased to exist in 1990, whereas the Republic of Moldova emerged as an independent state in 1991, and Czechoslovakia split into Slovakia and the Czech Republic in 1993.

In the first two decades after the collapse of the Soviet Union and the dissolution of the symbols of its dominance over Central Europe—the Warsaw Pact and the Council for Mutual Economic Assistance—a new geopolitical reality has come into being. NATO has become a new actor in the region, and in 1999 and 2004, ten Central European states became members of the alliance. In 2009, the accession of Croatia and Albania followed. Many of the new member states have had military involvement before and after joining NATO, with soldiers from Central Europe being deployed not only to Afghanistan and Iraq, but also to Bosnia and Herzegovina, Kosovo, Congo and Chad, to name only a few.

The European Union was the strongest political and economic force for the former Central European "People's Republics" as well as the Baltic states. The enlargement of the EU in 2004, in which eight countries of the region, as well as Cyprus and Malta, joined the community, was followed by the accession of Romania and Bulgaria three years later. The Western sphere of influence has moved eastwards, accepted by the societies of these countries.

On their way to Western structures, Central European countries initiated cooperation based on common goals and experience. Over the course of time, regional alliances have either maintained their purposes, like the Visegrád Group and the Council of the Baltic Sea States, or they have lost their *raison d'être* for most countries, like the Central European Free Trade Agreement and the Central European Initiative.

The region is still experiencing dynamic social changes. Migration, the search for identity, coming to terms with the past and re-establishing old institutions in public life are generally high on the agenda in many Central European countries. There have been also critical moments such as the Orange Revolution in Ukraine in 2004 or the Russian-Georgian war in 2008, which triggered reactions from the regional leaders.

This book is the first volume of Copernicus Graduate School Studies. Its aim is not to present all of the most important issues concerning Central Europe at the threshold of the twenty-first century, but rather to draw attention to chosen aspects of the regional reality. Some of the subjects may not seem to be vital but are certainly an interesting part of the political, economic or social landscape of the region, being in a continuous process of transformation.

The book consists of twenty-eight chapters gathered in seven parts. This arrangement intends to create a harmony between texts with a general approach, applicable to nearly all countries of the region, as well as chapters focusing on profound and at the same time narrow topics, characteristic of selected states.

In the first part, "Identity", crucial questions about the geographical and mental range of Central Europe are posed. It deals also with issues of the identity of selected nations.

The second part, "Central Europe in world politics", places the considered region in a wider context of contemporary international relations. It analyses the capabilities of the internal and external policy of governments in the postmodern era and complements the picture with examples of how Central European countries act in world politics.

The crisis of the eurozone and its effects on Central European states, the attitude of the USA towards the eastward enlargement of the community, the EU strategies in the region as well as the Slovenian presidency in the Council of the EU are the issues deliberated in the third part, "Central Europe in the European Union".

Part four deals with selected "Bilateral Relations" between Central European countries, while the authors of the fifth part, "Political and party systems", concentrates on trends which are characteristic for the whole region; e.g. strengthening the role of the national parliaments, as well as on profound case studies such as the crisis of Moldavia's political system.

The sixth part is focused on selected "Economic and Social Problems" of Central European states, dealing with barriers to economic growth of EU member states. An analysis of the side effects of transformation in particular states is made, with reference to migrations, imbalanced process of mass privatization, poverty etc.

The seventh and last part of the book, “Religious and Ethical Issues”, regards interesting aspects of non-Catholic churches and non-standard instruments of democracy in selected countries of Central Europe.

We hope that the reader will find this book a useful source of knowledge as we believe that Central Europe is still an “undiscovered island on changeable waters” of contemporary international relations.

PART ONE

IDENTITY ISSUES

CHAPTER ONE

MARTYRDOM AND COMMUNITY? CENTRAL-EUROPEAN IDENTITY AND POST-TOTALITARIAN TRAUMA

PATRYK WAWRZYŃSKI

Over the last hundred years, three processes have influenced the political understanding of Central Europe: World War I and the Treaty of Versailles, World War II and the Yalta-Potsdam deal, and the 2004–2007 enlargement of the European Union. The first gave Central European nations a formal opportunity to act as a causative entity in international relations. For two decades, Central Europe obtained formal frameworks which made it possible to define itself as a region. The second process established a new order and redefined the demographic and political landscape of Central Europe. The third restored the status of self-reliance to those nations and enabled them to fulfil their aspirations of participation in Western structures.

While the Treaty of Versailles constructed political frameworks, the democratization as well as the EU and NATO enlargement deconstructed the identity of Central Europe as a region. A broad approval of the aspirations of political elites as well as the implementation of Western standards in economy, political systems and civil society have invalidated a need for new frameworks of Central-European identity. After 2004, the question of the necessity of considering the presence of Central Europe in international relations, and if it is not more convenient to refer all present-day political divisions on the continent to the European Union, remains unanswered.

In the period between 1989 (the "Autumn of Nations" and the fall of communism) and 2004 (the enlargement of the EU) it became reasonable to believe that Central European identity was not merely a temporary phenomenon. The idea of Central Europe seemed to be an attractive alternative to the post-Cold War cultural landscape of the continent. Cooperation of the countries of the Visegrád Group (the V4) turned out to be a requirement of the historical moment. However, most notable was that regional collaboration became less important than the attempts to realize national interests within the EU.

Today, eight years after the enlargement, it is essential to ask about the future of the Central European identity. Most important European processes—the creation of the eurozone, the economic and financial crisis, the quest for a new EU model and Transatlantic security issues—have taken place without a common policy for the whole region. Thus, the present-day political agenda may not be a proper field in which to seek an answer to the question about Central European identity. Culture and the collective remembrance of the past might be preferable for constructing a suitable and actual definition of Central Europe as a subdivision of the continent, different both from the West (the "Free World" during the Cold War) and the East (the Russian Federation and states under its direct influence).

This chapter presents a theoretical approach to the Central European identity, a model based on historical experience and the cultural constitution of the state's identity. As a social constructivist, the author suggests understanding identity as a variable phenomenon that co-constitutes state policy and interlinks convictions and expectations. It is assumed that considering Central European identity as a desire to be Western identity is an underestimation of this phenomenon. Therefore, finding a new definition is the intended result of this chapter.

Landscape of Political Changes

Through a historical perspective, the concept of Central Europe is directly connected with a German vision of the continent's subdivisions and a presumed sphere of German dominance. The idea of *Mitteleuropa* was not just a vision of delimitation of regional borders, it was a political agenda, an instrument of hegemony, that if realized could position Bismarck's Germany as the most important European state.[1] Until the Treaty of Versailles, *Mitteleuropa* had been the most appropriate answer to the question about Central Europe. However, the new order after World War I constructed a political landscape of Europe in which Germany was incapable of dominating.

---

[1] J. Brachtefeld, *Mitteleuropa and German Politics, 1848 to the Present*, (London: St. Martin's Press, 1996), 26–30. See also B. Stråth, *Mitteleuropa. From List to Naumann*, "European Journal of Social Theory" 11 (2) (2008), 171–183.

After the Treaty of Versailles, the clearest definition of Central Europe included those states founded (or re-founded) on territories of three fallen empires: Austro-Hungary, Germany and Russia. Piotr Eberhardt has suggested an even simpler conception, describing Central Europe as "everything" between Germany and Russia, those states being borders of Western and Eastern subdivisions.[2]

In the interwar period, Central-European identity was not an important factor in state policy and did not influence international relations. Due to the egoism of states during the Great Depression, as well as the failure of the League of Nations and the concept of multilateral cooperation, regional initiatives were found lacking. Moreover, there were antagonisms and conflicts among newly-established states (e.g. between Poland and Czechoslovakia, Poland and Lithuania, Hungary and Romania, Hungary and Czechoslovakia or Bulgaria and Romania). Despite these unfavorable conditions, some symptoms of regional cooperation appeared, mostly as a result of regional superpower pressure and the Bolshevik danger emanating from Russia.

Even if there had been a possibility to create a Central-European identity in the interwar period, the rise of the Nazis in Germany changed the political landscape of the continent. The return of German expansionism and its militarist revisionism invalidated the concept of Central Europe and re-awakened the idea of *Mitteleuropa*. The *Anschluss* of Austria and the Munich Agreement in 1938, as well as the occupation of Czechoslovakia and the outbreak of the German-Polish War in 1939, completely changed the political status of the region. Central Europe ceased to be a subject and started to be an object of international relations.[3]

Nazi war triumphs and a secret protocol signed with the Soviet Union dividing Central Europe into two zones of influences led to a diffusion of totalitarian regimes and an escalation of violence and repression. Central Europe, especially Poland, became the main area of Shoah.[4] The policy of the Nazis, the annihilation of "non-Aryan races" and the acquisition of

---

[2] P. Eberhardt, *Między Rosją a Niemcami: przemiany narodowościowe w Europie Środkowo-Wschodniej w XX wieku*, (Warszawa: Wydawnictwo Naukowe PWN, 1996).

[3] A. M. Cienciala, *The Nazi-Soviet Pact of August 23, 1939: When Did Stalin Decide to Align with Hitler, and Was Poland the Culprit?*, in *Ideology, Politics and Diplomacy in East Central Europe*, edited by M. B. Biskupski, (Rochester: University of Rochester Press, 2003), 147–226.

[4] W. Laqueur, *In Place of a Preface*, in W. Laqueur, J. T. Baumel (eds.), *The Holocaust Encyclopedia*, (New Haven–London: Yale University Press, 2001), XIII–XIX.

territories for German colonists, had horrific results and destroyed a regional mosaic of nations and ethnic groups. It also led to an economic exploration and a total breakdown of the development potential of the region. Permanent demographic changes completed the immense devastation of Central Europe.

The end of World War II did not restore the political *status quo ante bellum*. Central Europe remained as an object of international relations, and as "spoils of war" it passed into the Soviet post-war sphere of influence. In fact, the promised free elections were forged in order to legitimize Soviet-enforced communist authorities. The region found itself under total Stalinist rule and was deprived of the possibility of acting as a causative entity in international relations for almost half a century. The vision of a dominated *Mitteleuropa* was realised, but the dominant force was not Germany. What is more, even Germany was divided and partially found itself as a sphere of external dominance.

Given that the Treaty of Versailles had excluded Germany from Central Europe, the agreements in Yalta and Potsdam (partially) restored its status as a Central European country. However, an interesting question remains: did only East Germany or both German states belong to Central Europe? Another question concerns the status of post-war Austria, which was also initially divided.

Despite the fact that post-war Central Europe was a variation of the idea of a dominated *Mitteleuropa*, the notion is not unequivocal. The Soviet sphere of influence in Central Europe included territories incorporated into the USSR—the Baltic states, the western territories of Belarus and Ukraine, Moldova and the Kaliningrad Oblast (a part of East Prussia)—as well as the formally independent countries Poland, Czechoslovakia, East Germany (initially as the Soviet occupation zone), Hungary, Romania, Bulgaria and, until 1948, Yugoslavia. Austria and West Germany, although they did not belong to the Soviet sphere of influence, were an object of allied powers' decisions and they were partially devoid of the right to self-determination. However, they did not acquire a Central European identity. Therefore, it would be an exaggeration to state that Austria and West Germany were part of the region during the Cold War. It can be assumed that their experience has created the potential to become Central European in the future, in case of a collapse of Soviet dominance. However, this assumption still remains a hypothesis.

Fig. 1.1. The political landscape of Europe in the 1980s

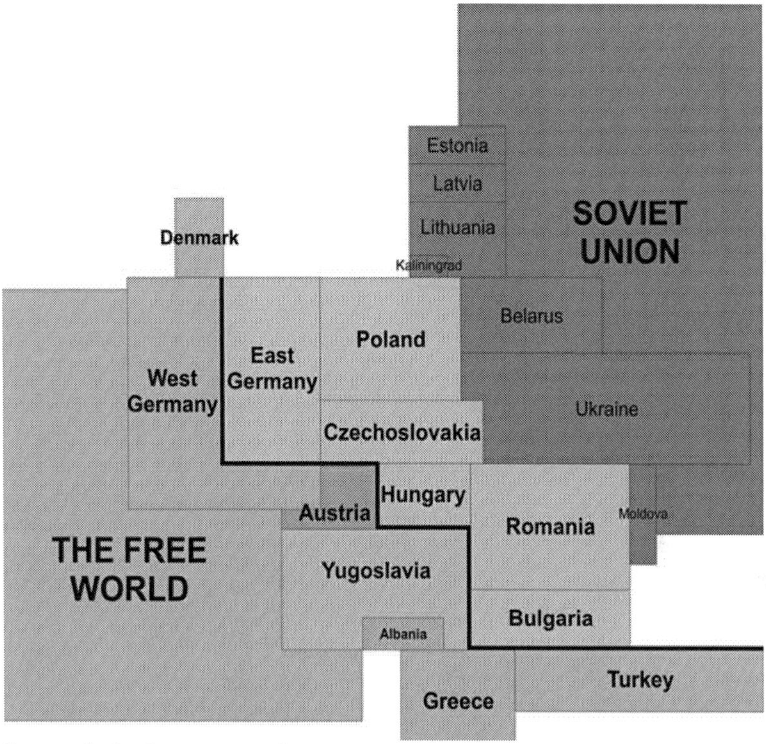

Source: Author's own research

In the simplified political landscape of Europe in the Cold War (see Fig. 1.1), subdivisions of the continent were not possible. The Iron Curtain divided Europe into the Western "Free World" and the Eastern "Soviet World". There was no space for states with an undefined status. Only three countries were able to position themselves between the two opposite blocs: Austria, Finland and Yugoslavia. Enver Hoxha's Albania realised a radical pro-Chinese vision of communism but it was possible only due to the unattractiveness of that state. Thus, a definition of Central Europe based on political divisions in the Cold War includes Austria and Yugoslavia as parts of the region. However, that definition cannot be accepted.

Fig. 1.2. The political landscape in Europe during the 1990s and 2000s

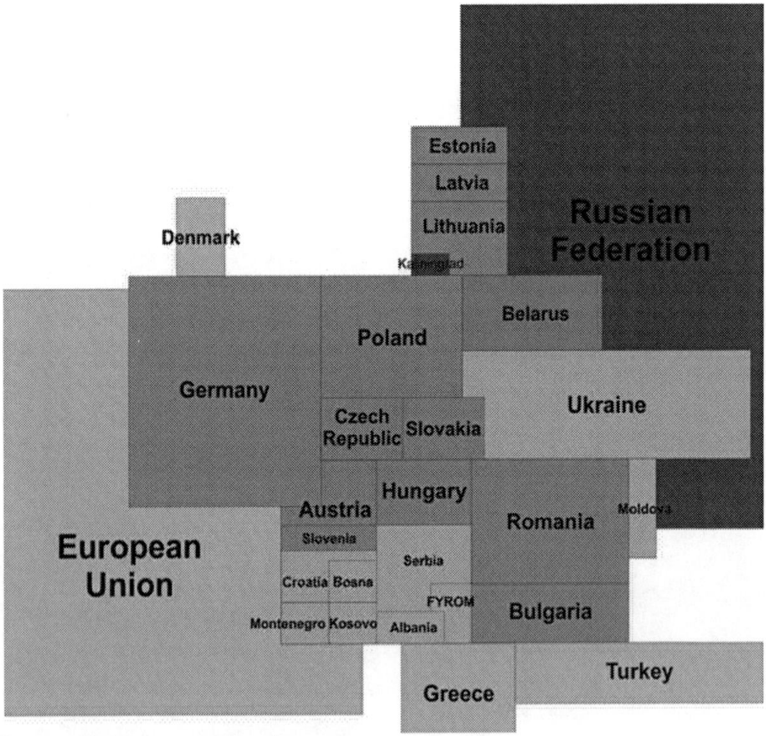

Source: Author's own research

Central-European identity in the Cold War might be best defined by considering the fact that the region was an object of competition between the superpowers and its status was somehow transitional. This hypothesis widens its range and includes West Germany along with all the formally independent states under the Soviet dominance. However, this vision can not be regarded as proper. Given the bipolar order in Europe and the antagonism between the blocs, a region integrating states from East and West was an illusion. Although the *Neue Ostpolitik* (New Eastern Policy) of the German chancellor Willy Brandt in the 1970s showed the potential of regional cooperation and a new regional identity, only a profound change of the political landscape, that took place in 1989, made those phenomena possible.

As has already been mentioned, the enlargement of the EU in 2004 was more crucial for understanding Central-European identity than the Autumn of Nations in 1989. The democratization of post-communist states was only a transitional time that led to a large implementation of Western standards in economy, politics and civil society. It can be assumed that a model for this process was the reunification of Germany, which in fact was an incorporation of East Germany and the transfer of the entire legal, political and social system.

The development of regional cooperation has been directly linked with the desire to belong to the West, and the cooperation lasted only as long as the full integration with the West was achieved. The Visegrád Group, the Central European Initiative (CEI) and the Central European Free Trade Agreement (CEFTA) were not instruments of a complex vision of regional integration. They were tools to make the accession to Western economical and political structures possible. The history of CEFTA is a perfect example. It was established as an economical "antechamber" for EU candidates and was supposed to be a practice in operating in a common market and dealing with problems that might occur after EU-accession. Currently, it plays that role for Albania, Moldova and six post-Yugoslav states (including Croatia, that will join the EU and leave CEFTA in 2012, and Kosovo, which is not universally recognized as an independent state).[5]

The lack of a profound regional cooperation and the privileged position of the EU as the main point of reference are evidence of the weakness of the political-based concept of Central European identity. Even less effective would be an attempt to construct a definition on the economic base. The debates on the EU fiscal pact proves that there is no unity even among Central-European EU-member states. The Czech Republic was the only one in the region to reject the project, although its authorities had been warned of the marginalization of their country in the EU.[6] It is significant that Prague did not find any allies in the region and all member states, except for the United Kingdom, accorded with the project. Similarly, during negotiations on the Lisbon Treaty, the Czech Republic and Poland, as the only Central European states, were against the change of the voting system in the EU Council, which would have strengthened the German position in the union.

The role of Germany and its identity in international relations is another issue concerning the definition of Central European identity. Given Germany's active support for the efforts of post-communist states to

---

[5] *Central European Free Trade Agreement—CEFTA 2006*, http://www.cefta.int/ (accessed March 5, 2012).

[6] N. Buckley, *Czech PM Sees Tensions Over EU Fiscal Pact*, "The Financial Times", http://www.ft.com/cms/s/0/6bf60fee-646c-11e1-b30e-00144feabdc0.html#axzz1oEizoWPb (accessed March 3, 2012).

become members of Western structures as well as its intense influence on the decomposition of Yugoslavia in the 1990s,[7] one can assume that after its reunification Germany has become again interested in the implementation of *Mitteleuropa*, and that Berlin had started to believe that Central Europe could be its sphere of economical and political influence. On the other hand, the reunified Germany can be dominant on the whole continent. As the development of European politics in the time of the global financial crisis shows, Germany, which has been interested in restoring *Mitteleuropa* since 1989, is currently able to widen its scope of dominance to the eurozone *en masse*.

Nowadays, after the great enlargement of the EU and the adoption of the euro by five presumably Central European states (Austria, Estonia, Germany, Slovakia and Slovenia), a definition of Central European identity based on economy or politics is not possible. Economical or political factors show that there is no cognitive need to subdivide Europe in a more complex way than the classic distinction between East and West. Thus, the question re-emerges: is it necessary to research Central European identity?

To understand the political landscape of Europe, it is still necessary to construct the concept of Central European identity. A definition might be possible provided that one uses different methods concentrating on other fields of the social construction of identity. The definition might not be just a result of elimination of particular states from the East and West.

The search for a theoretical groundwork may result in a question about Europe's attitude towards the United States' security policy during the presidency of George W. Bush. In February 2003, French President Jacques Chirac, commenting on the support of Central European states for the US military operation in Iraq, said that the political role of "New Europe" is to follow Western authorities and to implement their visions in the Transatlantic field. Chirac's statement may be considered to be the Western understanding of the role of Central Europe.[8]

---

[7] M. Waldenberg, *Rozbicie Jugosławii: jugosłowiańskie lustro międzynarodowej polityki*, (Warszawa: Wydawnictwo Naukowe Scholar, 2005).

[8] I. Traynor, I. Black, *Eastern Europe Dismayed at Chirac Snub*, "The Guardian", http://www.guardian.co.uk/world/2003/feb/19/iraq.france (accessed March 1, 2012).

Fig. 1.3. The deployment of troops to Iraq by European states in the 2000s

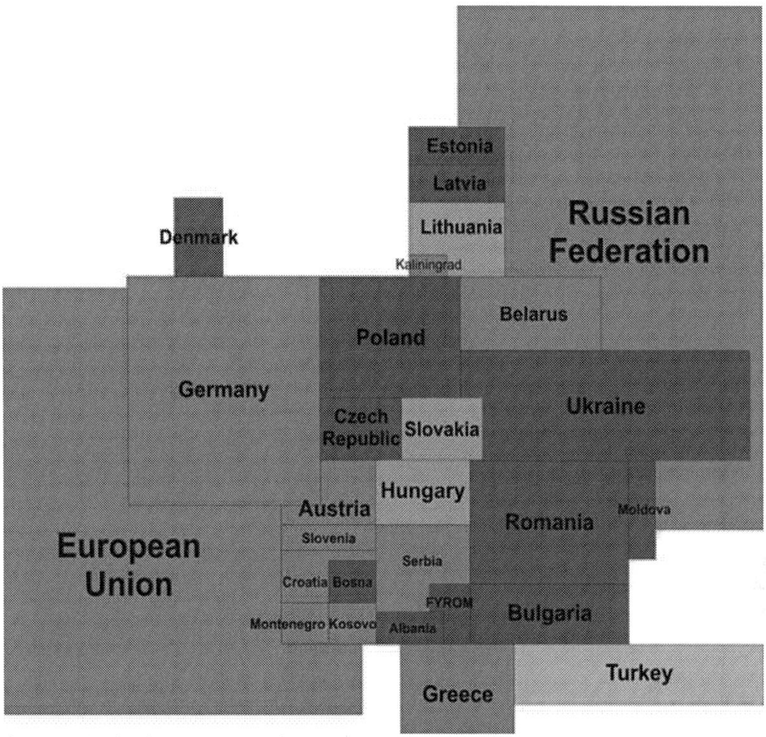

Source: Author's own research

Apparently, on the eve of the enlargement, Central Europe was still recognized as an object rather than a subject of international relations. This was the only moment after World War II that a Central European identity could be founded on a political basis. It was perhaps also an aim of Bush's US administration to form a pro-American bloc within Europe. The bloc would have been able to separate Western European states from Russia and to prevent their cooperation, which could be a menace to the concept of *Pax Americana*. Fig. 1.3. shows that this idea was partly implemented for a very short time. Central European states not only supported US foreign and security policy but also deployed their troops to Iraq, taking part in the war against Saddam Hussein's regime and the post-invasion occupation of the country. However, following Portugal and the Netherlands, Hungary withdrew its forces in March 2005, Lithuania in August 2007 and Slovakia in December 2007. In 2008, the mission was finished by Poland (in October), Bosnia and Herzegovina, Latvia, Macedonia (in November), Albania, Bulgaria, the Czech Republic, Moldova, Ukraine and Denmark (in December). Estonia and Romania withdrew their troops as late as in 2009. Nevertheless, the fact remains that, contrary to Germany and France, fourteen presumably Central European states took an active part in US military operations. That is a sign of the importance of the relations with the United States in defining the characteristics of the region.

Three Hypotheses Regarding Central European Identity

Three hypotheses may be useful in defining the groundwork of the concept of Central Europe. Their aim is to mark out borders of the region on the assumption that Central-European identity is not only a temporary identity of the countries that want to belong to the West.

Hypothesis 1: Central European states are only those countries lying geographically in the middle of the continent (according to Eberhardt, between Germany and Russia) that became member states of the EU and NATO after having accomplished the transition from communist to a democratic order, and implemented Western standards in economic, political and civil society. In this sense, Central Europe is the Czech Republic, Slovakia, Hungary, and Poland (as a heartland), Estonia, Latvia and Lithuania (as the Baltic sub-region), as well as Bulgaria, Romania, Slovenia and Croatia (as the Balkan sub-region).

Hypothesis 2: The previous hypothesis is too restricted. Due to historical factors, it is necessary to include Austria and Germany as part of the heartland. Both nations have maintained enduring and lasting relations with their Central European neighbours, influencing the vision of Germany's role in Europe. Moreover, a complete membership of Austria and Germany in the Western structures became possible after the collapse of communism, the result of the Autumn of Nations.

Hypothesis 3: Both previous definitions do not comply with the social phenomenon of identity and they do not indicate its relative durability. Thus, they cannot be accepted by the constructivist approach. Central European identity can be based on history but it cannot be limited to a historical fact due to its construction as a social phenomenon. Therefore, Central Europe is not only those states that have already implemented Western standards and joined Western organizations but also those geographically appropriate countries that emphasize their will to recognize themselves as subjects rather than objects of international relations. This definition includes post-Yugoslav states (Bosnia and Herzegovina,

Macedonia, Kosovo, Montenegro and Serbia), Albania, Moldova and Ukraine (if it continues its pro-European policy) as well as (potentially) Belarus.

Martyrdom and Community – a Concept of Central-European Identity

Verifying the above-mentioned hypotheses requires a theoretical model of regional identity that could be adequate in the case of Central Europe, and may be based on culture and memory.[9] The constituent of the Central European identity may be a post-totalitarian trauma,[10] referring to the totalitarian Nazi and Soviet regimes of the region.

Nazi rule led to *Shoah*, genocide, crimes against humanity, repression and economic exploitation. It destroyed the development potential of the region, caused ethnic changes and evoked a post-war trauma.[11] The hostilities inflicted unimaginable damages on Central European societies, making them victims of an evil that they were unable to stop. In the Nazi implementation of *Mitteleuropa*, Central Europe was a mere object of international relations. The concerned societies became fatalistic and incapable of counteracting the regional *Hecatomb*. A good example are the later excuses of German local authorities and servicemen. According to them, everybody only obeyed orders and did not support the Nazi policy. Similar excuses were used in the Polish debate about the Jedwabne massacre of July 1941.[12]

Communist rule preserved the changes brought about by the Nazis and caused new ones. Local attempts to restore subjectivity to Central European nations were suppressed either by the Soviet Union (in East Germany in 1953, in Hungary in 1956 and in Czechoslovakia in 1968) or by local communist regimes (in Poland in 1956, 1968, 1970, 1976 and 1980–81). All the opposition efforts in the USSR, especially in the Baltic States and Ukraine, were brutally pacified and punished. Moreover, the

---

[9] See: L. Khalili, *Heroes and Martyrs of Palestine. The Politics of National Commemoration*, (Cambridge–New York: Cambridge University Press, 2007), 4–7.

[10] Michael P. Jensen describes the theoretical model of the influence of martyrdom on identity. See M. P. Jensen, *Martyrdom and Identity: The Self on Trial*, (London–New York: T & T Clark International, 2010), 7–11.

[11] J. Withuis, A. Mooij (eds), *The Politics of War Trauma: The Aftermath of World War II in Eleven European Countries*, (Amsterdam: Aksant Academic Publishers, 2010).

[12] S. Kapralski, *The Jedwabne Village Green? The Memory and Counter-Memory of the Crime*, "History and Memory" 18 (1), (2006), 179–192.

centrally planned economy destroyed private initiative and exploited natural and social resources. The extermination and enforced emigration of traditional elites disturbed the continuity of local leadership. Annihilating liberal democratic movements and non-communist, anti-Nazi resistance forces led to an irreversible reduction of political potential and caused the ideological indolence of societies. The long rule of Soviet-enforced communist regime confirmed the fatalism and the conviction of being an object rather than a subject.

It is impossible to understand contemporary Central Europe without considering the post-totalitarian trauma that influenced state identities in the time of transition. It is also essential to point out that both the Nazi and the communist regime are the reason for a phenomenon:[13] the recognition of the region as an object of international relations as well as a field of competition and enforced domination. Although it might be an unpopular opinion, it is worth saying that Germany belongs to Central Europe because it complies with the conditions of participation in the regional identity. Germany is to be recognised as the "first victim of Nazi policy" because it experienced changes characteristic to Central Europe. After World War II it was treated as an object of international relations depending on decisions of superpowers.[14] Furthermore, both Brandt's *Neue Ostpolitik* in the 1970s and Helmut Kohl's support for post-communist countries in the 1990s were a result of German dealing with the post-totalitarian trauma and an attempt to be clear of guilt. The change in the vision of memory politics also shows this.[15]

To sum up, Central European identity may be conceived of as a variable social phenomenon constructed by three essential determinants: post-totalitarian trauma caused by both Nazi and Soviet political and economical dominance; the will to reestablish one's own subjectivity in international relations and the desire to self-define the state; the rejection of Eastern economic, political and social standards and implementation of Western ones. Crucial here is the first determinant referring to a common

---

[13] A. Weiss-Wendt, *Hostage of Politics:Raphael Lemkin on 'Soviet Genocide'*, "Journal of Genocide Research" 7 (4) (2005), 551–559.

[14] W. R. Smyser, *From Yalta to Berlin: The Cold War Struggle over Germany*, (New York: St. Martin's Press, 1999).

[15] S. Kattago, *Ambiguous Memory: The Nazi Past and German National Identity*, (Westport–London: Greenwood Press, 2001), 117–168. See also K. M. Zalewski, *The Berlin Republic. Evolution of Germany's Politics of Memory and German Patriotism*, (Warszawa: Ośrodek Studiów Wschodnich im. Marka Karpia, 2009), 37–60.

martyrdom. Central European societies are victims of totalitarian regimes and eyewitnesses of twentieth century genocide and crimes.

The three determinants of Central European identity mostly comply with Hypothesis 1. The only question concerns recognition of the dominance of communist Yugoslavia over Croatia and Slovenia as equivalent to the Soviet dominance over other countries. In fact, Josip Broz Tito's regime cannot be compared with Stalinist Soviet policy due to the scope of repression and damages. Crimes in Yugoslavia were committed on the authorities "own initiative", while the societies in the Soviet sphere of influence experienced a wave of enforced violence (this was probably one of the reasons why only Yugoslavia passed through a civil war after the collapse of communism). The subjectivity of states in the Cold War led to the suppression of self-determination. At the very beginning of the 1990s, those societies had a "sense of objectivity" and they were not convinced of their potential for self-definition.[16]

The countries of former Yugoslavia and Albania are a sub-division of Europe: the West Balkan region. Political changes in Slovenia and Croatia have shaped their identity in a Western (like Greece or Italy) rather than a Central European or Balkan sense. Moreover, Central Europe has not experienced the trauma of a civil war that, in turn, has deeply influenced the self-identification of post-Yugoslav nations.

The inclusion of Germany into Central Europe is to be reaffirmed. Chronologically, Germany was the first victim of the Nazi racist policy that caused irreversible changes in the local political and social landscape. Furthermore, Germany lost its subjectivity after World War II, and was divided into zones of occupation—in the eastern zone, a Soviet-enforced communist regime was installed.[17] The case of Germany shows how post-totalitarian trauma can be used to establish regional links, interdependence and influence. The reunified Germany was able to recognize itself as an advocate of post-communist states because it perceived itself as a part of the region in transition. Until the differences between western and eastern Germany are eliminated, the country cannot constitute its identity as purely Western. This conclusion leads to a paradox: the present-day Germany is simultaneously a Central-European and a Western state. The

[16] This consideration is proved by the international decision-making process on the future of Germany, the lack of immediate settlement of communist authorities (only partially in Romania), and the Red Army's troop deployment.

[17] See also the Soviet crimes against Russian Germans that are a part of German national memory: E. J. Schmaltz, S. D. Sinner, *'You will die under the ruins and snow': the Soviet repressions of Russian Germans as a case study of successful genocide*, "Journal of Genocide Research" 4 (3) (2002), 327–356.

current (at the time of writing) global financial crisis has seen Germany try to take advantage of this paradox by establishing a new common European identity instead of regional ones.

Verification of the second hypothesis partly leads to an answer to the question contained in the third hypothesis. There is no possibility of including the former-Yugoslav states and Albania in Central Europe. The cruelty of Hoxha's or Tito's regimes cannot be compared with Stalinist atrocities. The repression in Albania and Yugoslavia came from within the regime, while it came from the outside in the Soviet sphere of influence.

In the cases of Moldova and Ukraine there is one obstacle to their inclusion in Central Europe: they do not reject Eastern economic, political and social models and they do not implement Western standards. These states are in transition and it is hard to foresee the results. After the Orange Revolution it seemed that Ukraine would rapidly adopt the Western model and become an EU candidate. However, those expectations have not been fulfilled.

The question asked in the title of this chapter, concerning the connection between Central-European martyrdom and regional community, has to be answered in the negative. Post-totalitarian trauma does not constitute any martyrdom-based community but simultaneously constructs individual state identity and the character of the region. To establish a community it is necessary to share common interests. These are not present in contemporary Central Europe, especially after the enlargement of the EU. There are only common experiences, convictions and expectations. The political landscape is similar but the social architecture differs. A question fundamental for identity studies—"Why are we?"—requires an answer on two different levels. The first is the level of collective participation, the field of possible realizations of interests. The second is the level of memory and experience that forms the existence in the present form.

This theoretical concept of Central Europe comprises only the second-level answer. It is likely that Central European identity is to be conceived of as an empirical phenomenon constructed by common experiences and the will to re-establish one's own subjectivity in international relations. In a way, it is an identity of survivors and eyewitnesses of a mass crime. In a society, these type of individuals do not organize themselves but can understand each other in a way that non-survivors or non-witnesses cannot.

The author is a Ph.D. student at the Nicolaus Copernicus University in Toruń. In 2011, he was recognized as the Best Graduate of the University. Ha has received a scholarship from the Ministry of Education, Science and Culture of Meklemburg-Vorpommern.

Chapter Two

Central Europeans into Europeans: Common Identity and Individualization During the 1990s in the Central European States

Alexandra Tieanu

In 1984, referring to the nations living in Central Europe, the Hungarian writer György Konrád said:

> … we Hungarians, Czechs, and Poles huddle here on the western margin of the empire and on the eastern side of the Iron Curtain, with a cautious strategy of limited self-preservation and a troubled mind, because we don't want to identify with the East and we can't identify with the West.[1]

He continues by adding that "[w]e are by no means Western Europeans, but we don't belong to the East either, for the logic of empire doesn't attract us".[2] Talking about the reality that burdens the individual, Konrád says: "I am a Central European; here my attitudes are Western European, there they are Eastern European."[3] Konrád's perception was not singular among the Central-European intellectuals, politicians or individuals in general. In Czechoslovakia, Hungary and Poland, the idea of

* This study was possible due to an *Investing in people!* Ph.D. scholarship, project co-financed by the Sectorial Operational Program for Human Resources Development 2007–2013, Priority Axis 1. "Education and training in support for growth and development of a knowledge based society"; key area of intervention 1.5: Doctoral and post-doctoral programs in support of research; contract no: POSDRU/88/1.5/S/60185 – "Innovative Doctoral Studies in a Knowledge Based Society", Babeş-Bolyai University of Cluj-Napoca, Romania.

[1] G. Konrád, *Antipolitics*, (New York-London: Henry Holt & Co 1984), 91.

[2] Ibid., 124.

[3] Ibid., 128.

Central Europe came as a means to contest the official repressive communist regime during the 1970s and 1980s by constructing a discourse that denied the postwar geopolitical division of Europe between a free and democratic Western Europe and a Soviet-type monolithic Eastern Europe. After the fall of all these communist regimes, being Central European was seen as a way to quickly catch up with the rest of Western Europe, to project an idea of cultural and historical closeness that could guarantee an easier accession into the Euro-Atlantic structures. Being Central European, which for the nations located in this region meant feeling Western European but being perceived by the rest of Europe as Eastern Europeans, was the main dilemma of the 1990s. Therefore, people in Central Europe have, over the last three decades of the twentieth century, been through a series of shifts in their identity. From being Eastern Europeans, they constructed a separate identity and representation for themselves during the 1970s and 1980s as Central Europeans. Following the political changes of 1989, their Central Europeanness was no longer an advantage, but rather an obstacle for their Euro-Atlantic ambitions, so they had to present themselves as Europeans, as members of the European common family.

This chapter studies the manner in which the Central European states have gone from the Central Europeanness of the late 1980s to the Europeanness of the late 1990s in terms of defining themselves. The research will focus in a first instance on the construction of Central European representation during the 1980s and the manner in which it has influenced the relationship between alterity and identity in the region. After the fall of the communist regimes, the Central European discourse has adapted itself to the new geopolitical situation, transgressing from the intellectual circles to the political scene by acquiring new meanings in defining itself. For the period after 1990, the accent will be on the official discourses of the prominent politicians, who have used the discourse on Central Europe for political aims, trying to fulfil the Euro-Atlantic goals of each state. A case study illustrating this transformation in self-perception will start from the Polish journal *Gazeta Wyborcza*, a daily newspaper published in Warsaw. The change in terminology will be easily noticeable, as the term of "Central Europe" that predominated the first years of the 1990s was replaced gradually with "Europe" towards the late 1990s and early 2000s.

Becoming Central Europeans: Creating Central Europe during the 1980s

The idea of Central Europe has often dominated the intellectual and political thought of the past two centuries. It has been known under various names and each has had a different meaning. The representation of Central Europe changed not only its spatial delimitations, but also its political nuance depending on the viewpoint and on the historical period. Although there are usually four factors used to define a region (geographical, political, cultural and economic), geography rarely had much to do in the positioning of Central Europe, as it was decided by politics and culture. In the interwar period, several terms[4] were used to delineate a large or small region situated in the middle of the European continent. Germany preferred the term *Mitteleuropa* to delimitate its potential sphere of influence. The British and French concept of *Central Europe/Europe Centrale* was more concerned with creating a buffer-zone between Germany and Russia. The Czech term of *Central Europe/Střední Evropa*, the Hungarian *Danubian Region*, or even the Polish *Intermarium/Międzymorze* made reference to more or less the same small states that emerged after 1918 but had little success in the period.

After 1945, the installment of the Socialist regimes in the Eastern part of Europe meant the disappearance of whatever idea of Central Europe was previously advanced. The German *Mitteleuropa* reminded everyone of the horrors experienced during the war, while the other concepts of a Central Europe could not be accepted by the Soviet Union to denominate a region that was part of its communist empire. But at the end of the 1970s, a forgotten concept re-emerged as a mental protest against an oppressive

---

[4] See more on the different definitions and interpretations given to Central Europe in: P. M. R. Stirk, *Mitteleuropa: History and Prospects*, (Edinburgh: Edinburgh University Press, 1995); H. C. Meyer, *Mitteleuropa in German Political Geography*, "Annals of the Association of American Geographers" 36 (3) (1946), 178–194; J. Droz, *L'Europe Centrale. Evolution historique de l'Idée de "Mitteleuropa"*, (Paris: Payot 1960); , L. R. Johnson, *Central Europe: Enemies, Neighbors, Friends*, (New York-Oxford: Oxford University Press, 2002); J. Kłoczowski (ed.), *Europe Centrale entre l'Est et l'Ouest/ Central Europe between East and West,* (Lublin: Instytut Europy Środkowo-Wschodniej, 2005); E. Zamfirescu, *Mapping Central Europe*, (Hague: Netherlands Institute of International Relations, 1996); T. Garton Ash, *Mitteleuropa?*, "Daedalus" 119 (1) (1990), 1–21; K. A. Sinnhuber, *Central Europe-Mitteleuropa-Europe Centrale: An Analysis of a Geographical Term*, "Transactions and Papers" (Institute of British Geographers) 20 (1954), 15–39.

regime, representing the intellectuals' method of challenging the communist state after all open revolts had been crushed (in 1956 in Hungary, in 1968 in Czechoslovakia, and at different times in Poland). In these countries, the concept of "Central Europe" was used in its narrow version, referring solely to Czechoslovakia, Hungary, and Poland, as opposed to its broader version that included all the states between Germany and Russia that fell under Soviet influence after the war. The particularities of this narrow version of Central Europe were based not only on their similar revolts against communism, but also on cultural and historical common characteristics.[5] The specificity of this notion was that it had a profound cultural character as the political constraints did not permit anything else, and it came near to the idea of a "middle Europe", of "the lands between" a free Western Europe and a Soviet Eastern Europe.[6]

In 1983, the Czech author Milan Kundera published his essay *The Tragedy of Central Europe*, a work that gave maximum impulse to the debate on Europe and highlighted the particularities of the Central European region, its closeness to Europe, and its alterity to the Russian/Soviet civilization. According to Kundera:

> "Geographic Europe" (extending from the Atlantic to the Ural Mountains) was always divided into two halves which evolved separately: one tied to ancient Rome and the Catholic Church, the other anchored in Byzantium and the Orthodox Church. After 1945, the border between the two Europes shifted several hundred kilometers to the west, and several nations that had always considered themselves to be Western woke up to discover that they were now in the East.[7]

He continues, with what would be the expression that characterized Central Europe's destiny from 1945 until 1989:

---

[5] J. Szűcs, *Trei regiuni istorice* [*Three historical regions*], in I. Bibó, J. Szűcs, *Între Occident şi Răsărit [Between West and East]*, (Cluj-Bucureşti: Editura Kriterion, 2000); P. Hanák, *Central Europe: A Historical Region in Modern Times. A Contribution to the Debate about the Regions of Europe*, in G. Schöpflin, N. Wood (eds.), *In Search of Central Europe,* (Cambridge: Barnes and Noble, 1989), 57–69; P. S. Wandycz, *The Price of Freedom. A History of East Central Europe from the Middle Ages to the Present*, (London-New York: Routledge, 1992).

[6] J. Batt, *Introduction: Defining Central and Eastern Europe*, in S. White, J. Batt, P. G. Lewis (eds.), *Developments in Central and Eastern European Politics*, (Durham: Duke University Press, 2003), 9–11.

[7] M. Kundera, *The Tragedy of Central Europe*, "The New York Review of Books" 31 (1984), 33.

> As a result, three fundamental situations developed in Europe after the war: that of Western Europe, that of Eastern Europe, and, most complicated, that of the part of Europe situated geographically in the center—culturally in the West and politically in the East.[8]

Stressing the similarity to Europe and the desire to copy all that is European, Kundera's Central Europe finds its Other in Russia/the Soviet Union: "How could Central Europe not be horrified facing a Russia founded on the opposite principle: the smallest variety within the greatest space?"[9] Elsewhere, Kundera criticizes the "perfidious vocabulary that has transformed Central Europe into the East. Central Europe represents the destiny of the West, in concentrated form".[10]

Konrád also referred to Central Europe and to its peoples in his famous *Antipolitics. An Essay* stressing the "in-between-ness" of the region:

> … we Hungarians, Czechs, and Poles huddle here on the western margin of the empire and on the eastern side of the Iron Curtain, with a cautious strategy of self-preservation and a troubled mind, because we don't want to identify with the East and we can't identify with the West[11]

Referring not only to the geopolitical situation in Europe after the Second World War, Konrád also argues that the mentality and attitude of the Central Europeans are different from both Western and Eastern Europe: "It is here in East Central Europe that Eastern and Western culture collide; it's here that they intermingle."[12]

The Central European regional identity, like a national community, had to be constructed by means of discourse and symbols. A myth of Central Europe has therefore emerged, with subjective and nostalgic nuances, that haunted the underground intellectual debates behind the Iron Curtain. The Central Europeanness imagined in the 1980s was defined in the most favorable terms possible and had the character of a reality: in order to dismiss it, the opponents of this idea had to prove its falsity, since it was enough to affirm that Central Europe exists. Through this imagined reality, the dissident intellectuals aimed at rebuilding a consciousness that promoted

---

[8] Ibid.

[9] Ibid., 35.

[10] A. Finkelkraut, *Milan Kundera Interview*, "Cross Currents. A Yearbook of Central European Culture" 1 (1982), 29.

[11] G. Konrád, *Antipolitics*, 91.

[12] G. Konrád, *Letter from Budapest*, "Cross Currents. A Yearbook of Central European Culture" 1 (1982), 12.

values different from those of the communist regime.[13] The Central Europeans imagined their identity on four levels, but without making reference to the Socialist identity inspired by the new *Homo Sovieticus*. At the first level, there was the individual, as a unit of the community, in whose name the intellectuals and protesters fight for civil and political rights.[14] Secondly, there is the national level, since the nation was always considerably important for the Central European communities that lacked statehood for long periods of time. Above the nation, the communities from this region asserted from time to time their belonging to a common Central European identity. Lastly, the Central Europeans considered themselves as Europeans, as members of the European family. These four levels of identity have been quite obvious in the culture of Central Europe for the past two centuries, as the individual constantly related itself to the national or to the Central European and European community.

As a region in search of a distinct identity, Central Europe defined itself in opposition to Others. The most important Other for Central Europe during the 1980s was Russia/the Soviet Union, although some authors tend to differentiate between Tsarist and Soviet Russia.[15] Russia is considered the "Other", since Central Europe is "a drama of the West—a West that, kidnapped, displaced, and brainwashed, nevertheless insists on defending its identity"[16], and every process of identity-building needs to report itself to an external alterity in order to define itself.[17] The discursive construction of the relation between Central Europe and Russia was usually in Manichean terms of "we, the oppressed" and "them, the oppressors".[18] In cultural terms, it helped to consolidate a "sense of cultural distance"[19] between the two parts but as an imagined region, Central Europe did not refer only to its Russian/Soviet Other. There is also another relation of alterity, that with a similar Other: the Western European Other. In its connection to Europe, Central Europe was a

---

[13] G. Schöpflin, *Central Europe: Definitions Old and New*, in *In Search of Central Europe*, 18.

[14] V. Havel, *Viața în adevăr* [*Living in Truth*], (București: Editura Univers, 1997).

[15] M. Šimečka, *Another Civilization? An Other Civilization?* in *In Search of Central Europe,* 156–162.

[16] M. Kundera, *The Tragedy of Central Europe*, 34.

[17] I. B. Neumann, *Russia as Central Europe's Constituting Other*, "East Central Politics and Societies" 7 (2) (1993), 355; A. Hall, *The Constant:Russia,* in A. Bromke (ed.), *The Meaning and Uses of Polish History*, (New York: Columbia University Press, 1987), 209–216.

[18] Noticeable for example in Konrád's or Kundera's works.

[19] J. P. Arnason, *Introduction: Demarcating East Central Europe*, "European Journal of Social Theory" 8 (4) (2005), 388.

paradox: it sought to differentiate itself from the West, while at the same time it imitated it.[20] Historically, Central Europe as a region belonged to Europe and Western Europe, but it also distanced itself from it by means of its traditions and culture.[21] Western Europe was perceived as a superior civilization, an idealized utopia, an expression of a dynamic character as opposed to the rigidness and levelness of the East.[22] Towards the end of the 1980s, as a democratic wave swept through the region, Central Europe as a philosophical idea seemed to become a political project. In this moment, the Central European identity shifted in its characteristics and manner to perceive itself in relation to its Others, especially where Europe was concerned:

> It is characteristic that in their current searchings, Eastern Europeans are satisfied with the label "Central Europe" when it concerns their immediate socio-political preferences. But when philosophical aspirations, convictions, and attitudes towards history and politics come into play, Central Europe ceases to be the name of the new utopia. A name with a richer and somewhat more universal tradition is invoked instead. This name is "Europe".[23]

Central Europeans into Europeans: Common Identity and Individualization during the 1990s

After the fall of the communist regimes in 1989, the idea and concept of Central Europe was used not to suggest the distance from the Soviet Union/Russia but rather to stress closeness to Western Europe. The main attitude directing the political discourse and orientation in Central European states during the 1990s was that of "returning to Europe". In January 1990, the newly elected President of Czechoslovakia, Václav Havel, said: "We have the opportunity to transform Central Europe from a phenomenon that has so far been historical and spiritual into a phenomenon that is political."[24] But what was previously meant by Central

---

[20] C. G. Kiss, *Central European Writers about Central Europe: Introduction to a Non-Existent Book of Readings*, in *In Search of Central Europe*, 135.

[21] O. Halecki, *The Historical Role of Central-Eastern Europe*, "The ANNALS of the American Academy of Political and Social Science" 232 (1944), 9–18.

[22] B. Curyło, *Barbarians at the Gate ... The Ideas of Europe in Central-Eastern Europe*, "Central European Journal of International & Security Studies" 5 (1) (2011), 3.

[23] B. Torunczyk, *Kings and Spirits in the Eastern European Tales*, "Cross Currents. A Yearbook of Central European Currents" 7 (1988), 184.

[24] V. Havel, *To the Polish Sejm and Senate*, January 21, 1990,

Europe in terms of a community with shared culture and history was now only in a limited measure applicable to the meaning that Central Europeans gave to the term “Europe”. The “Europe” they wanted to be a part of was only in a small way that of the Western European culture, values, and traditions, but predominantly that of the Euro-Atlantic political, military and economic institutions. Nevertheless, the main objective of intellectual and political discourse focused on asserting their European values, contributions or historical connections, especially in the first years of the 1990s.[25]

An important shift in terms of self-perception in the Central European identity happened in the relationship this region had with its Others. As far as the Soviet Union, and later the Russian Federation, were concerned, the Central European states had a cautious attitude in the beginning, as they bore in mind the past experiences of their short-lived outbursts of sovereignty, but as they witnessed the decay and implosion of the Soviet Union they tried to assure the new Russian Federation that their efforts in obtaining member status in the Euro-Atlantic institutions were not directed against it,[26] nor did they want to jeopardize the European balance of military power. The new democracies in Central Europe sought to put considerable distance between their region and the Soviet Union, later the Russian Federation, by stressing the fact that Eastern Europe referred now only to the territories that belonged to the Soviet Empire and that they were successfully embarking on the road to democratic transition.[27] It was during these years that the concept of Central Europe was widely used as a tool of symbolic marginalization[28] where Eastern Europe was concerned,

---

http://old.hrad.cz/president/Havel/speeches/index_uk.html (accessed March 20, 2011).

[25] V. Havel, *New Year's Address to the Nation*, January 1, 1990, http://old.hrad.cz/president/Havel/speeches/1990/0101_uk.html (accessed March 20, 2011); J. Antall, *The Proposal to Dissolve the Soviet Military Bloc*, July 7, 1990, in G. Jeszenszky (ed.), *József Antall, Prime Minister of Hungary: A Historian in World Politics. Selected Speeches and Interviews*, (Budapest: József Antall Foundation, 2008), 250–254.

[26] J. Antall, *NATO: A Key to Stability in Europe* October 28, 1991, in *József Antall, Prime Minister of Hungary*, 272. See also T. Langsford, B. Tashev, *Old Europe, New Europe and the US*, (London: Ashgate, 2005), 240–243.

[27] An opinion expressed by T. Garton Ash, *Istoria prezentului. Eseuri, schiţe şi relatări din Europa anilor '90 [The History of the Present. Essays, drafts and reports from Europe of the 90s]*, (Iaşi: Polirom, 2002), 290–291 or G. Konrád, *Die Erweiterung der Mitte. Europa und Osteuropa am Ende des 20. Jahrhunderts*, (Vienna: Picus Verlag, 1999), 12–13.

[28] M. Janowski, C. Iordachi, B. Trencsényi, *Why Bother about Historical Regions? Debates over Central Europe in Hungary, Poland and Romania*, “East Central

being referred to as a space of authoritarian rule, socio-economic backwardness or political crises. Drawing on the studies made during the 1970s and 1980s, especially regarding socio-economic problems[29] or historical developments,[30] the trend already started in the intellectual debates was continued by re-inventing Eastern Europe[31] for the third time. Since the East[32] was different, being Central-European meant "less-Socialist"[33] and, therefore, more-European. In order to strengthen the difference between their countries and the rest of the former communist states, the Central Europeans tried to represent their successful transition to democracy and market-oriented economy as a "nearness"[34] to Europe, while the rest were still lagging behind. The exclusivist rhetoric[35] of Central Europe was seen during the 1990s especially in regard to South-Eastern Europe, or the Balkans. The tendency to marginalize the Balkans

---

Europe/ ECE" 32 (1–2) (2006), 18.

[29] See for example: I. T. Berend, G. Ránki, *Central Europe in the 19th and 20th centuries*, (Budapest: Akademiai Kiado, 1977); G. Konrád, I. Szelényi, *The Intellectuals on the Road to Class Power. A Sociological Study of the Role of the Intelligentsia in Socialism*, (New York-London: Harcourt, 1979).

[30] See for example P. S. Wandycz, *The Price of Freedom*; P. Hanák, *Central Europe: A Historical Region in Modern Times*.

[31] The expression "inventing Eastern Europe" belongs to Larry Wolff, who analysed how the area was constructed by means of mental representations during the eighteenth century by the Western Europeans. See: L. Wolff, *Inventing Eastern Europe. The Map of Civilization on the Mind of the Enlightenment*, (Stanford: Stanford University Press, 1994). The idea discussed in the present chapter, of re-inventing Eastern Europe for a third time during the 1990s is referred by Csaba Dupcsik, who speaks of a first invention of the East by Western Europeans during the eighteenth century, then by the Russians in the nineteenth century during the debate between Slavism and Europeanism, and finally during the 1980s and 1990s by the Central Europeans. C. Dupcsik, *Postcolonial Studies and the Inventing of Eastern Europe*, "East Central Europe/L'Europe du centre-Est: Eine wissenschaftliche Zeitschrift" 26 (1-2) (1990): 8–14.

[32] See an analysis on this in: C. Ingrao, *Ten Untaught Lessons About Central Europe: An Historical Perspective*, "Austrian Studies" 96 (3) (1996), 1–30.

[33] A. Miller, *Central Europe: A Tool for Historians or a Political Concept*, "European Review of History/Review Europeénne d'Histoire" 6 (1) (1999), 86–89.

[34] P. Chiantera-Stutte, *The Ambiguous Heritage of Mitteleuropa: The Resurfacing of Mitteleuropa as a Counter-image to the EU in Austrian Populism*, "Law and Critique" 14 (2003), 327.

[35] M. Todorova, *A Response to Iver Neumann's Forgetting the Central Europe of the 1980s*, in C. Lord (ed.), *Central Europe: Core or Periphery?*, (Copenhagen: Copenhagen Business School Press, 2000), 225–228. See also Todorova, *Imagining the Balkans*.

and differentiate was obvious in the Central European states towards the mid-1990s in the effort to underline their democratic and economic success in opposition to the economic disarray and ethnic conflict of the Balkans.

Another major shift that occurred in the Central European manner of self-perception was the gradual elimination of Central Europe from official discourse after the mid-1990s. Central Europe, as a term and idea, recalled past moments with different historical meanings and made reference to certain cultural traditions. Furthermore, after the efforts to reconstruct it as a mental representation during the 1980s, it implied also a transitional area, a space located geographically between the East and the West of the European continent and politically between democracy and totalitarianism. This understanding had now a rather pejorative nuance, since the Central Europeans strived to be accepted as equals among the rest of the Europeans. Referring to Europe, Havel says:

> Europe represents a common destiny, a common, complex history, common values, and a common culture and way of life. More than that, it is also, in a sense, a region characterized by particular forms of behavior, a particular quality of will, a particular understanding of responsibility.[36]

In the quest to surpass the terminology of Central Europe as a community of states with cultural traditions and historical ties, the Central Europeans were pleased when they were referred to as "the Visegrád Group" (a regional entity created by Hungary, Poland and Czechoslovakia in 1994) or as "CEFTA" (Central European Free Trade Agreement), as these meant that they were perceived in terms of their regional political cooperation or economic success. Representing themselves as Visegrád states or as CEFTA member states, they were proving their ability to cooperate and reform in order to accede to the Euro-Atlantic structures. The aim was now to shift Europe's symbolic boundaries[37] behind them, thus including them in the ranks of the developed countries and excluding the ones that still experience problems.

We have mentioned the four levels of self-perception among the Central Europeans. Taking into account the shifts that occurred after 1990, the third level, that of the Central European identity, was minimized in

[36] V. Havel, *A Hope for Europe*, "New York Review of Books", June 20, 1996, http://www.nybooks.com/articles/archives/1996/jun/20/the-hope-for-europe/?pagination=false (accessed December 10, 2011).

[37] P. Sztompka, *From East Europeans to Europeans: Shifting Collective Identities and Symbolic Boundaries in the New Europe*, "European Review" 12 (4) (2004), 489–490.

order to accommodate the new political goals of the state. This is obvious if we choose a case study, that of the articles that appeared in *Gazeta Wyborcza*[38], a major Polish newspaper. During the years after 1989, the predominant term used to refer to themselves was that of "Central Europe", due to the legacy of dissident intellectual discourse. As the idea passed into the political realm, especially after the creation of the "Višegrád Triangle/Group", the expression Višegrád became the symbol of delineating the region between 1991 and 1994. After 1994, as the Visegrád Group was showing signs of failure and the politicians were starting to affirm individual paths towards the European institutions for their countries, the terminology referring to Europe became more predominant. The concept of "Central Europe" remained in use, though, but with a dual definition: it denominated both the four countries that created Visegrád and CEFTA and all of the former communist states. The terminology had to be understood mainly as comprising the European Union, as proof that public discourse was also oriented towards the official national policy of each state.

However, despite building the Central European identity during the 1980s focusing on cultural and historical common traits and then transferring them into political and economic cooperation in the early 1990s, the Central European states soon began to compete with each other in what the Euro-Atlantic accession was concerned with. Even though "[a]ll the states in the region want to lose the term 'Central' as soon as possible and integrate into Western Europe"[39], it became obvious that they had more chances if they support[40] their cause alone, rather than jointly. Although during the previous years most of the declarations supported common efforts towards Euro-Atlantic integration, starting in 1994 there was an increased occurrence of the individualistic discourse on the part of all four states.[41] Good relations in the region are nevertheless a prerequisite for European security[42] and advancement in the negotiations

[38] "Gazeta Wyborcza", 1989–1998.

[39] J. Rupnik, *Europa środka*, "Gazeta Wyborcza", May 6, 1994.

[40] A. Jagodzinki, E. Kremien, *Wyszehrad w rozsypce*, "Gazeta Wyborcza", January 1, 1994, 3, 6. This article refers to the Czech Republic's and especially Prime Minister Václav Klaus' wishes to talk with NATO and the EU alone and not jointly within the frame of the Visegrád Group.

[41] See also R. Fawn (ed.), *Ideology and National Identity in Post-Communist Foreign Policies*, (London-Portland: Routledge, 2004).

[42] K. Skubiszewski, *Pozycja Polski w Europie: dziś i jutro*, "Gazeta Wyborcza", January 8–9, 1994.

with NATO and the EU, and therefore the meetings within the regional institutions, are never neglected.

Conclusions

After a considerable effort to represent themselves as Central Europeans in the context of the geopolitical constraints of the Cold War, the people of this region were willing to lose the attribute they had long desired for after 1989. Self-perception in the Central European states is, therefore, a result of the external circumstances of a certain period in time. The political dynamics in Europe have determined not only the relationships with their neighbours but also the manner in which the individual and the community perceive themselves.

Following the major shift in their collective identity during the 1980s, when the Eastern Europeans living in Czechoslovakia, Hungary, and Poland became Central Europeans, this process of regional identity-building proved very easily to deconstruct in the new political situation of the 1990s. Although the deconstruction of Central Europe was a gradual process, it went from Central Europeans to Visegrád states, then to CEFTA member states, and in the end to NATO and European Union member states in the timeframe of a decade. This allows for two observations to be made. Firstly, Central Europe as a cultural and historical idea proved to have a much more solid basis, since the debate on literature, culture and traditions continued during the 1990s and evoked a regional identity. Secondly, Central Europe as a political project proved to be a failure during these years, as it had no chances to succeed when rivaled by the much bigger project of the European community. Since becoming part of this larger Europe was the goal of each state, individual paths were destined to appear.

The author holds an MA in International Relations and European Policies, and a BA in History and International Relations. She is currently a PhD candidate in IR and European Studies at the Babeş-Bolyai University of Cluj-Napoca. She is affiliated to the Altiero Spinelli Center for the Study of European Governance. She is interested in European History, European Politics, the Idea of Central Europe and European Geopolitics.

CHAPTER THREE

SHARED MEMORY: THE SOURCES OF POLISH AND GERMAN PERCEPTIONS OF HISTORY AFTER SYSTEM TRANSFORMATIONS

KATARZYNA KĄCKA

The changes which occurred in Poland and Germany at the end of the 1980s and the beginning of the 1990s, together with the system and political transformation, led to economic, social and cultural transformations in both countries. Despite similar results, changes on both sides of the Oder and Lusatian Neisse Rivers took a different course. The transformation in Poland was complete, which, as a result, led to a search for new solutions in all areas of life. In Germany, on the other hand, the German Democratic Republic was absorbed by the Federal Republic of Germany, as a result of the so-called "reunification". So, in fact, changes meant that one country took over the principles of the other one.

Neighbourly relations between Poland and Germany are to a large extent determined by historical aspects, and this applies to virtually all levels of social life, from political relations to personal contacts. The system transformation in both countries also led to changes in the way the common past is perceived.

The mutual influence of Poles and Germans, due primarily to geographical and historical closeness, cannot be denied. Poles and Germans are connected by numerous historical events and similar fates, despite the fact that they fought against each other on numerous occasions. Polish and German cultures, though they are imprecise terms, continuously permeate one other. It cannot be different since a significant part of the areas currently situated in the territory of Poland used to belong to provinces of German states. Although the propaganda of the Polish People's Republic did everything to erase the memory of the German past of these areas, the

German character is still present and noticeable there. The theoretical concept of the mutual influence of both countries (*Beziehungsgeschichte*) was created in the second half of the twentieth century by Klaus Zernack, a German historian, one of the most eminent experts on the history of Eastern Europe. Changing the character of German research on Eastern European issues was his greatest merit. He succeeded in freeing it from the emphasis on the role of Germany in European history, and turned researchers' interest to Poland and Russia, among other things. He also expressed his skepticism of constructing national histories, considering them to be too limited and suggested extending the view of history to include, for example, the whole of or part of the continent. This position is very important for researching history of countries such as Germany, where the formation of the nation was "delayed". In his opinion, the notion of nation may not impose research limits, although its theoretical framework is one of many possibilities. This view is also represented by Moritz Csáky, a Viennese cultural expert, who rejects the assignation of exclusively national connotations to collective memory, identifying numerous places of remembrance with transnational character especially in Central Eastern Europe.[1] This position certainly works very well for the Polish-German neighbourhood. The main research question posed by Klaus Zernak regarding Polish-German relations was the following: "Isn't the persistence with which historical relations between Poles and Germans influences their current relations sufficient reason for considering the history of this mutual impact to be a *sui generis* factor?"[2] This question is still valid and it continues to inspire numerous scholars to look for new fields and methods of research which would "refresh" the way of thinking about Polish-German relations. As Ralph Schattkowsky claims, exploring history in order to describe it makes it possible to find such elements in it which best describe the evolution of a given phenomenon. All the more so that this search always involves "the awareness that it is impossible to present history in the form of total history (*histoire totale*)."[3]

---

[1] M. Csáky, *Das Gedächtnis der Städte. Kulturelle Verflechtungen: Wien und die urbanen Milieus in Zentraleuropa*, (Wien-Köln-Weimar: Böhlau Verlag, 2010).

[2] K. Zernak, *Das Jahrtausend deutsch-polnischer Beziehungsgeschichte als geschichtswissenschaftliches Problemfeld und Forschungsaufgabe*, in W. H. Fritze (ed.), *Grundfragen der geschichtlichen Beziehungen zwischen Deutschen, Polaben und Polen. Referate und Diskussionsbeiträge aus zwei wissenschaftlichen Tagungen*, (Berlin: Copress 1976), 5.

[3] R. Schattkowsky, *Społeczeństwo obywatelskie jako metoda i podejście w badaniach społecznych*, "Athenaeum. Polskie Studia Politologiczne" 31 (2011), 54.

The concept of second degree history created by Pierre Nora, a French researcher, is an interesting solution for political scientists, sociologists and historians undertaking the subject of Polish-German relations. It assumes moving away from writing exclusively political and event-related history, i.e. giving up the positivist model of historiography. In return, he suggests turning towards symbolic space, adding value to collective notions and pop-culture products. He also postulates the necessity of asking questions about memory, including collective memory and the role of memory in processes shaping collective identities. Thus, he sees a solution for contemporary history in the process of analysing the methods of "using" and assigning functions to the pasts for the current needs.[4]

When Pierre Nora's concept is used in practice, it may turn out that the example of Poland and Germany, a thousand-year-old history of relations between two neighbouring countries and societies, can combine research on the history of memory and the history of mutual relations.

Research on memory has been conducted on multiple platforms—sociological, cultural and political—for many years. Maurice Halwachs was its precursor, and coined the term "collective memory".[5] The results of his research conducted at the beginning of the twentieth century, which are still significant, affect the perception of this issue. However, the question of whether "collective memory should be regarded as the memory of a given group or memory in the group" was not answered by him: only Pierre Nora succeeded in answering it, deciding that there is no such thing as "memory of the group". Thus, he assigned memory to a specific society with its signs, gestures and symbols which are legible, recognizable and unambiguous for all of its members, and which they can also use for communication. This means that signs, symbols and rituals are somewhat material manifestations of collective memory. Pierre Nora also showed that the common approval of the concept of community memory completely changes the position of individuals in society. This particularly applies to the individual vs. group relations. So far, as he claimed: "Individuals had memory, communities had history."[6] The approach to collective memory by Barbara Szacka, Polish sociologist, is similar to this concept. In her opinion, this is a complex of notions from a group's past, all characters from this past and ways of remembering the past[7]. The

[4] P. Nora, *Pour une histoire au second degré*, "Le débat" 122 (2002), 24–31.

[5] M. Halwachs, *Społeczne ramy pamięci*, (Warszawa: Wydawnictwo Naukowe PWN, 2008).

[6] P. Nora, *Czas pamięci*, "Res Publica Nowa" 7 (2001), 41.

[7] B. Szacka, *Społeczna pamięć polskiej przeszłości narodowej w latach 1965–1988*, in B. Szacka, A. Sawisz (eds.), *Czas przeszły i pamięć społeczna*,

authors quoted above also agree that collective memory is always "burdened with the mark of the presence, of the collective thought of the group"[8]—it consists of elements referring to past events which are present in the current collective life.[9] It can be affected, among other things, by a set of ideas and norms developed by specific persons at specific times. In fact, apart from its visible manifestation in the form of signs, symbols and rituals, collective memory does not exist: "It is an artefact, a product produced anew in a discursive manner every day."[10] This opinion is perfectly depicted by the words of Italo Svevo, an Italian writer, from the beginning of the twentieth century:

> The past is still new. It keeps changing as life progresses. Its parts which appear to be forgotten reappear, while other, less important, disappear. The present time conducts the past like the members of an orchestra. It determines the use of specific tones. The part of memory intended for the one who will brighten or dim it reaches the present time.[11]

Therefore, memory is a set of elements which are a human product and they are of purely intellectual nature. They exist in a given group exclusively as intersubjective awareness. Thus, memory can also be constructed deliberately, a natural means of manipulation. This means that, in consequence, this is a specific product of various forms of political culture consisting of: a structure of symbolic space, ways of remembrance and historical politics. Undoubtedly, the current situation of a given society and state is one of the key factors shaping memory. Therefore, memory, as a specific product of the present time, subject to constant influences, often leads to tension between what is, what was and the way in which it functions in a society's imagination:

> collective memory, as any social phenomenon, has its history, it goes through 'cold' periods when it seems dormant and 'hot' periods when it wakes up and affects the surface of collective life, finds rich and diverse

---

(Warszawa: Uniwersytet Warszawski, 1990), 8.

[8] M. Król, *Wstęp do wydania polskiego*, in M. Halwachs, *Społeczne ramy pamięci*, (Warszawa: Wydawnictwo Naukowe PWN, 2008), XXV–XXVII.

[9] B. Szacka, *Historia i pamięć zbiorowa*, "Kultura i Społeczeństwo" 4 (2003), 4.

[10] M. Górny, H. H. Hahn, K. Kończal, R. Traba, *Wprowadzenie*, in R. Traba, H. H. Hahn (eds.), *Polsko-niemieckie miejsca pamięci*, Vol. 3: *Paralele*, (Warszawa: Wydawnictwo Naukowe Scholar, 2012), 11.

[11] Quoted from A. Wolff-Powęska, *Polacy – Niemcy. Kultura polityczna. Kultura pamięci*, (Poznań: Wydawnictwo Naukowe Instytutu Nauk Politycznych i Dziennikarstwa UAM, 2008), 42.

forms of expression, when it turns out to be a very significant expression of mentality.[12]

The process of Poland's systemic transformation and system changes which occurred after East Germany joined the Federal Republic of Germany took place, as all social processes do, with the participation of several generations. It is primarily their work and actions that shaped the events over the past few decades. Societies bearing the mark of totalitarian systems while building a new order were simultaneously looking for a new bond for their unity and identity. Their attitude towards the past was such a bond, among other things. Democratization processes are usually accompanied by a social crisis, which may at the same time be a crisis of remembering and forgetting. Transformations both in Poland and in Germany also provoked a clash between the social consciousnesses of different generations, taking place at the theoretical and practical levels. Thus, different and frequently extreme values and approaches were confronted in both countries. As a result, this dispute between the generations significantly affected the individual's axiological perception, the way of assessing current problems, the nation's history and the history of neighbourly relations.[13]

Changes to the political system induced the revision of the history of both countries. It was yet another point at which both Germans and Poles faced the necessity of looking back at their countries' history and the history of neighbourly relations. This process occurred in a parallel manner in both countries, despite the fact that the methods were not always the same. This gave rise to a stormy debate on remembrance (and also social forgetting). Events of the twentieth century proved to be the greatest challenge, especially World War II, in which both countries participated, although their roles were quite different. This happened for two reasons. Firstly, the unprecedented scale of war tragedy, and secondly (and this reason was far more prosaic) more recent events are more "easily" remembered, especially if their eyewitnesses are still alive. One of the questions which arose at the time, still valid today, was "what role will the past and the memory play in the new Polish-German relations?"

---

[12] B. Baczko, *Wyobrażenia społeczne. Szkice o nadziei i pamięci zbiorowej*, (Warszawa: Wydawnictwo Naukowe PWN, 1994), 201.

[13] R. Nazar, S. Popławski, *Transformacja i wartości. Aksjologiczne aspekty procesu transformacji w pokoleniowej perspektywie*, in W. Kaczoch, S. Popławski (eds.), *Transformacja i wartości. Aksjologiczne aspekty transformacji ustrojowej w Polsce*, (Zielona Góra: Oficyna Wydawnicza Uniwersytetu Zielonogórskiego, 1997), 132–133.

Unfortunately, the answer to this is ambiguous. Certainly, memory (and the policy connected with it) plays a significant role. However, this memory concerns the past of a specific state and requires internal solutions. Both countries developed their own strategies in this area. However, there exist some similarities between them, e.g. establishing institutions which deal with reviewing the past. Common past, on the other hand, appears in Polish and German relations, but seems to be a unilateral problem. Past events are usually recalled in Poland while solving current problems, but this is not always characterized by a good style. A disgraceful example of such behaviour involves comparing the construction of the pipeline from Russia to Germany under the Baltic Sea to the Ribbentrop-Molotov pact made by Radosław Sikorski, Polish Minister of Defence during the American-European summit in 2006: "We are particularly sensitive to agreements concluded over our heads. In the 20th century, we had Locarno, we had the Ribbentrop-Molotov pact. We do not want it to be repeated."[14] Fortunately, such events are incidental. It does not change the fact that our shared and difficult history often determines the behaviour of Polish politicians and affects contemporary decisions.

Considering the various approaches to historical issues, is it possible to find shared elements of memory in Poland and in Germany? And does the phenomenon of shared memory even exist? These questions are extremely difficult to answer, especially in view of the fact that memory in both countries has been shaped by different models of political culture. What is political culture then? There exist numerous definitions and interpretations of this phenomenon. For the needs of these considerations, the following interpretation may be adopted:

> values, attitudes and views, as well as the behaviour of citizens referring to the political world. These values are usually understood as fundamental, deeply rooted convictions and predispositions for actions referring to what is desirable for ourselves and for society and what should be valid.[15]

This definition makes it possible to analyse the notion in two dimensions. The first is the historical dimension, showing that all aspects contained in this notion stem from traditions, customs and cultural patterns of the individual societies. Thus, individual experience of individual

---

[14] B. Weglarczyk, *Gazowa zimna wojna*, "Gazeta Wyborcza", May 2, 2006.

[15] G. Meyer, *Kultura polityczna i demokratyzacja: podstawy, problemy i tezy*, in G. Meyer, S. Sulowski, W. Łukowski (eds.), *Kultura polityczna w Polsce i Niemczech. Wybrane problemy*, (Warszawa: ELIPSA, 2007), 11.

people and the historical experience of whole communities play an equally significant role here.

The second is the systemic dimension. It assumes that attitudes and political actions of citizens result from several interactions, e.g. with history, economy, politics and society. Therefore, what we call "political culture" is the effect of "permanent political socialization". It is manifested by the participation of persons as well as communities in assimilating values and opinions on politics and in using this knowledge in political activities. This process may also occur subconsciously, especially if socialization is controlled by the government, media, social groups and organizations. In consequence, political culture cannot be regarded as a constant phenomenon since it is subject to continuous influences and changes.[16]

The political cultures in Poland and in Germany were affected by various elements. An analysis of this phenomenon in the contemporary dimension cannot exclude the post-war history of both countries and the influence it has exerted after the transformation at the end of the 1980s and beginning of the 1990s. Undoubtedly, due to the different post-war political experience of Poles and Germans, it is difficult to apply the same system of notions here. This results from several broader problems. Firstly, after the end of World War II, there was no such thing as single German political culture. The reason for this is prosaic. As a result of decisions taken by the superpowers, two German states appeared on the map of Europe. They began to shape the politics of memory, building new standards of political culture independently of each other. Another significant factor which makes it difficult to compare both political cultures involves the existence of two, and previously three states in different political systems, which is also extremely important in the context of the systemic dimension of political culture and it strongly determines the shape of the individual categories of values.[17] Undoubtedly, it is necessary to show the legacy of the more than forty-year-old post-war history of both countries, to understand numerous aspects of the political culture of contemporary Poland and Germany. First of all, however, it is important to realize how the memory was shaped, what methods were used and, primarily, what marks it left in the memory of both societies.

---

16 M. R. Lepsius, *O kulturze politycznej w Niemczech*, (Poznań: Wydawnictwo Poznańskie, 2007), 12–13.

17 M. Zaborski, *Współczesne pomniki i miejsca pamięci w polskiej i niemieckiej kulturze politycznej*, (Toruń: Wydawnictwo Adam Marszałek, 2011), 32–33.

Germans are the only nation who experienced both type of dictatorships in the twentieth century. Additionally, the character of the contemporary German political culture was certainly affected by the division of the country, which had lasted almost half a century. It led, as M. Reiner Lepsius claims, to "the formation of very diverse political cultures".[18] The events of the previous century caused the countries to move away from the tradition of the German political culture rooted in the consciousness, although this happened in different ways. Undoubtedly, these discrepancies can still be seen today, and on numerous occasions they were an obstacle to the understanding between East and West Germany.

The journeys of the countries moving away from dictatorship after the war are marked in individual manners. Germany, Austria and Italy were affected by this problem to a similar extent after the end of World War II. The winning powers saw the possibility of the proper reconstruction of these countries in the democratization process, and this was favoured primarily by international conditions and democratic surroundings. It should be noted, however, that new system principles were imposed, especially in Germany. The establishment of the Federal Republic of West Germany and its subsequent inclusion in the North Atlantic Treaty and the European Economic Community enhanced the sense of security in West Germany. Political and economic stabilization were an additional factor stabilizing democratic transformations in this country.[19] The effort made in West Germany is undeniable. It took many years to overcome the non-democratic legacy and it occurred at two levels—the institutional and mental one.[20] In the political culture of West Germany, the category of the past was extremely strongly rooted. It was, first of all, a significant factor determining the direction of the policy implemented by the country. The reconciliation of the World War II past was the most important challenge of that period. Responsibility (and moral responsibility) for those events provoked politicians, regardless of the stand they represented, to make public declarations rejecting the war and considering the aspiration for peace to be the priority of the state's policy. A similar declaration was also made by Konrad Adenauer, the first German Chancellor.[21] Not only politicians, but also the entire society faced the problem of reconciling the

---

[18] M. R. Lepsius, *O kulturze politycznej w Niemczech*, 160.

[19] A. Wolff-Powęska, *Oswojona rewolucja. Europa Środkowo-Wschodnia w procesie demokratyzacji*, (Poznań: Instytut Zachodni, 1998), 24.

[20] W. Łukowski, S. Sulowski, *Kultura polityczna po obu stronach Odry*, in *Kultura polityczna w Polsce i Niemczech*, 240.

[21] K. Adenauer, *Wspomnienia*, (Warszawa: ABC Future, 2000).

past. The period of the allied occupation of Germany was one of the most difficult periods in the post-war history of the country. The burden of guilt and an attempt at "democratic repair" initiated by allied administration, induced a different kind of behaviour—from assuming full responsibility for the Third Reich's policy to its complete rejection—which is why, after the establishment of the Federal Republic of Germany, society received the so-called *Vergangenheitspolitik* (politics of the past) with enthusiasm. This was a period of about five years, during which it was attempted to reconcile with the National Socialist past and its consequences for Germans.[22] The federal amnesty of 1949 was an example of such activities—it was an official end of the "denazification" process, which also involved rescinding the punishment to thousands of former NSDAP members.

Change in the political point of view of the reconciliation proved to be an opportunity for Germans to start a new life in the post-war reality. Confusion was certainly the characteristic which predominated among Germans after World War II. For many, the unconditional surrender of the Third Reich meant not only losing the war, which after the six-year nightmare was not of great importance—it primarily meant the end of the values and ideals which were truly close to them. Additional difficulty also lay in the fact that virtually all Germans were blamed for the past events by the world. Thus, the *Stunde Null* concept (the zero hour) propagated by Konrad Adenauer, the German Chancellor at that time, was received enthusiastically. Its guidelines assumed cutting the Germans off from the National Socialist past. In consequence, this meant that the German state was entering a new road based on democratic foundations. Owing to this "active forgetting" (this notion was coined by Dolf Strenberg in 1949), questions about one's activity during the Third Reich's times became ultimately tactless.[23]

A new attitude proved to be symptomatic at that time. Many Germans began to present themselves as victims of the former system. It was emphasized that the policies of National Socialism gave just one choice to them: participate in the system or die. A process known as the "inclusiveness strategy" consisted of opposing "the small and evil Nazi clique" with "broad masses of honest Germans".[24] As a result, the memory

---

[22] N. Frei, *Polityka wobec przeszłości. Początki Republiki Federalnej i przeszłość nazistowska*, (Warszawa: Trio, 1999).

[23] W. Pięciak, *Niemiecka pamięć. Współczesne spory w Niemczech o miejsce III Rzeszy w historii, polityce i tożsamości (1989–2001)*, (Kraków: Wydawnictwo Uniwersytetu Jagiellońskiego, 2002), 102.

[24] K. Bachman, *Długi cień Trzeciej Rzeszy. Jak Niemcy zmieniali swój charakter*

of the Third Reich was reduced only to considering the harm and destruction resulting from allied bombing, the loss of some territories and expulsion from the opposite bank of the Oder and the Lusatian Neisse Rivers. In view of the Nazi past, interesting attitudes were also represented by the generation of young Germans who were born after the war and did not experience the tragedy personally. They began to fight for a new reality and new identity of the entire nation. However, this was connected with asking difficult questions to the generation of their parents. They did not reject the memory of the war, but decided to use it to propagate new values and to ultimately reject the Nazi ideology. This process is known as "overcoming the past"[25] and has become a part of the German political culture.

The form of political culture in the German Democratic Republic was influenced by a clear-cut division into private and national culture present in that state. The democracy deficit caused its citizens to "flee" from all that was national.[26] Almost entirely closing off the everyday culture in the private sphere was a side effect. A visible symptom thereof was the political absenteeism of the GDR citizens. Sustaining the division of the public and private areas enabled them to "show and maintain both political conformity and a private distance towards social and central ideas sanctioned by the state."[27] Notwithstanding the fact that, in the European opinion, the GDR created a model of state that suited the interests of the Soviet Union to the greatest extent, "the internal migration" of the citizens caused them to remain resistant to the national indoctrination.[28] Nonetheless, the East German political culture was the most imbued with socialist content of all the Eastern bloc countries. According to the programme of the Socialist Unity Party of Germany (SED, *Sozialistische Einheitspartei Deutschlands*) from 1976, the priority tasks of the party covered work on shaping the citizens into "a broadly developed socialist personality".[29] In a non-democratic state such as the GDR, the form of political culture was influenced by a few factors: a centrally managed and bureaucratized organization of the state, a closed political ideology sanctioned by the national authority, actually an exclusive presence of the normative conformity in the public space and, above all, the absence of

---

narodowy, (Wrocław: Atut, 2005), 82.

[25] B. Musiał, *Historiografia mityczna*, "Rzeczpospolita" 47, (2) (2001), 24–25.

[26] A. Wolff-Powęska, *Oswojona rewolucja*, 195.

[27] M. R. Lepsius, *O kulturze politycznej w Niemczech*, 160.

[28] A. Wolff-Powęska, *Oswojona rewolucja*, 195.

[29] Ibid., 176.

free expression of the public opinion, which was mainly a consequence of the total media control exercised by authorities.

Within political culture shaped in this manner, the politics of memory aimed to separate themselves entirely from the legacy of the Third Reich. In fact, everything that was related with National Socialism was undermined and destroyed systematically and consistently. One of the instruments applied therein, was the so-called wild "denazification". This method aimed, amongst other things, to eliminate individuals whose worldview opposed the new authority in the country. All those who in any way objected to the prevailing ideology in force, although they were not related with the previous system, were called "fascists or minions of a fascist".[30] The term fascist acquired a completely different meaning and it was pejorative. In the political struggle there were undertaken even extreme actions consisting in falsifying evidence of the Nazi past of those GDR citizens who challenged the new political reality in the country. Such peculiar instrumentalization of the anti-fascist ideology also played an additional role. Its objective was to justify repressive actions towards the citizens of the country performed by the authority. The most important point in favor of its implementation was the imperative of defence against a threat of the so-called Western vengeance. Distancing itself from the Nazi tradition in East Germany allowed for the creation of a positive, though one-sided, image of the country's history.

The GDR considered the anti-fascist legacy its own, demonstrating it even in a specific provision of the constitution from 1968, an adequate programming of contents conveyed by history lessons at school and the creation of culture which was also top-down controlled and managed. However, politics conducted in this manner actually led to "liquidation" of history limited in the mainstream to "enumeration of party conventions, plenary meetings, conferences, proclamations and plan indicators".[31] The Federal Republic of Germany was indicated by Germans from the East separating themselves from the Third Reich as continuation thereof.

As for the issue of memory, conventional ideology shaped in the country allowed them to take the side of the winner. This was also revealed through the creation and celebration of new holidays. The anniversary of the outbreak of World War II, September 1, was celebrated in the GDR as "International memorial day of the victims of fascist terror

[30] J. Holcer, *Rozważania o kulturze politycznej niemieckiego komunizmu*, in S. Sulowski (ed.), *Polska: Niemcy. Nadzieja i zaufanie. Księga Jubileuszowa na 80-lecie Urodzin Profesora Mieczysława Tomali*, (Warszawa: Politeja, 2002), 245.
[31] S. Wolle, *Wspaniały świat dyktatury. Codzienność i władza w NRD 1971–1989*, (Warszawa: Wiedza Powszechna, 2003), 23.

and the day of fight against fascism and imperialism". Yet, the actions of the GDR authority failed in one of the areas, namely that of identity of the country's citizens. Their identification with the state was marked by a contradiction. On the one hand, German society took pride in rebuilding the country. On the other hand, it was never possible to break the feeling of national community with Germans from the West. After all, "being a German" was always something more than "being a GDR citizen".[32]

In the time of the Warsaw capitulation after the defeat of the Warsaw Uprising, Polish political life was reviving two hundred kilometers southeastwards in Lublin, where new political culture in the spirit of socialism was starting to take shape. To Poles, the end of the World War II was both a time of joy in victory and the fear of being subjugated again, as the victory had not come from the expected side. Adam Krzemiński argues that it led to some kind of "schizophrenia" among Poles: "There is no doubt that during the war a majority of our society imagined the victory differently. There is also no doubt that in the spring of 1945, the majority felt relieved."[33] The new authority had to face the extremely difficult task of winning social support.

One of the instruments applied to create its political position was collective memory. Propaganda by the Lublin Committee began almost immediately. It was not sufficient to accuse Tadeusz Bór-Komorowski, commander of the Home Army, of treachery and publicly calling him a "drinking friend" of Erich von dem Bach, commander of the *Korpsgruppe*, during the suppression of the Warsaw Uprising and to accuse General Kazimierz Sosnkowski, Commander-in-Chief of the Polish Armed Forces, of being "a marionette of Hitler", and therefore a massive propaganda attack against all the soldiers of the Home Army started. They were called native "Hitlerites" and *Volksdeutch*, who created a network of "Home Army [National Armed Forces] Gestapo" to fight with the new authority. Similarly as in the GDR, all those who did not surrender to the currently prevailing political trends were called fascists.[34] Thus, to achieve a specific political effect, the events from the past were applied almost perfectly. Obviously, public opinion received the product in the form of adequately presented and interpreted facts. It was the authorities that

---

[32] A. Wolff-Powęska, *Oswojona rewolucja*, 177 and 195.

[33] A. Krzemiński, *Lekcje dialogu. Mowy, eseje i wywiady (Grass, Weizsäcker, Küng, Dönhoff, Habermas, Winkler, von Thadden i inni)*, (Wrocław: Oficyna Wydawnicza Atut - Wrocławskie Wydawn. Oświatowe, 2010), 137.

[34] A. K. Kunert, R. E. Stolarski (eds.), *"Bijące serce partii". Dzienniki Personalne Ministerstwa Bezpieczeństwa Publicznego,* (Warszawa: Oficyna Wydawnicza ADIUTOR, 2001), 352.

decided on inserting a given historical event in the symbolic space, official national propaganda or school textbooks. As a result, history was tabooed which manifested itself in attempted deletion of numerous subjects such as the activity of the Home Army or the Warsaw Uprising from the conscience of citizens. This task was doomed to failure, and the authorities were satisfied with "the absence" of these subjects at least in the public sphere.[35]

Norman Davies comments on this situation as follows: it was as if the soldiers of the Home Army did not exit. That is why, for over forty years the communist regime consistently refused to raise a monument of the Warsaw Uprising. The only monuments allowed in Warsaw commemorated abstract ideas of some unknown communist activists and the People's Army, anonymous civil victims or the ghetto heroes; it was simply prohibited, and others were in turn subjected to political manipulation.[36] The method of avoiding issues that were "troublesome" to the authorities was applied through the national promotion of those "correct" ones. The complete monopolization of mass media and functioning of censorship allowed the popularization of those historical events supporting the official political and party line, which was mandatory in the country. That is why anniversaries of the October Revolution, the July Manifesto or Labor Day were celebrated sumptuously.[37] Public space was also appropriately developed in that the schools were given patron names and street names were changed. In the first years after the war it was also noticeable that the authority took advantage of the antipathy of Poles towards Germans to realize particular political interests and to strengthen its position.

The propaganda of those days was frequently successful in reinforcing the image of "a bad German" in the conscience of Poles. Politicians, in order to win support, spoke about Germans with dislike and suggested that war criminals would be persecuted as soon as possible. German dislikes were magnified by propaganda actions; numerous propaganda movies were shot, and the image of Adolf Hitler became the favourite character of Polish satirists:

> … in *Szpilki* magazine Hitler is a person or rather a human creature which is devoid of satanic power and stripped off features of magnitude—he is a guy with a stupid moustache and falling cowlick. He loses his pants, he is a

[35] J. Z. Sawicki, *Bitwa o prawdę. Historia zmagań o pamięć Powstania Warszawskiego 1944–1989*, (Warszawa: Wydawnictwo DiG, 2005).
[36] N. Davis, *Powstanie '44*, (Kraków: Wydawnictwo Znak, 2004), 792.
[37] W. Roszkowski, *Stosunki polsko-niemieckie. Polityka i historia na przykładzie Polski*, "Przegląd Zachodni" 1 (2000), 34.

> schnitzel on the cook's table with a red star, he sits in a cage—and most of the cases he dangles from a gallows.[38]

The dislike towards Germans was revealed in numerous other ways. It was suggested that German language was to be abolished in school; people who publicly spoke German were met with hostile reactions; the words "Germans" or "German" were usually written in lowercase. Such writing may be also found in official documents, i.e. in the report "International Issues" by Edward Ochab, Minister of Public Administration.[39] Moreover, it is probable that the first novel printed in Poland after 1944, *The Teutonic Knights* by Henryk Sienkiewicz, also was not accidental.[40] Such a policy caused two memories, the official one and the informal one, both functioning in parallel. Along with the correct memory accepted by the authorities, there existed the informal memory which was often inconvenient for those in power.[41] Numerous events survived in the minds of Poles thanks to families, who passed the truth of the "prohibited" historical events from generation to generation; authorities whose actions opposed to popularization of propaganda contents; the clergy who risked celebrating a mass for national heroes whom the authority would rather forget. Norman Davies underlines that: "the memory of the Warsaw Uprising was tolerated only on the hallowed ground, but it was not tolerated in any other public places whatsoever."[42]

The system transformation which occurred during the 1980s and 1990s marked a new era in Polish-German relations. Political changes also entailed changes in other fields of both societies, and these were also related to the issues of memory. A phenomenon that appeared on a larger scale was the pluralization of memory (though obviously, it applied less to the societies of western lands in reunified Germany). Although those in power in democratic systems should by definition adopt a neutral approach in terms of influencing historical conscience, it is not always possible. In particular, both Poland and the reunified Germany had to face numerous historical problems that could have been perfectly applied in a political game. However, this subject shall not be discussed herein.

---

[38] E. Dymitrów, *Niemcy i okupacja hitlerowska w oczach Polaków. Poglądy i opinie z lat 1945–1948*, (Warszawa: Czytelnik, 1987), 166.

[39] *Referat ministra administracji publicznej Ochaba pt. "Zagadnienia międzynarodowe"*, Archiwum Akt Nowych, Ministerstwo Administracji Publicznej.

[40] M. Tomala, *Patrząc na Niemcy. Od wrogości do porozumienia 1945–1991*, (Warszawa: Polska Fundacja Spraw Międzynarodowych, 1997), 31.

[41] M. Zaborski, *Współczesne pomniki i miejsca pamięci w polskiej i niemieckiej kulturze politycznej*, 34.

[42] N. Davis, *Powstanie '44*, 792.

Undoubtedly, due to historical vicinity, the discourse of memory was dominated by two basic issues of the brown and the red past. In fact, both countries, in a different manner, experienced the existence of two totalitarian systems in twentieth century Europe. Despite the basic differences in their experience, there is no doubt that both categories of the past are an important element that constantly unites both nations. They may also be considered sources of Polish and German perceptions of history and the memory thereof.

The brown past, the tragedy of World War II, became permanent in the politics of both countries, which is not surprising when the number of victims and the scope of losses are considered.[43] Although there are opinions from different sides of the political scene, as well as those of a part of society, that this debate should now end, it is recurring issue on different occasions, especially on celebrations and anniversaries related to the war. There are also symbolic spaces in Poland and Germany related to those events almost everywhere, in the form of street names or numerous memorials. Undoubtedly, the time for an emotionless discussion about World War II has not yet come.

There is no doubt that the manner of remembering World War II in Poland is heavily influenced by the period of the Polish People's Republic and the enforced policy of the state. In fact, a large part of Polish society has considered Poles in the period of war as victims, until the present times, and numerous members of society have created an archetype of the Pole, harmed by the German.[44] It is necessary to underline though, that the background of such thinking may be traced back to much earlier times than the period of war. Being a victim is very "comfortable", as it puts the nation in a privileged position and gives rise to an irrational belief of being in the right.

Changes in Poland brought about new quality in the approach to the issue of Polish-German relations, and things which were not always easy for the Poles begun to appear, such as repression and persecution or the *Volksdeutsch* displacement. These problems were approached at completely different angles, free of "blank spots" and reticence. For the first time in years, Polish society was able to reject the imperative of "the collectivity of memory" and the way of thinking programmed by authority.

In reunified Germany, the issues of World War II are also present in the public discourse. The politics of memory as an element of political culture has been confronted with the remnants of the two separate German

[43] E. Dymitrów, *Pamięć i zapomnienie w stosunkach polsko-niemieckich*, "Przegląd Zachodni" 1 (2000), 2–3.

[44] M. Zaborski, *Współczesne pomniki i miejsca pamięci*, 34.

states. The East German transformation is considered a particular case of "a system change through reunification".[45] Contrary to other countries of the Eastern bloc, for which system transformation entailed referring back to the history and values of the proper nation, to East Germans it meant confrontation with the vacuity of identity. The GDR citizens became "co-authors" and "co-victims" of a double breakdown—the social and political system and, above all, that of the proper state.[46] This situation is best conveyed in the words of one East German writer: "Poles have their Poland, the Czech and Slovaks have their Czechoslovakia, Hungarians have their Hungary and we have Federal Republic of Germany."[47] Within only a year, East Germany was "absorbed" by an efficient democratic system with a well-functioning free-market economy. In practice, this meant ex-citizens of the GDR did not have the possibility of influencing the future reunified statehood.

Is there any room for the brown memory in the new reality shaped by different political traditions? The reply is affirmative. The presence of memory regarding World War II is unquestionable, although numerous Germans declared a dislike of scratching old wounds: "there is not a single day that goes without Hitler and the Nazis in some way or another—in the papers, movies, books, on the radio or television—knocking on our public conscience."[48] The speech of Martin Walser on October 11, 1998, upon his receipt of the German bookseller award, also gave rise to a stormy discussion. On that occasion, he expressed impatience with the never-ending German discussion about the war. He publicly wondered why there had been more questions about history asked in the 1990s than ever before. The reactions to this speech were extreme—from those in favor of such a view to the ones completely rejecting thereof.[49]

In the reunified Germany, attempts to normalize the history have been made since the system transformation. This process occurs in two basic fields. The first one refers to searching for the reasons for national pride by Germans. The examples of anti-Hitler opposition in the Third Reich, such as the activity of the Kreisau Circle and the White Rose resistance movement (a movie about one of its members, Sophie Scholl, entitled

---

[45] E. Bojenko-Izdebska, *Przemiany w Niemczech Wschodnich 1989–2010. Polityczne aspekty transformacji*, (Kraków: Księgarnia Akademicka, 2011), 7.
[46] A. Wolff-Powęska, *Oswojona rewolucja*, 169.
[47] Ibid.
[48] I. Kershaw, *Sieg Heil*, "Forum", 5 (2003), 49.
[49] J. Jabłkowska, *Spór o niemiecką pamięć w kontekście mowy Martina Walsera z 11.10.1998 r. (Friedenspreisrede)*, in B. Korzeniewski (ed.), *Przemiany pamięci społecznej a teoria kultury*, (Poznań: Instytut Zachodni, 2007), 65–85.

Sophie Scholl—the Last Days was shot in 2005), have almost become a legend. The other field refers to the recurring questions about guilt, although this debate acquired a different character in both German states shortly after the war. An exhibition presenting the crimes of the Wehrmacht in the 1940s, shown in over thirty German and Austrian cities, raised such a discussion. It is necessary to mention that the exhibition revealed shortcomings and frequently falsified the real image of World War II history. It is not relevant though, since the exhibition raised numerous questions, above all about so-called ordinary Germans that an entire generation put forward to the trial of history. It is worth mentioning that a part of this debate was transferred to Poland, where thousands of Poles lived in the areas included in the Reich and were drafted into the German army.

Another, equally important subject to be confronted by Poles and Germans was the red past and its memory. In Poland, the opinions about the Polish People's Republic are very frequently influenced by current social and political events.[50] Coming to terms with the past took place in two dimensions. The first one concerned the symbolic space in that all the monuments commemorating the heroes of that time were removed, the schools chose different patron names, and the street names were changed, though not without controversy. In the second dimension, it was necessary to deal with the past in the form of discussion on the cooperation with the previous regime. In Poland, this was hotly disputed throughout 1990s. The Institute of National Rememberance was founded and became an institution that collects and elaborates materials from the previous authority. The greatest challenge for the entire society was the wave of "disclosures" on so-called secret cooperators which sometimes went out of control. "Wild lustration" led to the accusations of persons who were actually the victims rather than the co-creators of the previous system.

In the case of Germany, the red past naturally applies to its eastern part, which previously constituted the GDR. West Germans are less interested in this problem and they tend to focus on the war. Contrary to Poles, Germans were not so consistent in removing monuments and memorials proper to the GDR. It was decided that some should remain, such as the monuments of Marx, Engels and Rosa Luxemburg, and the same applied to street names. An interesting element of the process of dealing with the past was the so-called "German-German literary dispute". Upon revealing documents produced in the structure of authority of the GDR, it turned out that numerous writers were involved in cooperation

[50] M. Zaborski, *Współczesne pomniki i miejsca pamięci*, 49.

with the secret service. Their attitudes were very frequently compared to the behavior of intelligentsia in the period of the Third Reich. To a larger part of the East German public opinion, such comparisons were unacceptable. A book entitled *The Black Book of Communism* appeared in 1997 and generated similar reactions. It was an important voice in the debate, and demonstrated the attempts to compare both systems were not unreasonable at all.[51]

Searching for the sources of Polish and German perception of history after system transformations is not a simple task. Certainly, they may be found in the politics of memory which is an element of political culture in both countries. Still, the complex past of Poland and Germany in the twentieth century is frequently blurred, indicating a great deal of problems, ambiguities and differences to be solved. Certainly, it is difficult to speak about a common Polish-German memory. However, there are events which are commonly remembered, although in a different manner:

> The virtue of universal histories was long believed in. Then writing of national histories that were separate from each other was long practiced. The problem of memory and searching for its anchoring points, its "nodes" or places revived national history through its immersion in the nature of specific identities. I have personally grown convinced that intensification of differences may generate similarities.[52]

The author holds a PhD degree and works as Assistant Professor at the Chair of History of International Relations at the Faculty of Political Science and International Studies, Nicolaus Copernicus University in Toruń. She deals with post-war Polish-German relations, foreign politicy as well as the history of diplomacy and theories of International Relations.

---

[51] Ibid, 70.

[52] Quoted after R. Traba, *Wprowadzenie*, in R. Traba (ed.), *Pamięć. Wyzwanie dla nowoczesnej Europy*, (Olsztyn: Borussia, 2008), 19.

CHAPTER FOUR

THE PROBLEM OF IDENTITY CREATION: GOVERNANCE OF INFORMATION IN THE POST-TOTALITARIAN UKRAINIAN CONTEXT

VIKTORIIA BOYKO

> Oh, East is East and West is West, and never the twain shall meet,
> Till Earth and Sky stand presently at God's great Judgement Seat;
> But there is neither East nor West, Border, nor Breed, nor Birth,
> When two strong men stand face to face, tho' they come from the ends of the earth!
>
> —Rudyard Kipling, 1889

Larry Wolff, Harvard University scientist, conducted research at the Harvard Ukrainian Research Institute under the auspice of Omeljan Pritsak in the early 1990s. His work *Inventing Eastern Europe*, published by Stanford University Press in 1994, has become an intellectual bestseller and brought the concept of East Central Europe *a la lettre* back to the international academic agenda, describing it in a sense of political geography and cultural cartography.[1]

He starts his book with a citation from Churchill's speech made in Fulton 1946, sadly known as marking the beginning of the Cold War: "From Stettin in the Baltic to Trieste in the Adriatic, an iron curtain has descended across the Continent", a rhetorical figure that coined the division of Europe in two parts: Western and Eastern Europe. For almost the next half a century it stood as a crucial structural boundary, both in the mind and on the map. Churchill outlined that "[t]he safety of the world requires a new unity of Europe". His speech in Fulton proved to be

[1] L. Wolff, *Inventing Eastern Europe. The Map of Civilization on the Mind of the Enlightment*, (Stanford: Stanford University Press, 1994), 419.

prophetic and his figure was cut in iron as a geopolitical fact of international relations.

However, the map of Europe, with its multitude of countries and cultures was mentally marked with Churchill‘s iron curtain, where the countries behind it were identified as "Eastern states of Europe", joined together in what he called a "Soviet sphere under totalitarian control".

What happend in 1989 was a breakdown of *status quo* imposed by Churchill—a revolution in Eastern Europe, or rather a series of related revolutions in the different Eastern states of Europe, which brought democratic elections, openness to market capitalism, withdrawal of Soviet troops and the eventually dissolution of the Warsaw Pact. The dissolution of the Soviet Union was, in a symbolic order, equal to the end of the great narrative (a metanarrative in the Jean-François Lyotard sense of the word) which also symbolised a twist in the plot of East Central Europe.

The division of Europe suddenly appeared to be over, erased, abolished. Larry Wolff claims that "Churchill's imaginary demarcation" was drawn much earlier, that the distinction of Central and Eastern Europe is older than Churchill and the Cold War: "The division of Europe happened not in Fulton—it happened at home. It was Western Europe who in the time of Enlightenment invented the Eastern Europe as its complementary other half—a sort of "Other".[2]

The essence of the problem of division between Western and East Central Europe could also be seen more clearly if we turn to the comparative analysis of philosophical fundamental principle.[3] Western philosophical thought, formed under the influence of the Renaissance and the philosophy of Descartes, Machiavelli, Hobbes, Locke, Grotius and Rousseau, views man as the measure of all things. The idea of the Cartesian *cogito*, the social contract theory and the interpretation of Locke and Rousseau were the basis for Western models of liberalism and democracy. For the area of Central and Eastern Europe, it is necessary to talk about a different socio-cultural paradigm. Here prevails the inherent philosophy of Socrates and the ideas of Christianity, the idea of the existence of the transcendent world of truth, goodness and justice. Man is

---

[2] I. Neumann, *The Uses of the Other. "The East" in European Identity Formation*, (Minneapolis: University of Minnesota Press, 1999).

[3] About the origin of the term *Mitteleuropa* and its transformation into the idea of Central Europe, and later on East Central Europe see: E. Busek, E. Brix, *Projekt Mitteleuropa*, (Wien: Ueberreuter, 1986); H. Łaszkiewicz, *A Quest for Identity: East-Central Europe and Its Historians,* in J. Kłoczowski (ed), *East-Central Europe's Position within Europe: Between East and West*, (Lublin: Instytut Europy Środkowo-Wschodniej, 2004), 60–74.

not a measure of all things, the social contract is not sufficient to determine the principles of coexistence among people, and the idea of *cogito* cannot find a fundamental ground in it.

In the dimension of intellectual discussions, for Milan Kundera, Czesław Miłosz, Adam Michnik, oppositionists of the 1980s, East Central Europe was a value they stood for during the great debate on the participation of the so-called Eastern bloc in the creation of identity of the whole of Europe. In the conceptions of Oskar Halecki, Jenő Szűcs, István Bibó and the school of Jerzy Kłoczowski, East Central Europe has played a symptomatic historical role in the creation of European identity.[4]

Contemporary theorists of identity of the nation or subregion have an enormous task (disregarding whether or not they split it into Central and Eastern Europe), and as Czesław Miłosz wrote, also the task of responding to the images and formulas that Western intellectuals have imposed on Eastern Europe. The emergence of new intellectual currents greatly facilitates this task by debunking "Orientalism" and creating a sound discursive space around the problem of the so called "in-between Europe region".

However, by turning from the philosophical to the political level one can observe how countries of East Central Europe were bound by the desire for integration into primordially European and Transatlantic structures in the last decades. This is manifest in a gradual shift in Europe, through getting rid of the need to distinguish between them and traditional members of the European Union, NATO and the final identification with Western society. These processes contributed to making the concept of East Central Europe politicized and unstable.

Certainly, the mental mapping process of East Central Europe has close ties with the way contemporary international politics is conducted, or as Prof. Jerzy Jedlicki, a bright historian from the Institute of History of Polish Academy of Sciences in Warsaw, mentioned: "[The] history of Eastern Europe of the twentieth century is a dimension *par excellence* for observations on how real memories about the past can sharpen and accelerate contemporary conflicts in international affairs."[5] In this article

---

[4] O. Halecki, *Historia Europy – jej granice i podziały*, (Lublin: Instytut Europy Środkowo-Wschodniej, 1994); J. Szűcs, *Trzy Europy*, (Lublin: Instytut Europy Środkowo-Wschodniej, 1995); I. Bibo, *Die Misere der osteuropäischen Kleinstaaterei*, (Frankfurt/Main: Neue Kritik, 1992); J. Kłoczkowski (ed.), *Historia Europy Środkowo-Wschodniej*, (Lublin: Instytut Europy Środkowo-Wschodniej, 2000), Vol. 1–2.

[5] J. Jedlicki, *Historical Memory as a Source of Conflicts in Eastern Europe*, "Communist and Post-Communist Studies" 3 (September, 1999), 225–32.

Jedlicki studies how the process of collective memory (remembering and forgetting historical events) related to Central and Eastern Europe crosses historical borders, and spills over onto political and international relations.

If we turn our attention to Ukraine on its way from a post-totalitarian to democratic state, we can see that it still has to pass through a number of transformations. Coping with the transformation process seems to be most observable from the perspective of transparency in the realm of information policies, as far as the last could be considered as a marker of transformation. In the Ukrainian case, the institutions involved in the issue of information policy creation can be counted on the fingers of one hand—such agencies include the Council of National Security of Ukraine and the National Institute for Strategic Studies. However, the state as the main actor has an overarching voice via a law passed in 2007 on the the Basic Rules of the Development of Informational Society in Ukraine in the Years 2007–2015, where we read: "Successful production and distribution of competitive national information products is one of the conditions necessary to establish stable national identity via, among others, creation of stable national memory."[6]

At this level, the preparedness of the state for the participation in information exchange is determined by the following criteria:

- quantity and quality of information products produced in the country and their own state,
- power, branching and resources available for further development of telecommunications networks,
- the state's ability to effectively regulate the production and dissemination of information (activity news agencies, media, cultural industries, foreign broadcasting organizations, etc.),
- the degree of accessibility for citizens of all public information sources (the concept of universal access),
- the practical protection of intellectual property and copyrights.

Moreover, according to the Ukrainian Law on Television and Radio Broadcasting, national audiovisual products are considered "programmes, films, audiovisual works produced by natural or legal persons of Ukraine" (Article 1).[7] The regulation of the domestic law of the matter does not

[6] *Law On the Basic Rules of the Development of Informational Society in Ukraine in Years 2007–2015*, http://zakon2.rada.gov.ua/laws/show/537-16, (accessed January 28, 2012).

[7] *Law On Television and Radio Broadcasting*,
http://zakon2.rada.gov.ua/laws/show/3759-12, (accessed Jauuary 28, 2012).

involve any restriction on a linguistic basis, although Ukrainian legislation gives absolute priority in the national media to a foreign product.

In France, which became a textbook example of a rigid policy in protecting its national identity, 60 % of air time is filled with French audio-visual products, out of which 40 % must be broadcast at prime time. Ukrainian legislation in this area is no less severe than the French one. Thus, the Law on Television and Radio Broadcasting states that "the total amount of broadcasting is supposed to be covered for at least 50 percent with national audiovisual product or musical works of Ukrainian authors or performers" (Part 1 of Article 9). Moreover, the Law on Cinematography stipulates "a set quota demonstration of national films, which is not less than 30 percent of the national screen time" (Article 22).[8] But unlike France, the aforementioned laws are in most cases not met.

It should be noted that public broadcasters in Western Europe are still the leading communicators in the field of public relations, making out around 20 % of the national space-frequency resource of information. There is a difference in Ukraine—public broadcasters covering about 5 % of the national information resource may soon become private, owned by foreign capital. The system of information needs deep social reforms in order to have its own identity and philosophy. However, the state for now is, unfortunately, on the periphery of the information field. A strategically important task of the state information policy is the introduction of digital broadcasting and the transition to this technology is now a global trend. According to the Regional Agreement "Geneva-06", which Ukraine is a part of, all European countries are obliged to cease analogue television broadcasts by 2015.

On November 27, 2007, the National Council on Television and Radio Broadcasting adopted the state programme of digital broadcasting in Ukraine. A full transition to this standard is to take place by July 2015.[9]

Here also the Program of the East Central European Initiative should be recalled, an intergovernmental organization comprising seventeen countries (Albania, Austria, Belarus, Bosnia Herzegovina, Italy, Macedonia, Moldova, Poland, Romania, Slovakia, Slovenia, Hungary, Ukraine, Croatia and the Czech Republic) established in 1989 for multilateral cooperation in East Central Europe and participation in European integration processes. One of the completed forms of cooperation between countries

---

[8] *Law On Cinematography*, http://zakon2.rada.gov.ua/laws/show/9/98-вр, (accessed January 28, 2012).

[9] *Resolution on the Introduction of the State Program of Digital TV and Radio Broadcasting*, http://zakon2.rada.gov.ua/laws/show/1085-2008-п, (accessed January 28, 2012).

of the region is a common approach to solving the problems of international information exchange, providing the basic rights and freedoms in the field of information, the creation of a united East Central European information highway, and the establishment of an information economy and introduction of information technologies in all spheres of society.

East Central European countries have inherited political and economic levers of control over the information field (telecommunications, broadcasting, mass media), which tightly follow the interstate and external circulation of information. Geopolitical change, such as the dissolution of the Soviet Union, has led to the progressive advancement of a number of East Central European states. However, there still remain some states having the monopoly on information resources, networks and communications, which is *sui generis* a normal state of things. On the other hand, the government regulation of media significantly slows down the process of European integration. The European Union initiated the development of information policy to apply information society and information economy.

As far as Ukraine is concerned, basic principles of the state information policy were declared, based on former state institutions competence, and a series of concepts, programmes and action plans were adopted. However, at the level of the practical implementation of information policy there are uncoordinated activities of various departments, inconsistency and a lack of transparency in the implementation of planned measures. As a result, Ukraine is not yet among the countries that can boast information independency. Currently, following situation is to be observed:

- an ineffective system of state regulation of national media space, a lack of a consolidated view of directions of its further development, a lack of qualitative cultural industry and of a national system of information disseminating on a global scale;
- a low level of presence in the global media space, and a high informational dependence on foreign governments and media organizations.[10]

Given the current state in the information sphere of Ukraine, the priority goal of information policy should be: (1) to create a strong and

[10] *Interview with Viktor Nabrusko, State Secretary of the National Union of Ukrainian Journalists*, http://www.telekritika.ua/bezpeka/2010-10-18/56680, (accessed January 26, 2012).

competitive national system of information production, capable of ensuring the consolidation of society on the basis of common values, goals, ideas and to promote the comprehensive development of personality as well as (2) further technological modernization to expand presence in the international division of labour in the field of ICT.

Here we come to understand that the main goal of information policy and information management in every state, and especially in a state with a totalitarian legacy, is the formation of a coherent identity of the nation. This would merge the nation around it, and fit with a wider geopolitical context. For Ukraine, it is a cognitive belonging to the historical and geographical phenomenon in East Central Europe.

In order to create a strong and competitive national system of information production, capable of ensuring the consolidation of society on the basis of common values, goals, ideas and promotion of the comprehensive development of personality, one needs this "common identity content", one that would integrate Ukraine inside the country but also with the rest of the world.

The so-called Copenhagen school of security studies headed by Barry Buzan coined the notion of "regional security complex", a formation where the interdependency between states that form this very security complex is very strong.[11] One can agree that Central Europe forms this kind of regional security complex. Therefore, constant by its nature identity creation process (disregarding whether it goes about the case of the specific country) Ukraine is very much dependant on the sound politics of information governance.

What has been analysed up to this point is a technical part of the issue but it is the semantic or content part that is of greater importance. Here it is worth remembering that Ukraine, belonging to the socio-cultural paradigm of East Central Europe, while creating its identity on the contemporary timeline, also contributes to the creation of the East Central European one.[12]

Symptomatic topics "fermented" in the last decade in the public information space of Ukraine deal with difficult questions of national

[11] B. Buzan, O. Wæver, *Regions and Powers: The Structure of International Security*, (Cambridge: Cambridge University Press, 2003), 564.

[12] In 1994, in "Warsaw Ukrainian Notes" a prominent medievalist, founder of the Institute of East Central Europe Jerzy Kłoczowski wrote about the historical tradition of Ukrainians belonging to Europe since the adoption of Christianity, later on empowered by the rise of an exceptionally dense network of Greek Catholic parishes from Przemyśl to Kiev. See J. Kłoczowski, *Ukraina a Europa Środkowo–Wschodnia*, "Warszawskie Zeszyty Ukrainoznawcze", (Warszawa, 1994), 15–20.

identity and memory politicy. Ukrainian authorities have plans for getting rid of "unnecessary documents" from the archives about the World War II period and on the Ukrainian rebellion army OUN UPA. This creates additional obstacles for researchers of that topic area. According to French philosopher Paul Ricœur, the role of history is not just to produce texts and images of the past but to formulate an introduction into the "culture of truth" as a moral value, a value in itself, and what we could potentially have in a couple of years regarding Ukraine would deal with the culture of "twisted" truth.

The event is very symptomatic for the whole post-totalitarian space, which deals not only with the problem of democratic values, but also with the problem of embryonic development of the information governance sector in Ukraine. Ironically, from the institutional perspective the only successful structure that deals with information governance in the realm of memory policy issues is the security service of Ukraine and its head Valeriy Khoroshkovsky.

The peculiarity of the Ukrainian situation is the unformed national identity, to some extent the result of cultural-linguistic assimilation, although it is better to talk of controversial identity. Data collection for the sociological survey "Lviv-Donetsk: sociological analyses of group identities and hierarchies of social loyalties", conducted in 1994 and 1999, also provides a clue to understanding this heterogeneous and compound phenomenon. It provides the possibility of considering the correlation between historical identity factors and the respondent's vision of a future political and international development of Ukraine, and its security relations as constituents of respondents' political orientation.[13]

The above-mentioned survey shows that representatives of eastern Ukraine perceive themselves as Ukrainians and they want their region to remain an inseparable part of Ukraine. However, they stress different characteristic traits of being Ukrainian, considered to be no worse than the Galician variant.[14] Whereas most of Galicians can be called supporters of the nationalistic variant of the Ukrainian identity narrative, its main traits cover Ukrainian language, the historical scheme of Mykhailo Hrushevskyi spiced with Golodomor and the Ukrainian Insurgent Army, the perception of Russia as an enemy or a threat to Ukraine, objection to integration into post-Soviet structures and the aspiration to establish Ukraine as a national state, where national identity would basically overlap the civil identity. By

---

[13] V. Sereda, *Regional Historical Identities and Memory,* "Україна модерна" 2007, Special edition, 160.

[14] *Львів – Донецьк: соціяльні ідентичності в сучасній Україні*, "Україна модерна", спеціяльний випуск, 2007.

contrast, in Donbas the prevailing narrative (which we can call Eastern-Slavic due to its Ukrainian historical continuity from Soviet discourse which complies with Russian language usage) perceives the Soviet period as a golden period in Ukrainian history and it does not tolerate NATO or the Ukrainian Insurgent Army. Certainly, this dichotomy cannot be sufficient while talking about the spectre of Ukrainian national identities, which can be intermediary, combined and dynamic.

***

The evolution of identities after the Orange Revolution does not weaken. On the contrary, it strengthens the distinction between the preferences of Donbas and Galicia. Confrontation between their elites, and hence masses, stresses more differences than commonalities. In particular, the project Lviv-Donetsk shows that in the early 1990s Donbas was closer to Galicia, whereas after the year 2000 an increase in centrifugal dynamics can be seen.

However, there is a dimension within which these two (or more) identities can coexist. This is the dimension of the internet, where most representatives of these identities can contribute to its creation but can have a floor to conduct a discussion. The low cost of internet products in comparison to print and television ones makes it possible to implement important contemporary projects that to a great degree construct such national identities as "Historical Truth", the Ukrainian version of "Wikipedia" in which the number of articles is five times as big as the Ukrainian Soviet Encyclopedia. Finally, there is also the possibility of a two-way flow of information, where each and every person can tailor the identity.

However, even the internet, an oasis of freedom, has recently felt the power of Ukrainian authorities. The international organization Reporters Without Borders has given a name to this affair—a cyber-war of netizens vs the Ukrainian government over the closure of the online resource, www.ex.ua, a Ukrainian file-sharing alternative to the American Megaupload (which was closed in January 2012), or the Pirate Bay. This was a popular web resource that, apart from the emphasized pirate content, also contained a vast amount of criticism on the current authority and the head of state. The closure resulted with a lightning speed DOS-attack on the official web pages of President Yanukovych, the Ministry of Internal Affairs and the National Bank, performed by the of Ukrainian organization "Anonimous". This resulted in the restoration of the resource, although in a refined version. This small event demonstrated the common effort of representatives of different national identities defending their right for information, and in a way creating a precedent of common ground.

Coming back to Churchill's prophecy, the thing that could break the "iron curtain" of alienation is the understanding that the East and West of Ukraine, just as the East and West of Europe, are categories of one symbolic order. In that situation, there is a need of "will"; the will for a free space for identity creation on the areas of "East" and "West", the will to accept these identities as they are under a common European roof. In this way, each creator of local identity will bear witness to a new European history.

The author holds an MA degree from the Kyiv-Mohyla Academy. She is a PhD Candidate at the Maria Curie-Sklodowska University in Lublin and the Volhynia National University of Lesia Ukrainka in Luck. Her fields of interest are national identity and nation building, the history of elites, the history of foreign policy and diplomatic structures, the Cold War, international security studies, and information security.

CHAPTER FIVE

MODERN LUSATIA: OPEN-AIR MUSEUM OR LIVING TRADITIONS OF THE REGION? A SURVEY BASED ON SORBIAN BROCHURES IN UPPER LUSATIA

JUSTYNA MICHNIUK

Lusatia is a region in the heart of Europe. It is not an administrative district or an independent state but a historical territory divided between the German states Saxony and Brandenburg as well as the Lower Silesia and Lubuskie voivodeships of western Poland. The word Lusatia sounds unfamiliar to most Germans or Poles. Few of them are able to say what exactly Lusatia is, where it is located or who lives there.

The Sorbs, a West Slavic nation living in Lusatia for more than 1,000 years, are not a homogeneous community. They are divided into Upper and Lower Sorbs speaking two different languages, with two religions and two separate mentalities. As the smallest Slavic nation, Sorbs are quite accustomed to divisions. In 1815, the Congress of Vienna decided to divide the region. A part of Upper Lusatia was given to Saxony and the rest of Lusatia became a part of Prussia. Nowadays, the land of Sorbs is divided into two different states of Germany.

It is hard to believe that such a small nation has lived through centuries of difficulties in preserving its culture, languages and tradition. Nowadays, as minority rights are more and more respected, Sorbs have the right to use their languages when in contact with municipal officials. The rights of the Sorbian minority are officially accepted and respected by local authorities. Analysing the variety of minority rights in Germany, one could say that any more could not be for the Sorbs. However, there is a difference between theory and practice.

According to statistics, less and less young Sorbs speak their language. The Lower Sorbian is on the list of endangered languages of Europe. Among teenagers, using the German language is regarded as an easier way to find a job and communicate at school, in a shop or on the street. When the number of speakers of a language is reduced to mere few thousand, its survival is threatened, and the progress of globalization, the unification of culture and a widespread use of social portals like Facebook are a challenge for the small Sorbian nation. At the beginning of the twenty-first century, a question arises of whether Lusatia has become an open-air museum or whether it remains a region of living tradition. A representative said that the Sorbian culture would die out only when the language is no longer spoken. Those words seem to be timeless.

This chapter demonstrates the discrepancy between the image of Sorbs presented in brochures available in Upper Lusatia and the present-day Sorbian reality. It is worth saying that a nation cannot be recognised by their old traditions and folklore alone, but also by their contemporary achievements.

The chapter is based not only on books (mostly in German), but also on the author's own survey conducted in Lusatia in 2010 to 2011. At that time, a large number of brochures was collected in places like the Town Museum, the Sorbian Museum, the Sorbian Cultural Information, offices of members of the German Bundestag, tourist information and so on. The brochures themselves differ from each other, and they can be divided into three basic groups:

(1) "Folklorised" brochures
(2) "Cultural" brochures
(3) Information brochures

The first group consists of presenting Upper Lusatia through the prism of Sorbian folklore. The most characteristic attributes are the depiction of Sorbian women in the national costumes of Upper and Lower Lusatia, bilingual traffic signs, the so called Easter riding, regional associations of Sorbs, and the church in Ralbitz.

The second group includes brochures giving information about cultural events in Lusatia concerning the Sorbian culture, customs and tradition. Information about museums, concerts, performances, Sorbian theatre, exhibitions, a Sorbian radio programme and tourist attractions are to be found there. The brochures are mostly bilingual, in Upper Sorbian and German.

The third group consists of brochures published by the town of Bautzen or the state of Saxony. Despite a bilingual German-Sorbian cover, the content is exclusively in German. In those brochures, information is provided about Sorbian educational offers, regional groups, buildings for public use as prisons, hospitals etc., as well as statistics on various aspects of regional life. Here, the printing date of the brochures is important.

The distinction points out to the large variety of brochures in today's Lusatia. Based on the three hypothetical groups, this chapter is an attempt to describe the image of the region at the beginning of the twenty-first century.

Fig. 4.1. Examples of "Folklorised" brochures

Fig. 4.2. Examples of “Cultural” brochures.

Coming to Bautzen for the first time by train, one can see a bilingual inscription *Bautzen/Budyšin* at the railway station. The town is located only 70 km from Dresden, but most inhabitants of the Saxony capital would probably not know where *Budyšin* is nor why the signboard at the Bautzen railway station is written in two languages. Most people living in the area might have heard about Spreewald, Lausitz, Ostereier, even about Jakob Bart Čišinski, but they unfortunately do not know who the Sorbs are.

Fig. 4.3. Examples of information brochures.

In general, folklore consists of legends, music, oral history, proverbs, jokes, popular beliefs, fairy tales and customs of a culture, subculture or a group. It is also a set of practices through which those expressive genres are shared. The word "folklore" was used for the first time by the English antiquarian William Thoms in 1846.[1] The above-mentioned definition

[1] *Folklore*, The Free Dictionary, http://www.thefreedictionary.com/folklore, (accessed

shows a very strong connection between folklore and the identity of a group, subculture or a nation. Sorbs, being the smallest Slavic nation in the twenty-first century, have a rich tradition, which makes Lusatia special. Nowhere else can one hear the Sorbian language, visit the Sorbian Institute and meet representatives of Sorbs struggling for preservation of their language in the media. The nation, being the heart of the region, has been living there since the sixth century. Nowadays, to preserve its culture it needs not only to promote its tradition but also to face the challenges of the contemporary world.

A motivation to write this chapter came from the work of Maria Mirtschin. In 2009, in her book *Fiktive Welten auf Postkarten*,[2] she described the Sorbian phenomenon based on postcards spread among tourists and citizens of Lusatia. The basic aim of a postcard is to send greetings and show the beauty of a place, while the fundamental aim of a brochure is to inform a visitor about a place. Folklore is an ally for both postcards and brochures, and the basis on which a picture of the land and its inhabitants can be created.

Maria Mirtschin wrote about the variety of postcard patterns, their history and the scenes from everyday life they depict. Generally speaking, she showed the "Sorbian world on postcards" or, to put it in a different way, the "fictive world of Spreewald", printed on a piece of paper. However, the aim of Maria Mirtschin was not to show that the Sorbs were a popular postcard pattern. As she wrote: "The personal fate of the people and their roots in a particular ethnic group was hardly important."[3] This clearly shows that a large amount of postcards from Lusatia were something unreal and fictive because they did not show the real nature of the land and people.

A similar picture is provided by the first group of brochures in Fig. 1.1, depicting Sorbian adults and children in national costume, Easter eggs and bilingual signboards. Does Lusatia look so colourful every day? In fact, walking the streets of Bautzen, Kamenz or even Crostwitz one will rarely see women and children dressed in a traditional Sorbian way. Fifty years ago, about 1,600 women wore traditional clothes on a daily basis,[4] with most in their twenties. Nowadays, the national costume is worn mostly by elderly women and during the national Sorbian festival, but not for young

---

January 12, 2012).

[2] M. Mirtschin, *Fiktive Welten auf Postkarten. Sorben in der Massenkultur*, (Bautzen: Sorbisches Institut, 2009).

[3] Ibid, 21.

[4] S. Hose, I. Keller, *Die Sorben aus volkskundlicher Sicht*, "*EUROPA REGIONAL*", 10 Jahrgang 2 (2002), 64.

Sorbs. In order to see traditional Sorbian costume now, one needs to come to Lusatia for Christmas or Easter.

Pictures provided by brochures, internet sites or TV influence common thought about a nation. Seeing a brochure with national costumes on the cover, one might think that Sorbs are an old-fashioned and closed community, and thus a kind of stereotypical perception takes place, based on limited knowledge about Sorbs.

In fact, contemporary Sorbs have developed modern institutions such as the Sorbian Institute, the Foundation for the Sorbian People, the Sorbian Artists Association, schools and Domowina regional associations. On the one hand, they respect their tradition. On the other hand, they are able to treat it with a sense of humour. Stereotypes, prejudices and Sorbian folklore may be laughed at, a good example being the sketches prepared by Sorbian students presented during Schadźowanka, an annual meeting of Sorbian intelligentsia.[5]

Folklore can be both a blessing and a curse for the Sorbs. It can both attract interest of tourists and produce an old-fashioned image of the nation. Therefore, the content of the "folklorised brochures" may seem one-sided, while in fact they contain much important information about Sorbs.

The "Cultural brochures" create an image of Sorbs as an active nation, which not only receives culture but also creates it. The leaflets advertise a bicycle path, the Kocor museum, and a theatre or concert performance. In Bautzen, the cultural centre of Upper Lusatia, one has the opportunity to watch a play not only in German but also in the Sorbian language, with a simultaneous translation. The German-Sorbian theatre is the only bicultural professional theatre in Germany. Around 1,000 events have taken place there, including twenty-five premieres, and it has a large repertoire of dramas and puppet shows. More than 140,000 people visited the theatre in 2011.[6]

"Cultural brochures" are also evidence of the Sorbian pride of their rich tradition and history as well as their will to transmit the knowledge to future generations of Sorbs and Germans. As one can see in the brochures, Sorbs are still living and continuing the tradition of their most famous artists and musicians, such as the important composers Alfons Janze, Jurij Winrar, Jan Bulank and Detlef Kobjela,[7] and the writers Jurij Koch, Kito

[5] G. Conradt, *Beiträge auf sorben.org zum Thema Schadzowanka*, http://www.sorben.org/tags/schadzowanka/index.html (accessed January 10, 2012).

[6] *Deutsch-Sorbisches Volkstheater Bautzen*, http://www.theater-bautzen.de/ (accessed January 10, 2012).

[7] M. Schönbach, *Nachts am Klavier—neue CD erinnert an Alfons Janze*,

Lorenz, Benno Budar, Benedikt Dyrlich, Róža Domašcyna and Měrćin Nowak-Njechorński. The latter is a hugely popular Sorbian painter, printmaker, writer and publicist, who recalled the legend of Krabat[8] presented in a 2008 film directed by Marco Kreuzpaintner.[9] However, it is highly problematic that all the best representatives of the Sorbian culture belong to older generations. Information about younger Sorbs, their educational and social situation, is missing in the brochures.

The function of information brochures is quite obvious: they create an image of Sorbs as a modern nation with their own institutions, educational structure and media. One of the most interesting brochures concerns the Council for Sorbian (*Wendish*) Affairs (*Rat für sorbische (wendische) Angelegenheiten*).[10] Article 25 of the Brandenburg Constitution guarantees the right of Sorbian people to protect, preserve and maintain their national identity and their traditional settlement area. This right includes promotion and teaching of the Sorbian language and culture as well as participation of Sorbian representatives in legislative processes regarding Sorbian issues.[11] In order to ensure those rights, the Council for Sorbian (*Wendish*) Affairs has been founded. It is entitled to attend meetings of committees of the Brandenburg Parliament and to express opinions on proposed laws.[12]

Another noteworthy brochure is the one called "Sorbs in Bautzen" ("*Die Sorben in Bautzen*"). It provides a lot of information about the history of Sorbs, their tradition, customs, important Sorbian personalities and their contemporary life in Bautzen (theatres, churches, media, organizations, education, restaurants etc.). According to the brochure, there is one Sorbian primary school out of a total six as well as one

---

http://sorbenland.info/nachts-am-klavier-neue-cd-erinnert-an-alfons-janze (accessed January 10, 2012).

[8] M. Nowak-Njechorński, *Mistrz Krabat dobry łużycki czarodziej*, (Katowice-Budziszyn: Śląsk, 1988).

[9] *Uczeń czarnoksiężnika*, Description of the film on the homepage filmweb.pl, http://www.filmweb.pl/film/Ucze%C5%84+czarnoksi%C4%99%C5%BCnika-2008-323371 (accessed January 9, 2012).

[10] *Rat für sorbische (wendische) Angelegenheiten/Rada za serbske nastupnosći*, http://www.landtag.brandenburg.de/de/meldungen%E2%80%9Erat_fuer_sorbische_%28wendische%29_angelegenheiten/rada_za_serbske_nastupnos%C4%87i%E2%80%9C/397073?_referer=396524, (accessed January 10, 2012).

[11] *Constitution of the Land of Brandenburg*, http://www.landtag.brandenburg.de/sixcms/media.php/5701/Verfassung_englisch.pdf (accessed January 10, 2012).

[12] *Landtag Brandenburg/Brandenburg parliament*, http://www.landtag.brandenburg.de/de/parlament/ausschuesse_und_gremien/rat_fuer_sorbische_%28wendische%29_angelegenheiten/396498?_referer=396501, (accessed January 10, 2012).

Sorbian high school out of four in Bautzen. It is essential to find new editions of brochures as the number of Sorbian schools decreases.[13]

In a brochure with an idyllic picture on the cover, a strong man holding a ladder on which his smaller friend stands, picking an apple from a tree. The question on the cover is “Is the support for minorities a privilege?” (“*Minderheitenförderung ein Privileg?*”). A short story inside the brochure depicts an example of Germans and Sorbs building good-neighbourly relations. They do not always achieve their aims (there is an insect in the apple), but at least they make efforts to cooperate.

The three analysed groups of brochures present three different aspects of the image of Sorbs. The nation expresses its distinctive character by means of folklore, culture and modern public life institutions. It is to be said that contemporary Lusatia is not just an open-air museum. So that the Sorbs are not perceived as merely a colourful folklore group, one needs to read with attention not only brochures but also guides and books concerning the small nation.

Die neue Gesellschaft Frankfurter Hefte wrote in 1997: “The Sorbian writer Juri Koch … expects a complete demise of his ethnic group in the next thirty years. This message may be sad but it might be realistic.”[14] It is to be hoped that the prophecy will not be fulfilled.

The author is a graduate in International Relations and she has a BA in Balkan Studies from the Nicolaus Copernicus University in Torun. She is currently a Ph.D. candidate dealing with the situation of Sorbs in Germany.

---

[13] *Sorben-Schule Crostwitz wird geschlossen*, http://www.lr-online.de/nachrichten/sachsen/Sorben-Schule-Crostwitz-wird-geschlossen;art1047,305948 (accessed January 10, 2012).

[14] “Die neue Gesellschaft Frankfurter Hefte”, 44 Jahrgang, (Bonn, 1997), 1089.

PART TWO

CENTRAL EUROPE IN WORLD POLITICS

CHAPTER SIX

GOVERNMENT IN A STATE OF CONFUSION: THE CHALLENGES TO NATIONAL SOVEREIGNTY POSED BY GLOBALISATION

OSKAR BRASZCZYŃSKI

To Fly or Not to Fly…

Konrad Lorentz, the famous Austrian zoologist and ornithologist, once described the habits of the Great Argus, an Asian bird. The male's constant flattering of females resulted in the evolution of his gigantic, broad and elongated secondary wing feathers. Consequently, he lost the ability to fly. I am inclined to see this as a metaphor of what happened to the nation state's sovereignty in the aftermath of trade liberalization, the policy of financial deregulation, the proliferation of interdependencies between global agents, and of globalization in general. But the inability of that beautiful bird to fly does not have to be seen from the negative perspective as the erosion of the traditional way of perceiving sovereignty. Apparently, having colourful and attractive wings was more important for males in comparison with flying, so at the level of elementary values procreation was more important than the effective transportation of oneself. Unfortunately, the Argus became languid and less militant, which now leads to their eradication when they encounter predators. They need to develop a defensive mechanism in the same way that governments need to acknowledge a new way of understanding sovereignty and to develop their new functions in the globalized world.

Terms, mechanisms …

The term globalization is both extremely imprecise and multidimensional. This phenomenon could be perceived in many different ways, which often invites confusion. Manfred Steger, in his book *Globalization. A Very Short Introduction,*[1] provides a complex analysis, taking into consideration many possible dimensions of globalization such as economic, social, political and cultural. To indicate the factors of globalization which affect national sovereignty, it is indispensable to point out only the main forces of this phenomenon, and to define only the core of it. Following Steger, globalization can be described as "a set of social processes"[2] which constitutes the pace towards greater integration at various levels and the proliferation of interdependences. He points out that these interdependences have social character and that they undergo constant creation, multiplication, stretching and intensification. To highlight precisely why globalization and sovereignty have points of contradiction, it is worth mentioning that by "deepening connections between local and the distant"[3], the phenomenon is associated with "deterritorialization".[4] Social performances take place regardless of the physical location of their agents thanks to contemporary methods of communication, which may be recognized as the main factor undermining sovereignty.

The term "sovereignty" is even more imprecise than globalization, as it is much older and different historical epochs have understood it differently, and so it is crucial to distinguish between the modern and the post-modern ways of considering this term. The modern understanding of sovereign state can be traced back to the Peace of Westphalia in 1648, which marked the end of the religious wars across Europe. The so called Westphalian model of sovereignty, simply put, recognized it in connection with territorial integrity and the principle of legal equality between particular states. *The Stanford Encyclopaedia of Philosophy* defines it as "supreme authority within a territory".[5] The lack of external agents performing in the territory of the defined nation state can be seen as the second factor determining the traditional way of understanding the term. Consequently, this kind of understanding excludes the existence of any supranational authority. After World War II, this exclusion contradicted

---

[1] M. Steger, *Globalization. A very short introduction*, (New York: Oxford University Press USA, 2003).

[2] Ibid., 13.

[3] Ibid., 13.

[4] W. Scheuerman, *Globalization*, in E. Zalta (ed.), *The Stanford Encyclopedia of Philosophy*, 2010, http://plato.stanford.edu/archives/sum2010/entries/globalization/ (accessed January 2, 2012).

[5] D. Philpott, *Sovereignty*, in E. Zalta (ed.), *The Stanford Encyclopedia of Philosophy*, 2010, http://plato.stanford.edu/archives/sum2010/entries/sovereignty/ (accessed January 2, 2012).

factors such as the emergence of human rights and institutions defending them, the policy of liberalization of markets, the constant increase of the flow of global capital, and the birth of international organizations such as the United Nations, the European Union, and OECD. For obvious reasons, these factors and organizations have tended to create the network of political and economic interdependencies known as globalization.

Therefore, the main challenge to sovereignty posed by globalization is the potential eradication of the traditional way of perceiving it. Governments are in a state of confusion when they consider their activities in accordance with the Westphalian model. Hence, the new or postmodern approach alleviates the confusion by the idea of shared sovereignty, as it is in the case of the European Union. Unfortunately, it can only alleviate the confusion. The process of continual strengthening of supranational organizations and transnational corporations, as well as the deepening disparities between the affluent and the poor, leads to an outflow of assets from the governments to the hands of the agencies of global governance. The result is a triggered wave of extreme nationalism and religious extremism, often leading to terrorist attacks, limitations of various freedoms, social discontents, and separatist movements; in short, aftermaths posing confusion. All of them ensue from one feature of globalization, the "uneven distribution of costs and benefits"[6] which makes interdependencies predominantly asymmetric.[7] This is exemplified mainly in the emergence of social movements such as Occupy Wall Street or the Bank Transfer Day campaign, to mention only two.

Supranational Agents

In order to understand the challenges to national sovereignty posed by globalization and to clarify the argument, it is fruitful to specify agencies taking part in the process of making governments powerless.

Never before have so many supranational agents competed for the prerogatives that once were the domain of the nation state. The constant process of loosening the autonomy of nation states is distinctive and takes place at various levels. New organizing centres of power include transnational corporations, NGOs (nongovernmental organizations), intergovernmental organizations such as the World Trade Organization,

---

[6] *Sovereignty and Globalization: Government in a State of Confusion*, http://www.idrc.ca/en/ev-34561-201-1-DO_TOPIC.html (accessed December 1, 2011).

[7] Ibid.

the International Monetary Fund and the World Bank at a global level, and the European Union, NAFTA, APEC and ASEAN at the regional level. This variety of global actors and "their ever-changing associations"[8] constitute key points of global governance. It became impossible for the particular nation states to experience globalization, or at least its effects, under protection. In the global network of interdependencies, you can observe that even diminutive governmental actions (especially connected with legal and economic measures) are restricted severely by the opinions of rating agencies, the possible response of world markets and supranational institutions and their legal acts. On the other side, it is distinctive also that coping with global problems (population growth, climate change etc.) cannot be the domain of the single nation state. This was one of the reasons for the creation of these supranational institutions. It had stemmed also from the assumption that "unilateralism will prove as futile as isolationism".[9] Moreover, Hannah Arendt argues that "power does not ordinarily mean bringing force to bear ... [but] is the capacity to act with others in pursuit of agreed objectives".[10] Hence, the challenges to national sovereignty posed by globalization may have been inevitable within the gradually growing awareness of global problems and the need to defend human rights. The main root of negative consequences of that phenomenon is connected to the liberalization of financial transactions, the collapse of the Bretton Wood system in 1971 (which provided the stability in the global economy, a phase called "[the] golden age of controlled capitalism" achieved mainly through establishing a gold-based fixed rate system), deregulation policy, instability, and the volatility of global markets in general.

Challenges to National Sovereignty Posed by Transnational Corporations

Global firms possessing huge economic power with subsidiaries in several countries now control the world's investment capital to a large extent. They also provide technological advances and have access to all international markets. Their leading position in the global economy is often maintained by merging with other corporations, as happened in the case of Disney-Pixar, Exxon-Mobil, AOL/Time Warner, Pfizer & Warner-Lambert among others. This has led to the stage in the global economy

---

[8] Ibid.
[9] *Sovereignty and Globalization*, 2011.
[10] Ibid.

characterized by the fact that the majority of the largest economies are transnational corporations (TNCs). Nation states flatter TNCs in pursuit of stimulating markets and enhancing their performance, mainly by means of deregulation policy and developing infrastructure in accordance with the corporations' needs. These favourable conditions have enabled TNCs to consolidate their global operations. Similarly to the Great Argus, nation states have become vulnerable to economic predators, such as global market speculators. Moreover, the liberal conditions of the global market and low transportation costs encouraged TNCs to disperse their manufacturing processes into lots of separated stages located in different geographical locations, mainly in countries famous for their cheap labour resources. These supranational networks of production allow TNCs to bypass trade unions on the national scale and limit costs of production by exploiting workers. Michael Chossudovsky, in his profound analysis *The Globalization of Poverty and the New World Order*,[11] points out that TNCs reduce labour cost levels to the smallest possible amount: "Real wages in the Third World and Eastern Europe are as much as seventy times lower than in the US, Western Europe or Japan: the possibilities of production are immense given the mass of cheap impoverished workers throughout the world."[12] Hence, the position of government as a provider of social safety is undermined. The nation's sovereignty is challenged by TNCs also because of the outflow of gigantic tax revenues due to the existence of offshore financial centres (OFCs), where governments do not interfere in the legitimization of the business sector and offer extremely low or no tax rates.[13] Thus, transnational corporations move their headquarters to OFCs to make better profits. Furthermore, the corporations have become organizing centres of economic power, determining trade flows on a global scale, the location of industries, and other economic activities. Their lobby puts constant pressure on national governments to obtain more privileges, both legal and economic, as they are often the largest job providers and their collapse could mean the collapse of a particular nation state. That is why, in a time of global recession, we face bailouts provided to TNCs by governments, as in the case of ING in Belgium and the Netherlands.

---

[11] M. Chodussudovsky, *The Globalization of Poverty and the New World Order*, (Ontario: Global Research, 2003).
[12] Ibid, 6.
[13] *Offshore financial center (OFC)*, http://www.businessdictionary.com/definition/offshore-financial-center-OFC.html (accessed December 3, 2011).

Challenges to National Sovereignty Posed by International Economic and Political Institutions

Manfred Steger points a crucial premise for this part of the argument:

> ... economic forms of interdependence are set into motion by political decisions but these decisions are nonetheless made in particular economic contexts. ... The economic and political aspects of globalization are profoundly interconnected.[14]

This statement allows for the discussion of the challenge to national sovereignty posed by both supranational economic and political institutions.

Bearing in mind the case of the Great Argus, governments' difficulties in managing disorganized networks of economic and political interdependencies have resulted in the creation of supranational institutions/agents such as: the United Nations (UN) and the European Union (EU) under political concerns, and the International Monetary Found (IMF), the World Bank and the World Trade Organization (WTO) under economic concerns. They could be now regarded as extremely privileged through their ability to impose austerity measures on the international economy, to regulate global trade, and to affect national sovereignty in general. The extent of the interference of economic institutions finds an overwhelming expression in the supply of loans to developing countries—forcing them to implement structural adjustment programmes often means forcing them to deregulate their economy in accordance with neoliberal theory. Hence, it is perceived as re-colonization, and the programmes facilitate TNCs[15] because they are consumed mainly by local businesses which are servants to them. These loans are often devoted also to service previous debts, so their actual positive impact on society is diminutive. In addition to this, the WTO provides legitimacy to strong economic agents: global banks, TNCs and their large-scale speculative acts performed against developing countries.[16] Moreover, compulsory cuts in budgets, as a part of adjustment programmes, limit educational development and increase disparities between the rich and the poor. Chossudovsky, who analysed the IMF and the World Bank using a sociological paradigm of conflict, adds one more point—that the WTO's trade deregulation policy, merged with new regulations relating to intellectual property rights, allows TNCs to

---

[14] M. Steger, *Globalization*, 62.
[15] M. Steger, *Globalization*, 53.
[16] M. Chodussudovsky, *The Globalization of Poverty*, 26.

"penetrate local markets and extend their control over virtually all areas of national manufacturing, agriculture and the service economy".[17] This kind of engineered collapse of state sovereignty is an overwhelming example of how globalization forces undermine national autonomy.

On the other hand, one can pick the positive example of the emerging "new" kind of sovereignty, as in the case of European Union which is called "shared sovereignty".

The roots of the EU are omitted, as it is not strictly connected with the core of the argument. Generally, the whole area of the EU is where two main concepts of sovereignty clash. The first is the previously mentioned traditional Westphalian approach. The second could be named the concept of shared sovereignty. These ideas cumulate in the question of whether we (as the EU) should do more together as a community. The word "together" is used to describe activities which are performed by two or more partners at the same time, with the use of the same or similar methods but with the existence of two separate organizing centres of these activities. This model is developed according to the traditional model of sovereignty. Performing as a community means deeper integration and creation of collective institutions, which will stand as an organizing centre for performed activities. This institution must be donated to by the member states mainly within this process, and members cede part of their sovereignty to acquire much better performing potential as a collective organism. The European Union is now developing more within the model of shared sovereignty, which can be exemplified in establishing a common currency—the eurozone and the free trade zone. On the other hand, supporters of the traditional model of sovereignty still stress their objections, as happened during an EU summit when the UK Prime Minister disagreed with joining the fiscal union, a set of potential punishments for EU members who do not respect debt measures and the set of legal clauses bringing public spending under control. In the aftermath of that decision, the alleged remedy for Europe's debt crisis, which is consuming the united economy and poses a severe danger to all member states, had to be turned into a multilateral agreement between the majority of member states. Not only is the UK's decision an eruption of the government's confusion connected with challenges to their sovereignty posed by globalization, but an expression of the irony of globalized order. Prime Minister David Cameron's decision was made to protect the British financial centre, the

[17] Ibid., 24.

supplier of the lion's share of the UK's wealth and at the same time one of the most powerful agents of globalization.

To conclude, due to the fact that the EU formed institutions which are capable of making decisions affecting member states directly, the status of being a member means a limitation of sovereignty. However, membership cannot be understood as the encroachment of sovereignty, mainly because ceding or sharing some national competences is voluntary and the common institutions cannot go beyond rights granted according to the subsidiary principle.

The Challenge to National Sovereignty Posed by International Nongovernmental Organizations (INGOs)

International Nongovernmental Organizations (INGOs) constitute an institutional phenomenon that did not exist before the twentieth century, and their rapid spread occurred mainly in 1990s. The potential of such organizations is rooted in their capability to unite diverse people, regardless of territorial boundaries, into collectives sharing similar interests. Due to their widespread structure, they may be influential on a global scale both politically and financially. Their potential to exert influence, and to put pressure on global agents, has increased over time and the reason for that may lie in the fact that by organizing lots of provocative happenings, they were spotted by the global media industries. The term INGOs covers a wide range of organizations, from environmentally-focused to human rights-focused. Sylvia Ostry from McGill University, in her paper entitled "Globalization and Sovereignty", points out that INGOs "… are post—Enlightenment, linked less by a rule of reason than by a rule of morality or values".[18] They draw public attention to important global issues like environmental problems (Greenpeace), governments' transparency (Transparency International), and human rights (Amnesty International). Their abstinence from violence wins them vast groups of supporters and public respect, which often force nation states to take their objectives into consideration. They perform as a collective conscience, shaming nation states' (from their perspective) wrongful acts. Obviously, this could be regarded as an attempt to undermine national sovereignty. Whenever the interests of nation states

[18] S. Ostry, *Globalization and Sovereignty*, J. R. Mallory Annual Lecture, McGill University, 1999, 6, www.utoronto.ca/cis/ostry/docs_pdf/mallory.pdf (accessed December 15, 2011).

and INGOs reach points of contradiction, the sovereign decision of governmental institutions may be questioned, as the example of Amnesty International's successful action shows, which in one case led to India's rejection of building a mine which would disrupt forestation and environmental laws and be offensive to indigenous communities on the hills.[19]

The other factor that makes INGOs powerful enough to challenge national sovereignty is their interdependence. They are mainly founded by donations from members and supporters and, what is more important, their goals do not stem from self-interest, so the arguments they form are taken by public opinion just as they are expressed, without pre-filtering. The sooner governments understand INGO's influential character and mechanisms of performing, the better mechanisms they will evolve to cooperate with them and to protect sovereignty.

What are the Possible Responses to the Challenge to National Sovereignty Posed by the Forces of Globalization?

Three main concepts can be distinguished which provide an answer to the above question.

The first one predicts a demise of the nation state in the traditional meaning. Hyperglobalizers, who support this idea, point to deterritorialization, a key aspect of globalization, as a reason for the lack of future resistance from governments in the global network of political and economic interdependencies. They anticipate that nation states, vulnerable to regulations imposed by supranational agents, will be overwhelmed by these more powerful bodies and they will turn into business cells linked regionally in "an almost seamless global web of production and exchange".[20]

The second concept is driven by globalization sceptics who disagree with the demise of the nation state and who claim the increase of its importance. They argue that political power still controls globalization, understood as a set of social, political and economic processes, which could have expanded globally after particular national decisions had been

---

[19] *India rejection of Vedanta mine a landmark victory for Indigenous rights,* http://www.amnesty.org/en/news-and-updates/indian-government-rejection-vedanta-bauxite-mine-landmark-victory-indigenous-rights (accessed December 18, 2011).

[20] M. Steger, *The Globalization of Poverty*, 62.

made. Globalization occurred in the 1980s and 1990s as a result of the policy of neoliberal governments in Europe, USA and Japan. Furthermore, they perceive nation states as the most important units in international relations due to each unique state's capability to strengthen or lessen its position in global markets. Last but not least, they notice that some spheres of life such as education, infrastructure and population movements are bound to remain in the hands of governments.

The third concept highlights a change in the role of nation states. This idea is clearly expressed by Eleonore Kofman and Gilian Youngs in their profound analysis *Globalization: Theory and Practice*: "... the state is developing into an enterprise association with key civic, public and constitutional functions ... subordinate to the global marketplace."[21] This idea assumes that states will have to become more flexible. They will be determined by the principle of competitiveness, which is alleged to eclipse the welfare principle, characteristic of the traditional functioning of nation states. The transformed state should enhance its effectiveness of returns on investment by developing the institution of public-private partnership.

Conclusion

Widespread belief that globalization processes affect national sovereignty are connected with the observed proliferation of political interrelations and interdependencies. Therefore, traditional human assumptions that political differences are organized along territorial borders[22] are undermined. Borders divide the space into known and unknown in accordance with natural human mechanisms of perception and collective identities. The loss of boundaries both physical and mental must have reached its expression in the global confusion, and Governments are also in that state. Like the Great Argus, they have lost their essential feature—the right to self-determination. Their sovereignty underwent profound change from total, created after the Peace of Westphalia in seventeenth century, to titular, which emerged in the postmodern times of the twentieth century.

The Great Argus cannot fly and is vulnerable to predator's attacks, who do not recognize its titular sovereignty. Like the nation states, it will have to develop mechanisms of self-defence.

---

[21] E. Kofman, G. Youngs (eds.), *Globalization: Theory and Practice*, (London: Pinter Pub, 1996), 136.

[22] M. Steger, *The Globalization of* Poverty, 56.

The author is a student of Individual Interfaculty Studies in Humanities at the University of Wrocław and International Business at the Wrocław University of Economics. He specialises in globalization and performance.

CHAPTER SEVEN

DILEMMAS OF POWER IN CENTRAL EUROPE ON THE THRESHOLD OF TWENTY-FIRST CENTURY

ADRIAN SZUMOWSKI

The end of the Cold War was a mark of a major change in the field of International Relations. The partition of the Soviet Union and the instantaneous end to a conflict which had been an axis and point of reference to international actors for years accelerated and revealed processes which became foundations of a new shape of international environment.

The notion of power is one of the basic concepts of International Relations. More importantly, it is heavily affected by the evolution of the international environment. Therefore, the need for the redefinition of power, especially the power of the state, creates a series of dilemmas for every actor.

This chapter's main aim is to identify and analyse the dilemmas of power, which are major challenges for Central European states. They are important for two reasons: first, those states are unique due to the complete change of their environment over the last twenty-one years. The principles and ideas which proved to be effective during the Soviet rule, such as the limited sovereignty doctrine, the leading role of communist parties, Marxist dogmas of social conflict, were supplemented with state-centred orientation in international environment. Central Europe is now on the brink of becoming part of the most advanced region of the world, which can be described as transnational, interdependent, fragmented and evolutionary. The second reason is a derivate of the first one: it is a requirement of the effectiveness of actions in the international environment of Central Europe, which in turn requires understanding of new ideas and redefining of the old ones.

The basic dilemmas of power in Central Europe can be found in two main areas. The first one concerns fundamental questions about the directions of the evolution of the nature of power. These dilemmas focus mainly on strategic issues like the primary components of power of the state, attitude toward new international actors, and the approach to new challenges in International Relations and related topics.

The second group are regional issues typical for Central Europe, which can be divided into two sub-groups. First are the dilemmas about the geopolitical, geoeconomical and geocultural position of Central Europe between two major power centres. Second is the question about Central Europe itself: should it be considered a separate and coherent entity or is Central Europe a group of independent actors, and part of a larger entity?

Those dilemmas are key in defining the power of Central Europe on every level: from military oriented "hard power", to "smart power" and "soft power". The correct definition of power is vital to the position of Central European actors in the twenty-first century. Central Europe has its own advantages and disadvantages which derive from its basic features, such as history, geopolitics, economy, religion and culture.

The end of the Cold War created the opportunity to reform the international environment towards the next stage of evolution in international affairs. Those events, especially the abrupt end of global hostilities, ended with the unanticipated fall of one of the adversaries and they accelerated tendencies, such as globalization, which in turn shifted the balance in international relations toward being less centralized.

During this shift, major challenges emerged aiming at the remaining international actors such as states. In order to remain effective and influential, they had to reassess obsolete notions and their resources in order to formulate new principles and blueprints of undertaking effective actions in the new international environment.

Power is one of the oldest and most prominent institutions of international relations. More importantly, it is a notion heavily affected by its evolution, a point of reference for many other international phenomena, processes and definitions, for instance the term "superpower".

Moreover, the notion of power is also becoming a more dynamic category of International Relations.[1] Those changes make power a dynamic and elusive notion, which is constantly changing and evolving in an unknown direction. Determinants of this evolution are common to many social dimensions such as development of societies, politics and international relations, the so called "megatrends of development" identified by scholars such as Balcerowicz.[2] However, the main problem is

---

[1] The explanation, analysis and description of power as a dynamic notion is a primary field of research for author of this chapter.

[2] The term was introduced by J. Naisbitt. Presently it describes universal

the proper identification of those megatrends. What is more important, as Edward H. Carr claimed in his work, is that the notion of power is not constant. If its nature is changing then so are its features and determinants. Therefore, the key factors which have been shaping power for one hundred or even fifty years are now obsolete. Military issues may be an example. They used to be treated as an embodiment of power themselves. While at the beginning of the twentieth century the strength of the army was the basic factor describing state power, nowadays, thanks to the securities revolution conducted by Barry Buzan, Ole Wæver and Jaap de Wilde,[3] power is dispersed among many different areas such as ecology, economy, societal and political issues. Together they have created new, coherent and enlarged international security perspectives. This also means that power followed the evolution of security toward those sectors, and in turn absorbed their logic and dynamics.

Thanks to changes in international relations, which have rapidly accelerated during the last twenty years, the notion of power has become elusive. Therefore, we are unable to speak about a single and coherent definition of power in international relations. In fact, different scholars tend to disagree with each other. According to a classification presented by John Rothgeb[4], three major groups of definitions can be identified.

First, power is defined as a resource at the disposal of the state. The basic parameters of those definitions are quantitative: the size of the armed forces, population, economy and natural deposits. One of the key scholars in this group is Robert Gilpin. It is empirical, concrete and measurable, relying on hard statistic data which are objective and comparable. And yet, they are not perfect. An important problem is the correct identification of key factors determining power and actors, as well as the question about the

---

civilization tendencies which are shaping international order and civilization themselves. Different scholars present a different perception of megatrends: J. Naisbitt introduced ten of them, P. Kennedy 7, National Defense Council report (*Global Trends 2015*) 7, H. McRae 5; M. Perczyński 4 and J. Pajestka 2. B. Balcerowicz named six megatrends: globalization, informatics revolution, uneven demographic explosion, environmental threats, political (democratization) and economic (capitalism) transformation as well as the clash of civilizations. Detailed info can be found in B. Balcerowicz, *Pokój i nie-pokój. Na progu XXI wieku*, (Warszawa: Bellona, 2002), 85–118.

[3] The whole project has been described in B. Buzan, O. Wæver, J. de Wilde, *Security: a new framework for analysis,* (London-Boulder: Lynne Rienner Pub., 1998).

[4] J. M. Rothgeb, *Defining Power: Influence and Force in the Contemporary International System*, (New York: St. Martin's Press, 1993), 19–22.

capability of an actor to convert resources to international influence.[5] That is why the majority of scholars describe resource-based power definitions in terms of "putative power"[6], "power potential"[7] or "power base".[8]

The second group is composed of definitions which identify power as a goal of foreign policy. One of the supporters of this point of view is Hans Morghentau. These definitions are equally problematic. First of all, the basic goals for international actors are composed of possible gains only, such as the improvement of security[9], political influence or economical income.[10] Secondly, power without goals causes nothing more than accidental and chaotic turbulences in international environment.[11] Without political objectives, goal-oriented definitions tend to degenerate toward resource-based definitions.

The third group concerns the definition of power as a control. This group is composed of a critical approach toward the latter groups of definitions. Its basic presumption states that power is connected with independent decision making and liberty of action.[12] Moreover, power is the ability to control the environment and other actors while simultaneously maintaining as broad choice of possibilities as possible. Considering power as a social activity has some serious implications. First of all, it binds power with a social context heavily based on actors and objects of perception and their hierarchy of preference, especially in the matter of desired outcomes in international surroundings. Secondly, power has to serve a political objective, which works as a prism, focusing actor activities. Thirdly, power is present only where resistance is present. Therefore, the hierarchy of preference for actors and objects has to be at

---

[5] For instance, is the DR of the Congo, the biggest state in Africa, more powerful than Japan? The latter is not only smaller, but lacking most valuable natural resources. Is the DR of the Congo more influential than the Roman Catholic Church (a transnational organization)? The essence of both questions concerns a quantitative analysis of power complemented with questions about its quality.

[6] K. Knorr, *The Power of Nations: The Political Economy of International Relations*, (New York: Basic Books, 1975), 9.

[7] R. Dahl, *The Concept of Power*, "Behavioral Studies" (1957), 203.

[8] R. O. Keohane, J. S. Nye, *Power and Interdependence: World Politics in Transition*, (Boston: Little, Brown, 1977), 11.

[9] K. N. Waltz, *The Origins of War in Neorealist Theory*, "Journal of Interdisciplinary Theory" 18 (4) (1988), 616.

[10] R. O. Keohane, *After Hegemony: Cooperation and Discord in World Political Economy*, (Princeton: Princeton University Press, 1984), 22.

[11] K. W. Deutsch, *The Nerves of the Government*, (New York: Free Press, 1966), 110.

[12] Ibid., 247.

least partially contradictory. According to Rothgeb's aphorism, "one cannot claim to be exercising Power when one tells a sleeping dog to lie down".[13]

Karl Deutsch, one of the scholars in favour of this definition, points out that from the perspective of international environment power is the ability to initiate or resist changes in international relations,[14] which means, paradoxically, that powerful actors do not have to learn.

Taking into account the various definitions, this chapter is based on the concept of power as a social construct. This definition proves to be well adapted to the present turmoil in international relations because it does not focus on tools, which are undergoing a serious change, as well as power-bearers and goals of using power. This definition is most valuable because of its successful attempt to extract the logic of power without focusing on its visual components.

The evolution of power in international relations caused not only a disambiguation of its definitions, but also a dilution of subject, means and strategies of displaying power in international relations. The most useful model for deepening the analysis was presented by Joseph Nye[15]. He distinguished three kinds of Power:

Hard Power refers to coercive tactics: the threat or use of armed forces, economic pressure or sanctions, assassinations and subterfuge or other forms of intimidation. Hard power is generally associated to the stronger nations, as the ability to change the domestic affairs of other nations through military threats and economic incentives. Realists and neorealists, such as John Mearsheimer[16], advocate the use of such power for the balancing of the international system. This kind of power is composed solely of military and economic means.[17]

Soft Power, on the other hand, is the ability to obtain desired outcomes through co-option and attraction. It is composed of cultural and legal areas of power display. Soft power can be wielded not just by states but also by all actors in international politics, such as NGOs or international

---

[13] J. M. Rothgeb, *Defining Power*, 21.

[14] K. W. Deutsch, *The Analysis of International Relations*, (New York: Prentice-Hall, 1978), 23.

[15] The division between "soft" and "hard" power was first introduced by J. S. Nye in 1990, but the most complex presentation of this notion was presented in J. S. Nye Jr, *Soft power. Jak osiągnąć sukces w polityce światowej*, (Warszawa: Wydawnictwa Akademickie i Profesjonalne, 2007).

[16] J. Czaputowicz, *Teorie stosunków międzynarodowych. Krytyka i systematyzacja*, (Warszawa: Wydawnictwo Naukowe PWN, 2008), 37.

[17] J. S. Nye, *Soft Power*, 34.

institutions. The term[18] was based on research conducted by Peter Bachrach and Morton Baratz.[19]

Smart Power is a term in International Relations defined by Joseph Nye as the ability to combine hard and soft power into a winning strategy.[20] Smart power essentially grasps means of displaying power in international relations, and is an attempt to formulate an overall blueprint for using soft as well as hard power in international relations.

***

As mentioned above, dilemmas of power of Central Europe can be divided into two basic categories. The first one concerns global issues, which occur between the international environment and the state structure, breaking the Westphalian state-oriented logic and formulating foundations for new international systems. Scholars tend to disagree over the identification of those factors. However, this chapter focuses on power, enabling a successful reduction of that list to four major factors:

- the globalization mechanism, the main driving force of evolution of international relations, and therefore responsible for generating other factors;
- the shift from a state-centered world order towards a multilateral world;
- the shift from traditional towards new security issues, such as terrorism, organized crime and ecology;
- the shift from focus to spread in the logic of power display.

First, and most prominent is the process of globalization, well known for its ambiguity. In reference to "globalization", various reactions occur. Some scholars focus primarily on the positive features of those processes, while others underline their negative impacts.[21]

There is no generally accepted definition of globalization. Some scholars underline the issue of creating a global and complex network of interpenetrating connections between various levels of social activity, from the global perspective, through national, local, to single individuals. This network allows the bypassing of some levels of control and the direct

---

[18] Ibid., 34–40.

[19] P. Bachrach, M. Baratz, *Decisions and Nondecisions: An Analytical Framework*, "American Political Science Review" (1963), 632–634.

[20] J. S. Nye, *Soft Power*, 188.

[21] W. Anioł, *Paradoksy globalizacji*, (Warszawa: Aspra-JR, 2002), 9.

access of previously protected spheres of social activity.[22] Others, underline the still increasing capability of global transfers of goods, capital, ideas and people, unprecedented in history, when it comes to their range, capacity and scope. To them, globalization is a channel which allows transit on a global scale. The third group focuses on connections between societies and governments, which creates a new global system.[23] The fourth group underlines the importance of adding a "new quality" of social relations which cannot be reduced to the global range. Those scholars stress the topic of qualitative improvement of social activity.[24]

The last group of scholars are the closest to grasping the essence of globalization. In fact, globalization is a process of creating a new field of social activity, a virtual space less dependent on geography and territory, where most of social activities eventually take place.

This creation is driven by two major forces—political decisions which create environments favourable for this particular path of development, and the technological factor, creating advanced tools, a process of creating new social space, mainly informatics and telecommunication devices but also improvements in social and economic organizations, so-called "technocapitalism".[25]

Those forces generate four mechanisms of globalization. The first one is the time-space compression[26], which is responsible for reorganizing global social activity on a basis which places more significance on geography than the Westphalian organization, focusing primarily on territory as the most important factor of social activity. The second mechanism is deterritorialization.[27] This mechanism allows for the creation of ties against geographical conditioning. It is responsible for the transfer of social activity to non-territorial virtual space. The third mechanism is the transnational social space[28], which is also called "post-

---

[22] R. Robertson, *Globalization: Social Theory and Global Culture*, (London: SAGE Publications, 1992), 27.

[23] M. Pietraś, *Procesy globalizacji*, in M. Pietraś (ed.), *Międzynarodowe Stosunki Polityczne,* (Lublin: Wydawnictwo Uniwersytetu Marii Curie-Skłodowskiej, 2007), 573.

[24] I. Clark, *Globalization and International Relations Theory*, (Oxford: Oxford University Press, 1999), 6.

[25] M. Pietraś, *Procesy globalizacji*, 582–583.

[26] M. Kempy, *Czy globalizacja kulturowa współdecyduje o dynamice społeczeństw postkomunistycznych*, "Kultura i społeczeństwo" 1 (2000), 9.

[27] J. A. Scholtke, *Beyond the Buzzword: Towards a Critical Theory of Globalization,* in E. Kofman, G. Youngs (eds.), *Globalization: Theory and Practice*, (London: Pinter Pub, 1996), 49.

[28] M. Pietraś, *Procesy globalizacji*, 575.

sovereign space".[29] It is a new space which is turning into a primary sphere of social activity and it can be depicted by two features. Firstly, it is just outside of a sovereign state control, which is to say that states are not privileged actors. They are *primus inter pares*, important but not exclusive actors. Secondly, what is more important, every attempt to expand the influence of the state is met with determined resistance.[30] The fourth mechanism is called "the world as a single place", and it is similar to the so-called "butterfly effect". There are two basic principles of this mechanism. The first one is objective and it refers to global effects of a single act undertaken in a distant part of the world. Globalization amplifies not only their range but also their magnitude, allowing them to be sensed as nearby events.[31] The second one is subjective and it causes a shift in the human perspective. The population of the world takes the shape of a civil society, thanks to new ways of communication via the internet or television.[32]

Those mechanisms are used to handle more and more global issues and they can be divided into five different paths concerning: economy, information, culture, politics and ecology. Each path has its own logic and characteristic. For instance, the economic globalization seems to progress swiftly and hastily[33], whereas the political one tends to be slow and mostly conservative.

The word "globalization" may seem to signify a global process. In fact, it is asymmetrical. Its beneficiaries are primarily three most developed regions: Europe[34], US and Japan.[35]

The last question concerns the impact of globalization on the international environment and its actors. This influence is profound,

---

[29] J. N. Rosenau, *The Dynamic of Globalization: Toward an Operational Formulation*, "Security Dialogue" 22 (1) (1996), 251.
[30] A recent example of his resistance were protests against the Anti-Counterfeiting Trade Agreement, which affected many governmental institutions, even in Central Europe.
[31] M. Pietraś, *Procesy globalizacji*, 575.
[32] M. G. Schecter, *Civil Society and Globalization: The Investigation of Contested Concepts*, in M. G. Schecter (ed.), *The Revival of Civil Society Global and Comparative Perspectives*, (Basingstoke: Palgrave Macmillan, 1999), 65.
[33] However, it seems that the cycle of economic crises—such as those started in 2008 in the US with Lehman Brothers bank bankruptcy—tend to slow it down for a while. Despite recent voices of discontent, it seems fairly unlikely to permanently stop globalization on this path.
[34] However, the question about Central Europe as a beneficiary of globalization is still open, lacking a decisive answer.
[35] M. Pietraś, *Procesy globalizacji*, 581.

ranging from the creation of a new level of international relations to changes in mechanisms of national governments and international governance. It encompasses limits and interdependences among them up to the transfer of power between the state and transnational actors, as well as new challenges for state sovereignty and the inner logic of power.

The second mechanism responsible for generating dilemmas of power on the global level is a shift from the state-centered world order towards a multilateral world. Globalization is causing a major change in the structure of international system.

The primary actors displaying power in the international environment are states. In the nineteenth and twentieth centuries they gained their present configuration and became the most prominent form of political organization. They are distinguished by three features. The first one is sovereignty, the most synthetic definitions being proposed by Lech Antonowicz as an independence, and by Ludwik Ehrlich[36], who distinguished two dimensions: the horizontal one, which means states are equal and independent from each other, and the vertical one, which means that a state government has supreme powers (law and force) over its territory and population. The second feature is territory of the state with its inhabitants being an exclusive power base of the particular government. The third feature is the fact that the state is the only legal actor entitled to exercise violence. Whoever is doing it without an explicit consent of the state, breaks the law.

This situation has steadily evolved from the conclusion of the Cold War. The process gained momentum after the events of 9/11. The state-centered system is supplemented with new actors who can be divided into four categories, described by the criteria of form organization, power potential and degree of independence.

The first category, international organizations created by states, should become a platform of negotiations and mutual cooperation. Therefore, they are equipped with the widest capabilities thanks to member states and their resources. However, they are bound with the will of their member states, and as such they function only in the narrow limits drawn by governments. A special case is the European Union. International Relations experts argue whether it is a special case of the first supranational sovereign actor, a hybrid of a state and international organization, or just a special case of massively potent international organization.

---

[36] L. Ehrlich, *Prawo międzynarodowe*, (Warszawa: Wydawnictwo Prawnicze, 1958), 123.

The second category includes international companies, i.e. companies founded in one state and operating in others. These entities have a strong position, especially in the economic sphere, and they are relatively independent from governments, having headquarters as well as divisions. However, they are sometimes entangled in cooperation with local governments, which can question their independence. Special subcategories are Private Military Companies (PMCs)[37], which are the most obvious and direct proof for the breach of the Westphalian order in the crucial field of military power.

To the third category there belong political organizations which represent nations without a state. It is the most debatable category for two reasons. Firstly, some states define them as criminal organizations and they treat them as such. Secondly, they break the monopoly of the state to use means of violence, which makes them operate on the edge of international law or even outside its limits. Antonowicz calls them states *in statu nascendi*[38], because their main aim is to create their own state. Those organizations have moderate capabilities when it comes to resources and power in international relations. However, conflicts with some particular states or a group of states effectively limit their influence.

The fourth category includes social and transnational organizations, which have been excluded from former categories. There are scores of them, from churches and transnational to criminal and terrorist organizations. Their power is marginal or moderate, focused primarily on one sector, and the attitude of states towards them varies. For instance, the Roman Catholic Church may be treated as a privileged entity in one state, while in another it may be barely tolerated, and in a few others even outlawed. The most important feature of this category is that it remains on the verge or even outside the perception of the state. The state cannot or does not want to interfere in their activities and the power they generate also remains outside the state control. However, it is hard to measure that power due to its diffusion in separate spheres of activity and the large quantity of those organizations.

---

[37] Such as Blackwater, Executive Outcome, Sandline International, etc. These are companies that service the military. Most of them work in the field of logistics and property protection and some provide training services, tactical support or even mercenaries. What is more, those companies are widespread in Western states as well. For instance, M. Kaldor points out that in the US there have been for many years twice as many security personnel as policemen. M. Kaldor, *New and Old Wars. Second Edition*, (Cambridge: Moden, 2006), 12.

[38] L. Antonowicz, *Podręcznik prawa międzynarodowego*, (Warszawa: Wydawnictwo Prawnicze LexisNexis, 2001), 88.

The third from the above-mentioned mechanisms is the shift from traditional towards new security issues, such as terrorism, organized crime and ecology. This shift is caused mainly by globalization processes. The traditional threats are composed of simple divisions between what is inside and what is outside. Therefore, security issues perceived as outside factors are usually connected with other actors such as a state. The question of dealing with these issues are connected largely with military activity. Since the Cold War, Weapons of Mass Destructions (WMD) belong to the security issues.

To sum up, old Westphalian security issues refer mainly to the physical survival of a state and less to the welfare of its citizens. They have been connected with other actors, gaining an apocalyptic dimension.[39]

Due to globalization mechanisms, security issues are now changing. It appears that they are becoming far less apocalyptic, but much more omnipresent, and they are loosely connected with the military dimension.[40] What is more important is that those issues appear to be only insignificantly connected with other actors.[41] It seems that the international environment itself is becoming more hostile.

What is more important is that the dynamics of international relations affects security, so that it evolves dramatically. A major breaking point were the events of 9/11, as the security of state borders turned out to be less important. A new security paradigm arose, named by Victor Cha as "intermestic security".[42] It assumes that both spheres—the international and the domestic one—should be considered as one environment which generates threats and challenges to state security.

Digital infrastructure and computer systems are also a security issue. The so called "cyberterrorism", "cyberattacks" and "cybercrime"[43] are hypothetical and anticipated threats to those structures. As the Anonymous attacks on the government websites of Greece and Poland in 2012 showed, those threats are serious. Due to the growing dependence of modern states and economies on informatics and the internet, they offer easy access to vital data, which opens another vulnerability of state and society.

---

[39] M. Pietraś, *Procesy globalizacji*, 586.

[40] Some communities point out at such bizarre symbols as Mickey Mouse and Coca-Cola as a challenge to their security.

[41] M. Pietraś, *Procesy globalizacji*, 586.

[42] V. D. Cha, *Globalization and the Study of International Security*, "Journal of Peace Research" 37 (3) (2000), 395.

[43] *Convention on Cybercrime*, Council of Europe, November 23, 2001, Budapest, http://www.conventions.coe.int/Treaty/en/Treaties/Html/185.htm (accessed March 5, 2012).

The fourth mechanism is directly linked with power in international relations. It describes a shift from focus to spread in the logic of power display.

Power, perceived as a social phenomenon, depends primarily on the context or, in other words, on the perception of actor, object and environment. Definitions of this kind are helpful in explaining puzzling international events, such as different attitudes toward US actions in the Persian Gulf in 1991 and 2003, by underlining the social context of executing power. It is crucial not only to interpret power, but also to identify its limitations and resources required for its display in an international environment.[44] Most scholars agree that there are four fundamental categories of power interpretation. Rothgeb named them: weight, domain, range and scope.

The weight is the capability of an actor to convince objects into conducting a desired action. There are four components: the inner organization of an actor, the nature of its aims, the perception of power in international relations and the quality of communication between the actor and its prey. The most important factor is the aim: the more general it is, the more probable is its success.[45] It is difficult to properly formulate a political aim due to the impact of certain mechanisms, especially globalization, which diminish the actor`s vision with scores of interdependences. The role of the law of unintended consequences is tremendous and it increases chaos in international relations.

The domain concerns the quantity and diversity of objects which the actor is capable of controlling. Key criterion is the geographical distance between them: if it is short, the capabilities of influence grow larger. The greatest capabilities are those in the immediate vicinity of an actor. However, the development of globalization[46] has reduced the impact of geography by a process called "virtualization" of the state.[47] Factors that help to describe precisely the domain are the capability of the identification of a target, the environmental attitude towards the actor and the resistance of the object.[48] Nowadays, the hardest factor is the identification of an object.[49] As mentioned before, some actors do not

---

[44] D. J. Baldwin, *Power Analysis and World Politics: New Trends vs. Old Tendencies*, "Word Politics" 31 (2) (1979), 168–169.

[45] J. M. Rothgeb, *Defining* Power, 39–40.

[46] The most synthetic approach to globalization was presented by M. Pietraś, *Procesy globalizacji*, 572–597.

[47] R. Rosecrance, *The Rise of the Virtual State*, 4–6.

[48] J. M. Rothgeb, *Defining Power*, 40–41.

[49] For instance, in 2001, the US invaded Afghanistan in order to capture or kill

possess permanent territory, which causes two major effects. First, the object has to be found before executing power. Second, the object is sometimes intertwined with third parties such as civilian organizations. It makes identification harder and makes the exercise of force more expensive in moral, economic and political terms. It may also cause unintended consequences in the international environment.

The range refers to the diversity of threats and gains an actor may offer. This variable is closely connected with available resources: not only natural deposits, money, but also technology, information and culture. It is connected with the effective management of those resources.[50] Changes in international relations are causing tremendous diversification of resources. As Nye states, the cultural attractiveness and legality dimensions are gaining more influence as an important component of power.

The scope says which behaviour of an object can be controlled by the actor. This field often contains elements of resistance, because independence from foreign control is the main paradigm for international actors. Resistance gets harder when actors try to control deeper functions of an object. The case of a threat to the fundamental identity can be seen in contemporary Iraq, where local organizations perceive coalition forces as a tool to reshape their identity. When resistance becomes harder, costs increase and effects become more and more fleeting. Subsequently, limiting the level of control to a particularly interesting activity of an object will allow the decrease in the cost of the action. What is more important is that delicate actions require precise tools and skills of decision makers.[51]

Regional issues typical for Central Europe can be divided into two sub-groups. The first one are the dilemmas about the geopolitical, geoeconomical and geocultural position of Central Europe between two major power centres. The second one is the question about Central Europe itself: should it be considered as a separate and coherent entity or should it be a group of independent actors?

The latter question is crucial. The main aim of this chapter is to analyse the dilemmas of power in Central Europe but the notion of Central Europe is ambiguous. There are several competing points of view. The narrowest definition is produced by the Visegrád Group, which sees Central Europe

Osama bin Laden, who was subsequently found in neighbouring Pakistan.

50 J. M. Rothgeb, *Defining Power*, 41–42.

51 Ibid., 42–44; K. J. Holsti, *International Politics: A Framework for Analysis*, (New York: Prentice Hall, 1983), 151.

as composed of four States: Poland, the Czech Republic, Slovakia and Hungary.[52]

Lyndon B. Johnson refers to two aspects of Central Europe, which in a narrow sense is composed of Poland, the Czech Rebublic, Slovakia, Hungary and Slovenia but in a broader sense it includes also Germany and Austria. The distinguishing features of Central Europe are the Roman Catholicism as a dominating confession, the historical presence of multinational empires and the self-perception by excluding people not belonging to Central Europe, such as Romanians.[53]

A wider definition of Central Europe was created in the nineteenth century by thinkers such as Johan Rudolf Kjellén and Karl Ernst Haushofer. This notion, called *Mitteleuropa*, attempts to estimate the geographical limits of German hegemony in military, economic and cultural terms. The maximum range of German influence consisted of the Baltic states, Poland, the Czech Republic, Hungary, Slovakia, Croatia, Switzerland, Liechtenstein, Austria and Germany, as well as parts of Ukraine, Russia, Romania, Serbia, France and Italy.

A noteworthy definition of Central Europe is to be found in the European Regional Development Fund of the EU. The programme invests over 321 million euro in public-private partnerships aiming at encouraging transnational partnerships in Central Europe. Following regions and states are named as belonging to it: Austria, the Czech Republic, German *Länder* (Baden-Württemberg, Bayern, Berlin, Brandenburg, Mecklenburg-Vorpommern, Sachsen, Sachsen-Anhalt, Thüringen), Hungary, the northern part of Italy (Emilia-Romagna, Friuli-Venezia Giulia, Liguria, Lombardia, Piemonte, Bolzano, Trento, Valle d'Aosta, Veneto), Poland, Slovakia, Slovenia and the western part of Ukraine (Chernivtsi, Ivano-Frankivsk, Volyn, Lviv, Zakarpattia).[54]

Another definition was presented by a UN group of experts in 2006. They considered Central Europe as a region with common religion and cultural heritage, without directly identifying the states. Common heritage can be described by the subsequent features. Firstly, the synchronic or diachronic existence of Catholicism and Protestantism, with Orthodoxy and Islam playing only marginal roles. Secondly, the influence of German and Jewish culture in addition to Slavonic, Roman and Hungarian layers.

---

[52] *About the Visegrád Group*, http://www.visegradgroup.eu/about (accessed March 5, 2012.

[53] L. R. Johnson, *Central Europe: Enemies, Neighbors, Friends*, (Oxford: Oxford University Press, 1996), 4–6.

[54] *Regions*, http://www.central2013.eu/about-central/regions/ (accessed March 5, 2012).

Thirdly, the early historical development of an urban system and an independent urban society in counterbalance to nobility, sovereign and the church compared, other than in Eastern and South Eastern Europe. Fourthly, the early occurrence of free farmers independent from feudal landlords. Fifthly, Central European traditions of local and regional self-government as a consequence of early political particularism. Sixthly, cultural, linguistic, denominational and ethnic variety within countries—Central Europe has historically been composed of mainly multicultural empires, such as Austro-Hungary or the Commonwealth of Poland and Lithuania. Seventhly, the geopolitical factor of political and economic orientation toward the continent; and finally, a historically delayed industrialization in comparison with Western Europe, but much earlier than the one in Eastern and South Eastern Europe.[55]

However, recent research points out that international recognition of Central Europe as a separate region is questionable[56], especially through the day to day practice of various international organizations and foreign ministries. Therefore, Central Europe as an international region is defined not as an entity of geographical features but as a commonwealth of interests and ties, which usually bypass the physical characteristic of a region, leaving only spatial continuity. Those ties and mutual interests have not only to be present but the decision makers have to be aware of them[57]. As a consequence, regions such as Central and Eastern Europe are divided into three separate entities: one became a subregion of Western Europe by joining Western institutions in 2004, the second integrated around the Commonwealth of Independent States and the third, the South Eastern Europe, joined the EU in 2007.[58]

It is a serious dilemma when it comes to power. First, Central European states need to determine their place in international relations. The Visegrád Group has to decide if it has interests as a coherent entity or its interests should be identified with an external centre of power. The decision has not been made so far. However, it seems that the orientation towards the surrounding of Central Europe (mainly the EU) prevails over

---

[55] P. Jordan, *A Subdivision of Europe into larger Regions by Cultural Criteria*, (Vienna, 2006), http://www.docstoc.com/docs/53115069/A-Subdivision-of-Europe-into-Larger-Regions-by-Cultural (accessed March 5, 2012).

[56] H. Dumała, *Regiony międzynarodowe w teorii i praktyce*, in I. Topolski, H. Dumała, A. Dumała (eds.), *Regiony w stosunkach międzynarodowych*, (Lublin: Wydawnictwo Uniwersytetu Marii Curie-Skłodowskiej, 2006), 26–30.

[57] Ibid., 19.

[58] Ibid., 21.

regional and mutual interests. Therefore, regional institutions have fairly limited capabilities.

***

The former question of geopolitical designations of power in Central Europe is a derivate of self-perception of Central European decision makers. For this chapter, three dilemmas will be identitifed. The first one is the question which neighbouring power centers should be considered as a role model for Central Europe.[59] The second one is the question about how power should be displayed, whether proactively or conservatively. The third dilemma is how to optimally configure state resources in order to achieve maximum effectiveness.

The first dilemma appears to have been decisively solved in 2004, as Poland, Hungary, the Czech Republic and Slovakia joined the EU. However, fifty years of the Soviet presence in Central Europe have left some marks on the cultural tissue of region. This dilemma focuses primarily on the acceptance of geocultural patterns of development. The historical burden consists of the Catholic and Protestant heritage, Western culture transmitted by Germany as well as the Orthodox tradition and a semi-Asiatic culture transmitted by the Russian Empire and the former Soviet Union. It seems that Western patterns became dominant due to the fact that their effectiveness was proven by achieving victory in the Cold War, and liberal democracy became a dominant global ideology. However, Central Europe has some heritage which leaves it vulnerable to Eastern influences.

Former members of the communist parties, security services and military officers are the main part of that heritage. This human factor has been shaped, trained and educated by the former regime, being to some extent its beneficiaries. Those people, often active statesmen and civil servants, allowed for the preservation of some elements of the former legal, educational, economical, political and moral systems. Polish sociologist Jadwiga Staniszkis highlights an example of this preservation pointing to a "continuity of law" of the People`s Republic of Poland in the

[59] This question skips more detailed models of development, because both Western and other civilizations include in fact various accents and shades that have a common foundation. For this reason, these considerations are focused on a most general level to show two distinct logics of a choice between West and East for Central European Actors. More detailed consideration on which model should be chosen in particular (Nordic, Mediterranean or American, etc) exceed the framework of this chapter.

reformed Republic of Poland.[60] A personal affiliation to Russian officials is hard to estimate but it is undoubtedly still present in Central Europe. There are two other factors which could possibly influence the geocultural shift in Central Europe. First, the economic dependence on external actors, especially on their energy resources as well as military equipment and logistic support. Second, a potential and fatal weakening of the Western influence—the US and the EU in particular—which may move Central Europe eastwards.

There is the second dilemma whether Central European actors should utilize more proactive or conservative strategies. There are two conditions. First, power is a social phenomenon heavily dependent on the perception as well as the self-perception of an actor. Those issues are as important as the power base and resources at the author`s disposal. Second, the Long Cycle Theory, created by George Modelski[61], explains global hegemony, though it may also be used to investigate power of other states. Cycles are composed of two variables: the self-perception of an actor and the actual power base. The main problem is to identify correctly the phase in a cycle and to seize opportunities successfully.

Some scholars, like George Friedman, tend to stress that the present cycle is approaching a breaking point where new power arise and old ones perish. According to his predictions[62], the first half of the twenty-first century will be prosperous for Central Europe. It will reach a new peak of power. Governments need only to seize the opportunities. Others tend to focus on balancing between hard and soft dimensions of power, and prefer to maintain a conservative stance in order to follow general European trends. This dilemma is still ongoing. Up to this moment, followers of conservative strategies have the upper hand but this attitude may change in the future mainly because of a relative weakening of neighbouring power centres, a process which it is hard to spot and evaluate.

The third dilemma concerns internal state organization. Focus is on sources of power and methods of using it in the twenty-first century as well as on threats and dangers to the state. This dilemma reflects how global megatrends affect the situation in Central Europe, an influence which can be described as ambiguous. On the one hand, European prosperity, especially in normative and economic terms, is unprecedented.

---

[60] J. Staniszkis, *Postkomunizm. Próba opisu*, (Gdańsk: Wydawnictwo słowo/obraz terytoria, 2005), 42.
[61] Principles and design were contained in the monograph: G. Modelski, *Long Cycles in World Politics*, (Seattle: University of Washington Press, 1987).
[62] G. Friedman, *Następne 100 lat. Prognoza na XXI wiek*, (Warszawa: Andrzej Findeisen/AMF Plus Group, 2009).

On the other, some negative trends and demographic implosions are presently occurring in EU member states. However, the parameters of the environment of Central Europe tend to promote the use of strategies heavily relying on soft power.

The future of Europe is not yet clearly defined. However, past experiences point to a most probable scenario of political, economic and cultural evolution, ending up in a form of intertwined and hybrid entity which Polish scholar Jan Zielonka calls a "neomedievial empire"[63] with heterogeneous actors, shifting and interpenetrating borders and overlapping political, economical and cultural systems. This environment requires not only high management skills, but also the capacity of anticipation and planning. Therefore, displaying power will require complex and precise strategies which will favour smart power because it requires not only the mechanical answer to international stimulus but also a process of deliberation and making conscious choices. What is important is that Central European states on the one hand have to become more virtualized[64] due to the growing importance of transnational social networks, which exist mainly in cybernetic or ideological space. On the other hand, it appears that underestimation of hard power was a serious misperception.

***

To sum up, Central European actors are facing series of major dilemmas of power. The first group are globalization, new security issues, new actors in international relations and the elusive shift in the nature of power itself. The second group is characteristic for Central Europe and it is composed of self-perception, logic of development, activity in environment and the logic of domestic power compositions. Those questions should be considered so that an effective strategy of actions in international relations can be formulated.

The author is a PhD student at the Maria Curie-Skłodowska University in Lublin. He specialises in power in International Relations.

---

[63] J. Zielonka, *Europa jako imperium: nowe spojrzenie na Unię Europejską*, (Warszawa: Polski Instytut Spraw Międzynarodowych, 2007), 191.
[64] R. Rosecrance, *The Rise of the Virtual State. Wealth and Power in the Doming Century*, (New York: Basic Books, 1999), 4–6.

CHAPTER EIGHT

INVOLVEMENT OF CENTRAL EUROPEAN STATES IN THE MILITARY OPERATIONS OF NATO

SEBASTIAN BORODIJ

Nobody expects a full-scale armed conflict in the Europe of today. However, this threat was very real after World War II and led to the creation of a bipolar world standing just a "button press" away from total annihilation. Fortunately, one of two blocks has since dissolved and mankind was spared this cruel fate. A peculiar vacuum in Central Europe subsequently appeared. For independent countries emerging from the former Soviet sphere of influence it was either a "go your own way" or "join the strongest" decision. In the last thirteen years, thirteen countries have joined NATO. With twenty-eight member states, it is the most powerful military alliance in the world, capable of operating not only in Europe but also on other continents, and has repeatedly been given United Nations mandates to protect UN peacekeeping forces or to apply Security Council decisions. The alliance adapted itself to a new environment after the fall of the iron curtain and is still adapting to the world after 9/11.

Central European countries that have joined the alliance gained support and benefits but were also given new duties and responsibilities to fulfil, and are now a vital and integral part of the alliance. With multiple threats to world peace it is important to know and understand NATO's actions and policies. The first part of this article depicts NATO history and evolution of its doctrine. The second part shows a glimpse of NATO operations involving Central European member states and their part in conducting them.

Brief History of NATO and Development of its Doctrine

The North Atlantic Treaty Organization was created in 1949 by representatives of twelve Western countries: Belgium, Canada, Denmark, France, Iceland, Italy, Luxembourg, the Netherlands, Norway, Portugal, the United Kingdom and the United States. It was supposed to be a military security alliance to deter the Union of Soviet Socialist Republics' (USSR) expansion on the European continent.

The cornerstone for NATO had been laid in Brussels in March 1948, when representatives of Belgium, France, Luxembourg, the Netherlands, and the United Kingdom met to create a mutual assistance treaty to provide a common defence system. The Brussels Treaty stipulated that the parties would provide all the military aid and assistance in their power should any of the five signatories be the target of armed aggression in Europe.[1] President Harry S. Truman urged US participation in NATO as a critical part of his policy of containment of Soviet expansion. This policy had begun with the Truman Doctrine of 1947 with military assistance to Greece and Turkey to resist communist influence. The North Atlantic Treaty was signed on April 4, 1949 in Washington, D.C. It formally committed the European signatories and the United States and Canada to the defence of Western Europe.

The USSR strongly opposed the NATO alliance. In 1955, Moscow created the Warsaw Pact, a military alliance which consisted of Albania, Bulgaria, Czechoslovakia, the German Democratic Republic, Hungary, Poland and Romania.

During the 1960s, French President Charles de Gaulle rejected the lead of the United States and Britain in Europe and pushed for a larger diplomatic role for France. The French developed their own nuclear capacity and in 1966, while still remaining a part of NATO, France withdrew its troops from the alliance and requested that NATO's headquarters and all allied units and installations not under the control of French authorities should be removed from French soil. The French armed forces returned under NATO military command in 2009. Anyway, NATO headquarters relocated from Paris to Brussels in October 1967 have remained there until now.

---

[1] T. Kośmider, J. Ślipec, J. Zuziak, *Europejska integracja militarna. Sojusze wojskowe XX wieku,* (Warszawa: Wydawnictwo Akademii Obrony Narodowej, 2011), 126–128.

In the 1970s an era of detente took place. The Nixon administration took the lead with a relaxation of tensions between the East and West. Strategic Arms Limitation Talks (SALT) were started in November 1969. In May 1972, the first series of SALT Treaties was signed. The Arab-Israeli War did little to ease world tensions when it erupted in October 1973 and the Soviets implied that they might intervene in the crisis due to the strategic importance of oil reserves in that part of the world. In 1979, the USSR invaded Afghanistan. The ongoing conflict caused the suspension of negotiations between the United States and the USSR on reductions of intermediate-range nuclear forces (INF) that had opened in 1981.

By the end of the 1980s, dramatic changes had occurred in the Warsaw Pact countries. Starting in Poland, democratic movements supported by millions of citizens swept communist parties from the political stage, creating a new era in international relations. In November 1989, the Berlin Wall was destroyed and ten months later Germany was unified again. When Russian troops withdrew from Eastern Europe in the early 1990s, the Warsaw Pact was dissolved. In response to these events, NATO members at a London summit conference in July 1990 declared that they no longer considered the Soviets to be an adversary. They also stressed cooperation and partnership with the emerging democracies of the former Warsaw Pact.[2] The North Atlantic Cooperation Council (NACC) was created in 1991 to draw Central and Eastern European countries into a closer relationship with NATO. The collapse of communism in Europe forced NATO to search for new roles beyond that of a mutual defence pact. One of the new tasks was to boost democracy and national security in the former Warsaw bloc nations. Consequently, in March 1999, fifty years after the creation of NATO, the Czech Republic, Hungary and Poland became members.

NATO strategic doctrine has undergone many changes and revisions since 1949. Originally, NATO had three main functions. Firstly, it averted the situation similar to that after World War I when the USA retreated from the European continent as well as from the League of Nations, thus leaving the badly "damaged" continent on its own. Secondly, it helped to control the defeated Germany after World War II and carry out de-Nazification and democratization processes. The most important function

[2] *NATO vademecum*, (Warszawa: Bellona, 1995), 35.

was of course the defence of Western countries from the USSR and communist influence.[3] Article 5 of the NATO treaty says:

> The Parties agree that an armed attack against one or more of them in Europe or North America shall be considered an attack against them all and consequently they agree that, if such an armed attack occurs, each of them, in exercise of the right of individual or collective self-defence recognized by Article 51 of the Charter of the United Nations, will assist the Party or Parties so attacked by taking forthwith, individually and in concert with the other Parties, such action as it deems necessary, including the use of armed force, to restore and maintain the security of the North Atlantic area.[4]

That means that any member party must use military force to help the assailed country or countries and that this response must be adequate. To fulfil this obligation, NATO has always needed a strategic doctrine, suited to challenge the world situation presents. According to the doctrine of "Shield and Sword", the European conventional forces were supposed to be a shield and the United States nuclear forces a sword in the event of an attack. More cold war doctrines involved "Contamination", "Far-ward strategy", "Massive Retaliation", "Massive Strike", "Flexible Response" and "Strategic Deterrent". What they had in common was that they were based on the use of nuclear power and they named the specific enemy the Warsaw Pact forces.[5]

After the end of the Cold War, NATO had to overhaul its goals and means to achieve them. It implemented the Partnership for Peace programme of practical bilateral cooperation between individual Euro-Atlantic partner countries and NATO. It allowed partners to build an individual relationship with NATO, choosing their own priorities for cooperation. Based on a commitment to the democratic principles that underpin the alliance itself, the purpose of the PfP is to increase stability, diminish threats to peace and build strengthened security relationships.

At the beginning of the twenty-first century, NATO was confronted with two dilemmas. First, even before 9/11 it was becoming clear that new threats, such as terrorism and the proliferation of weapons of mass destruction, were coming from outside of Europe, drawing the United

---

[3] S. Zakrzewski, *Ewolucja koncepcji strategicznej NATO*, in S. Zakrzewski (ed.), *NATO na początku XXI wieku,* (Poznań: Wyższa Szkoła Nauk Humanistycznych i Dziennikarstwa, 2008), 13.

[4] *North Atlantic Treaty*, full text in *NATO na początku XXI wieku*, 165–167.

[5] S. Zakrzewski, *Ewolucja koncepcji strategicznej NATO*, 14–20.

States' attention toward Central Asia and the Middle East. However, as long as NATO still considered itself to be solely about managing European security, any US focus away from Europe would have meant a focus away from NATO. The second dilemma resulted from the fact that the military capabilities of most allies were still optimized for a contingency that was becoming ever less likely: a large-scale war in Europe.[6] A new strategic concept was therefore needed. Finally, in 2010 a new NATO strategic concept was outlined during the Lisbon Summit. According to this, the core tasks of the alliance are collective defence, crisis management and cooperative security.[7]

Collective defence is the most important and vital task. A new type of threat is also defined, and rather than a country it is specific problems: proliferation of nuclear weapons, ballistic missiles and other weapons of mass destruction and their means of delivery; terrorism, cyber attacks and key environmental and resource constraints.

Crisis management must use a broader range of tools, more effective and comprehensive. NATO is going to be present in all stages of a potential crisis. Thus, the third task, cooperative security, preserves its importance. NATO is no longer limited geographically to the North Atlantic region. In order to achieve its main goals it must cooperate with the EU, Russia and every other organization which could help to secure peace and stabilization. On the one hand, the application of those declarations may turn out to be difficult. On the other, the ability of such a large organisation to redefine its goals according to the constantly developing situation in the world is encouraging.

NATO Involvement in Military Operations after the Cold War

NATO has been involved in many smaller and bigger military operations in the last twenty years. There were also few non-military operations (mainly humanitarian aid and logistic support) which are not our concern. What is ironic is the fact that during the years of Cold War

---

[6] M. Rühle, *NATO ten years after: learning the lessons*, http://www.nato.int/docu/review/2011/11-september/10-years-sept-11/EN/index.htm, (accessed February 20, 2012).

[7] *Strategic Concept for the Defense and Security of the Members of the North Atlantic Treaty Organization, Adopted by Heads of State and Government at the NATO Summit in Lisbon 19–20 November 2010*, http://www.nato.int/nato_static/assets/pdf/pdf_publications/20120214_strategic-concept-2010-eng.pdf (accessed February 21, 2012).

tension NATO forces were not involved in any military struggle. The goals named in the North Atlantic Treaty in 1949 were achieved only by means of deterrence, a situation similar to the old British strategy of fleet-in-being.

The first NATO military operation was the intervention during the devastating ethnic war in former Yugoslavia in the early 1990s. With UN forces (UNPROFOR) unable to bring security to the region, NATO was given a mandate to replace them. Almost 60,000 NATO troops in addition to forces from non-NATO nations were deployed to Bosnia. NATO was accountable for carrying out the Dayton Peace Accords. They had three major goals: the ending of hostilities, the authorization of a military and civilian programme going into effect, and the establishment of a central Bosnian government while excluding individuals that serve sentences or under indictment by the International War Crimes Tribunal from taking part in the running of the government.[8] The alliance peacekeeping force was named IFOR (Implementation Force) and after one year changed its name to SFOR (Stabilization Force). The mission was a successful one and ended in 2004, when it was succeeded by EU forces.

KFOR (Kosovo Force) has been the second big NATO operation. It started in 1999 when NATO-led peacekeeping entered the troubled territory of Kosovo under the mandate of the UN. The initial task of the alliance was to deter renewed hostility and threats against Kosovan Albanians by Yugoslav forces, to establish and maintain a secure environment in Kosovo including public safety and civil order, as well as to demilitarize the Kosovo Liberation Army.[9] Today, KFOR focuses on building a secure environment in which all citizens, irrespective of their ethnic origins, can live in peace. The mission is still active, with almost 6,000 soldiers involved from thirty countries.

September 11, 2001 marked a new chapter in NATO's history. The terrorist attack on the USA initiated events that have consequences to this day. NATO decided that the attack fulfils the requirements of Article 5 of the Treaty, which activated the defensive clause. This led to the launching of new military operations, two of which are briefly described below.

Operation Active Endeavour is the biggest maritime military action in NATO's history. It operates in the Mediterranean Sea and is designed to

---

[8] *Summary of the General Framework Agreement, Fact Sheet Released by the Office of the Spokesman*, U.S. Department of State, November 30, 1995, http://www.nato.int/ifor/gfa/gfa-summ.htm (accessed February 21, 2012).

[9] *NATO's Role in Kosovo*, http://www.nato.int/cps/en/natolive/topics_48818.htm, (accessed February 19, 2012).

prevent movement of terrorists or weapons of mass destruction.[10] It also has collateral benefits in enhanced security of shipping. Operation Active Endeavour is based on international law and directly supports United Nations resolutions against threats to international peace and security caused by terrorist acts. More than 100 ships were boarded during this operation which tightened the control of illegal trafficking lines in the Mediterranean.

The biggest NATO-conducted operation is the ISAF (International Assistance Security Force). It is a NATO-led security mission in Afghanistan established by the UN in 2001. It is supposed to support the Government of the Islamic Republic of Afghanistan that aims to reduce the capability and will of the insurgency. The ISAF supports the growth in capacity and capability of the Afghan National Security Forces (ANSF), facilitates improvements in governance and socio-economic development. The aim is to provide a secure environment for sustainable stability.[11] As of January 2012 more than 130 thousand troops are directly involved in military actions in Afghanistan.[12] The war against terrorism is far from being over, and many mistakes are still being made by politicians or military leaders. So far, however, NATO has been the only organization capable of mounting a full-scale mission in a region far from its members' boundaries. Moreover, the involvement of many member countries, as well as cooperation form non-NATO states like Russia and Ukraine, has made this action the biggest peacemaking and peacekeeping operation in world's history. Many flaws have been observed but they are an indication of human error, a faulty international law and the lack of dialogue between states, religious leaders and sovereignty seeking nations, rather than NATO actions themselves.

Central European States Military Presence in NATO

NATO member states differ from each other in many aspects. Anyway, they all must respect and fulfil commitments ensuing from their membership. One of the backbones of the alliance is the old "one for all, all for one" rule. It connects with another rule, saying that NATO countries help each other accordingly to their resources and conditions.

---

[10] *Active Endeavour*, NATO Shipping Centre, http://www.shipping.nato.int/operations/AE/Pages/Background.aspx (accessed February 20, 2012).

[11] S. Zakrzewski (ed.), *NATO na początku XXI wieku*, 199.

[12] *International Security Assistance Force (ISAF): Key Facts and Figures*, http://www.isaf.nato.int/images/stories/File/2012-01-23%20ISAF%20Placemat-final.pdf (accessed February 18, 2012).

Central European member states have done much to integrate with the old Western ones and are not afraid of taking risks by participating in NATO operations. This is therefore a good opportunity to trace the aforementioned states' involvement in NATO actions.

Albania

Along with Croatia, Albania is the youngest member of the alliance, being admitted in 2009. The popular support for NATO is very high in Albania. It derives from NATO's role in the Kosovo conflict and the historically based alliance between Albania and USA.[13] It has the smallest defence budget of any NATO member states and its military equipment is mostly obsolete or in poor condition.[14] However, Albania has received help from many alliance members on this matter. Many countries donated newer equipment to the modernising Albanian forces. Albania tries to be an active member state, focussing on the security of the Balkans region. Nevertheless, it has participated in NATO's missions abroad. Prior to being a member state, Albania took part of the IFOR and SFOR forces in Bosnia and Herzegovina.[15] Their forces consisted of only one platoon (roughly seventy men), but it was the first time that Albanian soldiers were deployed outside its country borders in a post-war mission. Albania is also taking part, to a lesser degree, in the KFOR mission, with four soldiers deployed and giving logistic support for other countries. Currently ISAF is the most important NATO-led operation in which Albania is taking part. 286 soldiers are deployed on Afghan soil in three remote locations.[16] As of 2012, Albanian forces have had one fatal casualty.[17]

---

[13] B. Górka-Winter, M. Madej (eds.), *NATO Member States and the New Strategic Concept: An Overview,* (Warszawa: Polski Instytut Spraw Międzynarodowych, 2010), 9.
[14] Ibid., 9.
[15] Maj. V. Nikolla, *Albania the land of eagles*, http://www.nato.int/sfor/indexinf/articles/030618b/t030618b.htm, (accessed February 22, 2012).
[16] *International Security Assistance Force (ISAF): Key Facts and Figures.*
[17] *Statement made by Albanian Minister of Defence Arben Imami on 23.02.2012*, http://english.albeu.com/albania-news/imami-gives-details-of-funeral-ceremony-for-captain-vogli-/65990/ (accessed February 25, 2012).

Bulgaria

Bulgaria joined NATO in 2004. It has a military force of about forty thousand professional soldiers. Bulgarian vision of NATO is somewhat ambiguous. On the one hand, it participates in NATO foreign operations and understands new asymmetrical threats like cyber terrorism. On the other, it pays attention to the risk of the outbreak of traditional conflicts, which undermines the new NATO policy and strategy.[18] At many levels, Bulgarians still perceive NATO as a Cold-War-like defence alliance, which can diminish the importance of NATO's new strategic concept. In any case, Bulgarian soldiers participated in the SFOR proving their skills and good training.[19] Ten Bulgarian soldiers are still serving as a part of KFOR mission. In 2011, Bulgarian frigate *BGS Drazki* participated in the NATO-led Unified Protector operation during the Libyan Crisis to help implement arms-embargo and a no-fly zone. Currently, approximately six hundred Bulgarian troops are part of the ISAF mission in Afghanistan, stationed in Kabul and Kandahar.

Croatia

Croatia has been a NATO member since 2009. As one of the countries involved in the Balkans Conflict during the 1990s, Croatia still considers some of the states that emerged from the former Yugoslav federation as unstable. Thus, participating in the alliance is a major step towards strengthening of national security.[20] Croatia is also aware of asymmetric threats that can be more dangerous to a small state. Therefore, it fully supports NATO involvement in fighting such forms of violence. Croatian forces are part of the KFOR mission (with twenty soldiers and two helicopters).[21] Croatia is also a major participant in the ISAF operation. 312 troops are currently in Afghanistan with the tasks of stabilization and training of local police and army units.

---

[18] *NATO Member States and the New Strategic Concept: An Overview*, 16.

[19] J. Baev, *Bulgaria's Experience in Peace Support Operations*, www.bmlv.gv.at/pdf_pool/publikationen/wg2_baev.pdf (accessed February 16, 2012).

[20] *NATO Member States and the New Strategic Concept: An Overview*, 25.

[21] *Kosovo Fore Key Facts and Figures*, http://www.nato.int/kfor/structur/nations/placemap/kfor_placemat.pdf (accessed February 24, 2012).
NATO operations /KFOR peacekeeping operation in Kosovo, http://www.osrh.hr/prikaz_en.asp?idi=301&kati=4, (accessed February 20, 2012).

Czech Republic

The Czech Republic was one of the first three former Soviet bloc nations to be invited to join NATO in 1999. Its military, however, was in a process of deep reorganization and it was not until 2005 that all adaptations were completed. There are many opinions about the role of NATO in the Czech society. Some view it as a *de facto* global stabilizer. Others regard it as an important military alliance and still others as a relict of the Cold War.[22] Czech forces took part in both SFOR and IFOR operations as a part of the Multinational Division led by the British. They have also taken part in the KFOR operation with seven soldiers operating still as of 2012. The total size of Czech presence in the ISAF operation in Afghanistan is 489 personnel as of February 8, 2012.[23] Most of them are stationed in Kabul and are responsible for the Kabul Military Airport.

Estonia, Latvia and Lithuania

Due to their similar security concerns and issues, it is good to discuss the presence of three Baltic countries in military structures in one paragraph. Those states joined NATO in 2004. Along with their bonds with the USA, they regard NATO as a cornerstone of their security and a symbolic affirmation of their belonging to the West.[24] Given the lack of an air force of the Baltic states, their sky is patrolled by the air force of other member states involved in the mission Allied Air Policing.[25] Despite their modest military capabilities and very small armies (no more than twenty thousand in total) they have ensured other NATO states that they would be able to support operations undertaken by the alliance, even outside the treaty area. A small contribution was made by those countries to SFOR and KFOR missions. Today, only one Estonian soldier is taking part in the latter operation. On the other hand, almost six hundred soldiers from all the Baltic states are currently operating under the ISAF. So far, thirteen have lost their life in the mission.[26] They mostly take part in Province Reconstruction Teams all over the country and help other states' special forces with their tasks.

---

[22] *NATO Member States and the New Strategic Concept: An Overview*, 29.
[23] *ACR Task Force ISAF*, http://www.army.cz/scripts/detail.php?id=14355 (accessed February 20, 2012).
[24] *NATO Member States and the New Strategic Concept: An Overview*, 37.
[25] Ibid. 39.
[26] *Constantly updated casualties numbers during the Operation Endouring Freedom,* http://icasualties.org/oef/ (accessed Febraury 26, 2012).

Hungary

Hungary has been a NATO member since 1999. It perceives NATO as a pillar of its security and the most powerful military alliance. According to the Hungarian point of view, NATO should not limit itself to be a defensive pact within its borders. Single states alone are not capable of neutralizing current threats to the world's security. Therefore, Budapest puts great emphasis on cooperation within the alliance. Hungary took an active part in both SFOR and IFOR operations in the past.[27] Currently, 413 soldiers are serving in the ISAF mission. One of their tasks is running the Provincial Reconstruction Team in Baghlan. Moreover, 261 soldiers are deployed in Kosovo as a part of the KFOR mission.

Poland

Poland joined NATO in 1999 with more than 240 thousand soldiers, mostly conscripts. In 2012, the Polish Army is professional with one hundred thousand soldiers and the biggest budget among the states that have joined NATO since 1999. Poland sees NATO as a key component of its security. It has taken part in almost every NATO operation, delivering in most cases the biggest contingent of forces among Central European countries.[28] Poland took an active role in the IFOR and SFOR missions, in which it even commanded a Nordic-Polish battle group. Two hundred and twenty-nine Polish troops are currently serving in KFOR as part of the Polish-Ukrainian battalion. Polish ships *ORP Condor* and *ORP Xawery Czernicki* are taking part in the Active Endeavour operation in the Mediterranean . Over a dozen Polish instructors are training Iraqi police and military under NATO's training mission (NTM-I). The Polish contingent in the ISAF mission is one of the biggest in the whole NATO with almost 2,500 soldiers mostly in Ghazni province. Thirty-seven Polish casualties is the biggest toll among the Central European NATO members.

Romania

Romania has been a NATO member since 2004. According to its strategy, territorial defence is still NATO's fundamental task. Nonetheless, the alliance must also be able to respond to asymmetrical threats beyond

---

[27] Lt. P. Mouret, *Hungarian's last inspections*, http://www.nato.int/sfor/indexinf/133/p08a/t02p08a.htm (accessed February 23, 2012).

[28] *NATO Member States and the New Strategic Concept: An Overview*, 79.

NATO's boundaries. Romania's goal is to specialize in training and using civilian specialists to deal with crises and reconstruction of political and social structures.[29] Romanian forces were part of the SFOR operation. Among others, they were responsible for explosive materials disposal.[30] Fifty-nine Romanian soldiers are in the KFOR while two Romanian ships (*Regele Ferdinand* and *Regina Maria*) are participating in the Operation Active Endeavour. Almost 2,000 Romanian troops are currently part of ISAF in Afghanistan's Zabul province. Romania has suffered the loss of nineteen soldiers since the beginning of the operation.[31]

Slovakia

As a NATO member since 2004 Slovakia sees its membership as the only real guarantee of security. Slovakia focuses on Article 5 of the Washington Treaty, which states the importance of collective and mutual defence. Slovakian authorities understand the importance of NATO actions beyond the treaty borders. However, in their view only willing member states should participate in such operations.The Slovak Army was part of the SFOR but it is no longer participating in KFOR mission.[32] ISAF is currently the main point of interest for Slovakian soldiers. Three hundred and twenty-nine troops are taking part in the mission in Afghanistan, mostly protecting the Kandahar Airbase and helping in engineering duties.

Slovenia

Slovenia joined NATO in 2004, the first former Yugoslav republic to do so. It is one of the smallest member states. Slovenia is very eager to participate in NATO operations, even those exceeding definitions of Article 5 of the Treaty. Currently, 7 % of all Slovenian soldiers are taking part in stabilization missions outside the country, which is the highest

---

[29] Ibid., 90.

[30] Capt. Russell Craig, *Moving heavy metal*, http://www.nato.int/sfor/indexinf/137/p14a/t02p14a.htm (accessed February 20, 2012).

[31] *Constantly updated casualties numbers during the Operation Endouring Freedom*, http://icasualties.org/oef/ (accessed February 25, 2012).

[32] Maj. L. Guzicka, *Slovaks in Sarajevo*, http://www.nato.int/sfor/indexinf/99/s99p14a/t00102514a.htm (accessed February 24, 2012).

mark among the Central European states.[33] Slovenia, as a Balkan state, is very interested in keeping this area safe and secure. More than three hundred soldiers are now participating in KFOR and many had participated in SFOR.[34] In Afghanistan, seventy-nine Slovenian soldiers are performing training, mentorship and liaison duties together with their Italian counterparts.[35]

Conclusion

NATO has undergone many changes in its history. Once enemies, Central European states are now part of the alliance, what points out to the importance of adopting new strategies and goals for this organization. Apart from being a defence pact, NATO tends to act as a world peacekeeper, what is clearly visible. The above described new member states from Central and Eastern Europe take an active part in fulfilling this role. None of them evade taking the risk of putting their soldiers' lives in danger whenever and wherever they are needed. The solidarity between all member states is a backbone of the existence of the alliance, and so far it has been obvious that NATO is one of the most successful international organizations in terms of importance and speed of response.

The author is a Ph.D. candidate at the Nicolaus Copernicus University in Toruń. His fields of interest are military operations, the history of wars and the US foreign policy.

---

[33] *NATO Member States and the New Strategic Concept: An Overview*, 98.
[34] M. Larson, *Slovenian flag flies at SFOR HQ*, http://www.nato.int/sfor/nations/various/slovenia/joins-sfor/slovenia.htm, (accessed February 25, 2012).
[35] *Slovenia in ISAF*, http://www.defencemanagement.com/feature_story.asp?id=15261, (accessed February 27, 2012).

CHAPTER NINE

TRANSFORMATION OF THE GEOSTRATEGIC POSITION OF ROMANIA AFTER 1989

KRZYSZTOF OLSZEWSKI

Romania is the second largest country in Central Europe. Its territory, amounting to 238,391 square kilometres, is populated by around twenty-two million people, and is the seventh largest population in the European Union. A significant part of Romania lies at the arc of Carpathians. The country possesses a 225 kilometre long coast on the Black Sea with the port of Constanţa. Romania guards the Eastern border of NATO and the EU. Its neighbours are Ukraine in the North and in the East, the Republic of Moldova in the East, Serbia and Hungary in the West as well as Bulgaria in the South, along the Danube river. As President Traian Băsescu said in his speech at the Bucharest Conference, taking place contemporarily with the NATO summit in April 2008, Romania lies in a region crucial for the global security. The Black Sea "offers a direct link with Russia and South Caucasus. Through Turkey ... the region is a neighbour with the Middle East. In a geostrategic drawing, the connection between the Caspian Sea and the Black Sea" brings the region closer to Central Asia.[1] Thus, the Black Sea region "is situated on the corridor linking the Euro-Atlantic community (as a security provider and energy consumer) with the Middle East area—the Caspian region—Central Asia (as an energy provider and security consumer)".[2]

---

[1] *Address by H.E. President Traian Basescu*, Bucharest Conference, Transatlantic Forum, April 1–3 2008,
http://www.summitbucharest.ro/documente/fisiere/en/Discurs_presedintele_Traian_Basescu_GMF.pdf (accessed June 2, 2012).
See also: K. P. Marczuk, *Rumuńska strategia bezpieczeństwa*, in K. P. Marczuk (ed.), *Dwie dekady zmian: Rumunia 1989–2009*, (Warszawa: Wydawnictwo Difin, 2009), 113.
[2] *The National Security Strategy of Romania. The European Romania, the Euro-*

In the bipolar geopolitical order of the Cold War, the geostrategic position of Romania under Nicolae Ceauşescu was quite insignificant, and Bucharest was rather a periphery of the Warsaw Pact. Romania was not the kind of "front state" in the East-West conflict, as Poland or Czechoslovakia were. Therefore, the Red Army withdrew from the country in 1958 without risking any geopolitical loss. In the 1960s and 1970s, Ceauşescu could even pretend to be "independent" form the Kremlin authorities. Thus, he became an attractive partner for Western countries regarding him as a "dissident" within the Soviet bloc. The attractiveness of Romania was precisely due to its membership in the Warsaw Pact. If it had tried to quit the alliance, its members could have reacted militarily.[3] Moreover, Romania outside the Warsaw Pact could have been downgraded to the position of Albania,[4] and that is why Bucharest remained a member of the alliance until its dissolution in 1991.

Only in the second half of the 1990s, when Emil Constantinescu was elected President, did Romania start to strive to connect its security with Western structures. Since then, it has been pursuing its political and economic interests with reference to NATO and the EU. Moreover, Bucharest has signed documents on strategic partnership with the USA, Great Britain, France, Italy, Spain, Hungary, Poland and Turkey as well as an agreement on economic strategic partnership with Germany.[5] In relations with Russia, Romania has pursued a pragmatic and active attitude in trying to build a relationship based on confidence and reciprocal benefits.[6]

Geopolitical Priorities in the Official Documents of Romania

From 1991 to 2001, Act 51/1991, regarding the national security of Romania, was the most important document in this respect. However, it

Atlantic Romania: For a Better life in a Democratic, Safer and More Prosperous Country, Romania. The President, Bucharest 2007, 32.

[3] A. Burakowski, *Geniusz Karpat. Dyktatura Nicolae Ceausescu 1965–1989*, (Warszawa: Instytut Studiów Politycznych PAN, Wydawnictwo TRIO, 2008), 117.

[4] Ibid., 40.

[5] *Report on Romania`s Foreign Policy 2005–2008*, Ministry of Foreign Affairs Romania, 12, http://www.mae.ro/poze_editare/2008.11.26_RaportMAE_eng.pdf> (accessed November 26, 2009).

See also: *Relaţii bilaterale. Turcia*, Homepage of the Ministry of Foreigh Affairs Romania, http://www.mae.ro/bilateral-relations/1746#791 (accessed June 4, 2012).

[6] *Report on Romania`s Foreign Policy 2005–2008*, 42.

determined the internal security matters of the country rather than its main geostrategic priorities. Since it was published in the Official Monitor on July 8, 1991 (only seven days after the dissolution of the Warsaw Pact) it did not mention Romania's potential aspirations to join NATO and the EU.[7] As a matter of fact, the country became a geopolitical vacuum as long as the post-communist authorities stayed in power until they lost the election in 1996.

In December 2001, a common assembly of Romanian Chamber of Deputies and Senate passed a new National Security Strategy entitled "Guaranteeing democracy and fundamental rights as well as a sustainable and constant economic and social development, accession to the NATO and integration with the EU." This was the first document of its kind in which Romania explicitly declared integration with Euro-Atlantic structures as a component of its national strategy. NATO and EU were called "the only two organisations capable of guaranteeing an independent position and sovereignty as well as permitting an economic, political and social development similar to that of democratic countries".[8]

The National Security Act of 2001 expressed Romania's aspirations to deepen its strategic partnership with the USA as well as to develop privileged bilateral relations with other EU and NATO member states.[9]

The document declared that Romania would pursue an active policy to boost security and stability in South Eastern Europe, South Caucasus and the whole region of Danube and the Black Sea.[10]

The most recent National Security Strategy from April 17, 2006, the first after access to NATO, focuses on Romania's security in the global and regional framework. Special relations with the USA and integration with NATO are emphasized in the title of the document: "The European Romania, the Euro-Atlantic Romania: For a Better life in a Democratic, Safer and More Prosperous Country."[11] According to the strategy, Romania

---

[7] K. P. Marczuk, *Rumuńska strategia bezpieczeństwa*, 119–120.
See also: *Legea 51/1991 privind siguranţa naţională a României*, Monitorul Oficial nr. 163 din 8 iulie 1991.

[8] *Hotărâre nr.36 din 18 decembrie 2001 privind adoptarea Strategiei de securitate naţională a României. Textul actului publicat în Monitorul Oficial nr. 822/20 decembrie 2001*, http://www.cdep.ro/pls/legis/legis_pck.htp_act_text?idt=31060 (accessed June 1, 2012).

[9] Ibid.

[10] Ibid.

[11] *The National Security Strategy of Romania. The European Romania, the Euro-Atlantic Romania: For a Better life in a Democratic, Safer and More Prosperous Country*, Romania. The President, Bucharest 2007.

pursues its national security "through our own means and through cooperation with our allies and partners, in accordance with the provisions of our strategies, the Alliance's strategic concepts and the EU's security strategy".[12] Building "Romania's new European and Euro-Atlantic identity" was named as one of nine main targets of the strategy[13] whereas the security guarantees within NATO were called "the most solid in Romania's history".[14]

Also the National Defence Strategy from 2010 emphasises that "Romania has never in its history benefited from such comprehensive guarantees of security as the ones deriving from being a member state of the North Atlantic Alliance as well as from the partnership with the United States of America."[15]

Romania's Entry into NATO

Romania initiated diplomatic relations with NATO in 1990. A year later, President Ion Iliescu offered its close cooperation with the alliance. In a letter to the Secretary General Manfred Wörner, he called NATO "the only organisation capable of securing stability and security of new democracies in Europe".[16] In 1994, Romania joined the Partnership for Peace, the first country of the former Warsaw Pact to do so. Two years later, Romanian soldiers took part for the first time in NATO manoeuvres on the Black Sea. In a resolution of June 1996, the Romanian Parliament asked the parliaments of NATO member states to support Romanian aspirations to join the alliance.[17] Soon, in the communiqué of the NATO summit in Madrid in July 1997, Romania was named as a candidate state.[18] In April 1999, Romania opened its air space for NATO air forces launching the operation in Kosovo. At the same time, Bucharest was granted the Membership Action Plan.

---

[12] Ibid., 4.

[13] Ibid., 19.

[14] Ibid., 26.

[15] *Strategia Naţională de Apărare. Pentru o Românie care garantează securitatea şi prosperitatea generaţiilor viitoare*, (Bucureşti, 2010), 3.

[16] *Cronologia relaţiilor România-NATO*, Homepage of the Romanian Ministry of Foreign Affairs, http://old.mae.ro/index.php?unde=doc&id=25433&idlnk=1&cat=3 (accessed June 1, 2012).

[17] Ibid.

[18] Ibid.

After the terrorist attacks on the World Trade Centre in New York in September 2001, Romania declared its airspace, maritime space and territory as fully available for NATO forces.[19]

In March 2002, Romania organised a meeting of the Vilnius Group in Bucharest, the association of ten countries aspiring to join NATO: Lithuania, Latvia, Estonia, Slovakia, Romania, Bulgaria, Slovenia, Croatia, Albania and Macedonia. During the event in the Bucharest Parliament Palace, the Deputy Secretary of State of the USA, Richard Armitage, encouraged the NATO aspirant countries to double their efforts to join the alliance.[20]

However, as the Polish journalist Tomasz Grabiński wrote in *Gazeta Wyborcza* at that time, there were two approaches to the NATO enlargement in the USA. According to the first, the alliance would assume as many new members as possible. It would then lose its military role and become a "political background" for the USA, comfortable and cooperative towards Russia. According to the other approach, NATO could not assume countries as having a low level of development and facing reform problems. NATO standards were to be kept high.[21]

In January 2002, *Berliner Zeitung* wrote that NATO had changed its approach to the enlargement after September 11, 2001. The real military potential of new members was to be less important than their political support for the alliance. NATO was supposed to be a "discussion club" rather than a military pact. This facilitated the accession of Central European countries including Romania.[22]

At the November 2002 NATO summit in Prague, Romania, along with six other Central European countries, was invited to start negotiations on the accession. Eighty percent of Romanians supported the transatlantic aspirations of their country. As George W. Bush said, Romania would be more secure and at the same time, it would make the alliance stronger.[23] On March 29, 2004, Romania joined NATO.

In order to become a part of the alliance, Romania had to fulfil a range of conditions. The army had to be reduced to one hundred thousand soldiers, including no more than five thousand officers. Moreover, the education and training of soldiers had to be improved. As the Polish

---

[19] T. Grabiński, *Pierwsi dla pokoju*, "Gazeta Wyborcza", 271, November 21, 2002, 13.

[20] T. Grabiński, *Kupą do NATO*, "Gazeta Wyborcza" 72, March 26, 2002, 6.

[21] Ibid.

[22] ANR, *"Berliner Zeitung". NATO przyjmuje siedem krajów?*, "Gazeta Wyborcza" 18, January 22, 2002, 7.

[23] W. Rogacin, *Bałkańska flanka*, "Newsweek Polska" 2 January 12, 2003, 38–39.

journalist Wojciech Rogacin wrote: "80 % of Romanian pilots were not able to operate airplanes used by NATO." Besides, border control as well as the fight against corruption and arms trafficking were to be improved.[24]

Owing to intensive reforms, the Romanian armed forces have been completely professionalised since January 2007. The army counts seventy-five thousand professional soldiers and fifteen thousand civil workers.[25]

Romania's role in NATO

Directly before the war against Iraq was declared in 2003, Romania and Bulgaria had become for NATO, as Wojciech Rogacin wrote: "more important allies than some merited member states". Earlier, the question of NATO membership of those two countries had been treated with scepticism by Washington. However, their strategic value increased significantly in the context of the invasion on Iraq. Therefore, in November 2002, they were invited to join the North Atlantic Alliance.[26]

In 2002, Prime Minister Adrian Năstase said that Romania would be an important ally within NATO due to its size, geostrategic position and military potential.[27] Rogacin, quoting the London analyst Daniel Keohane, wrote that after Romania's and Bulgaria's accession "the area of NATO would cover the space from the Baltic to the Black Sea while Turkey and Greece would gain a natural link with other member states. The alliance will stabilize its southern flank."[28]

According to another Polish journalist, Bartosz Węglarczyk, President George W. Bush wanted to assure peace in Europe by assuming seven countries at once in NATO. Thus, he would be able to concentrate on the war against terrorists in the Middle East as well as on the relations with China. The accession of Romania and Bulgaria, which would boost the importance of Southern Europe in NATO, was also supported by Greece, Turkey, Italy, Spain and France. Paris even wanted Romania to join NATO as early as 1999.[29]

According to Dominika Ćosić from the Polish weekly *Wprost*, Romania was "the most desired ally of NATO in the region". Bucharest was supposed to take over some functions that were the responsbillity of

---

[24] Ibid.

[25] K. P. Marczuk, *Rumuńska strategia bezpieczeństwa*, 122.

[26] W. Rogacin, *Bałkańska flanka*, 38–39.

[27] T. Grabiński, *Pierwsi dla pokoju*, "Gazeta Wyborcza" 271, November 21, 2002, 13.

[28] W. Rogacin, *Bałkańska flanka*, 38–39.

[29] B. Węglarczyk, *NATO + 7*, "Gazeta Wyborcza" 93, April 20, 2002, 1.

Turkey.[30] The significance of Romania increased due to its logistic advantages during the operations in Afghanistan and Iraq. Making its port in Constanţa and its air force base available for NATO, Romania became a transit point between Great Britain on the one hand as well as Iraq and Afghanistan on the other. Thus, the alliance was no longer exclusively dependent on Turkey. Furthermore, Romania's profit from the lease of the port facilities was a significant boost for its military budget.[31]

Rogacin held that the position of Romania and Bulgaria in NATO could become more important than that of Poland, the Czech Republic and Hungary, because the air bases of the former lie in a point of contact with regions which are a source of instability. For the purpose of the war in Iraq in 2003, NATO engineers installed additional equipment at the airports of Constanţa, Feteşti and Timişoara. Moreover, the morale and readiness of Romania and Bulgaria to prove their reliability as loyal allies were of value, given the "reserved" attitude of France and Germany at that time. Rogacin pointed out that Romania had already proven its loyalty as it sent a commando unit of "Red Scorpions" first to Kosovo and then to Afghanistan. During the war in former Yugoslavia, Romania provided the Americans with information of its secret service.[32]

"Out of Area" Military Operations

On the basis of the decision of its parliament from December 21, 2001, Romania has been taking part in the International Stability Assistance Force in Afghanistan. In July 2002, the 36th Infantry Battalion "Red Scorpions" was the first Romanian unit deployed in the theatre. Romania was the only former Warsaw Pact member to deploy a special battle unit as a part of antiterrorist forces. About four hundred troops were stationed at the Kandahar Airfield. It was the first Romanian military detachment involved in war operations since World War II.[33] In 2004, the above-mentioned Polish journalist Ćosić emphasized the success of the battalion that liquidated the biggest Taliban arsenal of weapons.[34]

---

[30] D. Ćosić, *Natonalizacja*, "Wprost" 18 May 2, 2004, 92–93.
[31] Ibid.
[32] W. Rogacin, *Bałkańska flanka*, 38–39.
[33] *Romanian Defence. 2004–2009. Five Years of NATO Membership*, Romanian Ministry of National Defence, http://www.mapn.gov.ro/publicatii/2011/revista_defense.pdf (accessed June 4, 2012), 18.
[34] D. Ćosić, *Natonalizacja*, 92–93.

From 2002 to 2009, the total number of Romanian troops engaged in operations in Afghanistan amounted to approximately 7,200.[35] In 2010, Bucharest increased its contingent to 1,600 troops.[36] According to NATO data from May 2012, there were 1,800 Romanian soldiers stationed there out of the total 129 thousand ISAF troops in Afghanistan. The Romanian contingent was the seventh biggest and it was larger than that of Spain, Turkey or Canada.[37]

Bucharest deployed its first operational forces in Operation Iraqi Freedom in July 2003. There were about 840 military personnel involved in the initial stage. Since August 2004, Romania has contributed to the NATO Training Mission in Iraq, which offered the Iraqi security forces preparation, equipment and technical assistance. In July 2009, Romania's six-year participation in Iraq was concluded.[38] During this time, attitudes among the Romanian society and political elites were very pro-American, and Romania did not want to pull out of Iraq before the deadline.[39]

Although the operations in Afghanistan and Iraq have been the most important, there have also been others in the last two decades. Since 1991, Romania has participated in several missions under the auspices of the United Nations,[40] NATO and, since 2004, the European Union.[41] Among others, it has been a part of the KFOR mission in Kosovo. Since 2005, Romania has been participating in the Operation Active Endeavour. In

---

[35] *Romanian Defence. 2004–2009. Five Years of NATO Membership*, 21.

[36] *Romania To Send More Troops To Afghanistan; Germany Mulls Raising Number*, Radio Free Europe, January 1, 2010, http://www.rferl.org/content/Romania_To_Send_More_Troops_To_Afghanistan/1936502.html (accessed June 4, 2012).

[37] *International Security Assistance Force (ISAF): Key Facts and Figures*, 10 May 2012, http://www.nato.int/isaf/docu/epub/pdf/placemat.pdf (accessed June 4, 2012).

[38] *Participarea României la operaţiunile şi misiunile Alianţei*, Romanian Ministry of Foreigh Affairs, http://www.mae.ro/print/1586 (accessed June 3, 2012).
Romanian Defence. 2004–2009. Five Years of NATO Membership, Romanian Ministry of National Defence, http://www.mapn.gov.ro/publicatii/2011/revista_defense.pdf (accessed June 4, 2012), 22.

[39] D. Ćosić, *Natonalizacja*, 92–93.

[40] For more, see: *Paticiparea României la operaţiuni ONU de menţinere a păcii*, Romanian Ministry of Foreigh Affairs, http://www.mae.ro/print/2114 (accessed June 3, 2012).
See also: *Romanian Defence. 2004–2009. Five Years of NATO Membership*, p. 26.

[41] See more: *Paticiparea României la misiunile PSAC*, Romanian Ministry of Foreigh Affairs, http://www.mae.ro/print/1884 (accessed June 3, 2012).
See also: *Romanian Defence. 2004–2009. Five Years of NATO Membership*, 25.

2007, Romania conducted operation BALTICA 07, consisting in the execution of Air Police Service for Latvia, Lithuania and Estonia.[42]

Romania's Vision of NATO

In the first years of its NATO membership, Romania had a clear vision of the future role of the alliance. In Bucharest's opinion, relations between NATO and Russia have been a strategic element of Euro-Atlantic security.[43] However, Romania has wanted Russia to fulfil its obligations within the Organisation for Security and Cooperation in Europe in 1999 to withdraw its troops from Georgian and Moldavian territories.[44]

Romania was one of eight NATO member countries that signed an appeal for issuing the Membership Action Plan to Ukraine and Georgia in March 2008. As the host of the summit next month, President Băsescu supported the initiative.[45] He also shared the opinion that "every independent state has the right to exercise its own choices and nobody [i.e. Russia] can veto them".[46]

Moreover, Romania has also supported the NATO accession of Albania and Croatia as well as Macedonia. Tirana and Zagreb were invited to join the alliance at the NATO summit in Bucharest in April 2008, and a year later they became member states. Romania has been also in favour of strengthening NATO's cooperation with Serbia, Montenegro, Bosnia and Herzegovina as well as the Republic of Moldova, Armenia and Azerbaijan.[47]

Romania, along with Poland and the Baltic States, has supported the concept of Secretary General Anders Fogh Rasmussen to strengthen NATO through maintaining the balance between the task of collective defence of territories of the member states and out of area operations. The anti-missile shield is supposed to be a common NATO project.[48]

---

[42] *Romanian Defence. 2004–2009. Five Years of NATO Membership*, 6.

[43] *Address by H.E. President Traian Basescu.*

[44] *Report on Romania`s Foreign Policy 2005–2008*, 42.

[45] Ibid., 17.

[46] *Rozpoczął się szczyt NATO w Bukareszcie*, „Rzeczpospolita", 2.04.2008, http://www.rp.pl/artykul/115248.html (accessed January 11, 2010).

[47] K. P. Marczuk, *Rumuńska strategia bezpieczeństwa*, 115.
See also: *Address by H.E. President Traian Basescu.*

[48] A. Słojewska, *Tarcza antyrakietowa będzie chronić całe NATO?*, "Rzeczpospolita", October 15, 2010.

Special Relations with the USA

Since 1997, Romania's relations with the USA have developed within the framework of the strategic partnership.[49] After the attacks on the World Trade Centre in New York, Romania has been strongly involved in supporting the USA. In *Gazeta Wyborcza* Bartosz Węglarczyk wrote that Bucharest "practically placed its territory, armed forces and secret services at Americans' disposal". Soon, American soldiers were stationed in Romania and the Romanian army was reformed at an accelerated pace.[50]

Controversies over the International Criminal Court

As an example of the character of the Romanian-American relations, an agreement of 2002 may be considered. As the International Criminal Court at the Hague started its activities in July 2002, an argument arouse between the European Union and the USA. The latter did not recognize the court. The Washington administration feared that it would sue American citizens. What is more, the USA signed bilateral agreements with individual countries guaranteeing the inviolability of US citizens. Polish journalist Joanna Kowalska wrote in *Newsweek* that poorer European countries aspiring to join both NATO and EU had found themselves "between hammer and anvil". For them, the agreement with the USA meant "a step backward on the way to the EU".[51]

On August 1, 2002, Romania was the first country to sign such an agreement. According to this:

> persons of the USA present in the territory of Romania shall not, absent the expressed consent of the Government of the USA, be surrendered or transferred by any means to the International. Criminal Court for any purpose … be surrendered or transferred by any means to any other entity or third country, or expelled to a third country, for the purpose of surrender to or transfer to the ICC.

Further, if Romania "extradites, surrenders or otherwise transfers a person of the USA to a third country", it will not agree "to the surrender or transfer of that person to the ICC … absent the expressed consent of the Government of the USA".[52]

---

[49] *Romanian Defence. 2004–2009. Five Years of NATO Membership*, 7.
[50] B. Węglarczyk, *NATO + 7*, 1.
[51] J. Kowalska, *Manewry między młotem a kowadłem*, "Newsweek Polska" 36, September 8, 2002, 56.
[52] *Agreement between the Government of the United States of America and the*

In Kowalska's view, the "submissiveness" of Romania evoked "a real fury" in Brussels. Bucharest presumably had jumped the gun instead of waiting for the official statement of the EU. On the other hand, President Ion Iliescu asserted that his country was not able to do it another way because the agreement was "a chance and a necessity". Washington officially denied to have exerted pressure on the government of Romania. Secretary of State Colin Powell said that signing the agreement had not been a condition for the access to NATO: "We do not intimidate our friends", he asserted. Anyway, Romania wanted to be "better safe than sorry" and signed the agreement.[53]

US Military Bases in Romania

As the Romanian journal *Adevărul* recorded, Romania, like Poland, was interested in the American military presence in the "New Europe". It would be an insurance against potential Russian pressure rather than against a hypothetical attack from Iran.[54] In December 2005, Secretary of State Condoleeza Rice and the Romanian Foreign Minister Mihai Răzvan Ungureanu signed the Access Agreement concerning the presence of US military forces on the territory of Romania. It was the first document foreseeing American military bases in an Eastern European former member state of the Warsaw Pact. About 1,500 soldiers were to be stationed in the country. Romania put three military training areas in Smârdan, Babadag and Cincu as well as the Mihail Kogălniceanu Airbase at the disposal of the US Army. Vessels and vehicles operated by or exclusively for United States forces were allowed to enter, exit and move freely within the territory of Romania. US aircraft, vessels and vehicles were freed from inspection.[55] Military facilities on Romanian soil were to

---

Government of Romania regarding the surrender of persons to the International Criminal Court, 1.08.2002, http://www.amicc.org/docs/US-Romania.pdf (accessed June 4, 2012).

[53] J. Kowalska, *Manewry między młotem a kowadłem*, 56.

[54] O.Nahoi, I.M.Ioniță, *România și Polonia parteneriat strategic*, „Adevărul", 08.10.2009, http://www.adevarul.ro/articole/romania-si-polonia-parteneriat-strategic.html (accessed October 19, 2009).

[55] *Agreement between the United States of America and Romania regarding the Activities of United States Forces located on the Territory of Romania*, Bucharest, 6.12.2005, http://www.state.gov/documents/organization/75826.pdf (accessed June 4, 2012).

See also: *American military bases in Romania and what they stand for*, http://www.mail-archive.com/news@antic.org/msg08353.html (accessed December 25, 2009).

be used by Americans to transfer forces to Afghanistan and the Middle East.[56] The presence of American soldiers in Romania may be perceived as an additional guarantee of security, along with the article five of the Treaty of Washington.

In October 2009, Vice President Joe Biden stated that the USA had no closer ally in the region than Romania, in which they have been strengthening their presence. Fifteen hundred American soldiers were already stationed in Romania in 2009. According to the Polish newspaper *Rzeczpospolita*, a new strategy from Washington aimed at deploying its troops in the vicinity of conflict zones, given that Afghanistan, Iran and Iraq were priorities of the American policy.[57]

Anti-Missile Shield

In September 2009, the USA modified its project of an anti-missile shield in Europe. The administration of Barrack Obama withdrew from the plan of the Bush administration to build a base of rocket launchers in Poland, along with early warning radars in the Czech Republic. A new concept foresaw the stationing of SM-3 rockets in two countries—one northern and one southern. The latter was supposed to be Romania.[58]

During his visit in Bucharest in October 2009, Biden was assured of the Romanian support for the project. He asserted that the new one was better than that planned by the administration of George W. Bush. Romania has benefited from the modification of the project, and the previous one had not foreseen the participation of Bucharest. Julian Chifu, head of the Conflict Prevention and Early Warning Centre in Bucharest, said that the invitation to take part in the project was proof for a strengthening of the strategic American-Romanian alliance and an increasing role of Romania in the US policy.[59] In his opinion, the strategic position of Romania was to be "radically improved".[60]

In February 2010, Romanian authorities accepted the plan of installing SM-3 rocket launchers on its territory. On September 13, 2011 in

---

See also: WJ, *Rumunia. Pierwsza baza USA*, "Gazeta Wyborcza" 284, December 7, 2005, 12.

[56] AFP, PAP, LWA, *Rumunia. Będą bazy USA* 281, December 3, 2005, 6.

[57] W. Lorenz, J. Przybylski, *Rumunia dostanie tarczę*, "Rzeczpospolita", October 23, 2009.

[58] Ibid.

[59] Ibid.

[60] W. Lorenz, J. Przybylski, *Rumunia dostanie tarczę antyrakietową*, "Rzeczpospolita", February 5, 2010.

Washington, Romanian Foreign Minister Teodor Baconschi and the Secretary of State of the USA Hillary Clinton signed an agreement concerning the construction of the ballistic missile defence system in southern Romania, at the military base of Deveselu. The avergae number of US forces members at the base will be approximately 150, and it cannot exceed 500. The parties declared that the system would be used exclusively for self-defence purposes.[61] The system is expected to start working in 2015.[62]

Discrepancies

One of the few geopolitical issues in which Romania opposed the position of the USA and most of NATO member states was the declaration of independence of Kosovo in February 2008. So far, Romania has not recognized that act. Bucharest supported Serbia in a case in the International Court of Justice. In its advisory opinion in July 2010, the court stated that the unilateral declaration of independence by Kosovo had been in accordance with international law.[63] In the dispute, Romania took the same position as Russia and China, contrary to the USA, Great Britain and France.[64]

Another issue in which Romania did not follow the United States was the intervention in Libya, in which Bucharest did not take part.[65] In this case, other Central European states also did not follow suit. Neither the Kosovo nor the Libya case caused any damages to the Romanian-American relations.

---

[61] *Agreement between the United States of America and Romania on the Deployment of the United States Ballistic Missile Defense System in Romania*, Washington, 13.09.2011, http://www.state.gov/documents/organization/173130.pdf (accessed June 4, 2012).

[62] W. Lorenz, J. Przybylski, *Rumunia dostanie tarczę antyrakietową.*

[63] *Accordance with international law of the unilateral declaration of independence in respect of Kosovo. Summary of the Advisory Opinion*, International Court of Justice, 22.07.2010, http://www.icj-cij.org/docket/files/141/16010.pdf (accessed June 4, 2012).
See also: *Report on Romania`s Foreign Policy 2005–2008*, 34.

[64] R. Ciubotaru, *România înfruntă SUA în lupta pentru Kosovo*, "Cotidianul", December 9, 2009,
http://www.cotidianul.ro/romania_infrunta_sua_in_lupta_pentru_kosovo-105211.html (accessed December 10, 2009).

[65] *Romania Rejects Military Intervention In Libya - President*, 12.03.2011, http://www.mediafax.ro/english/romania-rejects-military-intervention-in-libya-president-8056318 (accessed June 4, 2012).

Conclusions

Since 1989, the Romanian geostrategic position has undergone a remarkable change. From a peripheral member of the Warsaw Pact within the reality of the Cold War, Romania has evolved into the "southern pillar" of NATO within the reality of a world dominated by the USA. Before the collapse of communism and the death of the "genius of the Carpathians" Ceauşescu, Romania had strived to build socialism and strengthen its alliance with "brother" socialist countries. At the threshold of the twenty-first century, Bucharest aims at building its "new European and Euro-Atlantic identity".

In the twenty years after the breakthrough of 1989, Romania has gone a long way from being a "maverick" but, in fact, faithful ally of the Soviet Union to the position of a strategic and loyal partner of the United States.

Under Ceauşescu, Romania was hardly present on the international arena in terms of military power. From the 1990s it has become increasingly active as a participant of military operations outside its borders. Romania has gained the position of an active player in a region of an increased geostrategic importance.

The author is a graduate in International Relations at the Nicolaus Copernicus University in Toruń. At present, he is writing a PhD thesis concerning German-Romanian relations in the Cold War. His research focuses on German, Polish and Romanian foreign policy in the twentieth century.

Part Three

Central Europe in the European Union

CHAPTER TEN

LOST DYNAMICS OR DYNAMIC LOSS? EXPLORING THE VAGUE FUTURE OF EUROPEAN INTEGRATION

KAMIL FILIPEK

The second half of 2011 brought out some critical decisions regarding the future of the European integration process. On the wave of the global financial crisis, the European Union fell into a serious ontological trap that looms behind the desperate efforts of a few weighty European politicians to save the euro and some eurozone countries. The ongoing debate on the eurozone triggered old concerns about the future of the European project as a whole. "The Euro will not be safe until Europe answers some fundamental questions that it has run away from for many years" argues *The Economist*.[1] These fundamental (ontological) questions go far beyond the eurozone, the European Constitution, and the confederal vs. federal vision of Europe. They touch the basics of the European project and EU principles: cooperation, solidarity, subsidiarity, proportionality, diversity and cohesion.

This chapter tries to solve some of the important problems of the European integration on both a theoretical and a practical basis. Some complex issues are further discussed, such as the concept of Europe, the possible scenarios for European integration and the future of Central and Eastern Europe.

The Question of Europe

Contemporary problems arising in European integration cannot be understood without understating the meanings of Europe. Looking back

[1] *Starring into the Abyss*, in "The Economist", November 12, 2011, http://www.economist.com/node/21536872 (accessed February 22, 2012).

through the ages, the meaning of Europe has changed, matured, declined and clarified many times.

> Europe was not, and is not, an easily definable term with concrete and essential proportions, but has since Antiquity been discursively shaped through constant negotiation of who to in- and ex-clude. In such negotiation the boundaries of Europe have been repeatedly reshaped.[2]

The rich and odd history of the old continent has not yet been concluded, meaning we have to continuously discover the contemporary meaning of that beautiful and risky term. The indolence of creativity in the field of definition (conception) partly evokes the present problems of European integration.

For the purpose of this chapter, three types of definition of Europe are distinguished: axiological, organizational and processual. The axiological type of definition underlines the importance of values, both positively and negatively assessed, in the process of meaning creation. The value is a property of individuals, local communities and societies composing the complex picture of Europe. In order to build an axiologically coherent, definite and enduring image of Europe, it is necessary to highlight the set of values lying in its basis. Commonly agreed values justify legal activities resolving existing problems, dilemmas and doubts. They also limit the risk of instrumental interpretation of complex, regional history. This type of definition coincides with Pope John Paul II's vision of Europe and the European integration process:

> To give new impetus to its own history, Europe must recognize and reclaim with creative fidelity those fundamental values, acquired through a decisive contribution of Christianity, which can be summarized in the affirmation of the transcendent dignity of the human person, the value of reason, freedom, democracy, the constitutional state and the distinction between political life and religion ... it is of capital importance to remember that the union will lack substance if it is reduced to its merely geographic and economic dimensions; rather, it must consist above all in an agreement about the values which must find expression in its law and in its life.

The second type of definition is based on tangible, distinct, accessible features of the object. In this context, organization is perceived as a measurable, noticeable and detectable attribute of Europe. The Christian Church, the Treaty of Westphalia, the Council of Europe and most

---

[2] B. Stråth, *The Meanings of Europe*, www.helsinki.fi/nes/the meanings of europe helsinki.pdf (accessed February 17, 2012).

recently the European Union are great examples of organizations defining the ephemeral meaning of Europe. A sample of that type of definition was delivered by former German Chancellor, Helmut Kohl, in April 1992:

> In Maastricht we laid the foundation-stone for the completion of the European Union. The European Union Treaty introduces a new and decisive stage in the process of European union, which within a few years will lead to the creation of what the founding fathers dreamed of after the last war: the United States of Europe.[3]

The organizational approach overlaps with legal scientific reflection, emphasizing the importance of multilateral treaties signed by independent nation-states.[4]

The last type of definition underlines change, dynamics and development. The processual approach makes a break from the static, motionless vision of the object, assuming that Europe is a direct result of a wide range of processes, trends and phenomena taking place in the political, economic, social and cultural dimension, unifying various principles and assumptions operating in many different systemic contexts. It was proposed by sociologist Zygmunt Bauman:

> Europe is not something you discover; Europe is a mission – something to be made, created, built. And it takes a lot of ingenuity, sense of purpose and hard labour to accomplish that mission. Perhaps a labour that never ends, a challenge always still to be met in full, a prospect forever outstanding.[5]

These are, in nutshell, the most valuable definitions contributing to the contemporary meaning of Europe. Unfortunately, they rarely co-exist side by side. Because of different ontological roots, they are more mutually exclusive than additive. The last few years have witnessed the total domination of the organizational definition. Europe has been depicted throughout organization, agreement, treaty and compromise rather than

---

[3] C. Shore, *Building Europe. The Cultural Politics of European Integration*, (London: Routledge, 2000), 211.

[4] T. Raunio, *Much Ado About Nothing? National Legislatures in the EU Constitutional Treaty*, http://eiop.or.at/eiop/pdf/2005-009.pdf (accessed February 17, 2012); J. Biesenbender, *The Dynamics of Treaty Change. Measuring the Distribution of Power in the European Union?*, http://eiop.or.at/eiop/index.php/eiop/article/view/2011_005a/201 (accessed February 17, 2012).

[5] Z. Bauman, *Europe. An Unfinished Adventure*, (Cambridge: Polity Press, 2004), 2.

value and dynamism. Unluckily, the organizational twist is one of few important reasons for the contemporary crisis in the European Union and Europe. It is impossible to build a strong organizational order without a common axiological basis and the awareness of the inconstancy of goals and outcomes. Even the most sophisticated, technically stunning project encounters problems if there is no wider justification of action and conceptual margin left. Therefore, a shift towards the processual and axiological meaning of Europe is a good starting point for forthcoming deliberation and reflection.

The Dynamic Picture of Europe

If we assume that Europe is a process or a set of processes, it is necessary to explain the nature of this—its logic and possible development. Are we able to control this process? Can we identify the short and long-term goals? Which processes should be chosen in order to make the picture of the old continent legible? Many questions will arise when we realize how complex, spontaneous and dynamic the picture of Europe is. Therefore, every attempt to characterize Europe by the set of processes is exposed to criticism because of its selectiveness and arbitrariness. Nonetheless, some processual vision is needed to make our reasoning clear and logical.

One can say that Europe is a variable set of diverse, sometimes mutually exclusive processes contributing to regional integration and disintegration.[6] For example, in the economic dimension we can identify the powers of attraction and repulsion. Some European companies tighten mutual cooperation[7], and European governments have agreed to establish the European Coal and Steel Community, the European Free Trade Association, the European Economic Area, the Single Market (the Single European Act) etc. Over the last few months, a lot has been said (or speculated) about the fiscal union between eurozone countries. On the other hand, national interests prevail over agreed European economic goals. Russia, Germany, the Netherlands and France[8] decided to build the

---

[6] "The principle of the dialectic is that opposite elements (thesis and antithesis) combine to produce synthesis (new phenomenon)", M. O'Donnell, *A New Introduction to Sociology*, (Hong Kong: Nelson Thornes, 1987), 606.

[7] The greatest example is an advanced partnership made by Airbus because of different projects. Most of the Airbus suppliers come from Europe: http://www.airbus.com/fileadmin/media_gallery/files/ supply___world/Airbus-approved-suppliers-list-January2012.pdf (accessed February 22, 2012).

[8] N. Dulnev, *Nord Stream gas pipeline ready to deliver Russian gas to Northern*

"Nord Stream" pipeline despite the loud objections delivered by Estonia, Lithuania, Poland and Sweden.[9] The British withdrawal from the EU negotiations on the eurozone fiscal crisis may be also seen as a stimulus to new divisions in Europe.

Nevertheless, the economic dimension is just a little piece of Europe. The variable powers of attraction and repulsion are also present in the political, social, cultural and military domains. The dynamic proportion in two powers decides on the integration level of the old continent. The complex history of Europe reveals when the stabilising balance of power has been kept and lost. Tough historic lessons prove that in the interest of all European nations there should be as much control and elimination (or at least limitation) of the powers of repulsion destroying regional cooperation and solidarity as possible. We are aware that total control of the spontaneous and ephemeral processes shaping the variable picture of Europe is impossible. A certain dose of chaos is an inevitable feature of Europe's evolution. In order to support regional integration and cooperation, politicians and scientists should offer creative solutions limiting the scope of repulsion, disintegration and uncertainty.

The European Union at a Turning Point

The second half of 2011 and the beginning of 2012 brought some significant political decisions that shed light on the future of European integration. Particularly, the meeting of European leaders on December 9, 2011 proved that some critical changes are taking place in the European Union. The question arises of what happens with the EU? Will the EU survive? Do European leaders know where to go? Do they know how to get there? There are no simple answers to these questions. Even if some ideas and solutions seem to match existing problems precisely, we have to bear in mind that Europe and the European Union are variable processes and there are no ready (static or given) solutions for complex issues. Enormous flexibility and creativity is needed when the short-term political and economic goals of a few members prevail over the long-term regional interests and profits.

The global financial crisis narrowed down the scope of European integration (both from above and below perspective). The regional stage

---

Europe, http://www.telegraph.co.uk/sponsored/russianow/business/8760021/Nord-Stream-gas-pipeline-ready.html (accessed February 22, 2012).

[9] B. Solum Whist, *Nord Stream: Not Just a Pipeline*, Fridtjof Nansen Institute Report 15, (Lysaker: Fridtjof Nansen Institute, 2008), 18.

has been dominated by meetings and discussions focused on fiscal and monetary issues. The turmoil of the last few months suggests that the European project is only about money. Does it mean that the EU is starring into the abyss[10], as *The Economist* contends? Paradoxically, there is at least one advantage of those gloomy thoughts. Desperate efforts to save the eurozone uncovered the fragility of the European integration process, with most of the EU member states declaring their very shallow and instrumental approach to European integration. This approach has been demonstrated in two different ways. Some states used to treat the EU as a "milk cow" or "lifeline" (Greece, Ireland, Portugal, Spain, Poland) while others decided to keep away from the European problems and egoistically defend their own interests (Great Britain, Hungary, the Czech Republic). Unfortunately, it undermines the necessity of investment in common values: cooperation, solidarity, subsidiarity, welfare etc., which has been emphasized in the axiological definition of Europe. Will the eurozone problems reveal any wisdom?

Timothy Garton Ash warns that:

> We have to recognise that saving the euro is not a substitute for the larger political project, of which it was once meant to be both core and catalyst. The politics of fear may have saved the euro. We need a politics of hope to find a European answer to the Arab spring.

His vision is compatible with Anthony Giddens' remark:

> Stabilising the euro should be a bridge to longer-term change and a stimulus to the imagination. A new debate should be encouraged across Europe about how traditional limitations of the EU—its lack both of dynamic leadership and of democratic legitimacy—might be overcome.

The wisdom of the temporary slump seems to be clear. It is very risky to forget about the long-term goals of European integration. But what is really important is that those goals must stem from commonly agreed and shared values. It is reasonable to assume that the EU without an axiological base will not last long.

Contemporary problems of the EU are parallel to the "eurosclerosis" period from 1973 to 1986. At the beginning of the 1970s, the European integration was caught in an ontological trap laid by the global financial crisis and the inability of European leaders to think in terms of the future. Thanks to Jacques Delors, the eighth President of the European Commission (1985–1994), the political and economic crisis strengthened

---

[10] *Starring into the Abyss,* 2011.

the European integration process by the introduction of the single market in 1992.[11] To repeat this thrilling story, we need a lot of good political will and energy to save the European Union and Europe as a whole.

Lost Dynamics

At least one of two mutually exclusive options of crisis perception can be chosen: lost dynamics or dynamic loss. The "lost dynamics" metaphor describes the present state of European integration, but what is important is that it also catches the intrinsic problems of modern democratic systems. The European integration process is often depicted with "widening" (or "broadening") and "deepening" terms.[12] Widening refers to geographical enlargement of the EU while broadening concerns the reinforcement of the EU institutions and their internal policies. This is how the European Commission understands the European integration process:

> The members of the European family are joining their forces and capabilities to further enhance welfare and prosperity in a widened Union. ... However, in order to realise the full benefits of enlargement, the Community will have to revisit its policies, and make its institutions more efficient and democratic so as to better respond to the needs and expectations of the people of Europe.[13]

What is clear is that the European fiscal problems froze the pace of social, cultural but also political integration. Exclusive focus on finance limits the ability of the lower level actor, e.g. self-governments, NGOs and citizens to act in order to reinforce the EU institutions and their horizontal policies. American poet Ralph Waldo Emerson wrote: "Money often costs too much"[14], which finely describes the complex situation in the EU. When we talk about money there is no space for culture, people and sentiments. This is an example of how high-level politics can stop rank-and-file initiatives. Unfortunately, the fiscal mess also affects the pace of territorial growth of the EU. It is reasonable to assume that the enlargement process will slow down in the next few years (or even will be

---

[11] A single market was the direct result of the Single European Act forced by Jacques Delors.

[12] J.A. Karp, S. Bowler, *Broadening and Deepening or Broadening versus Deepening: The Question of Enlargement and Europe's 'Hesitant Europeans'*, "European Journal of Political Research" 45 (3) (2006), 369–390.

13 *Enlargement of the European Union: A Historic Opportunity,* (Brussels: European Commission, 2003), 1.

[14] R.W. Emerson, *The Conduct of Life*, (Boston: Ticknor and Fields, 1860), 94.

stopped completely). Croatia may be the last country allowed to join the European Union until the fiscal problems are resolved. Hopefully, the European political and intellectual elite will wake up on time and the idea of strong, united Europe on the global stage won't be lost.

As mentioned above, the lost dynamics are also an indirect consequence of the intrinsic problems of modern democracies. The global financial crisis only intensified the unresolved issues of democratic systems, free market economies and capitalism. Among the most searching problems are: (a) isolation of decisional process from social base (local communities, societies); (b) high level corruption, bribery, nepotism; (c) integration of elites (top-down integration); (d) implementation of sore economic reforms without social participation and consultation; (e) legitimacy crisis, alienation of politics, aversion to politicians; (f) crisis of national identity; (g) instrumental distribution of "us and them" stereotypes by political parties; (h) economization (monetarization and marketization) of social, cultural and political goals; (i) decline of nation-state; (j) mass media manipulation (The Fourth Estate); (k) socio-economic inequality increase (e.g. The Fourth World, decline of the middle class), and; (l) unlimited power of global financial actors (most recent). Those hidden issues exploded when the global crisis hit the European economy.[15] However, one has to bear in mind that the list presented is just a small piece of a huge process undermining modern democratic systems.

To escape from the lost dynamics position, European leaders have to: (a) widen the perspective of subjective debates and negotiations by social, cultural and axiological issues, and; (b) include the unresolved problems of modern democracies into the portfolio of urgent regional talks. The importance of money in the European integration process is unquestionable. It is obvious that without material support the integration would be only a political fiction, but as far as we know, financial issues are not the main problem. Regional chaos has arisen because some EU members did not agree to support those others in urgent need. The lasting disarray proves how weak and fragile the awareness of common goals and values is.

[15] For example, the Occupy Movement, an outburst of anger in London against injustice, mass protests in Greece and Italy against EU and reforms.

Dynamic Loss

The "dynamic loss" metaphor offers an alternative view on the present state of the European integration. It focuses on change, motion, progress and development. It assumes that even in the darkest night there is a hope of light. Lord Giddens argues:

> The list of problems the EU faces is truly formidable. It isn't surprising that confusion seems to reign and that many citizens are turning away from the union. Nationalism is on the rise again all over Europe. What cause is there for hope? Perversely, it lies in some large part in the shock experience of the crisis itself. Much more radical and immediate innovations open up in such a situation than in more placid times.[16]

Although optimism is inscribed into the logic of dynamic loss approach, there are some threats waiting for those ready to save the European Union. The dynamic loss process may lead to: (a) organizational acceleration; (b) decrease in a number of the member states, or; (c) a Europe with a variable geometry.

(a) Organizational acceleration

As we have tried to prove, the December 9, 2011 EU summit confirmed an axiological crisis limiting the scope and pace of the European integration process. However, fiscal issues discussed in the last few months should be treated as an initial, necessary step toward a stronger Europe. "Stop dithering. Only full integration can save Europe"[17], Nouriel Roubini and Nicolas Berggruen assure. They believe in the EU project and call for further integration:

> The greatest task of European leadership today is to re-sell the European idea. They need to remind the public that the absence of war, the freedom of mobility and the rising prosperity they have taken for granted since the end of the cold war has been due to the path toward unity and away from the nationalist demons of the past. To change course now is to put all of

---

[16] A. Giddens, *In Europe's dark days, what cause for hope?*, http://www.guardian.co.uk/world/2012/jan/25/anthony-giddens-europe-dark-days-hope (accessed February 23, 2012).

[17] N. Roubini, N. Berggruen, *Stop Dithering. Only Full Integration Can Save Europe,* http://www.guardian.co.uk/commentisfree/2011/sep/07/only-full-integration-save-europe (accessed February 24, 2012).

that at risk. That is why more European integration, not less, is the only solution.[18]

If we follow this, the logical long-term solution for the European Union is a political union.[19] Despite various understanding of such a concept, it is a great time to think about it in terms of political reality.

(b) Decrease in the number of member-states

Organizational acceleration, considered in a positive or negative light, may evoke new divisions in Europe. It is naive, dubious and politically risky to assume that all countries will speak with one voice in the debate about the future of the European Union. Regional voice affects (to an extent) a direct or indirect outcome of internal socio-political frictions in the decisional process at the EU level. Because of approaching elections, pressing social problems, political scandals etc., some countries may decide to get off the train running to political union. It is very probable that short-term logic of this kind drove Britain to leave the European train (hopefully gaining the speed now). Tactically, British Prime Minister David Cameron's decision seems to be right and justified in the eyes of an average Briton.[20] He temporary saved the City and did well at the Brussels summit. Yet his coalition partner Nick Clegg, who heads the smaller, pro-Europe Liberal Democrats, was not so straightforward: "I'm bitterly disappointed by the outcome of last week's summit, precisely because I think now there is a danger that the UK will be isolated and marginalised within the European Union", he said.[21] Time will tell if Cameron's decision was strategically right. The Polish Foreign Minister, Radosław Sikorski, quite aptly commented on the whole row:

---

[18] Ibid.

[19] For the idea of political Union in the European area see: S.J. Bodenheimer, *The Political Union Debate in Europe: A Case Study in Intergovernmental Diplomacy*, "International Organization" 21 (1) (1967), 24–54.

20 "A majority of voters back David Cameron's use of Britain's veto at the European Council, according to a poll. Despite rows at Westminster over the decision, the Prime Minister has the support of 62 % of the public, the Survation research for The Mail on Sunday found. Only 19 % said Mr Cameron was wrong to use the veto. Just over half—51 %—said the Prime Minister had done well at the Brussels summit"; http://www.huffingtonpost.co.uk/2011/12/10/opinon-polls-cameron-eu-veto_n_1141326.html (accessed February 25, 2012).

[21] *Cameron's Veto Stirs Controversy*, http://www.torontosun.com/2011/12/11/camerons-veto-stirs-controversy (accessed February 25, 2012).

> Your total sovereign, corporate and household debt exceeds 400 % of GDP. Are you sure markets will always favour you? We would prefer you in, but if you can't join, please allow us to forge ahead. And please start explaining to your people that European decisions are not Brussels' diktats but results of agreements in which you freely participate.[22]

If Britain, Hungary, the Czech Republic and/or Sweden choose isolation, the European Union will significantly shrink in the number of member-states.

(c) Europe with a variable geometry

This is a side effect of the dynamic loss process. A variable geometry Europe (multi-speed Europe, core Europe) is the controversial idea that "different parts of the European Union should integrate at different levels and pace depending on the political situation in each individual country".[23] Irreconcilable differences within the integration structure encourage the group (or groups) of the most developed countries to a functional separation. The concept of variable geometry overlaps with the idea of enhanced cooperation:

> Enhanced cooperation allows those countries of the Union that wish to continue to work more closely together to do so, while respecting the legal framework of the Union. The member states concerned can thus move forward at different speeds and/or towards different goals.[24]

The concept of a variable geometry Europe found its practical expression in the conclusion of the January 30, 2012 summit in Brussels. A complicated compromise (variable configuration) was achieved through the symbolic row between Poland and France. The variable configuration of meetings included: seventeen countries (the eurozone); twenty-three (the Euro-Plus Pact), twenty-five (the signatories of the fiscal pact), twenty-seven (the single market) and twenty-eight (involving Croatia).[25] It

---

[22] R. Sikorski, *Poland and the future of European Union*, Speech at Berlin, November 28, 2012, http://www.msz.gov.pl/files/docs/komunikaty/20111128BERLIN/radoslaw_sikorski_poland_and_the_future_of_the_eu.pdf (accessed February 25, 2012).
[23] *Multi-speed Europe*, http://en.wikipedia.org/wiki/Multi-speed_Europe
[24] *Enhanced cooperation*, http://europa.eu/legislation_summaries/glossary/enhanced_cooperation_en.htm (accessed February 26, 2012).
[25] *A Deal, But to What End?*, "The Economist", http://www.economist.com/blogs/charlemagne/2012/01/eu-summit (accessed February

shows that the European Union took a complex and risky ride towards a stronger Europe. Unfortunately, the voice of "young" member states, ready to support the European Union's brave reforms, has been rather neglected. Hopefully, variable geometry will be just a temporary, transitional phase to strengthen Europe, but it is very difficult to build regional solidarity and cooperation when some members are not fully recognized and appreciated.

Thus, the dynamic loss process is a very risky but inevitable phenomenon generating plenty of uncertainty and hope. In order to speed up the European Union has to strengthen solidarity, unity and set aside those members not interested in further integration (such as Great Britain and the Czech Republic). As Manuel Castells observed, "the larger the number of members, the more complex the decision-making process, threatening to paralyse European institutions".[26] It is very difficult to predict what legal instrument will be chosen by European leaders to achieve assumed goals and assumptions. Unfortunately, for the time being there are still more declarations and statements than concrete actions and results strengthening the European Union and Europe as a whole.

The Vague Future of European Integration

There are many extreme views on the future of European integration in the media and scientific literature. The vast range of quasi-theories and concepts runs from the pessimistic, "the end" pole, to the optimistic, "political union" stand. "The breakdown of the European Union is now more likely than the collapse of the single currency that was supposed to bind it together", Niall Ferguson warned in *The Washington Post*.[27] "The European Union can survive the euro crisis currently challenging the foundations of the regional alliance", Guido Westerwelle, German Foreign Minister counter-argues.[28] For the time being, it is quite irresponsible to predict what will happen in the next few months and years. Most of today's predictions are based on speculations and emotions rather than

---

25, 2012).

[26] M. Castells. *End of Millennium*, (Oxford: Blackwell Publishers, 2005), 345.

[27] N. Ferguson, *Why E.U. Collapse is More Likely Than the Fall of the Euro*, "The Washington Post", http://www.washingtonpost.com/opinions/why-eu-collapse-is-more-likely-than-the-fall-of-the-euro/2011/11/17/gIQAuY6wZN_story.html (accessed February 26, 2012).

[28] *German Official Says EU Will Survive Euro Crisis*, 20.01.2012, http://www.c-span.org/Events/German-Official-Says-EU-Will-Survive-Euro-Crisis/10737427328/ (accessed February 26, 2012).

extensive research and cold calculation. To avoid mistakes, one should focus only on certain trends and processes capable of shaping the European integration process in the future.

"The unification of Europe around the turn of millennium, when and if completed, will be one of the most important trends defining our new world", Castells argues.[29] Both "when" and "if" depend on how European leaders resolve the three following issues: (a) territorial enlargement; (b) fiscal problems, and; (c) European integration of long-term goals. Despite the accession of Croatia to the European Union[30], it is pretty certain that the enlargement process will be stopped until economic stability backs the EU. There is no real date of accession for: Albania, Bosnia and Herzegovina, Iceland, Kosovo, Macedonia and Montenegro. The latest row between France and Turkey[31] proved that the Turkish government is no longer interested in European integration: "The current fight comes at a time of heightened tension between Ankara and France and with the EU more generally, as well as Turkey's increasing self confidence on the world stage."[32] Economic success encouraged the Turkish government to freeze relations with the European Union, the United States and Israel and search for a new alliances on the global stage, e.g. Syria and Iran.[33] So, the (un)planned blockage of accession may be a temporary remedy for the fiscal problems of the EU, but at the same time it generates new international divisions and alliances, striking global stability and cooperation.

Because of the current fiscal mess, it seems reasonable to assume that strict and more-detailed fiscal rules will be written into the accession treaties of the future. Membership will be a more economic than political decision. Forthcoming accession treaties will be a direct result of lasting negotiations between the strongest European actors. Leaked information suggest that EU members will have to keep their deficits below 0.5 % of GDP or struggle with the European Court of Justice:[34] "But they will also

---

[29] M. Castells. *End of Millenium,* 338.

[30] Formally, Croatia is set to become the 28th member state of the European Union on July 1, 2013.

[31] H. Carnegy, D. Dombey, *Turkey and France Step up Row on 'Genocide'*, "Financial Times", http://www.ft.com/cms/s/0/0bae3b7a-2b2d-11e1-9fd0-00144feabdc0.html#axzz1nWd4m4a0, (accessed February 26, 2012).

[32] Ibid.

[33] B. Yinanc, *Israel's big question: Where is Turkey going?*, "Hürriyet Daily News", http://www.hurriyetdailynews.com/default.aspx?pageid=438&n=changing-realities-2010-01-05 (accessed February 26, 2012).

[34] L. Armitstead, *Eurozone waters down its tough fiscal rules in new treaty*,

be allowed to 'temporarily deviate' from the rules ‘in case of an usual event’ or in ‘periods of severe economic downturn’.”[35] Peculiar conditions and the lack of clear fiscal austerity may affect the whole process of European integration. As mentioned above, without financial support, integration would only be a political fiction. In any case, without clear fiscal austerity and political consequence the acceleration of European integration is simply impossible. Does this mean we are stuck in a vicious circle?

It is very risky to believe that outside influences would be able to push the European integration process forward. The United States, with their own internal fiscal problems, are no longer interested in huge, helpline investments into Europe.[36] Some financial help is considered from China but there are no transparent rules and dates of such a help. The only solution for the European Union is a political union. Although some theoretical goals are not yet evident, there is an urgent practical need for a strong legal framework enabling those interested in further integration to act. The new global reality reduces the space for internal (national) regional antagonisms and conflicts. Only strong regional entities are able to compete with others on the global stage. In such an entity, national interests and sovereignty are not lost but expressed in commonly agreed goals and assumptions. The modern vision of the European Union as a strong, reliable entity was developed by Ulrich Beck and Edgar Grande:[37]

> In the European Empire the concept of sovereignty is itself being transformed, i.e. sovereignty is developed into complex, cosmopolitan sovereignty. Two aspects characterize this transformation process. First, through the division of internal sovereignty and the consolidation of external sovereignty, the complexity of sovereignty is increasing … Moreover, the concept of European cosmopolitanism offers the possibility—only apparently paradoxical—of turning sovereignty losses into sovereignty gains.[38]

“The Telegraph”, http://www.telegraph.co.uk/finance/financialcrisis/9008470/Eurozone-waters-down-its-tough-fiscal-rules-in-new-treaty.html (accessed February 26, 2012).

[35] Ibid.

[36] J. Pace, *U.S. Will Not Help Pay for Europe's Debt Woes*, “Associated Press”; http://www.northjersey.com/news/US_rules_out_helping_pay_for_Europes_debt_woes.html (accessed March 1, 2012).

[37] U. Beck, E. Grande, *Cosmopolitan Europe*, (Cambridge: Polity, 2007).

[38] Ibid. 70.

The cosmopolitan vision of Europe requires “a lot of ingenuity, sense of purpose and hard labour”.[39] It is a good example of a mission or a game that never ends:

> The fact that Europe was created by the power of side effects, as the unintended product of the reflexive modernization of European national societies, does not mean that it was not, and cannot continue to be, the focus of strategic action … Europeanization must also be conceived as a strategic power game, a meta-power game, in which the rules governing the state's exercise of power—their institutional architecture, their scope and possibilities and conditions of their democratic legitimacy—are themselves newly determined.[40]

Due to Beck and Grande, such an understanding of the European project (or game) “must be analysed in as the (unintended) product of the competing strategies which have been employed over the past fifty years or more to shape the European experiment”.[41] Despite controversy with the cosmopolitan project, the awareness of the diminishing role of Europe on the global stage is growing. A global dynamic reality confirms that there is no alternative for decisive, regional action towards the political union.

The Vague Future of Central and Eastern Europe

The future of Central and Eastern Europe depends on: (a) internal relations between the strongest members of the European Union, and; (b) the dynamics of external (regional and global) political, economic and socio-cultural environment.

(a) Internal relations

Despite the latest Polish protests, it is reasonable to assume that the French-German axis will force countries of Central and Eastern Europe to choose one of the following options: (1) join mainstream Europe and engage into the European project based on the political union; (2) withdraw from the European integration process and form the “Isolationism Camp”; (3) join the second, third, fourth etc. ring of

---

[39] Z. Bauman, *Europe. An Unfinished Adventure.*
[40] U. Beck, E. Grande, *Cosmopolitan*, 136.
[41] Ibid.

integration and wait for the approval of the "ruling gang" to integrate further.

Formally, there is no pressure on CEE countries to choose one of these options. Informally, the future of Central and Eastern Europe is composed by the strongest EU players within the backstage negotiation. The lasting turmoil proves that the future of EU is drawn by Germany, France and Italy.[42] If CEE governments are permanently excluded from the decisional process, the European integration will become an illusion, a farce, a defeat and a failure. It is impossible to build a common democratic future based on the private vision of the strongest member-states.

The countries of Central and Eastern Europe are subject of external pressures built by actors from outside the European Union. Jadwiga Staniszkis emphasizes the "East European states' dependence on the Soviet Union since World War II, varying as it has in both content and form over time and from country to country".[43] After the revolutions of 1989 the form and strength of dependency has changed remarkably but it did not fully disappear. Russian political hegemony has been replaced by Western economic pressure of the International Monetary Fund, the World Bank, the World Trade Organization etc.[44] Despite the global democratization process, the CEE countries are not fully independent in their strategic decisions. In network geopolitics[45], various categories of actors, e.g. states, transnational corporations, criminal groups, terrorist networks, non-governmental organizations, global social movements and citizens organized in various associations, clubs, and unions affect the course of the decisional process. Thus, the vague future of Central and Eastern Europe is the resultant of massive, intersecting powers emitted by internal (European Union) and external (global) actors.

Conclusions

Europe's unfinished adventure has reached a turning point in its history. The unquestionable success of the last few decades of regional integration hangs by a single thread because of the eurozone problems

---

[42] Charlemagne, *No Drama, But a Whole Heap of Uncertainty*, "The Economist" http://www.economist.com/blogs/charlemagne/2012/03/european-summit (accessed March 4, 2012).

[43] J. Staniszkis, *The Dynamics of Dependency*, "The Wilson Center Papers", (Washington, 1987), 1.

[44] R. Swedberg, *The Doctrine of Economic Neutrality of the IMF and the World Bank,* "Journal of Peace Research" 4 (1986).

[45] K. Filipek, *Nowa geopolityka sieciowa*, "Przegląd Geopolityczny" 3 (2011), 76.

evoked by the global financial crisis. There is no simple and single solution for the negligence of the past, however the political union seems to be a reasonable and obtainable long term political goal. What's more, the euro project has uncovered how fragile, uncertain and volatile the pillars of European integration are. Politics cannot be isolated from axiology, conceptual thinking and the meta-theory of integration. It is clear that the most sophisticated, technically perfect institutions (e.g. the Economic and Monetary Union of the European Union, the European Central Bank) do not function well if there is no axiological justification for particular political actions. So, the inevitable political union project must be raised on a solid axiological and theoretical basis, otherwise the whole regional exertion and hard work will fail. "If Europe fails, it will suffer from low growth, economic domination and cultural domination", Dominique Strauss-Kahn, the former head of the IMF warns.[46] Hopefully, the rapid increase of EU problems will lead to a broad and systemic debate on the future of Europe.

The third type of definition, the so called "processual approach", allows scientists and politicians to grasp contemporary change, dynamics and uncertainty. As mentioned above, Europe is an endless mission, an enigma, something to be discovered. It is impossible to redefine it without a flexible, capacious and active attitude to regional politics, economy and culture. "However, the unification of Europe will probably not be fulfilled only by skillful political engineering … Europe will only unify, at various degrees and under forms yet to emerge, if its citizens want it", Manuel Castells says.[47] Its meaning, goals and assumptions must be constantly negotiated, adjusted and agreed. A new global reality does not tolerate regional dissent and conflicts. To achieve these ambitious strategic goals, it is necessary to step back from national stands and start thinking in regional terms. As the contemporary turmoil proves, in practice this is not so obvious and easy.

The author has a PhD in Economic Sociology. He also holds an MA in Sociology and International Relations. He works at the Center for Society and Culture of Eastern Europe at the John Paul II Catholic University of Lublin.

---

[46] *Starring into the Abyss,* 2011.
[47] M. Castells, *End of Millennium*, 364.

CHAPTER ELEVEN

ELEMENTS OF CONTINUITY IN THE US POLICY TOWARDS EUROPEAN INTEGRATION: THE CASE OF THE EU ENLARGEMENT OF 2004

OXANA LEKARENKO

Introduction

From the beginning of European integration, US administrations have been strongly interested in the success of European efforts to create a more united and prosperous Europe. This American support played an important role in creating the European Communities. The end of the Cold War created the necessary conditions to eliminate division and allowed former communist countries to start the process of returning to Europe. The eastward enlargement was the most prominent means by which the European Union could promote political stability and economic viability on the European continent. Political changes in Eastern Europe after 1989 forced the US policy-makers to reassess their approach to Europe if they wanted to maintain a "strong" American influence in the region. Eventually, the US administration supported both processes of deepening and broadening of the European integration. This article is an attempt to compare the main reasons for American support in the creation of the European Communities in 1950s and the US attitude towards the enlargement of the EU in 2004. These comparisons may enhance the deeper understanding of the main features of post-war American policy towards European integration in general.

The Main Motives for the American Support for the Creation and Development of the European Communities

Most of the contemporary historians of European integration have agreed that after the end of World War II American support played an important if not decisive role in the emergence and development of integration processes in Western Europe.[1] In the first post-war decade, the US administrations supported integration of the countries which belonged to one of the most important regions in the world. With the beginning of the Cold War, Europe occupied the central role in US foreign policy planning. The Cold War turned the countries of Western Europe into the main allies of the United States. However, as the Belgian historian Pascaline Winand argues, containing the Soviet Union by reinforcing the Atlantic Alliance through European economic prosperity and political stability was only one of the reasons for American support of the European integration. Other motivations, such as US interests in a liberal trading and democratic environment, existed before the beginning of the Cold War:

> American policy-makers calculated that European integration could help remove intra European trade and financial barriers and thus encourage the countries of a region to pursue more liberal trade policy in the global scale. The creation of European custom union would also facilitate access of American goods to European markets and simplify European countries' commercial policy towards the US. More economic prosperity would in turn foster political stability in Europe, thereby contributing to international and American security.[2]

During the Cold War, the German question was central to the American attitude towards a united Europe:

---

[1] See: J. G. Giauque, *Grand Designs and Visions of Unity: the Atlantic Powers and the Reorganization of Western Europe, 1955–1963*, (Chapel Hill-London: The University of North Carolina Press, 2002);
G. Lundestad, *"Empire" by Integration: the United States and European Integration, 1945–1997*, (New York: Oxford University Press USA, 1998);
P. Winand, *Eisenhower, Kennedy, and the United States of Europe*, (London: Palgrave Macmillan, 1997).

[2] P. Winand, E. Philippart, *From "Equal Partnership" to the "New Transatlantic Agenda": Enduring Features and Successive Forms*, in E. Philippart, P. Winand (eds.), *Ever Closer Partnership: Policy-Making in US-EU Relations*, (Brussels: P.I.E.-Peter Lang, 2001), 30–31.

> On the one hand, German resources were central for European recovery. On the other hand, Germany's independence had to be "contained". The preferred solution was to integrate Germany within an economically prosperous and politically unified Europe, which would channel German energies towards European recovery and unification, thereby contributing to political stability.[3]

Last but not least, the Americans hoped that the creation of a united Europe would allow the United States to reduce the American military and financial help to their European allies in the future, or as the President Eisenhower formulated it, "to sit back and relax a bit".[4] During the Cold War, the main motives of American support for the European integration did not undergo any significant changes, though American policy-makers were disappointed with some unpreventable consequences of the European unification process, such as rising discrimination of American goods in the European market.

The Cold War substantially limited the number of countries which could participate in the formation of the European Communities (EC). The division of the European continent brought about by the East-West conflict made it impossible for any of the members of the Soviet block to consider or to be considered for inclusion in the institutions of European cooperation. The European integration process was thus pursued without the participation of Poland, Czechoslovakia or Hungary, despite the manifest European credentials of each of those countries. Nevertheless, as the British historian Piers Ludlow points out, the reduction of the number of countries which could participate in the initial stages of the European integration was almost certainly a necessary precondition of the European integration's success. It is difficult to believe that in the beginning of the European unification process the EC could cope with such a large number of member states:

> Division of Germany had similar utility; it ensured a de facto equivalence in population and geographical size between France and Germany. This proved extremely valuable in allowing the structures of European cooperation to be set up on the basis of equality of representation and voting weight amongst all large member states: France, Germany, Italy (and from 1973 Great Britain).[5]

---

[3] Ibid., 31.

[4] *Foreign Relations of the United States. 1955–1957*, vol. 4, (Washington: United States Government Printing Office, 1986), 348–349.

[5] N. P. Ludlow, *European Integration and the Cold War*, in M. P. Leffler, O. A. Westad (eds.), *The Cambridge History of the Cold War*, vol. 2, (New York:

The American Reaction to the Political Changes in Europe after the End of the Cold War

The European integration contributed to the image of Western European success, stability and prosperity that did so much to destabilize communist regimes in Eastern Europe as the Cold War came to an end. The successor regimes which emerged from the "Velvet revolutions" at the end of 1980s not only adopted the rhetoric of a return to Europe but also took practical steps which could lead to their adherence to the EC. New leaders saw the EC as the main institutional vehicle for reintegration of their countries with Western Europe. Changes in Eastern Europe prompted Washington to reassess its policy towards the old continent and to recognize the unique role which the EC could play in stabilization of political and economic situation in Europe. The German question played a significant role again. With German reunification looming on the horizon, the European Community's political importance was magnified as a way of stalling a German Europe as opposed to a European Germany.

The signing of the Treaty of the European Union (TEU) in Maastricht in 1992, and the decline of the importance of the security dimension in transatlantic relations as a result of the end of the Cold War, brought Washington to the realization that the American economic and political influence in Europe was unlikely to be maintained unless the US wholeheartedly backed European integration. The US administration supported both processes of deepening and broadening of the European integration, which could have led to the emergence of an undivided, democratic and peaceful Europe. In his speech in Brussels in January 1994, President Bill Clinton stressed:

> My administration supports European Union and Europe's development of stronger institutions of common purpose and common action. We recognize we will benefit more from a strong and equal partner than from a weak one.[6]

Financial constraints on US foreign policy made the EU an attractive candidate for burden-sharing, notably in Central and Eastern Europe (CEE). The US recognized the important role that an integrated Western Europe could play in terminating the division of the continent and

---

Cambridge University Press, 2010), 190–191.

6 *Remarks to Future Leaders of Europe in Brussels*, January 1994, in *Public Papers of the Presidents. William J. Clinton. 1994*, (Washington: Government Printing Office, 1995), 9.

stabilizing its eastern part by enhancing trading relations with CEE states and providing considerable financial assistance, technical aid and support for democratic political structures in the region.

While supporting the EU, the United States considered that NATO would remain the core institute of the European security and North America's primary link with Europe. In other words, a united Europe would remain free, democratic and closely linked to its North American partners. American policy-makers argued that the EU lacked the kind of advanced, integrated military capability which remains the heart of NATO's strength and which continues to be needed to preserve European security:

> A revamped NATO, in which Washington could best communicate its views to its European partners, since it was a member of that organization, remained the principal means of influence of the US in Europe. Once again then American support for European integration was predicated upon embedding the EU within a tightly knit Atlantic community.[7]

The US Interests in the EU Enlargement

Enlargement was the most prominent means by which the EU could promote political stability and economic viability on the European continent. The Clinton administration enthusiastically supported the early accession of CEE countries into the EU. Eastward enlargement would help ensure that the region developed a democratic, free market orientation and that the EU bore most of the financial burden associated with this development. Additionally, the discipline of EU membership would help constrain the reemergence of ancient disputes regarding frontiers and ethnic minorities in CEE, like the creation of European Communities guaranteed the Franco-German reconciliation after the end of the World War II. But Washington's support for the EU enlargement was conditioned on the view that the entry of new EU members as full members of the WEU should be synchronized with their entry into NATO.[8] One of the attractions of NATO enlargement for the US was that new members like Poland, the Czech Republic, Hungary and eventually

---

[7] P. Winand, E. Philippart, *From "Equal Partnership" to the "New Transatlantic Agenda"*, 42–43.

[8] A. L. Gardner, *A New Era in US-EU Relations? The Clinton Administration and the New Transatlantic Agenda*, (Aldershot: Avebury, 1997), 32–38.

the Baltic states, would increase the weight of the Atlantic voice in the new Europe.[9]

The basic interests of the EU countries and the US in the process of the EU enlargement were similar: to encourage the development of a stable CEE and provide for expanding the community of "market democracies" towards the East. The general attempt to coordinate their policies in the region was undertaken at the July 1994 US-EU Berlin summit by the establishment of the ad hoc working group on Central and Eastern Europe. The New Transatlantic Agenda, adopted by the US and the EU in 1995, recommended the reinforcement of US-EU coordination of technical and financial assistance to consolidate democratic and market reforms in Central and Eastern Europe.[10]

The EU and the United States emphasized economic instruments for CEE integration into Europe, which included economic aid through the European PHARE[11] and American SEED[12] programmes, trade and investments. While both the US and the EU agreed on the centrality of economic assistance for democratic transformation in the CEE countries, the EU and its member-states were the major donors: "On the aid front, 53.5 per cent of all Western aid between 1990 and 1995 was provided by the EU and its member-states, and only 11.3 per cent by the United States; international financial institutions accounted for 24.8 per cent of the total."[13] The EU also developed more instruments for trade liberalization, particularly the Europe agreements. The EU traded more with the CEE countries than any other actor did. Eventually PHARE's aim switched from support of general reforms in the CEE countries to specific preparation for EU membership.

Nevertheless, the EU moved slowly in terms of the enlargement question. In the early 1990s, the EU's leadership was almost totally preoccupied with internal matters. Although the Maastricht treaty provided that any European state with a democratic system of government could apply to join the EU, the creation of a more tightly integrated economic

[9] M. Walker, *America's Mental Maps of a Greater Europe*, "International Affairs" 76 (3) (2000), 474.

[10] *New Transatlantic Agenda*, December 5, 1995, www.useu.usmission.gov/new_transatlantic_agenda.html (accessed January 30, 2012).

[11] PHARE—*Pologne et Hongrie Aide de la Reconstruction Economique*.

[12] SEED—Support for East European Democracy.

[13] L. G. Feldman, *The European Union's Enlargement Project and US-EU Cooperation in Central and Eastern Europe*, in F. G. Burwell and I. H. Daalder (eds.), *The United States and Europe in the Global Arena*, (New York: Palgrave Macmillan, 1999), 47.

and political union made accession more difficult. Since the June 1993 Copenhagen summit, the EU had declared publicly the need to find a delicate balance between deepening and widening. At the same summit, the criteria for EU membership were established. According to them a country can join the EU only if it meets all the membership criteria:

- Political: it must have stable institutions guaranteeing democracy, the rule of law and human rights;
- Economic: it must have a functioning market economy and be able to cope with competitive pressure and market forces within the EU;
- Legal: it must accept established EU law and practice, especially the major goals of political, economic and monetary union.[14] The last meant that the candidate countries had to meet the EU's 80 000 pages of rules and regulations known as the *acquis communautaire*. In all areas of the *acquis*, the candidate countries had to bring their institutions, management capacity and administrative and judicial systems up to the EU standards, both at national and regional level. That process could take plenty of time.

In addition, the expansion to the East represented for the EU a greater challenge than previous enlargements, due to the number of applicants, the magnitude of economic and social differences between them and current member states, the combined size of population and the vastness of territory. Bringing CEE states into the EU on an accelerated schedule would have been politically difficult and economically expensive for the EU.

The EU and NATO Enlargements: Two Separate but Parallel Processes

American policy-makers were concerned that political and economic reforms in CEE might falter if these countries were denied membership in both the EU and NATO. Since the EU was unlikely to offer membership to any of these countries in the near future, the US considered that NATO should fill the void. Compared to their EU counterparts, NATO members moved quickly on the enlargement question. The US took leadership in the process of NATO enlargement. It would strengthen NATO's position in Europe vis-à-vis the EU, which in turn would strengthen the US position

[14] *The criteria for EU membership*, www.europa.eu/pol/enlarg/index_en.htm (accessed January 25, 2012).

in European affairs. In 1995 the alliance established comparatively less stringent criteria for membership:

- a functioning democratic political system based on a market economy;
- fair treatment of minority populations;
- a commitment to the peaceful resolution of conflicts;
- the ability and willingness to make a military contribution to NATO operations;
- a commitment to democratic civil-military relations and institutional structures.[15]

In his speech in Washington in May 1997, Deputy Secretary of State Strobe Talbott noted:

> We hope that the enlargement of NATO, of which we are a member, will contribute to the conditions for the enlargement of the EU, of which we are not a member, but in which we have such a profound—I'd even say vital—interest ... From our vantage point, NATO enlargement and EU expansion are separate but parallel processes in support of the same overall cause, which is a broader, deeper transatlantic community.[16]

In July 1997 NATO leaders invited the Czech Republic, Hungary and Poland to start accession negotiations.

From their part, the EU's members saw NATO enlargement as a cost-effective and easier alternative to EU expansion, and therefore as a way of putting off EU enlargement.[17] Finally, the EU appreciated that the US had a special role to play in NATO and its enlargement. The US recognized the unique contribution the EU enlargement could make to the stability of CEE. However, the mutual acceptance of roles between the EU and the US happened as a natural consequence of cumulative experience, resources and the character of the two actors, rather than a result of formal assignment of tasks.[18]

Despite shared goals, the EU and NATO enlargement were two parallel processes with their own dynamics and schedule. In 1999, Poland,

---

[15] *The criteria for NATO membership*, www.nato.int/cps/en/natolive/topics_49212.htm (accessed January 25, 2012).
[16] M. Walker, *America's Mental Maps of a Greater Europe*, 470.
[17] M. E. Brown, *The United States, Western Europe and NATO Enlargement*, in F. G. Burwell and I. H. Daalder (eds.), *The United States and Europe in the Global Arena*, (New York: Palgrave Macmillan, 1999), 38.
[18] L. G. Feldman, *The European Union's Enlargement Project*, 49.

the Czech Republic and Hungary became members of NATO. In 2004, the same countries along with Cyprus, Estonia, Latvia, Lithuania, Malta, Slovenia and Slovakia joined the EU. The Bush administration welcomed the EU enlargement of 2004, asserting that it would help strengthen the "enduring partnership" between the United States and Europe. Some analysts even posited that enlargement could also decrease overall US-EU tensions because many new members of the EU turned out to be more pro-American. US businesses believed that they would gain access to a larger, more integrated European market, and saw enlargement as forcing further reform of the EU's regulatory policies.[19]

Conclusions

Although the strategic landscape in Europe has changed dramatically since 1989, there was more continuity in American attitude towards European integration than change. In the 1990s, the US enthusiastically supported the early accession of Central and Eastern European countries into the EU. There are a number of reasons for American support in the EU enlargement. Some of them were similar to those which led the United States to provide crucial support for the early stages of European integration. In the case of the EU eastward enlargement, at least three elements of continuity can be seen:

(1) The United States recognized the special role of the EU in providing economic prosperity and political stability on the European continent.
(2) American policy-makers expected that the EU would shoulder the main financial burden to encourage economic and political reforms in the CEE countries.
(3) The US administrations were interested in embracing the European integration process into the broader Atlantic framework.

[19] K. Archick, *European Union Enlargement*, Congressional Research Service (CRS) Report, July 3, 2008, www.digital.library.unt.edu/ark:/67531/metacrs10580/m1/1/high_res_d/RS21344_2008Jul03.pdf (accessed February 2, 2012).

The author is an associate professor at the Department of Modern and Contemporary History and International Relations at the Faculty of History, Tomsk State University, Russia.

CHAPTER TWELVE

THE EU STRATEGIES FOR THE BALTIC SEA AND THE DANUBE REGION: A COMPARATIVE VIEW

MARTIN KOSCHKAR

Introduction

There may be different concepts of regionalization in Europe, such as the "Europe of Olympic Circles"[1], the "Europe of Regions"[2], or the rather new concept of macro-regions. Nevertheless, the driving power behind a lot of these concepts is the increase in importance of the European Union over the last two decades. With the enlargements of 1995, 2004, and 2007 the EU has become a central actor and point of reference for all member states. These states share common values, common laws, and common ways of decision making.[3] During this process, already existing wider regions like the Area of the Danube or the Baltic Sea Region became a part of the EU. The new form of intra-EU-regionalization through the concept of macro-regions reverts on these already historical or natural "pre-constructed" regions. In 2009, a strategy for the Baltic Sea Region was introduced by the EU. In 2010, a second strategy for the Danube Region followed. Both new instruments will have influence on the future development of regional governance in Central Europe. This chapter regards this new type of regionalization by comparing the two regions and their strategies. This is accomplished by following three guiding questions: What is a macro-region? Do the Baltic Sea Region and the

---

[1] The concept is presented in: E. Antola, *Political Challenges in the Baltic Sea Region*, (London: Konrad Adenauer Foundation, 2009).
[2] As presented from the Committee of the Regions, http://www.cor.europa.eu/pages/HomeTemplate.aspx (accessed February 22, 2012).
[3] E. Antola, *Political Challenges*, 14.

Danube Region fulfil the theoretical aspects of a macro-region? Where are the main similarities and differences between the two macro-region strategies of the European Union?

To answer these questions the paper is divided into five parts. After the introduction the second part tries to give a closer definition of the term "macro-region" based on the existing documents of the European Union and research papers which address this rather new concept of regionalism. The third part will introduce the new element of European governance concerning this concept: The EU macro-region strategies. The fourth part will concentrate on the comparative view between the macro-regions and their strategies. The paper will close with conclusions to answer the guiding questions followed by a short outlook on the future development.

Defining a "Macro-Region"

The so-called "macro-region-concept" symbolizes a new form of regionalism within the European Union. In recent years, the concept has found its way into normal EU "vocabulary" and seems to be faced with great expectations from organs of the EU. Besides this fact, a clear and legal definition of the term "macro-region" is still missing.[4] The concept can be located in the scientific field of international studies and it is based on the experience of transnational EU cooperation programmes like INTERREG.[5] The most important frame-condition for the development of the concept was the east-enlargement of the EU in 2004.[6] The widened territory of the EU was the fundament for new ideas in the field of regional policy especially in the Baltic Sea Region where a large number of already existing regional cooperational entities had to face the growing influence of "Brussels". Interestingly, the idea of a new strategic concept for a region within the EU was born out of a group of EU-parliamentarians in 2005, the so-called Baltic Europe Intergroup.[7] From this time onwards, the theoretical and practical development of the "macro-region-concept" went

---

[4] C. Schymik, *Modellversuch Makroregion*, (Berlin: Stiftung Wissenschaft und Politik, 2011).

[5] A. Dubios, S. Hedin, P. Schmitt, J. Sterling, *EU-macro-regions and macro-regional strategies—A scoping study*, "Nordregio Electronic Working Paper" 4 (Stockholm, 2009).

[6] C. Schymik, *Modellversuch Makroregion,* 10.

[7] A. Stocchiero, *Macro-Regions of Europe: Old wine in a New Bottle?*, "Working Papers" 65, 2010 (ENG), http://www.medgov.net/site/files/download/old_wine_in%20_new_bottle.pdf (accessed February 16, 2012); C. Schymik, *Modellversuch Makroregion*, 11.

shoulder to shoulder with the term of the "macro-region strategy". With the idea of a strategy for a "macro-region", a new political instrument in the field of EU regional policy was born.[8] However, the fundament for the strategy will always be the region. In 2009, the European Commission introduced, based on the words of the former EU-Commissioner for regional policy Pawel Samecki, its definition of a "macro-region" as: "an area including territory from a number of different countries or regions associated with one or more common features or challenges … geographic, cultural, economic or other".[9] This is a very broad and unspecific definition, but at first sight one main issue of the concept is presented: cooperation among states. Through the perception of the European Commission, increasing cooperation among the member states can lead to further integration and an advancement of central policy areas. Two normative reasons for a "macro-region" are presented in a working paper of 2009. Firstly, a macro-region may help to solve cross-border problems like environmental issues which know no lines of demarcation, and secondly, a group of states may handle the influence and aspects of the ongoing denationalization and globalization much better than a single nation-state.[10] Additionally, a macro-region can handle topics more "flexibly" than the whole twenty-seven member states of the EU.

Besides these motivations, five theoretical aspects can be considered in the concept. The broad definition explains firstly the functional aspect of a macro-region. The term of "common features or challenges" allows a flexible, problem-orientated construction of a region based on a cross-border issue. The functional aspect may be called the core of the region which binds the national actors together. Depending on the perspective, the functional aspect can differ. Therefore, a "macro-region" with more than one common issue can be "multifunctional".[11] Regarding this issue, the region can be constructed, deconstructed or reconstructed.[12] The

---

[8] C. Schymik, *Die EU-Strategie für den Ostseeraum*, in Europäisches Zentrum für Föderalismus-Forschung Tübingen (ed.), *Jahrbuch des Föderalismus 2011*, (Baden Baden, 2011), 378.

[9] *Macro-regional strategies in the European Union,* http://ec.europa.eu/regional_policy/cooperate/baltic/pdf/macroregional_strategies_2009.pdf (accessed February 16, 2012).

[10] Ibid.

[11] Like ecological, historical, cultural, economic aspects; as presented in: C. Schymik, *Modellversuch Makroregion*, 7–8.

[12] E. Stratenschulte, *Von der Ostsee in die Welt?—Schlussfolgerungen der Ostseestrategie für weitere markoregionale Strategien in Europa*, in E. Stratenschulte (ed.), *Das europäische Meer—Die Ostsee als Handlungsraum*, (Berlin: Berliner Wissenschafts-Verlag, 2011), 159.

cooperation in the region is secondly described as transnational and thirdly as territorial. Transnational means that more than two states should participate. Recalling the functional aspect, a whole state does not have to participate—only the functional subnational regions can be part of the macro-region and this further than in a bilateral way on the territory of the European Union[13]. Therefore, the macro-region lies within the territory of the EU. It should be a new level in the so-called *sui generis* multi-level-system of the European Union. This is important in not confusing the whole EU as a macro-region in understanding the concept. Always more than two but less than all EU member-states cooperate in a macro-region.[14] Fourthly, a macro-region is open for neighboring countries of the EU. When the core of the region lies in the EU and the functional aspects are fulfilled, third countries can participate.[15] The last aspect describes a macro-region as symmetrical, which is important for politics and decision-making in the region. The territory of a region should always be balanced between the participating countries. With no hegemonic state, the interest in cooperation is also balanced which fosters cooperation in general.[16]

These aspects are the guidance for the "creation" of a macro-region. Based on the documents of the EU, a critical "construction-obstacle" regarding the macro-region concept is discussed. For a long-term subsistence of a macro-region, the process of constructing the region needs to be mutual: top-down by declarations of political leaders and bottom-up by a supportive civil society for a social interaction in the region.[17] Other authors underline the potential of a "macro-region" for new political actions based on the macro-region strategies of the EU.[18] Both arguments address how a theoretical "macro-region" can be established.

The Strategies

Since the EU-enlargement in 2004, the Organs of the European Union, especially the ambitious European Commission, have introduced two macro-region strategies: the EU strategy for the Baltic Sea Region (EUSBSR) and the EU strategy for the Danube Region (EUSDR). Already the names of the strategies place them in the wider geographic perspective

---

[13] C. Schymik, *Modellversuch Makroregion*, 22.
[14] *Macro-regional strategies in the European Union*; A. Dubios, S. Hedin, P. Schmitt and J. Sterling, *EU-macro-regions*, 19.
[15] E. Stratenschulte, *Von der Ostsee*, 164.
[16] C. Schymik, *Modellversuch Makroregion*, 22.
[17] E. Stratenschulte, *Von der Ostsee*, 160–161.
[18] A. Dubios, S. Hedin, P. Schmitt and J. Sterling, *EU-macro-regions*, 19.

of Europe. The strategies are named after two natural resources: On the one hand, the Baltic Sea as an almost EU-interior sea after 2004, and on the other the Danube as a connecting river from the "Black Forest to the Black Sea".[19] How, based on this, both regions fulfil the theoretical aspects of macro-regions will be discussed in the next section. However, as a basis for comparison, the governance-approach of the strategies must be reviewed: firstly by discussing the structure and development of the macro-region strategies, and secondly by enlightening the new form of governance based on the multi-level-system of the EU.

Structure and development

Both strategies are similarly designed. They are composed of two documents: a strategic paper and an action plan.[20] The strategic paper can be understood as the written overarching vision for the development of the region.[21] With the intention of bonding the whole region, the strategic paper has to look after the common needs, problems and interests of the region itself and the participating actors of the region.[22] Therefore, the governance-approach can be seen as cross-border, interdisciplinary and multi-actor. This implies also the need for an overarching actor to introduce such a sort of instrument. In both cases, this role is taken by the European Commission.[23] The main topics of the strategic papers are named "pillars", and they are in both documents divided into a larger number of "priority areas".[24] All aspects are designed as development goals. Therefore, the implementation is focused in the second part of the

---

[19] K. Böttger, *Die EU-Strategie für den Donauraum: Ziele erreichen, indem man Probleme umschifft*, in Europäisches Zentrum für Föderalismus-Forschung Tübingen (ed.), *Jahrbuch des Föderalismus 2011*, (Baden Baden, 2011), 411.

[20] For the Baltic Sea Region: *Communication of the European Commission concerning the EU Strategy for the Baltic Sea Region*, KOM (2009) 248 final, June 10, 2009. Action Plan: *Working paper regarding the Communication for the EU Strategy for the Baltic Sea Region*, SEC (2009) 712. For the Danube Region: *Communication of the European Commission concerning the EU Strategy for the Danube Region*, KOM (2010) 715 final, December 8, 2010. Action Plan: *Working paper regarding the Communication for the EU Strategy for the Danube Region*, SEC (2010) 1489 final.

[21] Less than fifteen pages in both cases, the "vision" described in the EUSBSR, *Communication of the European*, KOM (2009) 248 final, June 10, 2009, 12.

[22] A. Dubios, S. Hedin, P. Schmitt and J. Sterling, *EU-macro-regions,* 24.

[23] A. Stocchiero, *Macro-Regions of Europe*, 4 and 6.

[24] In both cases four pillars divided into 15 (EUSBSR) and 11 (EUSDSR) priority areas.

strategy: the action plan. The plan consists of many projects which handle the topics of the strategy in a cross-border way, and were produced in a bottom-up process out of the region. This is the most important fact for the organization of the strategies. Through the participating actors of the projects, the strategy tries to use the responsibility and the knowledge of the regional actors to reach the goals for their own region.[25] This was a focus of the strategy during the development since 2004. A main part of the development consists of a broad consultation process in the regions. This was important to develop the "vision" of the strategic paper out of the needs and interests of the regional actors and also to generate active partners for projects to accumulate the action plan. For example, during almost two years of the EUSBSR consultation process over one hundred written inputs were sent to the European Commission to shape the content of the strategy.[26] Similar steps of development were undertaken for both strategies; however, the timeline differed slightly.

As already mentioned, the concept of the macro-region strategies has a parliamentarian background out of the Baltic Europe Intergroup in 2005. In 2007, the idea was carried further through the European Commission which launched the consultation process for the EUSBSR in the same year. In 2009, the consultation came to an end and the final strategy was presented during the Swedish presidency and adopted by the Council of the European Union. In 2008, the first steps for the EUSDR were undertaken and the consultation process started in 2010. In December 2010, the final EUSDR was presented. It was adopted by the Council during the Hungarian presidency in the first half of 2011.[27] Besides the importance of a consultation process, two other aspects of the macro-region strategies can by recorded. Firstly, the final presentation of the strategies was based on the initiative of national member states out of the region, which handled the strategies as a project of their EU-presidency.[28] Secondly, the Baltic Sea Region was the first region for a macro-region strategy of the EU. Therefore, the EUSBSR is sometimes seen as a role

---

[25] Described by the European Commission in the review of the EUSBSR, *Report of the European Commission on the Implementation of the EU Strategy for the Baltic Sea Region*, KOM (2011) 381 final, June 22, 2011.

[26] C. Schymik, P. Krumrey, *EU-Ostseestrategie für den Ostseeraum—Kerneuropa in der nördlichen Peripherie?*, (Berlin: Stiftung Wissenschaft und Politik, 2009), 6.

[27] C. Schymik, *Modellversuch Makroregion.*

[28] For example, after the first ideas for the EUSBSR neither the German (2007) nor the Finnish (2006) presidency of the European Union carried on with the concept. In 2007, the Swedish government decided to make the strategy to a priority project of their own presidency in 2009.

model for the development of the EUSDR.[29] This statement is supported by the similar structure of the strategies and is also grounded in the "longer" history of the EUSBSR which already allowed the possibility of the first results and experiences of implementation.[30] These lessons learned in praxis can also be seen as a role model for the Danube Region.

New type of governance based on three "Nos"

The type of governance which shapes the development of the strategies is based on the new level of the macro-region as a political sphere inside the European Union. The aforementioned strategies place a lot of responsibility laid on regional actors. This can be seen in the projects but also by the role of national governments as coordinators of the priority areas of the strategies.[31] All in all, the strategies introduce a new type of cooperation between the EU, the member states in the regions, and neighboring states of the EU which are functionally connected to the macro-region. The frame for the further development is the European Union in form of the European Commission as an external "coach" for the strategies[32] but also as a "motor" of the process. The broad approach of the strategies addresses governance questions in three aspects: governance as multi-level, multi-actor, and multi-sector.[33] The last two aspects are represented by the consultation process, the projects of the action plans (both multi-actor) and by the overarching "vision" of the strategy which brings together different needs and interest for a holistic approach (multi-sector). The aspect of multi-level governance is connected with the new level of the macro-region. All other levels of the EU multi-level system are participating in the strategies—the supranational EU-level in the form of the European-Commission, the national-level in the form of the coordinators of the priority areas and the sub-national and local level in the form of project-partners for the implementation of the strategies. Yet, some authors argue that just despite these strategies, currently the macro-

---

[29] K. Böttger, *Die EU-Strategie,* 411.

[30] *Report of the European Commission*, KOM (2011) 381 final, June 22, 2011.

[31] The coordinators are listed in the action plan, in the case of Germany the subnational governments of the connected German federal lands take this part. For further information see the two action plans: *Working paper regarding…*, SEC (2009) 712. *Working paper regarding*, SEC (2010) 1489 final.

[32] *Macro-regional strategies in the European Union.*

[33] Based on different aspects out of the working-paper: Ibid., also mentioned in: A. Stocchiero, *Macro-Regions of Europe*, 6.

region-level cannot be seen as a full active political level in this system.[34] This is due to the so called “three Nos” of EUSBSR and EUSDR which shape the strategies in praxis. As a basic condition, both strategic papers formulate that the strategies have to operate with no new institutions, no new law and no new money.[35] These three “Nos” were very important during the consultation processes to reach a low-level compromise which can be accepted by all actors faced by the fear of changed budgets, new stressing administrations or institutional “monsters”.[36] Therefore, no new laws for a coerced implementation of the strategies in form of an EU-directive or something similar may be imposed. No new money above the already existing funding instruments of the EU may be scheduled in the EU-budget and no new institutions to coordinate the strategy may be created. In praxis, both strategies follow these conditions. However, a High Level Group of EU-officials was established for better coordination facing the multi-sector aspect of the strategies.[37]

Besides these aspects, the macro-region strategies seem to have a clear influence of intra-regional cooperation within the EU and can support different policy areas,[38] at least the discussion on aspects of regional development. The governance of a macro-region was theoretically reviewed and analysed in a two-sided way. Neo-functionalists agree with the concept by underlining the strengthened role of the European Commission in the field of regional policy. Federalists agree with the concept by pointing out the increasing influence of regional and local actors during the process of implementation.[39] The two opinions may be somewhat contradictory, but at least they point out different perspectives on the concept. This sort of discussion fosters the further development of macro-regional strategies theoretically as well as practically. The European Commission has been invited to deliver a report on the progress of the macro-regional strategy concept based on the experience of the EUSBSR and EUSDR in 2013. This denotes the next milestone in the process.

---

[34] C. Schymik, *Modellversuch Makroregion*, 10.

[35] Initially presented in the strategic papers but also repeated by the Council conclusions, for example in the case of the EUSDR: *Council conclusions on the European Strategy for the Danube Region*, April 13, 2011.

[36] Regarding for example the bad experience of the Union for the Mediterranean Sea, E. Stratenschulte, *Von der Ostsee*, 166.

[37] C. Schymik, *Die EU-Strategie*, 384.

[38] *Macro-regional strategies in the European Union.*

[39] C. Schymik, *Die EU-Strategie*, 386–387.

Comparative View

As presented in the previous part, the structure of the two macro-region strategies is similar (strategic paper and action plan). Besides this formal similarity, the comparison will concentrate on three aspects. Firstly, it will be discussed how the two regions (the Baltic Sea and the Danube) match up with the theoretical concept of macro-regions. Secondly, the governance of the regions in form of the macro-region strategies will be reviewed in content, and the influence of the three "Nos" will be discussed in praxis.

The Baltic Sea and the Danube Region as "macro-regions in praxis"

The regions form the basis for the strategies. In the EUSBSR and EUSDR, the strategic papers define their understanding of these regions (see Table 12.1). Both regions consist of eight EU-member states. Germany is the only member state which belongs to both macro-regions, but not Germany as a whole state, just the functional regions which are connected to the Baltic Sea and the Danube are part of the macro-region: in the former, the northern federal lands of Schleswig-Holstein, Hamburg and Mecklenburg-Western Pomerania, and in the latter the southern federal lands of Bavaria and Baden-Württemberg. In both cases, additional third countries as non-EU-members belong to the regions. The area of each region symbolizes one fifth to one quarter of the whole European continent. A quantified comparison shows that the Baltic Sea Region is wider than the Danube Region but less populated. The overall GDP is higher in the Danube Region but in conjunction with the population, the GDP per capita is almost similar in both regions.

The five theoretical aspects of a macro-region can be tested for both cases. The pre-constructed aspect of the Danube and the Baltic Sea Region is very important for the first theoretical aspect of a macro-region: the functional dimension. At first sight, their names already present a clear functional part for both regions. With the Danube as a river and the Baltic Sea as a common sea between the coastal states, two ecosystems build the core of the regions. The functional aspect of environmental questions creates a common region.[40] However, the abutting perspective differs. A common sea can be seen as more connective than a river of almost 3,000

[40] E. Stratenschulte, *Von der Ostsee in die Welt?*, 160–161.

Table 12.1. The Regions

Criteria	Baltic Sea Region	Danube Region
People	71 million	89 million
Territory	1279.000 km^2	769.000 km^2
GDP	1375 billion Euro	1620 billion Euro
EU Member States	Denmark	Romania
	Sweden	Bulgaria
	Finland	Hungary
	Estonia	Slovenia
	Latvia	Slovakia
	Lithuania	Czech Republic
	Poland	Austria
	Germany (The Federal Lands of Mecklenburg Western Pomerania, Hamburg and Schleswig Holstein)	Germany (The Federal Lands of Bavaria and Baden Württemberg)
Others	Russia, Norway, Belarus	Bosnia Herzegovina, Croatia, Moldavia, Montenegro, Serbia, Ukraine

Source: Own table based on data from Schymik (2009).

km.[41] This may be a small problem for the cooperation in the Danube Region when this functional aspect cannot overcome the heterogeneity of the included nation states.[42] Also, in other functional dimensions the Danube Region seems to be more heterogenic than the Baltic Sea Region. Considering the Hanseatic League, the Lutheranism or the Swedish Empire, it is quite easy to find more connective issues in the History of the Baltic Sea.[43] In the case of the Danube Region, besides the Austria-Hungary Empire, nationalism and heterogeneity seem to be more evident.[44]

---

[41] Ibid., 165.

[42] Mentioned by the Commissioner of regional policy Johannes Hahn, presented in: T. Rostoks, *In place for an Introduction: Why the Baltic Sea Strategy*, in Z. Ozolina, I. Reinholde, T. Rostoks (eds.), *EU Strategy for the Baltic Sea Region. A year after and beyond*, (Riga: Zinātne, 2010), 9–40.

[43] B. Henningsen, *On identity—No identity*, (Copenhagen: Baltic Development Forum, 2011); B. Henningsen, *Die Ostsee als Handlungs- und Kulturraum: Geschichte, Politik und Kultur*, in E. Stratenschulte (ed.), *Das europäische Meer—Die Ostsee als Handlungsraum*, (Berlin: Berliner Wissenschafts-Verlag, 2011), 9–20.

[44] K. Böttger, *Die EU-Strategie*, 413–414.

Both regions are territorial and transnational. Regarding the area and the number of states, the European part always symbolizes the core of the regions. With eight member states, the regions present in each case 30 % of all EU member states. Both regions unite member states of different "ages": with Germany and Denmark old member states, with Finland, Sweden and Austria member states of the enlargement of 1995, and in both cases several "young" member states of 2004. Beyond this, the Danube Region includes Romania, Bulgaria (2007) and Croatia (2013) as the youngest members of the European family.[45]

The symmetrical aspect of a macro-region cannot be completely fulfilled in praxis. However, no region is faced with a hegemonic state which dominates the area. For example, in the German or Polish case just the functional adequate sub-regions are counted in the macro-region, and an over-estimation of these states is avoided. Therefore, the Baltic Sea Region can be seen as almost symmetrical. In the case of the Danube Region, the southern federal lands of Bavaria and Baden-Württemberg dominate slightly in the comparison of population-rates with the smaller states of the region.[46]

Both macro-regions are open for third countries. In the Danube Region, the number of non-EU-states is higher: six to three, compared to the Baltic Sea Region. Consequently, the third countries take a much more active part in the Danube Region than in the Baltic Sea Region.[47] In the northern case, the integration of Russia is especially important to reach an inclusion of all Baltic Sea coastal states. States are included which will stay outside of the EU even in a long-term perspective.[48] In the southern area, the Danube Region can be seen as a "gate to Europe" which includes states with an at least long-term perspective of EU-accession, like Montenegro or Serbia.[49]

All in all, both regions fulfil the theoretical aspects of a macro-region, and show a lot of similarities in structural questions. In the end, the

---

[45] Ibid., 411.

[46] *Verstärkte Zusammenarbeit im Donauraum* – Interview with E. Stratenschulte, www.european-circle.de (accessed February 1, 2012).

[47] C. Schymik, *Modellversuch Makroregion*, 12.

[48] For the Case of Russia, the EUSBSR symbolizes a new way of cooperation with EU-member states additional to the overall cooperation with the EU in general, R. Bengtsson, *The Baltic Sea Region in 2011*, in B. Henningsen, T. Etzold (eds.), *Political State of the Region Report 2011*, (Copenhagen: Baltic Development Forum, 2011), 12.

[49] As mentioned in the strategy paper: *Communication of the European Commission*, KOM (2010) 715 final, December 8, 2010.

construction of the two regions seems to be easier in the Baltic Sea case because of a better pre-constructed foundation.

Governance of common needs with the three "Nos" in praxis

The fields of the four "pillars" of each strategy cover almost the same topics. Although the names differ, the four main topics can generally be summarized as: environmental sustainability, economic development, infrastructure, and security.

Table 12.2. The names of the "pillars"

EUSBSR	EUSDR
An Environmentally Sustainable Region	Connecting the Region
A Prosperous Region	Protecting the Environment
An Accessible and Attractive Region	Building Prosperity
A Safe and Secure Region	Strengthening the Region

Source: author's own research.

Together with the "priority areas", the specific meaning of the "pillars" leaves room for interpretation. Questions of education, tourism, energy or transport are also included. Once more, the contents of the strategies show the multi-sector character of the concept. Beneath these similarities, the main focus of the strategies differs. The EUSBSR puts more emphasis on the problem of environmental sustainability. The statements of the strategic paper are in this topic directly linked to the rather new field of the EU maritime policy,[50] a unique feature of this topic. Other aspects of the EUSBSR and EUSDR are more "visionary", process-oriented and not directly linked to a specific policy field of the EU. By naming the maritime policy, the EUSBSR is directly connected to specific European laws.[51] This characteristic symbolizes the highest priority of the Baltic Sea Region strategy and considers the urgent environmental problems of the region.[52] The development of this topic will be very important for the success of the whole EUSBSR, not only for the concept as an instrument of governance but also as a project which is supported by the civil society.

---

[50] As the "philosophical fundament" of the strategy, E. Antola, *Political Challenges*, 5.

[51] *Communication of the European Commission*, KOM (2009) 248 final, June 10, 2009.

[52] C. Schymik, *Die EU-Strategie*, 379–380.

The EUSDR stands back in this field. Although the sustainable development of the Danube's ecosystem is addressed, it is of course not connected to the specific maritime policy. Some goals of the environmental development even seem to be contradictory to other goals, such as the support for an increase of river traffic.[53] A high priority of the EUSDR is the field of security. Both strategies understand security as questions of "soft security" but the EUSDR provides a wider interpretation of the topic. In the EUSBSR, security is mostly connected to the topic of maritime safety in shipping and transport. The Danube case also questions organized crime, corruption, effectiveness of institutions, and border security.[54] This difference may be connected to the higher influence of non-EU countries in the region. As a "gate to Europe", the Danube Region needs to consider the external border of the EU.

All topics of the strategies are implemented in the regions through the projects of the action plans. This is a process of an ongoing development because they are designed as "rolling action plans"[55], where new projects can be added when they match up with the goals of the strategies.

Because of the three "Nos" of the strategies, both concepts have to operate within the already existing laws, funding and institutions in the regions. This mirrors the interpretation of the council conclusions which pointed out that strategies should work with the existing framework to make them more efficient.[56] In the issue of law, the EU law seems to be an important factor. Beneath the already mentioned outlook towards the field of EU maritime policy, other aspects of the strategies have to build on existing laws in the region. Once again, the EU presents itself as a harmonizing actor. The national legislation is influenced by the EU-level and formerly national disparities are flattened. Nowadays up to 60 % of national legislation in member states of the EU is "induced" by the European organs. A connective lawful frame for running the strategies may be a supportive factor for the projects of the EUSBSR and EUSDR. In comparison between the two regions, the future development has to show how the higher influence of non-EU-countries in the Danube Region may affect the attractiveness to develop and implement cross-border

[53] K. Böttger, *Die EU-Strategie*, 413–414.

[54] C. Schymik, *Modellversuch Makroregion*, 14.

[55] As the update of the EUSBSR-action plan, http://ec.europa.eu/regional_policy/cooperate/baltic/index_en.cfm (accessed February 25, 2012).

[56] *Council Conclusions on the European Strategy for the Danube Region*, April 13, 2011.

projects between EU-member states and neighboring states.[57] In this case, the Baltic Sea Region seems to have an advantage because fewer countries with non-EU-laws have to be integrated.

The fact of "no new money" generates the need for a closer look at the already existing funding instruments in the regions. The existing funding instruments of the EU (e.g. the European Fund for Regional Development) should be used in a goal-oriented way.[58] The European Commission quantifies the relevant budget which may be used by the strategies, with up to 50 billion and 95 billion Euros for EUSBSR and EUSDR respectively.[59] This is an overall amount for the entire programme period of EU regional policy for 2007 to 2013 in the specific regions. Due to the fact that the strategies were introduced during the programme period, this amount cannot be achieved in praxis.[60] Therefore, the quantified advantage of the EUSDR must be viewed in perspective. In fact, the existing funding areas of the EU symbolize again an advantage for the EUSBSR. The macro-region of the strategy is congruent to the Baltic Sea Region Program. Therefore, projects of the EUSBSR can be organized within one funding area. By 2013, the area of the EUSDR will be separated into the funding areas of Central Europe and the South East Europe Program.[61] Cross-programme projects have to be coordinated between these two areas. The existing financial problems should be considered by the European Commission in the plans for the new programme period starting in 2014.[62]

To build strategies on the existing institutions in the regions is an attractive aspect to reach "local ownership"[63] for projects with motivated actors. Institutional transnational networks in the regions are an advantage to implement the cross-border projects of the strategies, and both areas have experience with regional cooperation. For example, in 1856 a European Danube Commission was established which brought the two

---

[57] E. Stratenschulte, *Von der Ostsee in die Welt?*, 166.
[58] R. Bengtsson, *The Baltic Sea Region*, 12.
[59] C. Schymik, *Modellversuch Makroregion*, 15.
[60] V. Pop, *Baltic Sea Strategy yields few results after one year*, http://euobserver.com (accessed Feberuary 10, 2012).
[61] For all programme areas see: http://ec.europa.eu/regional_policy/information/maps/index_en.cfm#2 (accessed February 25, 2012).
[62] V. Pop, *Baltic Sea Strategy yields few results after one year*, http://euobserver.com (accessed February 10, 2012).
[63] *Verstärkte Zusammenarbeit im Donauraum*, Interview with E. Stratenschulte, www.european-circle.de (accessed February 1, 2012).

regions together,[64] however the overall development of this factor was very different. Since 1990, a broad multi-level system of regional cooperation has been established in the Baltic Sea Region which brings together nation-states, sub-regions, cities and the civil society.[65] For example, the Council of Baltic Sea States celebrates its twentieth anniversary in 2012. There is no comparable cooperation in the Danube Region. A catch-up development therefore seems to be necessary. In 2009, the Council of Danube Cities and Regions was established. Assessments argue that the actual state of the Danube regional cooperation is on the level of the Baltic Sea Region cooperation of the early 1990s.[66] The institutional cooperation of the region is a clear fundament for new projects or coordination processes connected to the EUSBSR. Once again this represents an advantage for the EUSBSR.

Conclusions

Putting together the different thoughts presented in the political and scientific papers, a "macro-region" can be described as a multifunctional, transnational constructed part of the EU, which can be enlarged by functional associated third countries. The territory is balanced between the participating states and bounded together by interaction of a political top-down and civil bottom-up perspective. This definition follows the most important theoretical aspects presented in the literature concerning macro-regions. It also underlines the development of a new form of intra-EU regionalization[67] by introducing a new level of governance between the national level of the EU member-states and the supranational level of the EU organs. The aforementioned EU multi-level-system is extended. This implies new ways of governance in the form of the macro-region strategies.

The Baltic Sea Region and the Danube Region fulfil the theoretical aspects of a macro-region. The Danube Region can be characterized as less symmetrical than the Baltic Sea Region but with a higher influence of non-EU-countries. The governance-approach of the two macro-region strategies is almost identical. Similar topics are addressed by the strategies in both regions but the main priority differs. In the EUSBSR, environmental sustainability is the main focus, while the EUSDR

---

[64] K. Böttger, *Die EU-Strategie*, 411.

[65] Overview in: C. Gebhard, *Unravelling the Baltic Sea Conundrum*, (Baden Baden: Nomos, 2009).

[66] C. Schymik, *Modellversuch Makroregion*, 14.

[67] A. Stocchiero, *Macro-Regions of Europe*, 3.

addresses safety and security questions because of the external border of the EU. The framing conditions for running the Baltic Sea Region Strategy can be seen as a role model. The implementation of the strategy can build on the specific experience in the field of regional cooperation and the benefit of a clearly structured funding area. The actors of the Danube Region need to improve on this development during the upcoming years.

The further development of the EUSBSR and EUSDR will regard the first experiences with the concept in praxis. This can be expected for the field of EU-funding areas and programmes from 2014 onwards.[68] On the national level, the milestones of the concept were always connected to political will and awareness. This factor can decide on future success. EU-presidencies of member states out of the Baltic Sea or the Danube Region have to prove this ambition. The first steps are made and first success was achieved through projects of the action plans. However, the strategies still need to become more "visible" in the regions and the indicators to measure the success need to be developed further.[69]

The experience of the EUSBSR and EUSDR will also help to enhance the theoretical concept of macro-region strategies. The expected discussion will also have to focus on other possible macro-regions in Europe.

The author is a research assistant at the Chair of Comparative Politics at the Department of Political and Administrative Science at the University of Rostock. His PhD project concerns the cooperation of parliaments and parliamentarians in the Baltic Sea region.

[68] T. Nuotio, *The Annual Report 2010 on Implementation of the EUSBSR of the Central Baltic IV Interreg A Programme 2007–2013*, http://www.centralbaltic.eu/documents/doc_download/1412-2010-report-eusbsr-implementation-by-the-central-baltic-interreg-iv-a-programme-2007-2013 (accessed February 15, 2012).

[69] As reviewed by the Council: *Council Conclusions on the review of the European Strategy for the Baltic Sea Region*, November 15, 2011.

CHAPTER THIRTEEN

ACHIEVEMENTS OF THE SLOVENIAN PRESIDENCY OF THE EU COUNCIL

AGATA BIERNAT

Slovenia is one of the smallest European countries. Its population amounts to around two million people and its area is 20.273 square kilometers. For centuries, Slovenia had been dominated by large nations and dynasties. After World War I, Slovenians, along with Croats and Serbs, founded the Kingdom of Serbs, Croats and Slovenians, later renamed the Kingdom of Yugoslavia. From the end of World War II until its declaration of independence in 1991, Slovenia was part of the Federal People's Republic of Yugoslavia, later the Socialist Federal Republic of Yugoslavia.[1] Fifteen years after gaining independence, in 2004 Slovenia became a member of the European Union.

On January 1, 2007, Slovenia officially adopted the euro and in the first half of 2008 it presided over the Council of the European Union. A country with a population of two million people headed a community of twenty-seven countries and almost five hundred million citizens. Janez Potočnik, the European Commissioner for Science and Research, said that there were many reasons why Slovenia was selected:

> We are the first of the so-called "new" member states to have adopted the euro. We have a strong economy, with gross domestic product about 80 % of the EU average. We realized very quickly after our country's creation that serious macro- and micro-economic reforms were necessary for our own development, regardless of our perspective of membership of the European Union. Slovenia was able to take full advantage of the assistance

[1] M. Mrak, M. Rojec, C. Silva-Jáuregui (eds.), *Slovenia: From Yugoslavia to the European Union,* (Washington: World Bank Publications, 2004), xx.

> offered before accession to be in a position to make the most of our membership when it came about.[2]

Slovenia took over the Presidency of the Council of the European Union as the first of the 2004/07 accession countries, the first post-communist and the first Slavic country. It was also the last country to hold the first trio-arranged presidency and the smallest, except Luxembourg, ever to hold the presidency. It was a sign of great trust and a recognition of Slovenia's achievements as well as a great responsibility. Ari Vatanen, a Finnish Member of the European Parliament representing France, said: "Slovenia was always the most advanced country in Yugoslavia and deserved to be the first one to hold the title of EU presidency. It has paved the way for others in the east."[3] There is no doubt that Slovenia has been an extremely dynamic society in the last twenty-five years. The deep social changes it has experienced not only involved an economic and political transition from socialism to capitalism and a liberal democracy, but also the creation of an independent state.

Slovenia as a Part of Trio Presidency

Trio Presidency was established under the Lisbon Treaty. According to the Article 1 of the European Council Decision of December 1, 2009 on the exercise of the Presidency of the Council, the:

> Presidency of the Council, with the exception of the Foreign Affairs configuration, shall be held by pre-established groups of three Member States for a period of 18 months. The groups shall be made up on a basis of equal rotation among the Member States, taking into account their diversity and geographical balance within the Union. Each member of the group shall in turn chair for a six-month period all configurations of the Council, with the exception of the Foreign Affairs configuration. The other members of the group shall assist the Chair in all its responsibilities on the basis of a common programme. Members of the team may decide alternative arrangements among themselves.[4]

---

[2] *Hill & Knowlton's Guide to the Slovenian Presidency of the European Union January–June 2008*, 9 http://www.hillandknowlton.be/sites/default/files/Slovenia 2008.pdf (accessed January 4, 2012).

[3] A. Gough, *Slovenia's EU Presidency in Review*, http://www.slovenia-life.com/ ljubljana/articles/?category=perspectives&name=Slovenia-EU-Presidency-in-Review, (accessed January 8, 2012).

[4] *European Council Decision of 1 December 2009 on the exercise of the Presidency of the Council (2009/881/EU)*, http://eur-

Slovenia concluded the first Trio Presidency formed by Germany and Portugal. The trio system was agreed at the meeting of Permanent Representatives to the EU in March 2006 and approved by the General Affairs and External Relations Council in June 2006. It replaced the previous one-year operational programme and the three-year strategic programme for the Union by an eighteen-month programme of three successive Presidencies.[5]

The central issues of the German-Portuguese-Slovene trio plan were the continuation of the EU's reform and constitutional process, implementation of the Lisbon Strategy for Growth and Employment as well as further progress towards the completion of the European area of freedom, security and justice.[6] Furthermore, their aim was to step up cooperation in the sphere of the EU's joint action on foreign policy. The programme was a consensus among the three member states guided by the General Secretariat of the Council. Furthermore, it is important to highlight that each Trio state draws up its own national presidency programme, largely based on the so-called “inherited agenda” of the EU Council.

Preparations for Slovenia's Presidency of the Council of the EU

EU Council presidency has been one of the most demanding and complex tasks of Slovenia since its independence and a challenge in terms of organization and logistics. It has been not only a project in the field of European affairs, but an all-Slovenian project.[7] Therefore, careful

---

lex.europa.eu/LexUriServ/LexUriServ.do?uri=OJ:L:2009:315:0050:0050:EN:PDF (accessed January 6, 2012).

[5] S. Kajnč, *The Slovenian Presidency of the EU Council: How the 16th Member State Performed*, http://www.realinstitutoelcano.org/wps/portal/rielcano_eng/Content?WCM_GLOBAL_CONTEXT=/elcano/elcano_in/zonas_in/europe/ari105-2008 (accessed Janaury 11, 2012).

[6] *Information on Trio presidency Germany-Portugal-Slovenia*, http://www.eu2007.de/en/The_Council_Presidency/trio/index.html (accessed January 2, 2012).

[7] The presidency of the Council of the European Union was a great issue for Slovenia. The Government as well as the society were convinced that this was a huge opportunity for their country. They wanted to be active during the six-month time. It has to be noted that Ljubljana`s presidency “organized 166 official events: 26 were at the ministerial or higher level, including the EU-US Summit, 13 informal ministerial meetings, a meeting with the Conference of Presidents of the

preparation was required. Moreover, due to significant changes in the EU after the last two enlargements, the complexity and variability of all parameters which need to be taken into consideration by the presiding country increased enormously.

First of all, it has to be emphasized that Slovenia was well prepared for the presidency. In January 2005, Ljubljana launched a detailed preparation programme to facilitate a successful conduct of its mission and take advantage of the opportunities the presidency brings. Experience has shown that a country needs at least three years to prepare for the office. In 2005, organizational and technical frameworks were defined. With regard to defining general political guidelines and priorities, the preparations are headed by the Prime Minister, Janez Janša.[8] A special working group was established dealing with operational management and implementation, headed by the State Secretary for European Affairs, Janez Lenarčič, head of the Government Office for European Affairs.

Although the government was in charge of the preparation of Slovenia's presidency, it was important for the political elite to keep the National Assembly as closely involved in the preparation and management

---

European Parliament, the Government's meeting with the European Commission, and 10 troika meetings with third countries. A total of 140 events were held at the sub-ministerial level. In Slovenia, most events were held at the modern Brdo Congress Centre at Brdo pri Kranju. Soon after the beginning of Slovenia's presidency, the construction of this congress centre turned out to have been a wise decision, as it enabled efficient organization of meetings." *Report on the Slovenian Presidency of the European Council, (January 1 to June 30, 2008)*, Ljubljana, 8, http://www.svez.gov.si/fileadmin/svez.gov.si/pageuploads/docs/predsedovanje_eu/REPORT_ON_THE_SLOVENIAN_PRESIDENCY_OF_THE_EU_COUNCIL.pdf (accessed January 6, 2012).

[8] To achieve all the goals, the Slovenian government established the "Core Working Group for the EU Presidency" led by the Prime Minister. Its members have been the Minister of Finance, the Minister of Foreign Affairs, the Minister of Public Administration and the State Secretary for European Affairs. The Core Working Group had also to ensure a harmonized management of the EU presidency, formulate general political directions and priorities of the presidency as well as monitor the course of preparations. Therefore, the "Operational Group for the Preparation of Activities and Holding the EU Presidency" was established. This group was led by the State Secretary for European Affairs and it was composed of representatives of individual ministries and other governmental offices that were included in preparations for holding the EU presidency. This Operational Group coordinated, directed and monitored the work of individual sub-groups, ministries and other organs, D. Fink-Hafner, D. Lajh, *The 2008 Slovenian EU Presidency: A New Synergy for Europe? A Midterm Report,* p. 34, http://www.sieps.se/sites/default/files/84-20082op.pdf (accessed January 11, 2012).

of the presidency as possible.[9] This was considered to be a condition for the government's successful management of the presidency and an important parliamentary dimension of the presidency itself.

On May 17, 2007, the majority of Slovenian parties represented in the Parliament signed the "Agreement on the cooperation of political parties, the group of unconnected deputies and representatives of national minorities in the National Assembly of the Republic of Slovenia for the successful implementation of the preparation and presidency of the EU". The initiator of the document was the Slovenian Prime Minister. Informally, it was known as an "agreement on 'non-attacking' the government during the EU Presidency".[10] The only parties not to sign were the Liberal Democracy of Slovenia and the Slovenian National Party, who shared the opinion that the proposal was simply not acceptable. Nonetheless, even the biggest opposition party, the Social Democrats, approved the agreement. The government had a comfortable majority in the National Assembly and was not afraid of opposition. This being the case, Janša expressed many times his dissatisfaction with the lack of support by the opposition.

The preparations focused on five areas referring to the presidency programme: human resources, public relations and promotion, events logistics, and the presidency budget. Slovenia designated 62 million euros for the presidency. According to official statistics, round 3,000 public servants were officially involved to meet the staff demand:[11] 2,610 of them worked in Ljubljana and 165 were located at the Permanent Representation of Slovenia to the EU in Brussels.[12] The project also included 133 external experts and 245 students. Of 315 new fixed-term jobs approved by the Government, 289 people were actually employed. Apart from the management and coordination structures, the presidency involved all ministries and government offices as well as other state bodies. Some of the experts in Brussels headed individual bodies of the

---

[9] D. Zajc, *The Slovenian Parliament and the EU Presidency*, in A. Agh, J. Kis-Varga (eds.), *The global crisis and the EU responses: The perspectives of the SBH team presidency*, (Budapest: "Together for Europe" Research Centre, 2009), 311.
[10] Ibid., 39.
[11] S. Kajnč, *Channels of Cooperation: A Case Study of Slovenia's Presidency of the EU*, p. 2, http://www.ceps.eu/files/book/1788.pdf (accessed January 8, 2012).
[12] *Report on the Slovenian Presidency of the European Council, (January 1 to June 30, 2008)*, Ljubljana, 6,
http://www.svez.gov.si/fileadmin/svez.gov.si/pageuploads/docs/predsedovanje_eu/REPORT_ON_THE_SLOVENIAN_PRESIDENCY_OF_THE_EU_COUNCIL.pdf (accessed January 6, 2012).

EU Council and represented the EU at the international level. Others coordinated activities in Ljubljana. The recruitment was completed at the beginning of 2006.

The slogan of the Slovenian EU presidency was "Si.energy for Europe". Along with priority issues, it was supposed to be incorporated into every action and the approach taken throughout the presidency. Five particular priorities were:

- future of the Union and timely entry into force of the Lisbon Treaty,
- successful launching of the new Lisbon Strategy cycle,
- a step forward in addressing climate-energy issues,
- strengthening of the European perspective for the Western Balkans,
- promoting dialogue between cultures, beliefs and traditions in the context of the European Year of Intercultural Dialogue.[13]

The main question remains: did Slovenia manage to fulfill all of them?

Future of the European Union and Enforcement of the Lisbon Treaty

By signing the Lisbon Treaty in December 2007, the European Union member states committed to ratify it at the earliest possible date. During the Slovenian EU presidency, nineteen countries did it while in others the ratification procedures were under way. It is has to be mentioned that the Slovenian National Assembly ratified the treaty with seventy-four votes as the second member state after Hungary on January 29, 2008.[14] Only six MPs of the small, right-wing Slovene National Party voted against, after their proposal to hold a referendum on the issue had been rejected by other parliamentarians.

Slovenian ratification was slightly overshadowed by the negative result of the referendum in Ireland.[15] The vote, which raised existential concerns over the bloc's future, "had to do with conditions in Ireland" and Slovenia

---

[13] D. Fink-Hafner and D. Lajh, *The 2008 Slovenian EU Presidency: A New Synergy for Europe? A Midterm Report,* 44, http://www.sieps.se/sites/default/files/84-20082op.pdf (accessed January 11, 2012).

[14] *Državni zbor je danes z glasovi 74 poslancev ratificiral Lizbonsko pogodbo*, http://www.dnevnik.si/novice/slovenija/295711 (accessed January 18, 2012).

[15] *Uradni rezultati: Irci zavrnili Lizbonsko pogodbo; Janša obžaluje negativen izid*, http://www.dnevnik.si/novice/eu/326465 (accessed January 18, 2012).

was not to be blamed. In fact, the Irish "no" was beyond the influence of the presidency or any other member state.

Successful Launching of the New Cycle of the Lisbon Strategy

One of the most significant moments of the Slovenian EU presidency was the launch of the new three-year cycle of the Lisbon Strategy for growth and jobs for the period 2008 to 2010 and the approval of a time frame for the climate and energy package at a meeting of the European Council in Brussels in spring 2008.[16] As far as the Lisbon Strategy was concerned, it was agreed that radical changes in the content were not necessary but the process should be continued with a focus on implementation of reforms.

Another achievement of Slovenia was the launch of the European Research Area, the so called Ljubljana Process, in mid-April. The initiative is mentioned in the Lisbon Treaty, which gives it a strong legal backing and raises this policy area within the mandate of the EU. The definition of the ERA has evolved during the ten years of its existence, but the new Commissioner for Research, Innovation and Science, Máire Geoghegan-Quinn, recently encapsulated it as "a single, unified research area in Europe, within which researchers and knowledge can move around freely".[17] The major aim of the Ljubljana Process was to establish closer cooperation among participants in the European Research Area. A significant contribution was to be the European Institution of Innovation and Technology (EIT) with its head office established in Budapest in April 2010.

A Step Forward in Tackling Climate and Energy Issues

From the environmental point of view, the climate and energy package was one of the most important issues in Slovenia's EU presidency.

---

[16] *Achievements of the Slovenian Presidency of the EU Council. A press release*, June 30, 2008, http://www.eu2008.si/en/News_and_Documents/Press_Releases/June/0630SVEZdosezki.html (accessed January 19, 2012).

[17] *The 2010 Guglielmo Marconi lecture at the Lisbon Council's innovation summit*, March 5, 2010, http://europa.eu/rapid/pressReleasesAction.do?reference=SPEECH/10/68&format=HTML&aged=0&langu age=EN&guiLanguage=en, (accessed Janaury 19, 2011).

Apparently, the energy issue was a hard nut to crack, involving the entrenched interests of such powerful actors as the Commission, France and Germany. The solution was far from ideal but it was a compromise, like others during this presidency.

Slovenia's role was to facilitate progress in the discussions on the four main proposals comprising the package. During the French presidency, an agreement was to be reached not only among the member states but also with the European Parliament.[18] The EU wanted to play the role of a global leader in the run-up to the climate summit in Copenhagen in December 2009. The presidency did manage to get member states' commitment to seek an early agreement but, as always, some difficulties emerged on the way.

There is no doubt that Slovenia's presidency will be remembered for having paved the way for an EU agreement on key energy and climate issues. It also worked hard on a number of specific environmental agenda issues, including leadership on biodiversity. Here, the presidency re-ensured EU leaders' support for the "Natura 2000" project at a time when the climate change was dominating all environmental debates at the spring council meeting.[19]

A failure of the Slovenian presidency was that no visible effort was made to put the Soil Framework Directive back on the agenda after its being blocked by the environment Council.[20]

Strengthening the European Perspective for the Western Balkans

The Western Balkans issue, especially the Serbian one, was the real priority for Slovenian presidency, and it tried to act as actively as possible to achieve all of the goals. The stability of the Western Balkans is still of utmost importance for security and prosperity of the entire EU. Therefore, Ljubljana focused on supporting the progress of the EU accession process

---

[18] *EEB's Assessment of the Environmental Results of the Slovenian Presidency of the EU. January to June 2008*, 1, http://www.eeb.org/publication/EEB_ASSESSMENT_Slovenia_FINAL_July08.pdf (accessed Janaury 12, 2012).

[19] Ibid.

[20] *The Slovenian presidency: good on energy and biodiversity, bad on soil, agriculture and waste*, Homepage of the European Environmental Bureau, http://www.eeb.org/index.cfm/news-events/news/the-slovenian-presidency-good-on-energy-and-biodiversity-bad-on-soil-agriculture-and-waste/ (accessed Janaury 18, 2012).

of the countries that had been stabilizing, enhancing democratic and economic reforms and mutual cooperation in the last ten years.

From the security point of view, the main areas of Slovenia's interest have been the Balkans as well as the South Eastern Europe in general. Ljubljana's presidency tried to convince other member states that building the European perspective for the Western Balkans countries should remain one of the major topics on the EU agenda. Slovenia concentrated on completing the network of Stabilization and Association Agreements with those countries. It was also important to strengthen their cooperation in several areas.

On April 29, 2008, in Luxembourg the Stabilization and Association Agreements (SAA) between Serbia and the EU was signed[21] by the Serbian Deputy Prime Minister Božidar Đelić, the EU's Enlargement Commissioner Olli Rehn and the Slovenian Foreign Minister Dimitrij Rupel. The signing ceremony was attended by President Boris Tadić and Foreign Minister Vuk Jeremić. For Belgrade, it was a key step towards the future full membership in the EU.

On June 16, 2008 the EU signed the SAA with Bosnia and Herzegovina, following the country's approval of a police reform, which was one of EU's key demands.[22] The document consists of ten chapters, which include the general principles, political dialogue, regional cooperation, free movement of commodities, movement of the labour force and a harmonization of the law.

The EU Council confirmed the revised Accession Partnership with Croatia. In the accession negotiations with Zagreb, the Slovenian presidency opened four chapters (transport policy, energy, free movement of workers, social policy and employment). On the other hand, in the accession negotiations with Turkey, the Slovenian presidency opened two negotiation chapters (company law and intellectual property law). As regards Cyprus, the EU Council adopted amendments to the Green Line Regulation.[23]

Some commentators questioned Slovenia's added value in the Western Balkans in the middle of the presidency, but Ljubljana was able to act as a

---

[21] *Srbiji odškrnili vrata v EU*, http://www.dnevnik.si/novice/eu/316481 (accessed January 15, 2012).

[22] *Report on the Slovenian Presidency of the European Council, (January 1 to June 30, 2008)*, Ljubljana, 5, http://www.svez.gov.si/fileadmin/svez.gov.si/pageuploads/docs/predsedovanje_eu/REPORT_ON_THE_SLOVENIAN_PRESIDENCY_OF_THE_EU_COUNCIL.pdf (accessed January 6, 2012).

[23] Ibid., 18.

bridge between the EU and the region.[24] Minister Rupels' visits to the region as well as numerous lower-level meetings were a sign of Slovenia's will to be a regional leader and a broker.

Moreover, sectoral initiatives were launched under Slovenian leadership, such as the "Bled initiative" to include the Western Balkan states in the EU framework on cooperation in the field of civil protection. Slovenia also pursued the idea of creating a Regional School of Public Administration (ReSPA), an international organization entrusted with the mission of boosting regional cooperation in the field of public administration in the Western Balkans.[25] The letter of intent to establish the ReSPA was signed by officials from Albania, Montenegro, Serbia, Bosnia and Herzegovina, Croatia, Macedonia and Kosovo. A critical observer will always claim that more could have been done, but these are examples of initiatives that have been undertaken and skilfully developed and negotiated.

The issue of Kosovo was a kind of test for Slovenia, emphasizing that Prishtina declared independence during the Slovenian EU presidency[26] and Ljubljana declared its support. The fact that Slovenia's decision had not been a coincidence was proven by the publication of protocols of negotiations between the Political Director in the Ministry of Foreign Affairs of Slovenia Mitja Drobnić and diplomats of the US Department of State and the National Security Committee held in December 2007.[27]

---

[24] S. Kajnč, *The Slovenian Presidency of the EU Council: How the 16th Member State Performed*, http://www.realinstitutoelcano.org/wps/portal/rielcano_eng/Content?WCM_GLOBAL_CONTEXT=/elcano/elcano_in/zonas_in/europe/ari105-2008 (accessed January 11, 2012).

[25] The ReSPA Initiative was initially formulated following the June 2003 Thessaloniki Agenda. Its development was later organised into different phases. The Host Country Agreement (HCA) was signed by Montenegro and ReSPA on 22 June 2011, http://www.respaweb.eu/ (accessed January 19, 2012).

[26] It also recalls that Kosovo's declaration of independence was no surprise for the EU at that time and it had been long clear that unanimity in this matter was impossible. See: S. Kajnč, *The Slovenian Presidency of the EU Council: How the 16th Member State Performed*, http://www.realinstitutoelcano.org/wps/portal/rielcano_eng/Content?WCM_GLOBAL_CONTEXT=/elcano/elcano_in/zonas_in/europe/ari105-2008 (accessed January 11, 2012).

[27] A. Kumar, *EU Presidency Experiences Focused on Rules of Origin for West Balkans Countries*, 5, http://oliver.efri.hr/~euconf/2011/docs/plennary/3.%20Kumar.pdf (accessed January 19, 2012).

Drobnić resigned after his notes had been revealed. They highlighted not only the impact of the USA on Slovenia but also the role of the EU and the United Nations in accelerating the proclamation of independence by Prishtina.[28] What matters is that the incident did not disrupt the general framework of European engagement in the region. Moreover, there were not any external or internal political forces exercising pressure on the Slovenian government not to recognize the independent Kosovo. Ljubljana had been involved in previous secret political preparation. The integrity of Slovenia after the recognition of Kosovo was not threatened because its society is homogenous and consists in more than 80 % Slovenians.

Slovenia, as the first former Yugoslav republic, officially recognized Kosovo on March 5, 2008. The Slovenian Parliament voted with fifty-seven votes in favour in comparison to four against.[29] Minister Rupel said that the decision should be regarded by Belgrade as a part of European and international policy and not as an act against Serbia.

The first three priorities were a kind of basic agenda, being also in part a continuation of German and Portugal presidency. The fifth priority, promoting intercultural dialogue, can be seen as a symbolic one. In turn, the fourth priority focusing on the Western Balkans was the true Slovenian political priority.

---

[28] "Drobnic's resignation is a direct result of the affair that broke out after the Ljubljana daily *Dnevnik* published details from notes taken during Mitja Drobnic's conversation with top US administration representatives, in which, among other things, the US wanted Slovenia to be the first to recognize the independence of Kosovo. In the document, the US Deputy Assistant Secretary Rosemary DiCarlo explained how she had advised the Albanians to call a session of the Kosovo Parliament, during which they would declare independence for a Sunday, because the Russian Federation would not have enough time to call a Security Council meeting." During the meeting, Assistant Secretary of State for European and Eurasian Affairs Daniel Fried expressed his opinion that six European Union member states would not recognize Kosovo at first, but if at least fifteen out of twenty-seven EU member states did it, it would be more than enough. Fried explained that Slovenia's leadership would be of key importance in the role of the EU Presidency, adding that the US avoided making any statements in regards to Kosovo's independence but that it would be among the first countries to recognize Kosovo if its authorities announced independence after the Serbian presidential election. Fried also said that the US was also trying to have as many states outside the EU as possible recognize Kosovo during the first days after the declaration. *Resignation at Slovenian EU presidency over Kosovo*, http://www.kosovocompromise.com/cms/item/topic/en.html?view=story&id=507 &sectionId=1 (accessed January 21, 2012).

[29] *Slovenija je priznala Kosovo, Srbija je že protestirala*, http://www.dnevnik.si/novice/slovenija/303309 (accessed January 23, 2012).

Promoting Dialogue of Cultures—The Most Symbolic Priority?

The Slovenian presidency started with an opening event dedicated to the European Year of Intercultural Dialogue. It was launched by the Commission President José Manuel Barroso and the Slovenian Prime Minister Janez Janša in Ljubljana on January 8. In December 2007, Ján Figel', the European Commissioner for Education, Training, Culture and Youth said:

> In the 21st century, Europe faces a new challenge: how to become an intercultural society, based on a respectful exchange of views between individuals and groups with different cultural backgrounds, on an equal basis. We want to go beyond multicultural societies, where cultures and cultural groups simply coexist side by side: mere tolerance is not enough anymore. We need to give an impulse for a true metamorphosis in our societies, so that we can create an intercultural Europe where cultures exchange and interact constructively, and where there is universal respect for human dignity.[30]

For this occasion Slovenia prepared numerous discussions and events aiming at strengthening intercultural dialogue and encouraging understanding, tolerance, solidarity and a sense of common destiny, especially among young people. Moreover, during the Slovenian presidency, the Euro-Mediterranean University was established in Piran in June 2008.[31] It is a part of a wider international network of universities. Its mission includes: approving the quality of higher education through the implementation of postgraduate (MA and PhD) study and research programmes with a special focus on cultural diversity.

Summary

On the regional level, Slovenia has gradually managed to create a positive image and play a crucial role within the EU in dealing with the issues involving the Western Balkans. Slovenia is now perceived as an important actor in solving the region's conflicts as it provides ideas and initiatives. Moreover, it is able to act as a broker. After some struggle, the

---

[30] *Slovenia: Official Launch of the European Year of Intercultural Dialogue*, http://www.prp.be/en/detail_1114.aspx (accessed January 21, 2012).

[31] *Homepage of the European-Mediterranean University*, http://www.emuni.si/en/strani/29/emuni-university.html (accessed January 24, 2012)..

Slovenian presidency of the EU Council managed to achieve unity on the issue of Kosovo's declaration of independence, which is clear evidence of Slovenia's ability to act as a bridge between the EU and the Western Balkans.

On the most general level, European politics worked as usual. Presiding the Council and relations with other institutions ran smoothly. There were no major mistakes. Despite the fact that Slovenia faced such issues as the collapse of financial markets, spiralling energy and food prices, growing tensions in the Western Balkans and Russia, not to mention the process of ratification of the Lisbon Treaty.[32] There is no doubt that these matters would also be a huge challenge for other, even bigger EU member states.

To conclude, it has to be mentioned that Slovenia tried to cooperate with Germany and Portugal as a Trio member. It is beyond question that the Trio programme was a more important point of reference for Slovenia than for the other two states, for whom it was much easier to fulfil most of their priorities.[33] Nonetheless, the Slovenians tried hard to continue the good work of the German and Portuguese presidencies, for example on strengthening the competitiveness and innovation within the EU Lisbon Strategy for Growth and Jobs. Slovenia brought to a higher level the Central Asia strategy of the German presidency and the renewed relations with African countries as a priority of Portuguese presidency.[34] Frequent cooperation during the Slovenian presidency has been positively assessed, as far as information and advice on negotiations with member states are concerned.

Slovenia's success has prevailed over its errors. As always, the EU remains a work in progress. Ljubljana's experience at "the head of the table" proved that the 2004 enlargement did not leave the EU "exposed to mismanagement by incompetent outsiders or a plethora of tiny new member states".[35] Therefore, Slovenia can definitely be seen as an

---

[32] *More than two cheers for Slovenia*, http://www.europeanvoice.com/article/imported/more-than-two-cheers-for-slovenia/61535.aspx (accessed January 21, 2012).

[33] S. Kajnč, *The Slovenian Presidency of the EU Council: How the 16th Member State Performed*, http://www.realinstitutoelcano.org/wps/portal/rielcano_eng/Content?WCM_GLOBAL_CONTEXT=/elcano/elcano_in/zonas_in/europe/ari105-2008 (accessed January 11, 2012).

[34] Ibid.

[35] *More than two cheers for Slovenia*, http://www.europeanvoice.com/article/imported/more-than-two-cheers-for-slovenia/61535.aspx (accessed January 15, 2012).

example for other small countries. It was well prepared for the EU Council Presidency and it did a good work at the helm of the EU.

The author holds an MA in Political Science and a BA in Balkan Philology. She is a PhD candidate at the Nicolaus Copernicus University in Toruń. Her interests focus on Turkey's foreign policy and political processes in the Western Balkans, with particular emphasis on the process of European integration in the region.

PART FOUR

BILATERAL RELATIONS

CHAPTER FOURTEEN

THE FOUNDATIONS OF THE POLISH-ROMANIAN STRATEGIC PARTNERSHIP

LUCYNA CZECHOWSKA

Introduction

In 2009, Poland and Romania signed two statements which expressed the will of building a strategic partnership between them: Joint Declaration of the President of Poland, Lech Kaczyński and the President of Romania, Traian Băsescu on bilateral relations[1] (March 5, 2009), and Joint Declaration of the President of Poland, Lech Kaczyński and the President of Romania, Traian Băsescu on Polish-Romanian strategic partnership[2] (October 7, 2009). The aim of this chapter is to determine if those countries fulfilled one of the most important conditions of that new institution in the contemporary international relations which is strategic partnership—the convergence of foreign policy strategic goals and standpoints.

The time frame of this chapter ranges from 2004 to 2009, chosen due to the breakthrough in the Euro-Atlantic integration process of both countries. Poland entered the European Union whereas Romania joined the North Atlantic Treaty Organization and successfully concluded its

---

[1] *Wspólna deklaracja Prezydenta Rzeczypospolitej Polskiej, Lecha Kaczyńskiego i Prezydenta Rumunii, Traiana Basescu ws. współpracy dwustronnej*, March 5, 2009, http://www.prezydent.pl/archiwum/archiwum-aktualnosci/rok-2009/art,9,97, lech-kaczynski-zwolennikiem-jak-najblizszych-relacji-miedzy-polska-a-rumunia.html (accessed November 15, 2011).

[2] *Wspólna Deklaracja J.E. Pana Lecha Kaczyńskiego, Prezydenta Rzeczypospolitej Polskiej oraz J.E. Pana Traiana Basescu, Prezydenta Rumunii dotycząca polsko-rumuńskiego partnerstwa strategicznego*, October 7, 2009, http://www.prezydent.pl/archiwum/archiwum-aktualnosci/rok-2009/art,12,695, wspolna-deklaracja-o-partnerstwie-strategicznym.html (accessed November 15, 2011).

membership negotiations with the EU. On the other hand, in 2009 Warsaw and Bucharest, by signing the above-mentioned declarations, for the first time expressed their will to develop special relations.

This chapter has been based on the author's own definition of strategic partnership in the field of Political Science. According to this definition, strategic partnership/special relations should be considered as a bilateral relationship, characterized in the same time by an institutional flexibility and a unique rapprochement as well as by an intensity of contacts between states maintaining their formal sovereignty, being convinced about a cohesion of their strategic goals and opting for a long-term cooperation in order to implement those goals. Institutional flexibility means that states are not obliged to sign a formal international agreement or even an informal declaration[3] in order to begin cooperation in that formula. Thus, entering and quitting a created relationship is extremely easy. Unique intensity of contacts and extraordinary rapprochement signify that the highest authorities of both countries meet and talk much more frequently with each other than with other partners (at least those from the same region). Formal sovereignty means that although the parties develop a very close relationship in which one affects the other and they often create joint institutions (for example a parliamentary assembly), they do not give up their exclusive right to introduce laws that apply to their citizens. Mutual conviction about the convergence of their priorities signifies not only that the states are aware of wanting similar things but also that they share the faith that bilateral cooperation would help make their wishes come true. A long-term cooperation distinguishes the strategic partnerships from temporary diplomatic coalitions which are formed for the sake of short-lived goals and then dissolved right after achieving them.

To answer the question documents of both sides have been examined, in which the states presented guidelines of their foreign and security policy in the given period. The following Polish sources have been used: statements of the Ministers of Foreign Affairs (2004 Włodzmierz Cimoszewicz; 2005 Daniel Rotfeld; 2006 Stefan Meller; 2007 Anna Fotyga; 2008–2009 Radosław Sikorski), statements of the Prime Ministers (2004 Marek Belka; 2005 Kazimierz Marcinkiewicz; 2006 Jarosław Kaczyński; 2007 Donald Tusk) and The National Security Strategy of the Republic of Poland (2007). The following Romanian sources have been used: government programs (2005–2008 Călin Popescu-Tăriceanu; 2009–2012 Emil Boc), the speeches of the President of Romania during a

[3] It is worth mentioning that, usually, states do sign informal statements expressing the will to elevate their bilateral cooperation to the level of strategic partnership and defining their common goals.

meeting with the heads of diplomatic missions accredited in Bucharest (2005–2009 Traian Băsescu) and The National Security Strategy of Romania (2007).

What is meant as Cohesion of Strategic Goals?

Before coming to Poland's and Romania's priorities expressed between 2004 and 2009 the very essence of their strategic goals should be described.

There are several classifications of purposes. A first distinction worth mentioning is the one between strategic and tactical objectives. It refers to the difference between goals related to a long-term strategy and those related to short-term tactics derived from a concrete strategy. Since the objectives studied in this chapter have descended from key documents presenting guidelines of Polish and Romanian foreign and security policies in the given period, it is to be assumed that all of them are of strategic nature.

From the perspective of this research it has been helpful to discern intrinsic, reputational and strategic values proposed by Glenn Snyder. Due to their final character,[4] most important are the intrinsic values (such as independence, human rights, and prestige in the international arena). Strategic and reputational interests, in turn, are instrumental. The degree of their implementation is not significant because of themselves, but due to their contribution to the achievement of other objectives.[5] Reputational values are of psychological nature; their essence is the perception by other countries (for example, the image of a reliable ally, or of a stable economy). Strategic values are mainly oriented towards the future. Their relevance and role depend on the importance attached to the anticipated state of reality by policymakers and their willingness to take risks (for example, control over strategic trails or territories, ethnic homogeneity of the state, and the guarantee of crucial supplies).[6]

Convergent strategic goals of partners do not necessarily stand for identical goals. According to Hans Morgenthau:

---

[4] These are not used to achieve any other values.

[5] The reputational interests are instrumental to the intrinsic ones, but can also be a means of achieving the strategic values and vice versa.

[6] A. Dybczyński, *Środowisko międzynarodowe a zachowania państw*, (Wrocław: Wydawnictwo Uniwersytetu Wrocławskiego, 2006), 60–61, 65.

> The Anglo-American alliance with regard to Europe provides the classic example of an alliance serving identical interests; the objective of one partner—the preservation of the balance of power in Europe—is also the objective of the other. The alliance between the United States and Pakistan is one of many contemporary instances of an alliance serving complementary interests. For the United States it serves the primary purpose of expanding the scope of the policy of containment; for Pakistan it serves primarily the purpose of increasing its political, military, and economic potential vis-a-vis its neighbours.[7]

A little more attention should be paid to differing goals of partners. Each country has a set of hierarchical objectives in various fields. Finding two states with identical priorities must be considered as extremely unlikely, so usually partners enter an alliance with varied proportions of identical, compatible, different but nonexclusive and completely opposing interests. Part of the compatible priorities may evolve into more general, common goals. In the course of cooperation even some initially mutually exclusive interests may become convergent (by establishing a common position or by ignoring differences). That process is much more likely to occur if they have radically different places in the hierarchy, and where a matter fundamental to one party has only marginal significance for the other. However, to make it happen a quantity and importance of identical goals must take precedence over the opposing ones.[8]

Identical, Compatible and Different but Non-exclusive Goals

International security

The study has shown that most priorities expressed by the parties in identical or very similar ways concerned international security.

[7] H. Morgenthau, *Alliances*, in J. Friedman, C. Bladen, S. Rosen (eds.), *Alliance in international politics*, (Boston: Allyn and Bacon, 1970), 82.
[8] G. Liska, *Alignments and Realignments*, in J. Friedman, C. Bladen, S. Rosen (eds.), *Alliance in international politics*, (Boston: Allyn and Bacon, 1970), 110.

Table 14.1. International security

-	Euro-Atlantic security is indivisible
-	Transatlantic ties and the cooperation between Europe and the United States should be maintained
-	North Atlantic Treaty Organization remains a primary structure of the collective security in the Euro-Atlantic area
-	Transformation of NATO in order to adapt it to the twenty-first century realities is crucial
-	Support to the "open door" policy of NATO
-	Support to the role of NATO as a forum for political consultation for the Euro-Atlantic area
-	Military presence of the US in Europe should be maintained
-	Confirmation of one`s value as an ally through an active participation in international operations (for example in Iraq and Afghanistan)
-	Fight against international terrorism should be carried on, first of all through preventive actions, and if they fail also through military missions
-	Development of European defence capabilities under the condition of avoiding duplication or competition with capabilities, command structure, strategy and doctrine of NATO

Based on the key documents presenting the guidelines of Polish[9] and Romanian[10] foreign and security policies in the given period.

[9] *Informacja Ministra Spraw Zagranicznych RP Włodzimierza Cimoszewicza o podstawowych kierunkach polityki zagranicznej (przedstawiona na 16. Posiedzeniu Sejmu w dniu 14 marca 2002 roku)*, http://www.msz.gov.pl/Expose,2002,1647.html (accessed September 7, 2011); *Exposé Prezesa Rady Ministrów Marka Belki*, http://www.kprm.gov.pl/archiwum/4751_11525.htm (accessed April 19, 2007); *Government information on the Polish foreign policy presented by the Minister of Foreign Affairs, Prof. Adam Daniel Rotfeld, at the session of the Sejm on 21st January 2005*, http://www.msz.gov.pl/Ministers,Annual,Address,,2005,2157.html (accessed April 19, 2007); *Exposé Premiera Kazimierza Marcinkiewicza*, http://www.kprm.gov.pl/archiwum/4751_14848.htm (accessed April 19, 2007); *Government information on Polish foreign policy in 2006 pesented at the session of the Sejm on February 15, 2006 by the Minister of Foreign Affairs of the Republic of Poland, Stefan Meller*, http://www.msz.gov.pl/Ministers,Annual,Address,2131.html (accessed April 3, 2012); *Exposé Premiera Jarosława Kaczyńskiego*, http://www.kprm.gov.pl/archiwum/1433_18017.htm (accessed April 19, 2007); *Informacja Rządu na temat polskiej polityki zagranicznej w 2007 roku*, http://www.msz.gov.pl/Exposé,2007,23170.html (accessed July 19, 2011); *National Security Strategy of the Republic of Poland*, Warsaw 2007, p. 10,

Far-reaching analogies used to understand national and international security as well as methods of their preservation[11] were, undoubtedly, the most important common denominators linking the partners in the considered period. For both countries, joining NATO took place ahead of their accession to the European Union.[12] It became a long-awaited proof of

---

http://merln.ndu.edu/whitepapers/Poland-2007-eng.pdf (accessed April 3, 2012);
Exposé premiera Donalda Tuska,
http://www.premier.gov.pl/premier/przemowienia/id:19/wai:1/ (accessed February 2, 2008);
Informacja Ministra Spraw Zagranicznych na temat polityki zagranicznej RP w 2008 roku, http://www.msz.gov.pl/Expose,2008,27479.html (accessed July 19, 2011);
Minister of the Foreign Affairs, Mr Radosław Sikorski, on the goals of Poland's foreign policy for 2009,
http://www.msz.gov.pl/Minister,of,the,Foreign,Affairs,,Mr,Radoslaw,Sikorski,,on,the,goals,of,the,Poland%E2%80%99s,foreign,policy,for,2009,25449.html (accessed April 3, 2012).

[10] *Government program 2005-2008*,
http://www.forumpartnerships.zsi.at/attach/RO_05_NS_G_GovernamentProgramme.pdf (accessed March 20, 2012);
Alocuţiunea preşedintelui României, Traian Băsescu, la întâlnirea de început de an cu Şefii Misiunilor Diplomatice acreditaţi la Bucureşti (Bucureşti, 18 ianuarie 2005), http://cms.presidency.ro/?pag=68&sid=5922 (accessed November 9, 2011);
Discursul preşedintelui României, Traian Băsescu, la întâlnirea de început de an cu Şefii Misiunilor Diplomatice acreditaţi la Bucureşti (Bucureşti, 20 ianuarie 2006), http://cms.presidency.ro/?pag=68&sid=5923 (accessed November 9, 2011);
Alocuţiuea preşedintelui României, Traian Băsescu, la întâlnirea de început de an cu Şefii Misiunilor Diplomatice acreditaţi la Bucureşti (Bucureşti, 19 ianuarie 2007), http://cms.presidency.ro/?pag=68&sid=5924 (accessed November 9, 2011);
The National Security Strategy of Romania, Bucharest 2007,
http://merln.ndu.edu/whitepapers/Romania2007_English.pdf (accessed November 9, 2011);
Discursul preşedintelui României, Traian Băsescu, la întâlnirea de început de an cu Şefii Misiunilor Diplomatice acreditaţi la Bucureşti (Bucureşti, 23 ianuarie 2008), http://cms.presidency.ro/?pag=68&sid=5925 (accessed November 9, 2011);
Chapter 21 – Romania's Foreign Policy,
http://old.mae.ro/index.php?unde=doc&id=5047&idlnk=1&cat=3 (accessed November 9, 2011);
Alocuţiunea preşedintelui României, Traian Băsescu, la întâlnirea de început de an cu Şefii Misiunilor Diplomatice acreditaţi la Bucureşti (Bucureşti, 21 ianuarie 2009), http://cms.presidency.ro/?pag=68&sid=5926 (accessed November 9, 2011).

[11] For example that a fight against international terrorism should be carried, firstly, through preventive actions, and secondly, through military operations.

[12] Poland joined the NATO in 1999 and the EU in 2004. Romania, in turn, became

belonging to the West and a basic guarantee of their national security. As stated by President Băsescu in January 2010: "Romanian security is inconceivable without a strong transatlantic relation, whose pillar is the North Atlantic Treaty Organization."[13] Both parties also believed that the alliance is the best forum for political consultations between North America and Europe[14] and therefore should remain a primary structure of the collective security in the Euro-Atlantic area.

What is more, according to the head of the Polish diplomacy in 2006: "NATO—while retaining its original attributes of a defensive alliance—should develop the capacities that can serve suppression of terrorism, its state and non-state backers. This requires an appropriate modification of the military doctrine, allowing the operation of expeditionary forces of the alliance beyond the treaty zone."[15]

From the above-mentioned standpoints shared by both parties derived other similarities, such as the determination to adjust the army to NATO requirements[16] and the desire to confirm its value as an ally by a fervent fulfilment of all undertaken commitments. As a result, the countries treated their contribution to a wide range of international operations[17] as a matter of honour. They repeatedly declared "an active participation in peacekeeping and security activities regionally and globally and effectively countering both traditional and asymmetrical security risks and threats"[18], Moreover, the partners manifested to keep their troops in areas where prospects for stabilization were most uncertain (especially in Afghanistan).

The states also shared the opinion that the alliance should be open for all European countries[19] and strive for an effective cooperation with the

---

a member of the alliance in 2004 and the European Union in 2007.

[13] *Discursul preşedintelui României, Traian Băsescu, la întâlnirea de început de an cu Şefii Misiunilor Diplomatice acreditaţi la Bucureşti (Bucureşti, 20 ianuarie 2010)*, http://cms.presidency.ro/?pag=68&sid=12012 (accessed April 3, 2012).

[14] *National Security Strategy of the Republic of Poland*, p. 10; *The National Security Strategy of Romania*, 27.

[15] *Government information on Polish foreign policy in 2006.*

[16] *Government program 2005-2008*, s. 124-128; *Exposé Premiera Kazimierza Marcinkiewicza.*

[17] In addition to the alliance operations, Poland and Romania were also engaged in missions under the auspices of the EU, the UN and the United States.

[18] *The National Security Strategy of Romania*, 7.

[19] *Alocuţiunea preşedintelui României, Traian Băsescu, la întâlnirea de început de an cu Şefii Misiunilor Diplomatice acreditaţi la Bucureşti (Bucureşti, 21 ianuarie 2009)*; *Minister of the Foreign Affairs, Mr Radosław Sikorski, on the goals of the Poland's foreign policy for 2009.*

states partaking in the Partnership for Peace programme. As different but nonexclusive purposes there should be considered the will expressed by both states to increase their impact on the decision-making within the organization.[20]

Poland's and Romania's attitude towards the White House was also linked with security issues. Both countries believed that the US was their key strategic partner and supported the American military presence in Europe. A good example of the importance attached by Bucharest to its relationship with Washington can be seen in the following: "At the same time, the Romanian Government will promote a privileged relation with the United States of America"[21], which was included in a section of the government programme entirely devoted to the European integration. Likewise, Warsaw mentioned a crucial role of its cooperation with the United States in each document presenting the guidelines of Polish foreign and security policy in the considered period.

Very similar was the Polish and Romanian approach to the European defence capabilities. Although they supported the ESDP and they even declared some contribution to its development,[22] the countries claimed that their involvement hinged on respecting the so called "3 x D" rule.[23]

Matters of the European Union

Due to their mutual membership in the European Union, the partners shared some convergent goals and standpoints on EU matters.

[20] *Government program 2005–2008*, 124 and 132; *Exposé Premiera Jarosława Kaczyńskiego*.
[21] *Government program 2005–2008*, 5.
[22] The declarations of Bucharest foresaw participation in the implementation of the European Headline Goal 2010 and in the creation of a crisis management system. They also mentioned promotion of better emergency and victim assistance plans and protection of personal data. The Polish party, in turn, listed a contribution to development of an emergency response, rapid reaction forces, battle groups, participation in stabilization, peacekeeping, humanitarian, rescue and training missions, development of a multilateral military cooperation with EU countries and participation in European programs reinforcing the EDA.
[23] "3 x D" rule: no duplication, no discrimination and no decoupling.

Table 14.2. EU matters

-	European Union as a strong, integrated, efficient and effective structure
-	Supporting the free movement of labour force inside the UE
-	EU should be a key actor on the global level
-	Development of the Common Foreign and Security Policy as well as the European Security and Defence Policy
-	Strengthening the EU's energy policy, which should be based on diversification, increased ties among EU countries and renewable energy sources
-	Implementation of programmes in the field of Justice and Home Affairs, including improved border security and the immigration policy
-	Further development the European Neighbourhood Policy as the main structure capable of ensuring a stable and secure environment in Eastern and Southern Europe
-	Further enlargement of the European Union

Based on the key documents presenting the guidelines of Polish and Romanian foreign and security policies in the considered period (see Table 14.1 for the full list).

Assuming that the EU membership should contribute to Polish and Romanian civilizational progress, both countries supported the deepening of the integration within the organization and rising importance of Brussels in the international arena. According to words of the Romanian President: "We want a strong Romania in a strong Europe."[24] The Polish Prime Minister said: "The strong Union is the integrated Union"[25], and the partners agreed on the fact that the European Union should not only be a common market but also a platform for economic, social and political cooperation. Moreover, both parties insisted on a non-discriminatory treatment for Romanian and Polish workers in the EU and supported the free movement of labour force inside the community.[26]

In terms of the EU's external relations, the main axis of the agreement between Warsaw and Bucharest seemed to be the progress of the European Neighbourhood Policy and support for the European aspirations of its recipients (in the first place Moldova and Ukraine,[27] then the South

---

[24] *Alocuţiunea preşedintelui României, Traian Băsescu, la întâlnirea de început de an cu Şefii Misiunilor Diplomatice acreditaţi la Bucureşti (Bucureşti, 18 ianuarie 2005).*

[25] *Exposé premiera Donalda Tuska.*

[26] *Chapter 21—Romania's Foreign Policy*; *Informacja Rządu na temat polskiej polityki zagranicznej w 2007 roku.*

[27] Due to their different geographical location, Poland is more active in promoting

Caucasus countries). The partners also agreed that the integration of the Western Balkan countries and Turkey should proceed as soon as possible within the pre-accession requirements.[28]

Besides the development of the CFSP, ESDP and ENP, the parties devoted great attention to the European energy security based on the diversification of energy sources, renewable energy and strengthened links among member states.[29] What is more, they both recognized the potential for energy cooperation with the states of South Caucasus and Central Asia.[30] Although the countries were concentrated on different energy projects,[31] there was no open competition between them. The desires of both countries to maximize their potential as transit countries for energy sources should also be understood as different but not mutually exclusive goals.

Poland and Romania acknowledged also "a responsibility to apply without cracking common European policies in Justice and Home Affairs"[32], including the improved border security and the immigration policy.

Similarly as in the case of NATO, the partners wanted a greater influence on EU actions and policies,[33] including the preparation of the future financial perspective, so that their interests were adequately represented.

Ukraine whereas Romania is above all supporting Moldova.

[28] Poland also supported the efforts of Romania and Bulgaria for their accession to the EU and the NATO.

[29] *Discursul preşedintelui României, Traian Băsescu, la întâlnirea de început de an cu Şefii Misiunilor Diplomatice acreditaţi la Bucureşti (Bucureşti, 23 ianuarie 2008)*; *National Security Strategy of the Republic of Poland*, 16–17.

[30] *Chapter 21—Romania's Foreign Policy*; *Discursul preşedintelui României, Traian Băsescu, la întâlnirea de început de an cu Şefii Misiunilor Diplomatice acreditaţi la Bucureşti (Bucureşti, 23 ianuarie 2008)*; *Informacja Rządu na temat polskiej polityki zagranicznej w 2007 roku.*

[31] Poland promoted in particular: the construction of the Odessa-Brody-Płock pipeline and the LNG terminal in Świnoujście. The flagship projects of Romania were the Nabucco pipeline, the Pan-European Oil Pipeline (PEOP) and the LNG terminal in Constanţa.

[32] *Alocuţiunea preşedintelui României, Traian Băsescu, la întâlnirea de început de an cu Şefii Misiunilor Diplomatice acreditaţi la Bucureşti (Bucureşti, 18 ianuarie 2005).*

[33] *Alocuţiunea preşedintelui României, Traian Băsescu, la întâlnirea de început de an cu Şefii Misiunilor Diplomatice acreditaţi la Bucureşti (Bucureşti, 19 ianuarie 2007)*; *Government information on the Polish foreign policy presented by the Minister of Foreign Affairs, Prof. Adam Daniel Rotfeld.*

The similarities and the dissimilarities in bilateral relations maintained by Poland and Romania inside the European Union are worth noting. Both capitals manifested the strategic partnership between them and the Republic of France as well as a kind of special relationship with the United Kingdom of Great Britain and Northern Ireland. Moreover, both of them attached great importance to cooperation with neighbouring member states.[34] Although the parties expressed in a similar way their desire to deepen their European integration by developing close ties with individual EU members, Romanian documents showed little interest in the countries outside its closest neighbourhood. Doubtless, Warsaw had far broader bilateral relations inside the EU in the considered period.[35]

Global challenges

Warsaw and Bucharest shared a congruent point of view on global challenges.

Table 14.3. Global challenges

-	Combatting global problems: terrorism, proliferation of weapons of mass destruction and climate changes;
-	Promotion of democracy, human rights and arms control;
-	Supporting the United Nations System reform, which would adapt it to challenges of the twenty-first century;
-	Promotion of multilateralism, respect for the international law and development of mechanisms for cooperation in the spirit of the UN Charter and the CSCE Final Act;
-	Improvement of effectiveness of universal and regional international organizations;
-	More active and efficient Council of Europe regarding human rights and implementation of the rule of law;
-	More dynamic work of the Organization for Security and Cooperation in Europe.

Based on the key documents presenting the assumptions of Polish and Romanian foreign and security policies in the given period (see table 14.1 for the full list).

Given their similar historical experiences over the past seventy years, both countries showed a strong commitment to multilateralism, the

[34] In case of Poland they were Germany, the Baltic states and the members of the V4, whereas for Romania they were Hungary and Bulgaria.
[35] Which is understandable as Poland has been a member state longer than Romania.

international law and the universal values such as human rights and democracy.[36] Above all, Poland and Romania aimed at the development of international mechanisms for cooperation and structures committed to protect the spirit of the UN Charter and the CSCE Final Act, for instance in "sustaining the International Court of Justice, the International Criminal Court, as well as the European Court of Human Rights, including the respect of its decisions".[37]

Both states favoured the UN reform, which they considered to be the only universal organization and therefore still necessary forum for the settlement of international issues and reducing international tensions. Poland opted for the establishment of the Peacebuilding Commission, the Human Rights Council and a reform of the Economic and Social Council. It also demanded a greater efficiency and representativeness of the Security Council (by granting an additional non-permanent seat to the Eastern Europe regional group and establishing a common EU representative in the SC)[38]. Bucharest, on the other hand, was in favour of "resizing of commissions and its specialized bodies" as well as "the enlargement of the Security Council with new permanent members such as Japan and Germany".[39]

What is more, the partners announced their involvement in the work of regional institutions, in particular the Organization for Security and Cooperation in Europe, the Council of Europe and the Organization for Economic Cooperation and Development.[40] They repeatedly declared their willingness to work actively in the most important structures of the Euro-Atlantic area, and were equally committed to solving global problems. Poland and Romania expressed the will to fight against climate changes, international terrorism and the proliferation of weapons of mass destruction.[41]

Both partners considered their relations with countries from other continents as an opportunity to boost their economic growth, and declared

---

[36] *Informacja Rządu na temat polskiej polityki zagranicznej w 2004 roku.*

[37] *Government program 2005–2008*, 132.

[38] *Informacja Ministra Spraw Zagranicznych na temat polityki zagranicznej RP w 2008 roku*; *Government information on Polish foreign policy in 2006.*

[39] *Government program 2005–2008*, 132.

[40] *National Security Strategy of the Republic of Poland*, 14; *Chapter 21—Romania's Foreign Policy.*

[41] *Informacja Ministra Spraw Zagranicznych na temat polityki zagranicznej RP w 2008 roku*; *Exposé Premiera Jarosława Kaczyńskiego*; *Alocuţiuea preşedintelui României, Traian Băsescu, la întâlnirea de început de an cu Şefii Misiunilor Diplomatice acreditaţi la Bucureşti (Bucureşti, 21 ianuarie 2009).*

their will to enhance a multidimensional cooperation with most powerful Asian and South American states: China, Japan, South Korea, India and Brazil.

As far as African states are concerned, development policy was important. According to the Polish Minister Stefan Meller:

> Our centuries-long tradition of struggle for freedom and independence and, particularly, the experience gained in our successful transformation, constitute a kind of rich political know-how, which predestines Poland to concern itself with human rights and the right to democracy and free market. This is also connected with the fulfilment of our obligations to provide development aid – something that will gain increasing prominence in our international activity. We will support efforts to attain sustainable development, reduce poverty and hunger and find new sources of financing aid for the least developed countries.[42]

Although Warsaw and Bucharest considered Israel to be a significant partner, they were also striving to make better use of their "good relations with Arab states, with a view to promoting our economic and cultural interests so as to facilitate dialogue among civilizations".[43]

Moreover, the parties tried to take a stand on almost every matter of international importance, for instance the Iranian nuclear system. To quote the head of Polish diplomacy in 2006: "I wish to pledge Poland's support for the efforts of our allies and partners aimed at finding satisfactory resolution to the problem of the Iranian nuclear programme."[44]

Regional policy

Due to their different geographical location, the priorities of Polish and Romanian regional policy had little in common.

The most obvious common goal in that field was the promotion of freedom, democracy, stability and security in the Eastern neighbourhood of the European Union.[45] Poland and Romania also recognized the need to solve ongoing conflicts in the former Soviet Union. They declared their commitment but also counted on the visible presence of the Euro-Atlantic community. To quote Minister Włodzimierz Cimoszewicz: "In the Euro-

---

[42] *Government information on Polish foreign policy in 2006.*

[43] *Chapter 21—Romania's Foreign Policy.*

[44] *Government information on Polish foreign policy in 2006.*

[45] *Alocuţiunea preşedintelui României, Traian Băsescu, la întâlnirea de început de an cu Şefii Misiunilor Diplomatice acreditaţi la Bucureşti (Bucureşti, 19 ianuarie 2007)*; *Exposé Premiera Kazimierza Marcinkiewicza.*

Atlantic area for years there still have been hotbeds of conflict, including Transnistria, the Caucasus and the South Caucasus. We hope for progress in solving them."[46] Both Poland and Romania were in favour of the withdrawal of foreign troops illegally stationed on the territory of some countries in Eastern Europe and the Caucasus. Because of their own geostrategic goals, Warsaw was much more involved in defending the territorial integrity of Georgia.[47] On the other hand, Bucharest supported Moldova above all as can be seen in the government programme from 2009: "Romania will continue to support the Transnistrian conflict settlement and the EU constant and consistent involvement in finding a viable negotiated solution, with full respect to the national sovereignty and the territorial integrity of the Republic of Moldova."[48]

Table 14.4. Regional policy

-	Promotion of freedom, democracy, stability and security in the Eastern neighbourhood of the EU;
-	Sharing their know-how in conducting reforms;
-	More visible commitment of the West (EU, US) in solving frozen conflicts in the former Soviet Union;
-	Withdrawal of foreign troops illegally stationed in some countries of Eastern Europe and South Caucasus;
-	Supporting the European aspirations of Moldova, Ukraine, the Western Balkans, Turkey and the South Caucasus countries;
-	Supporting peaceful transformation of the Balkans;
-	Clear perspective of the NATO membership for Ukraine and Georgia.

Based on the key documents presenting the assumptions of Polish and Romanian foreign and security policies in the given period (see Table 14.1 for the full list).

Poland and Romania also expressed their will to share their experiences in the field of transformation[49] and to "play a substantial role in the process designed to define and implement the NATO and EU stabilization, cooperation and security assistance policies in Central, Eastern and South Eastern Europe".[50] Both declared participation in achieving the objectives of the Stability Pact with South Eastern Europe as well as promoting

---

[46] *Informacja Ministra Spraw Zagranicznych RP Włodzimierza Cimoszewicza o podstawowych kierunkach polityki zagranicznej.*

[47] *Minister of the Foreign Affairs, Mr Radosław Sikorski, on the goals of the Poland's foreign policy for 2009.*

[48] *Chapter 21—Romania's Foreign Policy.*

[49] For example granting study scholarships.

[50] *The National Security Strategy of Romania*, 29.

further enlargement of the alliance and the European Union in that direction.

In the context of regional policy, Poland devoted its attention to the Baltic region, Belarus, Ukraine, Russia and the cooperation within the Visegrád Group. Romania, on the other hand, was focused on the Black Sea region and relations with the Western Balkans. Consequently, there was a large group of priorities that one of the parties considered as important and the second totally ignored. For instance, Kosovo was a subject relevant for Bucharest and omitted by Warsaw. As President Băsescu noted in 2006: "the development of a state within an existing state can be a dangerous precedent".[51] Although this matter has not been discussed in the Polish documents and therefore cannot be used as an example in this study, it should be mentioned that Warsaw recognized the independence of Kosovo in 2008.

Completely Opposing Goals

The most noticeable difference of positions between the partners can be seen in the Eastern Dimension of the EU, as far as its centre of gravity is concerned.

As the Polish Minister Anna Fotyga said:

> The accession of Romania and Bulgaria to the European Union on 1 January 2007, opens up new opportunities for cooperation with those countries, including the Eastern Dimension of the European Neighbourhood Policy. However, we would not like the integration of Romania and Bulgaria to shift the European Union's interest in the East only to this direction and we will not focus on the cooperation within the Black Sea area.[52]

The Romanians, in turn, declared their consistent support for "the enhancement of cooperation within the Black Sea Economic Cooperation Organization and the Black Sea Synergy"[53], as well as their desire to gain as much of the European interest in these initiatives as possible. It is worth noting, however, that later in the same document, as well as in several others, Bucharest stated its support for the Eastern Partnership as a complementary project to the already existing instruments. What is even

---

[51] *Discursul preşedintelui României, Traian Băsescu, la întâlnirea de început de an cu Şefii Misiunilor Diplomatice acreditaţi la Bucureşti (Bucureşti, 20 ianuarie 2006).*

[52] *Informacja Rządu na temat polskiej polityki zagranicznej w 2007 roku.*

[53] *Chapter 21—Romania's Foreign Policy.*

more symptomatic is that the Polish documents do not even mention the Black Sea Synergy, devoting all of their attention to the perspectives of cooperation within the EP.

The above-mentioned initiatives have very similar goals[54] and beneficiaries.[55] Therefore, they are considered by many observers as competitive towards one other. Without doubt, the centre of gravity issue of the EU Eastern Dimension can be regarded as a potential source of conflict between the partners. However, neither party has emphasized this contradiction so far. On the contrary, they have been trying to focus on what they had in common.

Conclusions

The analysis of strategic objectives of both countries in the period under consideration has shown a far-reaching cohesion of visions of the contemporary world and Europe. Poland and Romania attached great importance to the Euro-Atlantic cooperation within the North Atlantic Treaty Organization as a basic guarantee of their security, and considered the United States as a valuable military power still needed in Europe. In the same time, the parties declared their desire to be an influential part of a strong, integrated and effective European Union. Moreover, in their opinion Brussels should be one of the key players in the modern international arena. In terms of global politics, both states were committed to the United Nations System reform and supported the maintaining of relevance of regional structures for cooperation. In addition, they strongly believed that global challenges ought to be responded to by the global community as every state shares the responsibility for the future of forthcoming generations. Although their regional policies were concentrated in different areas, the partners had similar points of view on what the West should do in its closest neighbourhood. Both Warsaw and Bucharest believed that the EU and the US ought to engage in the settlement of ongoing conflicts in the former Soviet Union as well as to promote democracy and human rights by, *inter alia*, financial encouragement.

---

[54] *Black Sea Synergy*, http://ec.europa.eu/external_relations/blacksea/index_en.htm (accessed March 18, 2010);
Eastern Partnership, http://ec.europa.eu/external_relations/eastern/index_en.htm (accessed March 18, 2010).

[55] The difference is that the Eastern Partnership is dedicated to Belarus, while the Black Sea Synergy is not. On the other hand, the recipient of the BSS could be (besides Moldova, Ukraine, Georgia, Azerbaijan and Armenia) Russia and Turkey.

What is more interesting is that most of their common goals and standpoints are of a long-term nature. They did not come into being in 2009 when the first joint declaration on special relations was signed. What, then, were the foundations of the Polish-Romanian strategic partnership?

Beside an impressive amount of identical, compatible as well as different but non-exclusive priorities, there was one important matter in which the objectives of both countries were contradictory—the centre of gravity of the Eastern Dimension of the European Neighbourhood Policy. From the Polish point of view it should be its eastern border and the initiative of the Eastern Partnership (introduced in May 2009). Romania, on the other hand, promoted the Black Sea Synergy (introduced in February 2008). Presumably, it was not a coincidence that Warsaw declared its will to build special relations with Bucharest in the same year the EP was introduced. While most states sign that kind of statement when some new common goal appears, Poland and Romania did it the other way round. It seems that a potential conflict of interests was for them the starting point for a strategic partnership. As a result, the parties decided to make their initially contradictory goals congruent by establishing a more general, common position—the development of the whole European Neighbourhood Policy.

It is difficult to estimate how enduring a relationship based on the logic of avoiding the negative effects of a potential competition in the EU may be. For now, the motto: "Keep your friends close but your enemies even closer" seems to be working. The authorities of both countries claim that the Eastern Partnership and the Black Sea Synergy complement one another and they declare their support for both structures. What is more, it may be presumed that Poland and Romania can easily find more common strategic objectives in the forthcoming years given their similar historical experience in the past century, their traditional sympathy and their broadly coherent visions of the future. Based on, *inter alia*, a mechanism of permanent consultations at the highest level and joint bodies,[56] the architecture of bilateral relations should create favourable conditions for this process. To sum up, efforts made by the partners so far may lead to a real strategic partnership in the future.

[56] For instance the Polish-Romanian Parliamentary Group and the Consultative Committee of the Presidents of Poland and Romania.

The author holds a PhD in International Relations. She is a researcher at the Nicolaus Copernicus University in Toruń. Her research interests focus on the theory of alliances, Polish foreign policy, the external policy of the European Union and the European Neighbourhood Policy.

CHAPTER FIFTEEN

THE IMPACT OF BILATERAL RELATIONS BETWEEN THE REPUBLIC OF POLAND AND THE RUSSIAN FEDERATION ON THE POLITICAL STATUS OF EASTERN CENTRAL EUROPE (1991–2010)

KATARZYNA MĄCZNIK AND TOMASZ WICHA

Theoretical Background

Central Europe is a part of a continent divided on the basis of an analysis of two geopolitical axes—East-West and North-South. Both strategic conditions and cultural as well as historical aspects are to be taken into account in this chapter.[1] Interpreting the location of the region, Central Europe is classified as an area with a compact inhabitation of both Roman and Russian population and surrounded by seas—the Baltic, the Adriatic, the Mediterranean and the Black Sea.[2]

Defining the territory of Central Europe is problematic and may lead to limitless discussions in the field of Political Science. Depending on which criterion one applies, divergent territory is classified as Central Europe. In its strictest sense it includes Poland, the Czech Republic, Slovakia and Hungary,[3] states that co-operate within the Visegrád Group.

---

[1] D. Dzierżek, W. Paruch, *Europa Środkowa—idee i koncepcje*, in E. Nowak, R. Riedel (eds.), *Polska i Europa Środkowa. Demokratyzacja. Konsolidacja. Europeizacja*, (Lublin: Wydawnictwo Uniwersytetu Marii Curie-Skłodowskiej, 2010), 21.

[2] Ibid., 22.

[3] E. Kużelewska, *Strategia polityki zagranicznej RP*, in J. Stachura (ed.), *Współczesne międzynarodowe stosunki polityczne*, (Białystok: Wydawnictwo Wyższej Szkoły Ekonomicznej, 2010), 313.

In the present study, the eastern part of Central Europe is defined as including Lithuania, Latvia, Estonia, Belarus, Ukraine, Georgia, Armenia, Azerbaijan and Moldova. Over the centuries, some of those countries have been the involved in wars between Poland and Russia. Moreover, a wish to impact foreign policy and political status of the eastern states of Central Europe was visible in late 1990s. There were strong differences in the perception of the foreign policies of Poland and Russia concerning the region. The reasons for this disparity were historical and economic conditions, and the political aspirations of each party can be assessed as high, which was the main point of divergence.

In 1989 and 1990, the establishment of democracy and the forming of new political systems in eastern Central Europe started as an implication of many internal and external factors. The crisis of communism was one of the key reasons for the process. The attempt to modernize and reform the system was named perestroika.[4] Changes in the political system of the Soviet Union started in 1985 when Mikhail Gorbachev became the General Secretary of the communist party. The reforms that he launched resulted in the gradual downfall of communism until the dissolution of the Soviet Union on December 25, 1991. As a result, fifteen new independent states emerged, free to shape their home and foreign policy.

The relations between Warsaw and Moscow in the years 1991–2010 influenced the formation of the political systems of the states in the eastern Central Europe. The disparity in perceptions concerning the region can be found in history as there have always been disputes between Russia and Poland to control the area between the Baltic and the Black Sea. Through political, social and economic actions, the authorities of Poland and Russia have tried to influence foreign policies of the states of the eastern Central Europe. This has resulted in a weakening of bilateral relations between the Republic of Poland and the Russian Federation and led to alterations in the political systems in the region.

The Strategic Dimension of Polish and Russian Policies towards Eastern Central Europe

Polish-Russian impact on the political status of eastern Central Europe has historically had economic and political dimensions. Not only common Slavic origins but also disparities and conflicts have influenced bilateral relations between Poland and Russia. Throughout the centuries, first the

[4] K. Trembicka, *Demokratyzacja systemów politycznych w Europie Środkowo-Wschodniej w latach 1989–1990*, in *Polska i Europa Środkowa*, 107.

former and then the latter aspired to rule over the region of Eastern and Central Europe.[5] The bilateral relations with Russia belong to the most complex and multidimensional challenges in Polish foreign policy.[6]

From 1944 until 1989, communist Poland was a satellite state of the Soviet Union, which significantly limited Warsaw's foreign policy. Visions of a future independent state were created by Polish elites in emigration. Finally, as late as in 1991, the newly sovereign Poland had an opportunity to establish its own policy towards the states of eastern Central Europe, including strategic cooperation. Four of those countries are direct neighbours of Poland.

Poland has been interested in establishing European standards in the eastern states of Central Europe, such as democracy, human rights, minority rights and legal proceedings. Polish authorities have aimed at integrating the region into NATO and the European Union, as well as weakening Russia's position in the area.[7] Initiatives undertaken have focused on the stabilization of the states of Eastern Europe and South Caucasus.

Taking into account the geopolitical changes on the continent, the government of Tadeusz Mazowiecki redefined Poland's foreign policy goals, with a two-dimensional policy conducted towards Eastern Europe.[8] The core of the idea was to maintain good relations with Russia and the former Soviet republics. Given the dissolution of the Soviet Union, the background for individual relations with each of the states was to be introduced.[9]

Krzysztof Skubiszewski, the first Minister of Foreign Affairs of the Republic of Poland after the fall of communism, mentioned the following tasks of his Eastern policy: maintaining the peaceful process of transformation in the region, promoting independence of the new states

---

[5] R. Kupiecki, K. Szczepanik, *Polityka zagraniczna Polski 1918–1994*, (Warszawa: Fundacja Studiów Międzynarodowych, 1995), 66.

[6] M. Orzechowski, *Stosunki pomiędzy PRL/RP a ZSRR/FR w latach 1989–1991*, in A. Gil, T. Kapuśniak (eds.), *Polityka wschodnia Polski. Uwarunkowania. Koncepcje. Realizacja*, (Lublin–Warszawa: Instytut Europy Środkowo-Wschodniej, 2009), 49.

[7] A. Szeptycki, *Nowa odsłona polskiego mesjanizmu na Wschodzie?*, in S. Bieleń (ed.), *Polityka zagraniczna Polski po wstąpieniu do NATO i Unii Europejskiej. Problemy tożsamości i adaptacji*, (Warszawa: DIFIN, 2010), 290.

[8] K. Marzęda, *Pozycja geopolityczna Polski po roku 1989*, in *Polityka wschodnia Polski*, 62.

[9] K. Skubiszewski, *Polska polityka zagraniczna*, in *Rocznik Polskiej Polityki Zagranicznej 1991*, (Warszawa: Polski Instytut Spraw Międzynarodowych, 1993), 21–22.

and aiming at stability in the whole post-Soviet area. Finally, the Polish government focused on establishing active bilateral relations with the members of the Commonwealth of Independent States and those post-Soviet countries that did not also participate in the Commonwealth. Skubiszewski promoted regional cooperation as a constituent of Polish political interests, and Warsaw took part in the Council of the Baltic Sea States, which included Estonia, Latvia and Lithuania as well as Belarus and Ukraine with an observer status.

Another Polish government, led by the coalition of the Democratic Left Alliance and the Polish Peasants' Party, introduced a new concept in the Eastern policy—Partnership for Transformation. The project, presented by the foreign Minister Andrzej Olechowski in Cracow, marked three strategic tasks. The first one was to achieve sustainable development and bilateral relations with the post-Soviet states, especially Russia, Belarus, Ukraine, the Baltic states, Kazakhstan and Moldova, assuming that Russia would accept Polish integration into NATO. The second aim was to cooperate on promoting stability and security in the region. The third one was to boost economic cooperation.[10] The Polish project was rejected by Russia, which did not wish to cooperate within the region as it had its own concepts of foreign policy towards the region of Eastern Europe.

From 1993 until the end of the decade, the Polish foreign policy towards the states of eastern Central Europe was associated with constant mutual critique, limitations on political meetings and a very slow increase of Polish presence in regional markets.[11] Weakening of bilateral relations did not help to establish closer cooperation with the post-Soviet states.

The core of a new foreign policy of the Russian Federation was formulated by Mikhail Gorbachev and it was referred to as the "new thinking".[12] The aim of the concept was the dissolution of the Soviet Union and the establishment of a new position of the Russian Federation after the reforms. The West was no longer perceived as an enemy, and Western states started to be presented as political allies. Nuclear power was no longer a point of arguments on the international arena.[13]

---

[10] M. J. Całka, *Polska polityka wschodnia w 1994*, in *Rocznik Polskiej Polityki Zagranicznej 1995*, (Warszawa: Polski Instytut Spraw Międzynarodowych, 1995), 50–52.

[11] R. Kuźniar, *Polityka wschodnia III RP – sukcesy pragmatyzmu, porażki prometeizmu*, in *Polityka wschodnia Polski*, 183.

[12] A. Bryc, *Cele polityki zagranicznej Federacji Rosyjskiej*, (Toruń: Wydawnictwo Adam Marszałek, 2004), 22.

[13] S. Bieleń, *Tożsamość międzynarodowa Federacji Rosyjskiej*, (Warszawa:

Geopolitical factors played the most important role in Russian politics during 1990–1995. The changes put forward referred to the "close vicinity", i.e. the post-Soviet space, including the Commonwealth of Independent States and the Baltic states. Russia treated eastern Central Europe as its sphere of domination.[14] The establishment of the CIS was supposed to make potential chaos after the dissolution of the Soviet Union impossible.

The differences in the concepts of Polish and Russian foreign policy towards the region of Eastern and Central Europe in 1991–1995 were an implication of the disparate perceptions of the role of Poland and Russia on the international arena. Moscow strived to rule over the post-Soviet region whereas Warsaw aimed at bringing an end to the Russian domination in eastern Central Europe.

The next stage in the Polish foreign policy started in December 1995 when Aleksander Kwaśniewski became President of Poland, with a view to a new beginning in the bilateral relations of Poland and Russia, with security and economic issues separated from each other. It was the Polish integration into NATO that remained the divisive factor for both states.

Jerzy Buzek and his right-wing government did not revive relations with Russia. One of the critical points here were the negotiations with the European Union initiated by the Polish government in December 1997. Moscow demanded information from the EU concerning potential disadvantages for Russia resulting from the extension of the European community.

In the years 1995–2000, the course of Russian foreign policy was under discussion. On the one hand, Atlantic-oriented circles wanted Russia not to oppose NATO and to take into account its potential access into the alliance.[15] On the other hand, so-called Euro-Asians blamed the authorities for focusing on the West and neglecting other points of political reference. The Euro-Asians emphasized the geopolitical importance of Eastern and Central Europe and common goals with the region, especially economic ones. However, they did not deny the significance of the relations between Russia and the West, especially in terms of economy and security.[16]

Oficyna Wydawnicza Aspra-Jr, 2006), 63.

[14] B. Łomiński, *Europa Środkowa w polityce zagranicznej Rosji*, in B. Łomiński, M. Stolarczyk (eds.), *Polska i jej sąsiedzi w latach dziewięćdziesiątych. Polityczne i ekonomiczne aspekty współpracy i integracji*, (Katowice: Wydawnictwo Uniwersytetu Śląskiego, 1998), 162.

[15] A. Bryc, *Cele polityki zagranicznej*, 23.

[16] S. Bieleń, *Tożsamość międzynarodowa Federacji Rosyjskiej*, 71–78.

The most pragmatic approach was based on the principle of polyarchy.[17] The concept of a dynamic balance formed the core of Russian diplomacy when Evgeny Primakov was Minister of Foreign Affairs. The crux of the project consisted in the assumption that coming back to a bipolar world was not possible. Thus, Russia was not supposed to bind itself with any alliance but to keep a balanced approach on the international arena.

The Commonwealth of Independent States was barely active in the period 1995–2000. Russian activities focused rather on an individual cooperation with the states of eastern Central Europe. After the dissolution of the Soviet Union, the closest relations were maintained between Moscow and Minsk.

After the accession into NATO in March 1999, Poland started a new stage in its policy towards Eastern Europe. The priority was to shape bilateral relations with post-Soviet states, strengthening and supporting their security and economy. A Western orientation in the internal and external affairs of those states was supposed to appear. Moreover, a prospect for a future membership in the European Union was set for Russia and other post-Soviet countries.[18] In a statement given in the Polish Seym, the Minister of Foreign Affairs Bronisław Geremek spoke about promoting international relations in Eastern and Central Europe and introducing constant cooperation within the NATO-Russia Council. The undertaken initiatives were aimed at weakening Russia's position in Europe and strengthening the role of NATO member states. As one of them, Poland had an opportunity to support the states of Eastern and Central Europe.

Russia opposed the Polish accession into the EU on the grounds that it would have a negative impact on the region. The Kremlin decided to stop the aspirations of Ukraine and Georgia to integrate into NATO and EU.

The victory of the Law and Justice Party in the parliamentary and that of Lech Kaczyński in the presidential election in Poland in 2005 resulted in the application of a hard policy towards Russia.[19] The government of Kazimierz Marcinkiewicz declared their wish to keep good bilateral

---

[17] K. Łastawski, *Koncepcje polityki zagranicznej i bezpieczeństwa Federacji Rosyjskiej*, in *Federacja Rosyjska w stosunkach międzynarodowych*, A. Czarnocki, I. Topolski (eds.), (Lublin: Wydawnictwo Uniwersytetu Marii Curie-Skłodowskiej, 2006), 65.

[18] K. Marzęda, *Pozycja geopolityczna Polski po roku 1989*, in *Polityka wschodnia Polski*, 63–64.

[19] R. Zięba, *Główne kierunki polityki zagranicznej Polski po zimnej wojnie*, (Warszawa: Wydawnictwa Akademickie i Profesjonalne, 2010), 184.

relations with Russia but in practice they were limited to official meetings.[20] The Minister of Foreign Affairs Stefan Meller claimed that Poland did want to promote a partnership with Russia, especially in the field of economy, stressing the historic and cultural vicinity of both countries.

At the same time, Polish authorities continued to support democratic movements in the CIS countries, particularly in Ukraine and Georgia. An effort was made to launch "a colour revolution" in Belarus.[21] The Polish government declared they would support civil society by making access to information easier. A summit on energy was called by Poland (with Lithuania, Ukraine and Georgia) to find independent sources of natural gas and petroleum. In the programme of the Law and Justice party, the will of creating a close partnership with the eastern states of Central Europe is explicitly stated, and the strategic partnership with Ukraine is also emphasised.

In the years 2005–2010, the Polish Eastern policy, led by President Lech Kaczyński, was based on the notion of sovereignty of a state. Kaczyński realised that Polish security depends on a strategic alliance with the eastern states of Central Europe that would allow Poland to be a partner of Russia and strengthen Warsaw's position in comparison with the Kremlin.[22]

After a premature parliamentary election in 2007, the government was formed by the Civic Platform and the Polish Peasants' Party. It stressed an improvement in the bilateral relations with Russia rejecting the foreign policy of the Law and Justice party. It was emphasised verbally by the Prime Minister Donald Tusk that Poland would not have the most difficult relations with Russia among the EU member states. In that case, the European majority was supposed to influence the Polish policy towards Russia.[23] As public opinion in Europe was moved by the Georgian-Russian war in 2008, President Kaczyński, along with the leaders of Lithuania, Latvia, Estonia and Ukraine, blamed Russia for having fomented the conflict. This also met with criticism in Poland, and the government of Donald Tusk opposed the diplomatic initiatives of President Kaczyński.

---

[20] M. Kaczmarski, W. Konończuk, *Rosyjski dylemat w polityce zagranicznej Polski po 1999 roku*, in *Polityka wschodnia Polski*, 206.
[21] R. Zięba, *Główne kierunki polityki zagranicznej Polski po zimnej wojnie*, 185.
[22] *Na Zachodzie interesy, na Wschodzie bezpieczeństwo*, Interview with Krzysztof Szczerski from April 5, 2011, Website of "Arcana", www.portal.arcana.pl,, (accessed October 12, 2011).
[23] Ibid.

In May 2008, Poland and Sweden launched an initiative to implement the EU project of Eastern Partnership. It consisted in the strong engagement of the EU in promoting democratic transformations in Ukraine, Belarus, Moldova, Georgia, Armenia and Azerbaijan. The strategic aims of the EaP were the establishment of political association, facilitation of trade between the partner states and the EU, liberalisation of the visa programme and the creation of a political structure based on four thematic platforms for cooperation in the future.[24] The crux was to present the project in a way so that it would not be perceived as anti-Russian. The draft of the initiative was accepted by the European Council in June 2008. In May 2009, the project officially came into force.

The strategic goals of the Polish policy towards the states of eastern Central Europe in the years 1991–2010 can be evaluated as ambitious. Polish politicians strived to promote democracy in the region, strengthen energy security and facilitate the integration process with the EU and NATO. Most of the goals have not been fulfilled as the countries concerned (Belarus, Georgia and Ukraine in particular) were not capable of introducing deep political changes. What is more, member states of the EU were not interested in worsening EU-Russia relations, given the Russian ambitions to keep the region under its control.

Polish and Russian concepts concerning the policy towards Eastern Europe were disparate due to their different perceptions of the region's role in the international arena. The concepts have been changing since 1991 due to changes in the political situation in the continent.

The Russian-Polish Dispute on the Direction of Changes in Eastern Central Europe

The states which appeared from the dissolution of the Soviet Union had to define their own foreign policies. Different opportunities and visions concerning internal and external affairs led to different "ways to democracy" among those states. Despite the breakdown of its empire, Russia tried to maintain its sphere of influence. The Kremlin's concepts concerning eastern Central Europe diverged from the Polish ones, which resulted in a worsening of bilateral relations between both states.

Lithuania, Latvia and Estonia were the first Soviet republics to declare independence from March to May 1990. In the first stage of the dissolution of the USSR, Russia did not oppose the initiatives undertaken

---

[24] *Partnerstwo Wschodnie*, Website of the Ministry of Foreign Affairs of the Republic of Poland, http://www.msz.gov.pl (accessed August 20, 2010).

by the Baltic states. Later, Polish and Russian politicians undertook practical initiatives towards new Eastern European states. Poland defended the status of those countries as subjects of international politics, whereas Russia strived to promote a "service" policy towards the region.

The presidential election in 2004 was one of the most important events in the history of independent Ukraine. The core question that appeared during that election was whether there was a chance for Ukraine to get "closer" to Europe and to become democratic.[25] The events revealed Polish and Russian divergent concepts of foreign policy, with Poland supporting a West-friendly candidate Viktor Yushchenko and Russia being in favour of the rather Russia-oriented Viktor Yanukovych.

The Orange Revolution was a response to the electoral fraud, which had been supposed to install Yanukovych as President. Poland was the first EU member state to protest against the fraud. The revolution led to changes in Ukraine. Yushchenko was elected President in a repeated poll. The influence of Russia was weakened and the Polish-Russian bilateral relations worsened.[26]

Poland, the EU and the Council of Europe, as well as, indirectly, the United States of America, played a significant role in solving the crisis and calling a presidential election once again. Moscow treated it as a Western alliance and a victory of the Polish concept concerning the region. Russia lost its role as a dominant and mediator in disputes in post-Soviet republics. The support of the EU resulted in a new definition of Ukrainian foreign policy, while the authorities in Kiev explicitly expressed their will to integrate with the EU and NATO.

The political situation in Belarus was of utmost importance to Polish authorities as well. Russia wanted to integrate Minsk and Moscow, which would strengthen their economic and political cooperation. The active initiatives of the Kremlin aiming at close relations with Belarus omitted other members of the CIS, indicating a change in the Russian approach to integration and a wish to rebuild its position in the region by small steps. The authorities in Moscow wanted to regain their lost sphere of influence. They focused on the key goal of integrating Russia and Belarus on Russian conditions, which would mean the practical incorporation of Belarus into the Russian Federation.[27]

---

[25] T. A. Olszański, *Wybory prezydenckie na Ukrainie październik-grudzień 2004*, "Prace Ośrodka Studiów Wschodnich" 21 (5) (2005).

[26] V. Avioutskii, *Aksamitne rewolucje*, (Warszawa: Wydawnictwo Akademickie Dialog, 2007), 91.

[27] W. Konończuk, *Trudny "sojusznik". Białoruś w polityce Rosji*, "Prace Ośrodka Studiów Wschodnich", 2008, 7.

Georgia remained important in the international arena because of its geopolitical situation. Until 2000, only Russia had been interested in the affairs of Georgia. Later on, due to political changes, Tbilisi started to strive for a closer relation with the EU. The above-mentioned support of Polish President for Georgia in its conflict with Russia in 2008 affected the relations of Poland and Russia in a negative way. By getting support from Poland, Georgia struggled to integrate with the EU and to limit the domination of Russia.

After accession to the EU, Poland promoted the integration of eastern Central Europe. Their greatest wish, to become a member of NATO and the EU, was visible in Georgia and Ukraine. Thus, Polish-Russian clashes took place in 2004 in Ukraine and in 2008 in Georgia, since Poland wanted those countries to gain as much independence from Russia as possible. Formally, the Kremlin did not have instruments to block the integration of Ukraine into the Western structures and it used informal channels instead. Moreover, Ukrainian military issues inhibited the process of integration.[28]

Russia feared losing its geopolitical influence to the West and was treated as a competitor in the region. The accession of Georgia into NATO was perceived as a danger. The events during the war in August 2008 revealed differences between Russia and Poland in the perception of eastern Central Europe. Lech Kaczyński condemned Russia for its aggression, and formulated a note about the territorial integrity of Georgia.[29] He claimed that the Polish support for Georgia was unconditional and far-sighted, even if it caused a long-lasting confrontation with Russia.[30]

The Russian-Georgian war was a serious sign for the international community and the CIS. It revealed the political and military domination of Russia in the region, and security could have been treated as a ploy to achieve strategic political and economic goals.

---

[28] M. Dobraczyński, *Ukraina wobec Wschodu i Zachodu*, in *Polska i jej sąsiedzi*, 187.

[29] B. Cichocki, *Polityka Polski wobec Rosji*, in *Rocznik Polskiej Polityki Zagranicznej 2009*, (Warszawa: Polski Instytut Spraw Międzynarodowych, 2009), 119.

[30] *Musimy zmienić Unię*, "Rzeczpospolita" 19 (16) VIII (2008) (8092), http://archiwum.rp.pl (accessed February 10, 2011).

Conclusions

Polish and Russian policies towards the states of eastern Central Europe in 1991–2010 were disparate. Polish politicians used to undertake actions to establish and influence the political status of the region. After the accession to the EU Polish politicians launched initiatives concerning Ukraine, Georgia, Armenia, Azerbaijan and Moldova. Initiatives towards Baltic states abated after their accession to the EU and NATO in 2004.

The bilateral relations between Poland and Russia underwent different stages. A barrier in the improvement of those relations was the Commonwealth of Independent States. Moscow and Warsaw used to have disparate concepts concerning the development of the region, especially Ukraine and Belarus. Poland wanted to see them as democratic states integrated with the EU and NATO. That did not exclude the positive relations of Kiev and Minsk with Moscow. However, Poland was perceived as an informal leader of the states unfriendly to Russia.[31]

Rebuilding the Russian sphere of influence led to clashes with Polish interests, especially in the case of Ukraine and Georgia. In the early 1990s, when Russia made an attempt to integrate post-Soviet states in the CIS, Poland did not oppose. Only the intensification of Russian initiatives and attempts to influence politics in the states of the eastern part of Central Europe led to Warsaw's reactions and affected the bilateral relations in a negative way. Russia strongly opposed the attempts to promote democracy in the countries of the CIS, particularly the attempt of 2006 to launch a "colour revolution" in Belarus.[32] The energy summit of Poland, Lithuania, Ukraine and Georgia, struggling to find independent sources of natural gas and crude oil, was also contrary to Russia's interests.

The Polish-Russian relations influenced a sequence of changes in the political status of the states in the eastern part of Central Europe, particularly Ukraine, Georgia, Lithuania, Latvia and Estonia. The political breakthrough in Ukraine in 2004 was a result of a struggle between two visions—Polish and Russian one. As far as Belarus was concerned, despite Polish attempts to make Minsk independent from Moscow, Russia managed to boost integration with Minsk.

Lack of political stability in eastern Central Europe will lead to strengthened external initiatives, and it will be a point of interest to the EU to stabilise the region. Thus, the relations between Poland and Russia will

---

[31] M. Kaczmarski, W. Konończuk, *Rosyjski dylemat w polityce zagranicznej Polski po 1999 roku,* 213.

[32] R. Zięba, *Główne kierunki polityki zagranicznej Polski po zimnej wojnie*, 185.

most probably influence the political status of the states in eastern Central Europe.

Katarzyna Mącznik is a Ph.D. student at the University of Maria Curie-Skłodowska in Lublin. Her interests focus on Eastern Europe in general as well as sociological and economic changes in Eastern and Central Europe

Tomasz Wicha is an M.A. student at the University of Maria Curie-Skłodowska in Lublin. His interests focus on political and economic changes in Eastern and Central Europe.

CHAPTER SIXTEEN

HUMAN RIGHTS IN RELATIONS BETWEEN POLAND AND BELARUS

WIESŁAW WACŁAWCZYK

Since 1975, when the Final Act of the Helsinki Conference was signed, human rights became a hot-button issue in relations between the Soviet Union and the United States. The latter, accompanied in its efforts by other Western states, tried to make the protection of these rights the litmus test of the relations under discussion. In the 1970s and 80s, the West used the question of human rights as leverage to force the Soviet Union to liberalise the communist system. Such an approach to the question at issue seemed to serve the vital interests of the United States, since by playing the card of human rights it could enhance its political image in the eyes of the world community. As Mary E. Stuckey observes, "[w]ith its foreign policy at the service of universal human rights, America could conceivably avoid the charge of cultural imperialism".[1]

With the fall of communism in the countries of the former Eastern bloc, the Universal Declaration of Human Rights became an issue in bilateral and multilateral relations. It soon turned out that the meaning of rights stipulated in this document was subject to various interpretations. In states that had not been parts of the Soviet Union, such as Poland, Hungary or the Czech Republic, there was a greater understanding for first generation rights such as freedom of speech and to assembly or the right to fair trial, than in the former Soviet republics like Belarus, Ukraine or Russia. The latter states were eager to emphasise the role of second generation rights, i.e. the economic, social, and cultural rights, while ascribing less importance to the aforementioned first generation rights. In 2000, Gábor Kardos wrote: "Hungary, the Czech Republic, and Poland, formerly part of the Soviet *Zwangsordnung*, as well as former parts of

---

[1] M. E. Stuckey, *Jimmy Carter, Human Rights and the National Agenda*, (College Station: Texas A&M University Press, 2008), 16.

Vienna's empire, now have reasonably well-functioning liberal democracies", which "is the fundamental reason for their sincere if imperfect commitment to international human rights standards – both at home and abroad".[2] It may be added that after 1990 the three countries in question have developed, to different degrees, a sense of mission in the field of human rights education on the international arena.

This has obviously been the case for Poland in its relations with Belarus. In the period 1945–1989, Poland was regarded as one of "communism's weakest links"[3], and after the collapse of the Eastern bloc it became a member of the Council of Europe in 1991. A year later the lower chamber of the Polish Parliament, Seym, ratified the European Convention for the Protection of Human Rights and Fundamental Freedoms (the European Convention on Human Rights), which was adopted by the Council of Europe in 1950. Since 1993, residents of Poland have had the right to file individual complaints to the European Court of Human Rights in Strasbourg. Belarusians have not had this right up to this point, since Belarus is still not a member of the Council of Europe. Therefore, in its relations with Belarus, Poland treats the question of human rights as a means of propagating "European values". At the same time, however, Warsaw considers these values to be assets that helped define the guidelines of its Eastern policy after 1989. As Timothy Snyder puts it, "[i]n supporting the sovereignty of eastern neighbors, in spreading European norms, and then transmitting European influence, the Poland of the 1990s was behaving as a sovereign nation-state with defined interests and goals".[4]

In November 1992, the assumptions of Warsaw's Eastern policy were presented to the Seym by Poland's Foreign Minister Krzysztof Skubiszewski. The Minister spoke "of the Polish concept of a Europeanised East, the opening of that part of the continent to Europe, and the inclusion of this region's states into European institutions".[5] It was

---

[2] G. Kardos, *Human Rights and Foreign Policy in Central Europe: Hungary, the Czech Republic, and Poland* in D. P. Forsythe (ed.) *Human Rights and Comparative Foreign Policy*, (Tokyo: United Nations University Press, 2000), 244.
[3] G. Sanford, *Communism's Weakest Link – Democratic Capitalism's Greatest Challenge: Poland*, in G. Pridham, E. Herring, G. Sanford (eds.), *Building Democracy? The International Dimension of Democratisation in Eastern Europe*, (London: Leicester University Press, 1997), 170.
[4] T. Snyder, *The Reconstruction of Nations: Poland, Ukraine, Lithuania, Belarus, 1569–1999*, (New Heaven-London: Yale University Press, 2003), 292–293.
[5] R. Kuźniar, *Poland's Foreign Policy after 1989*, (Warszawa: Wydawnictwo Naukowe Scholar, 2009), 94–95.

obvious that such specified goals of the country's foreign policy had to include the question of human rights, and also involved the historical background of international relations in the region.

Belarus has had a fixed place in the history of Poland. Being part of the Grand Duchy of Lithuania, it was united with the Kingdom of Poland in 1386 when the Act of Krėva was signed. In 1569, Belarus became part of the Polish-Lithuanian Commonwealth, a large European state that ceased to exist in 1795 when it was finally partitioned by Russia, Prussia, and Austria. Until 1918, Belarus found itself under Russian control. A brief period of independence (March to December 1918) was terminated in January 1919 when it was declared the Byelorusian Socialist Soviet Republic. As a result of the Polish-Soviet War (February 1919 to March 1921), Belarus was partitioned between the Soviet Union and Poland. It became independent on December 8, 1991 when the Soviet Union was formally dissolved.

For Belarus, relations with Poland were a matter of concern, due to their difficult past. However, the latter recognised the Belarusian independence on December 27, 1991, and in March 1992 it established diplomatic relations with Minsk.

Roman Kuźniar notes that Belarus remains a "special case" for Poland:

> This country has huge significance for Poland's geopolitical situation in Central Eastern Europe. Belarus is the direct neighbour lying between Poland and the mainland of Russia, for which it is in turn a strategic link with Central Europe and the West. The ethnic and cultural differences between Russia and Belarus are blurry, which tempts Russians to think of Belarus as a Russian province ... Another important factor in Poland's policy towards Belarus is the large Polish minority living there.[6]

It is worth adding that the latter factor became one of the important and practical reasons for Warsaw making the question of minority rights in Belarus its object of special concern.

In June 1992, Stanislav Shushkevich, the pro-European Chairman of the Supreme Soviet of Belarus, visited Warsaw. The result of this visit turned out to be the Treaty on Good-neighbourly Relations and Good Cooperation, signed by both parties on June 23. The Treaty contains provisions concerning the rights of the Belarusian minority in Poland (about 300,000) and the Polish minority in Belarus (about 400,000). It secures the "free maintaining, development and expression of one's own ethnic, cultural, linguistic and religious identity without any form of

[6] Ibid., 89–90.

discrimination and in conditions of full equality before law".[7] The Treaty confirmed the inviolability of the present border between both states and created a framework for close cooperation in security, political and economic affairs. Of special importance for Poland, considering the fact that parts of the Belarusian territory belonged to it for centuries, was the intention of constructing an infrastructure aimed at protecting the historical and cultural heritage of both countries.

The promising beginnings in Polish-Belarusian relations after 1991 were not a coincidence. To a great degree, they were a consequence of Poland's readiness to renounce its claim to the territories east of the Curzon line as proposed by the Russians during the Yalta agreements. This readiness was in line with Jerzy Giedroyc's views on the Polish *raison d'etat*. A Lithuanian Pole, the founder of the most influential Polish émigré publication *Kultura*, Giedroyc (1906–2000) soon understood that Poland should come to terms with its borders established after World War II. Here is how Snyder expands on the issue:

> Giedroyc believed that a newly independent Poland would be something other than a revival of interwar Poland, and that preparations should begin immediately. Giedroyc understood that the Second World War had reposed without resolving Poland's Eastern questions, and worked to create a platform upon which new solutions could be sought by a future sovereign Poland. Although Giedroyc rarely wrote, his editorial decisions marked out a *Kultura* line on eastern policy.
>
> *Kultura* treated Poland's postwar Eastern border as the Eastern frontier of a future sovereign Poland. This may seem like common sense, but it was very controversial among Poles and unusual among East European *émigrés* in general. This border was first drawn by the Molotov-Ribbentrop pact in 1939 and confirmed by the Yalta accords of 1945, events that Poles regarded as the great diplomatic betrayals of the twentieth century. Giedroyc's innovation was to see these territories not as Polish lands lost to the Soviet Union but as contested territories that could now serve nations comparable to the Polish nation.[8]

By renouncing any territorial claims to Belarus, Ukraine and Lithuania, Poland wanted to create an atmosphere of confidence and credibility in relations with these countries in order to effectively conduct its Eastern policy. The pillars of this policy were contacts with Russia and friendly

---

[7] *Chronology for Poles in Belarus*, http://www.unhcr.org/refworld/country,,MARP,,BLR,,469f38691e,0.html (accessed February 29, 2012).

[8] T. Snyder, *The Reconstruction of Nations*, 220.

relations with the mentioned post-Soviet republics. Although it seemed extremely difficult to reconcile these two objectives, Warsaw made this double-track policy the basis of its political activity in the region. Its main target was to draw the three new states into the orbit of Western influence. While Lithuania quickly found its way there, Ukraine, and especially Belarus, posed much a greater challenge in this respect.

Human rights soon became an issue in Warsaw's Eastern policy. For Poland, they were both the value upon which it wanted to build its new political system and the means of attracting its eastern neighbours to the West. At the same time, the Polish authorities understood that by showing respect for human rights, and campaigning for them on the international arena, Warsaw could gain credibility in the eyes of Western states. Thus, vindicating human rights became the imperative of Polish foreign policy in Eastern Europe.

In relations with Belarus, the bigesst challenges to this policy appeared after Alexander Lukashenko came to power in 1994. He reversed the pro-European and moderately pro-Polish course of Belarusian policy initiated by Stanislav Shushkevich and Prime Minister Vyacheslav Kebich. At the beginning of Lukashenko's presidency, the main and actually only goal of his foreign policy was to get the country closer to Russia. It seemed that this reorientation of political priorities was welcomed by a vast majority of the Belarusian population, which felt a stronger affinity with Russia than with Poland or any other European country. In 1996, Moscow and Minsk signed an association agreement, and in 1997 President Lukashenko and President Boris Yeltsin founded the Union of Russia and Belarus.

Warsaw could do nothing to stop this course of events. Both Russia and Belarus were hostile to the idea of NATO's orientation towards the East; they perceived it as a threat to their security and vital political interests in the region. Therefore, Poland, which was an eager candidate for NATO membership, and found it more and more difficult to keep diplomatic contacts with Belarus. The last high-ranking Polish politician to visit Minsk was Minister Bronislaw Geremek, who, as the chairman-in-office of the Organisation for Security and Cooperation in Europe, opened the OSCE Advisory and Observers' Group in February 1998.

Under President Lukashenko, the protection of human rights in Belarus became an irksome issue. This should come as no surprise if one assumes that the role of human rights is "to transform the human being from a passive witness into an active participant in all world events".[9] This idea is

---

[9] V. Kudriavtsev, E. Lukasheva, *Postcommunist New Thinking on Human Rights*, in P. Juviler, B. Gross, V. Kartashkin, E. Lukasheva (eds.), *Human Rights for the 21st Century: Foundations for Responsible Hope: A U.S.-Post-Soviet Dialogue*, (New

alien to the current Belarusian President. In 1996, the Constitution of Belarus was amended to better fit his political aspirations. In its new shape, the constitution enabled Lukashenko to enormously strengthen the power of the President and to marginalise the role of the Parliament, whose composition became, to a considerable degree, subject to the former's will and decisions.

In order to exercise his broad power freely and effectively, President Lukashenko has seriously abridged freedom of the media. He declared war on the opposition media right after winning his first presidential election, and since then has been consistent in fighting them. In 2004, Miklós Harasti, the OSCE Representative on Freedom of the Media, observed that the situation of the Belarusian media was characterised, *inter alia*, by:

> [c]oercive administrative measures taken against journalists, including deportation for alleged biased reporting of political events; Suspension and closure of independent outlets; Denial of access to state-owned printing facilities for independent newspapers ... Restrictive and arbitrary application of the Media Law against independent newspapers that are critical of the Government ... Application of libel and insult laws to silence critical voices in the non-state media ... High level of state control over the electronic media ... Significant restrictions on access to independent information outside the capital.[10]

Warsaw has actively tried to secure the Belarusians access to media independent of the Lukashenko's government. In 1999, Radio Ratsiya was founded in the town of Białystok, situated in the north-east of Poland. Its main goal was to give the Belarusian minority in Poland information and opinions that differed from those provided by the official media orchestrated from Minsk. Due to lack of funds, the radio stopped broadcasting in 2002. In 2006, it resumed as before in the Belarusian language. Since then, it has been financed by the Polish Ministry of Foreign Affairs. In 2009, Radio Ratsiya began to broadcast from Biała Podlaska, a town located close to the Belarusian town of Brest, thanks to which it can also be heard there.

Another medium that started broadcasting for Belarusians in 2007 from the territory of Poland is Belsat TV. According to *The New York Times*, it is at present "the first and only independent satellite channel for Belarus, broadcasting news and current affairs as well as cultural and

York-London: M.E. Sharpe, 1993), 94.

[10] *Freedom and Responsibility: Yearbokk* 2004, (Vienna: OSCE Representative on Freedom of the Media, 2005), 219–220.

children's programmes".[11] The *Wall Street Journal* reported on January 29, 2011, that Belsat TV:

> funded by the Polish government, has become an increasingly critical source of independent information for people in Belarus since security forces beat and arrested hundreds of participants in a massive street protest that followed last month's disputed presidential election.[12]

Since the beginning of Lukashenko's presidency, the Polish authorities have tried to conduct a "critical dialogue" with Minsk. In its resolution of January 22, 1999, named The Message to the Belarusian People, the members of Seym expressed their concern over the delegalisation of the Supreme Council of the Republic of Belarus. They wrote:

> The Seym of the Republic of Poland gives a moral support to the deputies of the Supreme Council of the Republic of Belarus of 13th convocation, who have been denied the possibility of exercising their mandates. Many of these deputies are subjected to repression, including imprisonment. We demand the release of Andrey Klimau and Vladimir Kudinau. We solidarise with all people persecuted for their convictions and freedom activities. We are convinced that talks between the authorities and opposition groups could lead to solving the current problems in Belarus. They could enable it to get out of the self-imposed state of isolation.[13]

In Minsk, the Seym's *Message to the Belarusian People* was interpreted as a form of interfering with Belarus's internal affairs. However, it did not discourage Warsaw from continuing its policy of "critical dialogue" with Lukashenko's regime. In March 2000, on the eve of the eighty-second anniversary of the proclamation of the Belarusian People's Republic, two Seym deputies, Mariusz Kamiński and Marian Krzaklewski, arrived in

---

[11] *From Poland, Satellite TV Tries to Pierce the Belarus Media Muzzle*, "New York Times", April 24, 2011, A8, http://www.nytimes.com/2011/04/24/world/europe/24belarus.html?_r=1 (accessed March 7, 2012).

[12] G. Fairclough, *Dissent Hits Belarus via Warsaw: Polish-Supported Broadcasts Key Tool in Battle Against Lukashenko Regime*, "Wall Street Journal", January 29, 2011, http://online.wsj.com/article/SB10001424052748704680604576110221620742008.html (accessed March 7, 2012).

[13] *Uchwała Sejmu Rzeczypospolitej Polskiej z dnia 22 stycznia 199 r. Posłanie Sejmu Rzeczypospolitej Polskiej do Narodu Białoruskiego*, "Monitor Polski" 4 (16) (1999): 1/1. http://static1.money.pl/d/akty_prawne/pdf/MP/1999/4/MP19990040016.pdf (accessed March 7, 2012).

Minsk to take part in a demonstration commemorating the event. The former was detained by police before the demonstration, while the latter managed to read a message to the Belarusians, which contained words of support for their efforts to install democracy in the state.[14] On September 10, 2004, the Seym passed a resolution expressing concern over the dissolution of the Belarusian Labour Party. The text reads *inter alia*:

> The Seym of the Republic of Poland expresses deep concern regarding the delegalisation of the Belarusian Labour Party and repressions directed against other political groupings, persecution of independent trade unions as well as independent institutions of higher education (Belarusian Humanities University) and stifling freedom of speech by the authorities. The Seym members call on the authorities of the Republic of Belarus to cease their practices of discrimination, which are targeted at the institution of civic society; they express their conviction that only by showing unconditional respect for the norms of democracy and inalienable rights and freedoms of man and citizen can Belarus return back to the European family of free nations.[15]

Poland consistently reacted to violations of human rights in Belarus. When in 1999 Viktar Hanchar, the former Deputy Prime Minister, disappeared from Minsk and was presumed to have been abducted and killed with his friend, businessman Anatol Krasouski, the Polish Ministry of Foreign Affairs announced a statement in which it expressed concern over the fate of the missing people. Hanchar and Krasouski were not the only ones. Earlier, in May 1999, Jury Zacharanka, the former Minister of Internal Affairs, who, like Hanchar, had become disillusioned with President Lukashenko and turned against him, was also reported as a missing person. In July 2000, Dzmitry Zavadski, a Belarusian camera operator working for the Russian Public Television ORT, disappeared without traces while being on his way to the Minsk airport, where he was to meet his colleague Pavel Sharamyet. The suspicions that all of the mentioned people could have been murdered for political reasons were shared by most of the opposition activists in Belarus. They contributed to the further deterioration of relations between Minsk and the Western countries.

---

[14] A. Bieńczyk-Missala, *Prawa człowieka w polskiej polityce zagranicznej po 1989 roku*, (Warszawa: Wydawnictwa Uniwersytetu Warszawskiego, 2005), 198.

[15] *Uchwała Sejmu Rzeczypospolitej Polskiej z dnia 10 września 2004 r. w sprawie łamania praw człowieka i obywatela na Białorusi*, „Monitor Polski" 39 (679) (2004), 1811, http://dokumenty.rcl.gov.pl/M2004039067801.pdf (accessed March 7, 2012).

Towards the end of the 1990s, Poland suggested that the Belarusian authorities should meet with representatives of the opposition parties and organisations in order to discuss the most urgent political issues in the country.[16] Warsaw also willingly joined the appeals of the Organisation for Security and Cooperation in Europe, the European Union and the Council of Europe, in which these organisations called on Minsk to amend its election law so that it could secure fair, open and democratic elections. The Belarusian authorities did not listen to these suggestions, and regarded them as a form of European meddling in Minsk's internal affairs. The subsequent election in Belarus was flawed in many ways. Among the most common irregularities, notable examples are name refusals to register independent candidates, anomalies in forming election committees, restricting access to the media for certain candidates and parties, and vilifying the opposition.[17]

In spite of these violations of human rights and democratic rules by the Belarusian authorities, Poland did not want to break its relations with Minsk. Warsaw was determined to continue its policy of "critical dialogue" with the Lukashenko's administration even in the face of the European Union's lack of understanding and interest in it. When in June 1998, after the Belarusian authorities had forced the Western embassies to move out of the Drozdy estate near Minsk, Warsaw did not join the sanctions imposed by the West on Belarus (announcing selected Belarusian politicians, including President Lukashenko, as *persona non grata* in the interested Western countries). Trying to carry on with its tactics of "critical dialogue" in relations with Minsk, Poland found itself in a difficult situation at that time. Here is how Roman Kuźniar describes the dilemmas of the Polish policy to Belarus at the turn of the century:

> Without much hope for changing Minsk's internal and external directions, Poland did not want that Russia treat Belarus as its simple, strategic extension towards Europe. On the one hand, Warsaw presented the same stance as the EU members and the US on infringements of democratic standards and regular and serious violations of human rights in Belarus, while on the other—it opposed against isolation or self isolation of its direct neighbour. If Poland planned—and was clear about it—to support gradual change in Belarus, it had to maintain at least a marginal level of dialogue and communication with it. Poland also needed to support and somehow protect the Polish national minority of several hundred thousand

[16] A. Bieńczyk-Missala, *Prawa człowieka w polskiej polityce zagranicznej po 1989 roku*, 199.
[17] Ibid.

> people. For these reasons, it was impossible for a policy towards such a partner, with such objectives, to be both effective and coherent.[18]

Although aware of the weaknesses of their Eastern policy, the Polish authorities were determined to stick to the main line. When in 2002 both the EU and US increased sanctions on Belarus, after Lukashenko's administration practically paralysed the work of the OSCE's Advisory and Monitoring Group in Minsk, Warsaw did not officially join the restrictions, although the Polish government "fully shared the EU's opinion on the activity of the Belarusian authorities".[19] Poland's reluctance to impose radical sanctions on its eastern neighbour was positively received in Minsk, however it did not bring any changes in President Lukashenko's foreign policy. In spite of tensions in its bilateral relations with Russia, Belarus was still more interested in a strategic alliance with Moscow than in close links with Warsaw. Although Minsk agreed to conduct a dialogue with its western neighbour, it did not intend to reform its political system. The question of human rights remained a serious problem in Polish-Belarusian diplomatic contacts, since the latter side was adamant in its reluctance to accept any suggestions regarding this issue. Lukashenko's Belarus took a pragmatic approach to the bilateral relations with Poland, emphasising the importance of economic ties, i.e. trade and business exchange. At the same time, it consistently ignored Warsaw's efforts to discuss issues concerning Minsk's foreign and domestic policy.

In spite of that, Poland did not give up the idea of promulgating democratic values behind its eastern border. In the first years of the twenty-first century, Belarus became one of the most popular destinations of Polish non-governmental organisations that were active in the field of human rights education. At that time, dozens of volunteers and staff members of these organisations visited Belarusian towns to give lectures and conduct workshops on civil society, civil liberties, or journalistic standards. Among the most active Polish NGOs in Belarus were the Helsinki Foundation for Human Rights and the Eastern European Democracy Centre. Their representatives met with leaders of Belarusian NGOs and started cooperation with them. Many Polish human rights defenders found their way to Belarusian activists and politicians who opposed Lukashenko's policy and opted for closer links with the West. The activists and politicians under discussion were e.g. Alaksandar Milinkievič, who was an opposition candidate in the Belarusian presidential election of 2006, Ales Bialiatski, the head of the Viasna

[18] R. Kuźniar, *Poland's Foreign Policy after 1989*, 271–272.
[19] Ibid., 273.

Human Rights Centre, or Zhanna Litvina, who has been for many years (and still is) the chairwoman of the Belarusian Association of Journalists (BAJ).

In the discussed period of time, hundreds of members and volunteers of Belarusian non-governmental organisations and opposition parties participated in human rights courses, training and conferences organised in Poland. In this field, the most active role was played by the above-mentioned Helsinki Foundation for Human Rights. In 1990, it began to organise in Warsaw special courses for residents of the former republics of the Soviet Union. Those courses, conducted in the Russian language, were attended by members of NGOs, lawyers, journalists, politicians, and representatives of other professions from countries of Eastern Europe (Belarus, Moldova, Russia, Ukraine), the Caucasus (Armenia, Azerbaijan, Georgia), and Central Asia (Kazakhstan, Kyrgyzstan, Tajikistan, Turkmenistan, Uzbekistan). One of the courses under discussion, the Summer School on Human Rights, has been held yearly since 1990, and Belarusians have made up a significant part of the participants of this course.

It is worthwhile to add that in the period of 1999–2003 the Helsinki Foundation for Human Rights held a special programme focused on Belarus. During that time, its volunteers and staff members intensively travelled to all major towns in this country, met with representatives of Belarusian NGOs and held lectures and workshops on human rights.

Apart from the Helsinki Foundation, there were other Polish non-governmental organisations who played an important role in raising the awareness of human rights in the Belarusian society. Notable among them are the Stefan Batory Foundation, the earlier mentioned Eastern European Democracy Centre and the Press Freedom Monitoring Centre.

The administration of the Lukashenko's regime did not turn a blind eye to these activities of Polish NGOs, and contributed to a deterioration of bilateral relations between the two countries. In 2005, the Belarusian authorities, horrified by the events of the Orange Revolution in Ukraine, introduced strict regulations concerning the registration of parties and associations. In May of the same year, they annulled the convention of the Union of Poles in Belarus during which Andżelika Borys, perceived by Lukashenko's administration as too independent, was chosen as the new president of this organisation. Four months later, the Belarusian authorities held another convention of the Union. Neither Borys nor her adherents were allowed to participate in it, so that the members of the organisation could elect a new president, more submissive to the regime. Since then, there have been two organisations called the Union of Poles in Belarus.

Thus, the Belarusian authorities managed to weaken the Union, which, according to their accusations, could initiate in Belarus a revolution similar to those that had taken place in Ukraine, Georgia or Kyrgyzstan.

At the beginning of 2006, analysts wrote in the *Rocznik Strategiczny* [*Strategic Yearbook*]:

> Polish policy towards Belarus was characterised by ever-more limited room for manoeuvre, as well as an ever-clearer shortage of instruments by which the desire to antagonise the bilateral relations on the part of the Belarusian authorities could be reacted to.[20]

These words were written after Poland had called off its ambassador from Minsk and the diplomatic links between the two countries were brought down to the level of *chargé d'affaires*.

The impasse in Polish-Belarusian relations in the middle of the first decade of the twenty-first century has not been broken until the present day. The signs of thaw in these relations in 2008 (Poland reduced the price of visas for the Belarusians) and 2009 (Polish Deputy Prime Minister Waldemar Pawlak paid a visit to Minsk) did not mark a breakthrough in the tense standoff between the two states. Although a representative of President Lukashenko took part in the meeting inaugurating the EU's Eastern Partnership project (in Prague May 7, 2009), Minsk ostentatiously ignored the EP's summits in Warsaw (September 29–30, 2011) and in Prague (March 5, 2012). The absence of the Belarusian delegation during these meetings may be regarded as an obvious sign that President Lukashenko is not going to change his militant policy to Poland and the European Union. The Eastern Partnership, a project presented to the EU's General Affairs and External Relations Council by Polish Foreign Minister Radosław Sikorski and Swedish Foreign Minister Carl Bildt, is perceived in Minsk as another initiative aimed at the democratisation of Belarus.

According to Ryszard Zięba, the Polish policy towards Belarus may finally bring about positive results.[21] Indeed, it is to be assumed that although Minsk still seems to be impervious to human rights concerns and democratic ideals, this situation is likely to change in the future. The most important reason for which Warsaw should carry on with its present policy to Belarus is that there is no alternative to it. Human rights determine to a great degree the identity of contemporary Europe through its most important institutions. Being an EU member, Poland has an obligation to

---

[20] Ibid., 351.

[21] R. Zięba, *Główne kierunki polityki zagranicznej Polski po zimnej wojnie*, (Warszawa: Wydawnictwa Akademickie i Profesjonalne, 2012), 242.

promulgate the idea of human rights behind its eastern border. This defines, at least to a large extent, its *raison d'etat*.

The author is habilitated doctor of Political Science at the Nicolaus Copernicus University in Toruń. He specializes in human rights and mass communication issues.

PART FIVE

POLITICAL AND PARTY SYSTEMS

CHAPTER SEVENTEEN

STRENGTHENING THE ROLE OF NATIONAL PARLIAMENTS BY CONSTITUTIONAL COURTS OF THE CENTRAL EUROPEAN MEMBER STATES[+]

JANA ONDREJKOVÁ

Introduction

For the numerous lawyers from Central European states who perceived the accession process to the European Union as a confirmation of the attained level of democracy after the Velvet Revolution, it may sound somewhat blasphemous to say that the original concept of European integration was not designed as a democratic project.[1] There are different aspects explaining this past:

(1) The historical and political context (especially the lessons learned from the failure of previous broad integration plans and the preference for Monnet's French technocratic and outcome-based approach).[2]

(2) The comparative point of view, where the democratic element was neither stronger nor weaker than that in similar international organizations.[3]

[+] The paper was written within grant project No. P408/12/1255 "The Key Concepts of Constitutional Theory in the Age of Changes of Paradigms".

[1] See: G. F. Mancini, D. T. Keeling, *Democracy and the European Court of Justice*, "Modern Law Review" 2 (1994), 2175, and foll., especially the first part, titled *The Undemocratic Nature of the European Community's Original Constitution.*

[2] P. Craig, G. de Burca, *The Evolution of EU Law. 2nd edition*, (Oxford: Oxford University Press, 2011), 15–16.

[3] Consider, for example, the role of the then Assembly in the Council of Europe whose main purpose was to "facilitate parliamentary supervision of intergovernmental

(3) The derivation of legitimacy through the involvement and decisive position of the democratically accountable national representatives at the European level;

(4) In most states, the general requirement of a parliamentary assent for the international law to be in some form valid in the national legal order can be considered as sufficiently protecting the principles of democracy.[4]

In fact, it was only in 1979 when the first direct election to the European Parliament took place. This does not deny the importance of other sources of legitimacy of the EU,[5] but democracy[6] is highlighted as one of the basic values of the EU (Art. 2 TEU).

Search for a New Balance in Democratic Legitimacy Sources

Inasmuch as the European Parliament (even after the significant spread of the EU competences) remains the only EU institution that can claim its own direct democratic legitimacy, it can prove useful to focus on the intergovernmentalistic argumentation about legitimacy through national institutions acting at the European level. However, in order to fulfil these claims in parliamentary systems[7] (e.g. Germany, Italy or the Czech Republic) it would be necessary that:

---

decision-making processes". F. Arndt, *Parliamentary Assemblies, International*, in *Max Planck Encyclopaedia of Public International Law*, www.mpepil.com (accessed March 1, 2012).

[4] As for the supranational elements in the Founding Treaties, it is necessary to remember that the explicit use was connected only with the ECSC High Authority whose tasks were substantially more of an executive rather than legislative nature. For a detailed analysis see: R. Barents, *The Autonomy of Community Law*, (Hague: Kluwer Law International, 2004), 27 and foll.

[5] See: C. Lord, P. Magnette, *E Pluribus Unum? Creative Disagreement about Legitimacy in the EU*, "JCMS" 1 (2004), 183–202, which discusses the following vectors of legitimacy: indirect, parliamentary, technocratic and procedural.

[6] Nevertheless, the requirements and consequences of different normative models of democracy differ. See: J. Habermas, *Three Normative Models of Democracy*, "Constellations" 1 (1994), 1–10. This type of argumentation is used in D. Chalmers, G. Davies, G. Monti, *European Union Law. 2nd edition*, (Cambridge: Cambridge University Press, 2010), 132–136 (participatory democracy and republicanism).

[7] In France and other semi-presidential systems, the division of powers in the international agenda between the parliament and the head of state, both directly

(1) In the area of policymaking, the government is not expected to follow its own policies in international relations without being accountable to the national parliament.
(2) In the area of law-making, the national parliament is not to be circumvented in its legislative, public deliberation, public control and other functions by the government's actions at the European level.

In states with a dualistic approach to international law, not only the obligations accepted by the executive at the international level were to be in most cases ratified with an ex ante approval by the parliament, but the actual implementation of these obligations *ex post* in domestic law was mainly in the hands of national parliaments. This allowed the national parliaments to have more detailed control over individual obligations and for preserving the domestic legal rules against external modifications.[8]

The two above-mentioned propositions were nevertheless affected by the commencement of European integration. The law and policymaking at the European level was to become partly independent from directly elected national bodies via qualified majority voting (QMV) that concerned more areas after the transitional period ending in 1966, and through the interference of the ECJ (the principle of direct effect not limited to the regulations, and the principle of primacy). While these facts were explained and evaluated in detail from the point of view of European integration,[9] less attention was paid by the lawyers to the shift in competences between the legislative and executive branches in the member states.[10]

The same arguments that made the European law more effective (QMV, direct effect, primacy) made the link between the citizens and the adoption of general rules increasingly less effective.[11] Meanwhile, the new

elected, would require outlining in details, but the core of the argument about the accountability of the government and the powers of the parliament remains.

[8] See: J. Kysela, P. Ondrejek, J. Ondrejkova, *Narrow Gate? The Process of Entering International and EU Agreements into the Constitutional Order of an EU Member State: the Example of the Czech Republic*, "CYELP" (2011): 229–231.

[9] J. H. H. Weiler, *The Transformation of Europe*, "The Yale Law Journal" 8 (1991), 2403–2483.

[10] Even if one questions whether the national parliaments possess more power vis-à-vis the governments in domestic issues when compared to the safeguards related to the European decision-making.

[11] Although the national parliaments developed some new ways of compensation of the loss of their original influence. For historical overview see: K. Auel, *Introduction: The Europeanisation of Parliamentary Democracy*, "The Journal of

channel of democratic legitimacy was being strengthened at the European level—the empowerment of the European Parliament not only by Treaty amendments, but also through the case law of the ECJ.[12] A similar process of the formal[13] increase in the powers of national parliaments at the EU level is brought into focus when we rearrange article 12 TEU (the active contribution of the national parliaments to the good functioning of the Union) in more or less chronological order: (d) participation in the revision procedures in accordance with the art. 48 TEU, (b) notification of application for accession, (e) engagement in inter-parliamentary cooperation, (a) information on draft legislative acts, (b) control of subsidiarity, and (c) involvement in the decision within the framework of the area of freedom, security and justice. However, even if some constitutional courts repeat this empowerment claim uncritically in their decisions, it is useful to look behind the wording and search for mere extensions of previously existing safeguards.

The Impact of the Lisbon Treaty on National Parliaments

Previously all revisions of the founding treaties and accessions had to be ratified by the member states in accordance with their respective constitutional requirements, which meant the involvement of national parliaments or referendum. The current wording of the art. 48 TEU in fact brings substantial changes for other national institutions. With regard to the art. 48 (6) TEU, it is for the member states to decide the constitutional requirements for the approval of the simplified revision procedure decision mentioned therein. Otherwise, it could be doubtful what kind of ratification procedure should be used or whether the ex-ante constitutional review of international treaties (or ratification acts) is applicable. Similar concerns apply to the general passerelle clause (art. 48 (7) TEU). According to this, the national parliaments are the only institutions envisaged to express their veto within a limited time. However, this results in the exclusion of other bodies regularly involved in the ratification procedure, including the constitutional court, which could normally be asked to assess the constitutionality of the treaty or its changes. In the

Legislative Studies" 3–4 (2005), 307–309.

[12] For more details see: B. Rittberger, *Building Europe's Parliament*, (Oxford: OUP Oxford, 2007).

[13] As opposed to more "factual" efforts of the national parliaments, e.g. the use of procedures that bind their parliaments to defend a particular position in the council, creation of the specialised parliamentary committees or establishment of links and coordination with other parliaments.

instance of the specific passerelle clauses (ex. art. 31 TEU relating to the Common Foreign and Security Policy), neither the national parliaments (with one exception in art. 81 TFEU) nor the other above-mentioned bodies are counted on the level of EU law. As such, art. 48 TEU would have meant the empowerment of the national parliaments only when compared to the situation of their absolute omission. Nevertheless, this was not the case. On the contrary, these simplified revision procedures can weaken the position of other national actors usually involved in the process of the amendment of the international treaties.[14]

The same applies to the other cases. The inter-parliamentary cooperation began approximately in the 1980s, and the first declaration on information rights was annexed to the Maastricht Treaty of 1992. The ability to issue opinions on the principle of subsidiarity dates back to the 1997 Protocol on the role of national parliaments in the European Union annexed to the Treaty of Amsterdam. What differs is the regard which must be now given to them in the so-called yellow and orange card procedures, but the actual significance of this procedure is questionable.[15] This protocol had also already mentioned the rights in the area of freedom, security and justice.[16]

At the same time, however, these "strengthened" provisions may lead to a cleavage between the governments and their national parliaments, up to the exploitation of one's position against the other. The national parliaments can now assess the EU policies and legislative proposals independently of their governments and express their opinions autonomously, but this also means the loss of the "parliament-card"[17] the government might otherwise be willing to use.[18] However, this new direct link of national parliaments to the EU is not the only reason why current political theories of the relationship between the governments and the national parliaments needs rethinking. Up to now, these theories were

---

[14] Simplified revision in substantive issues is exceptional, consider e.g. art. 108 of the UN Charter or art. 121 and 122 of the ICC Statute.

[15] See: Chalmers sub 6, 130–132.

[16] For a more detailed critical assessment of the changes brought by the Lisbon Treaty with regard to national parliaments, see: F. Jacobs, *Evolving relations between the European Parliament and the national parliaments in the aftermath of the Lisbon Treaty*, http://euce.org/eusa/2011/papers/7k_jacobs.pdf (accessed March 1, 2012).

[17] As a parallel to a "constitutional card", see: M. Kumm, *The Jurisprudence of Constitutional Conflict: Constitutional Supremacy in Europe before and after the Constitutional Treaty*, "European Law Journal" 3 2005, 281.

[18] I am grateful to Jan Kysela for this remark.

more general and treated the whole area of EU issues in national parliaments similarly. After the Lisbon Treaty a distinction was created between the issues that the national parliaments would be directly involved with, in the explicit wording of the EU Treaties and in issues where a unanimity in the Council still prevails. However, the third area of matters of utmost importance for national parliaments was set up by those players who were largely omitted in previous theories on the government-parliamentary relationship—the constitutional courts.

In order to support this argument, we can assess the changes brought to the national parliaments by the Lisbon Treaty from a domestic point of view. It could be reasonably felt that, where there is only a formal recognition of previously used channels of involvement of national parliaments, no substantial changes of existing procedures are necessary.[19] As a result, related questions arise: did the procedures change after the Lisbon Treaty? Or, more generally, are these rights sufficiently guaranteed by existing corresponding procedures? And, in case the answers are positive, who was the *spiritus movens* of the change?

Legal Changes in the Rules of Procedure of the Czech Parliament

The Czech Republic may be an interesting example to demonstrate the importance of these questions. In the Czech Republic, the key provision governing the involvement of the chambers of Parliament in EU issues, since accession to the EU, is art 10b of the Constitution:

> (1) The Government shall inform the Parliament regularly and in advance on issues related to obligations arising for the Czech Republic from its membership in an international organization or institution stipulated in Section 10a. (2) The Chambers of Parliament express their opinions on the decisions of such an international organization or institution in a form provided for by their rules of procedure. (3) An Act on the principles of conduct and relations between both Chambers and in their external

[19] This claim can be substantiated also by COSAC 13th Biannual Report on EU Practices and Procedures (May 2010) drawing on the questionnaire about the new powers of National Parliaments after the entry into force of the Treaty of Lisbon. *Thirteenth Bi-annual Report: Developments in European Union Practices and Procedures Relevant to Parliamentary Scrutiny*, http://www.cosac.eu/en/documents/biannual/13br.pdf/ (accessed March 1, 2012).

relations may entrust the exercise of the competence of the Chambers under Subsection 2 to a joint body of the Chambers[20]

Even the Czech Constitutional Court in its first judgment on the Lisbon Treaty of November 26, 2008 did not condition the ratification of the Lisbon Treaty by the enactment of an adequate act regulating the procedures corresponding to forms of involvement of the national Parliament newly listed in the Lisbon Treaty. The court limited itself to the view that such an act would have been desirable in the case that this treaty entered into force (see sec. 153, 165, 166 of the judgement—all related to the art. 48 (6, 7) TEU—and sec. 174, speaking in general about the duty, foremost of the government, to prepare a regulation enabling the full realisation of the role of the national parliament). Subsequently this act, in fact an amendment of the rules of procedure of the respective chambers[21], was not proposed by the government. In the Czech Republic, as opposed to other states where the government coupled the ratification procedure with the adoption of laws detailing new procedures, it remained for the elected representatives to draft a proposal that was then approved as Act No. 162/2009 Coll.[22]

The enlarged involvement of national parliaments according to the Lisbon Treaty as such seemed to require the introduction of only two kinds of procedures (relating to two passerelle clauses, art. 48 (7) and art. 31 TEU, and the subsidiarity check with possible action to the Court of Justice). Nevertheless, the Czech Parliament extended its involvement also to the simplified revision procedure of internal policies and action of the Union (art. 48 (6) TEU), other specific passerelle clauses (art. 153 (2), art. 192 (2), art. 312 (2), art. 333 (1, 2) TFEU),[23] and to the flexibility clause (art. 352 TFEU). According to the new wording, the government is not allowed to give its consent in the name of the Czech Republic in these

[20] *Constitution of the Czech Republic*, http://www.psp.cz/cgi-bin/eng/docs/laws/1993/1.html (accessed March 1, 2012). Meanwhile, no act mentioned in sec. 3 have been adopted.

[21] The Czech Constitutional Court also mentioned the suitability of the procedure of a constitutional review of the simplified revision procedures (sec. 165 of the judgment of 26 November 2008). This however was not part of the amendment.

[22] For more details from behind the scenes see: J. Kysela, *Implementace Lisabonské smlouvy v pravidlech jednání Parlamentu ČR* [*Implementation of the Lisbon Treaty in the Czech Parliament's Rules of Procedure*], "Časopis pro právní vědu a praxi" 1 (2010), 40–51.

[23] For a handy overview of passerelle clauses see: *Legislative procedures*, http://europa.eu/legislation_summaries/institutional_affairs/treaties/lisbon_treaty/ai0016_en.htm (accessed March 1, 2012).

enumerated decision-making procedures in the EU institutions without the prior approval of both of the chambers of Parliament (not just their EU issues committees). Special accelerated procedures were set up for these cases in both chambers. This is a modification to the general procedure where the government is only required to reflect the position of the chambers in the formulation of its own position for the meetings in EU institutions.

Therefore, even if we consider the self-restraint of the Czech government in the drafting of the amendment as an expression of respect for the parliamentary rules of procedure, the question remains as to whether the government should have provided more assistance concerning its expertise in the actual employment of similar important EU procedures that were not covered by this amendment. Probably inspired by the German Federal Constitutional Court judgment of June 30, 2009,[24] this aspect of applying a too lenient approach to the use of specific "exception" or "dynamic" provisions in the TEU and TFEU was contested by a group of senators in early September 2009 before the second application for the review of the constitutionality of the Lisbon Treaty. On October 6, 2009, the Constitutional Court dismissed this application with the argument that, in most cases, the procedure is formulated as the decision of the respective chamber to refuse the government's proposal and that the sufficiency of a simple majority for refusal is a more stringent condition than if the super-majority was necessary. However, in cases where the positive decision of the chamber is required, it must be ascertained on a case-by-case basis through which a majority (one half or three-fifths) is to be met. The Constitutional Court did not express its opinion on the fact that other so-called brake clauses[25] were not covered by this amendment, and that the new procedure of constitutional review was not established. One month later, on November 3, 2009, the Constitutional Court gave its second judgment on the Lisbon Treaty and did not elaborate further on the position of the national Parliament. Only in sec. 135 of the judgment did it use the general phrase about the empowerment of the national parliaments by the Lisbon Treaty as a counter-argument against the claim of the unconstitutional democratic deficit of the decision-making procedures at the EU level.

---

[24] *Headnotes to the judgment of the Second Senate of 30 June 2009*, http://www.bundesverfassungsgericht.de/entscheidungen/es20090630_2bve000208en.html (accessed March 1, 2012).

[25] *Passerelle clauses, brake clauses and accelerator clauses*, http://europa.eu/legislation_summaries/institutional_affairs/treaties/lisbon_treaty/ai0019_en.htm (accessed March 1, 2012).

The specific lesson learned from the above-mentioned development in the Czech Republic seems to be that the Lisbon Treaty is considered by the Constitutional Court to be a significant improvement in the position of the national Parliament. The government, which has prominent expertise in EU law and procedures, was, however, reluctant to propose the respective amendments and it was therefore a result of the initiative of individual members of Parliament to prepare the complex amendment for the rules of procedure. This amendment did not cover all the fields indicated in the first judgment of the Constitutional Court on the Lisbon Treaty, neither did it regulate in detail other clauses with a similar structure as the passerelle ones, and some questionable matters e.g. concerning the voting majorities, were left to future practice and the possible intervention of the Constitutional Court.

If we look to the situation in Poland and Slovakia, we can find similar patterns. On November 27, 2009 the groups of Seym Deputies and Senators initiated a constitutional review procedure, among other reasons, grounded on the fact that:

> The legislator's consent to bind the Republic of Poland with the indicated provisions of the Treaties is not accompanied by the statutory regulation stipulating the participation of the Seym and the Senate in the process of determining the stance of the Republic of Poland in every case of possible adoption, by the European Council or the Council of the European Union, of a legal act on the basis of any of the [*dynamic Treaty provisions*].[26]

The constitutional tribunal, in its judgment of November 24, 2010, discontinued the proceedings with regard to this part of the application since, in the meantime, the cooperation of the Council of Ministers with the Seym and the Senate in matters relating to the Republic of Poland's membership in the European Union became subject to the new act of October 8, 2010 of the same name. The constitutional tribunal expressly refused to follow the path of the German Federal Constitutional Court and specify the powers of the Parliament with regard to the EU issues, because of the "vital differences between the Constitution of the Republic of Poland and the Basic Law for the Federal Republic of Germany, when it comes to regulating the systemic foundations of European integration".[27] However, during detailed review, the tribunal several times used the

---

[26] *Judgment of 24 November 2010 Ref. No. K 32/09*, http://www.trybunal.gov.pl/eng/summaries/documents/K_32_09_EN.pdf (accessed March 1, 2012).
[27] Ibid.

references to the new act on the cooperation[28] without excluding the possibility that this act itself could be subject to the constitutional review. This act also goes beyond the minimal involvement prevised by the TEU and TFEU.[29]

In Slovakia, the Constitutional Court did not review the Lisbon Treaty as such (as opposed to the decision on the constitutionality of the Constitutional Treaty of February 27, 2008[30]) and the question concerning the involvement of national parliaments was never raised. The amendment of the rules of procedure of the Parliament reflecting its new rights under the EU law was, however, approved only in June 2011 and was published under the No. 187/2011 Coll. As in the Czech case, the amendment was prepared by the parliamentary committee and the government only indicated the necessary changes to the draft that would better fit the procedures on the EU level. The Constitutional Act 397/2004 Coll. on the cooperation between the national council of the Slovak Republic and the government of the Slovak Republic in the affairs concerning the European Union did not change.

Assessment of the Role of Constitutional Courts

Summarising the arguments presented above, it is difficult to assess the contribution of the Lisbon Treaty to the powers of the national parliaments in a black-or-white manner. After the comparison of the previous wording of the Treaties and Protocols, the only truly new right seems to be the subsidiarity control procedure, no matter how effective in fact it could be.[31] With regard to the involvement of the national parliaments in the broader debate, this is more of a solemn recognition of the processes that have been in operation for several years. Also, the rights of the national parliaments under the new simplified revision procedure could be considered as strengthened only if there had previously been no ratification

---

[28] *Act of 8 October 2010 on the cooperation of the Council of Ministers with the Sejm and the Senate in matters relating to the Republic of Poland's membership of the European Union*, http://www.cosac.eu/upload/application/pdf/f51d6748/Ustawa_o_wspolpracy_2010_EN.pdf (accessed March 1, 2012).

[29] See: Ibid., art. 11–16.

[30] *II. ÚS 171/05-175*, http://www.concourt.sk/rozhod.do?urlpage=dokument&id_spisu=182952 (accessed March 1, 2012).

[31] See: footnote no. 15.

procedures. Moreover, all these improvements are compromised by the possible shortcomings identified in part three.

Therefore, in what manner could the Lisbon Treaty be considered a significant empowerment of the national parliaments? Paradoxically, it may be in the sense that it has made them less dependent on their own governments in representing national interests at the EU level. Even in cases where the mandate for the government is approved by a razor-thin majority, or where the government decides to diverge from the mandate, or perhaps the government's position is outvoted in the EU institution, the parliamentary minority is entrusted with new safeguards.[32] The fact that some parliaments themselves prepared the respective revision of their rules of procedure, and thereby remedied the inaction of the government and extended their own involvement into other dynamic clauses, can be considered as the expression of their interest and willingness to interfere more substantially with EU issues than ever before.

This new involvement could be crucial since pure political accountability of the national executive (prime minister and ministers) to the national parliament for the execution of their mandates on the European level can be of limited importance in practice.[33] Also, the softer modes that the national parliaments created to compensate for their loss of powers (adopting or approving government positions, establishment of special committees or informal cooperation with other parliaments and EU

---

[32] For a prior assessment of the possibilities of the parliamentary opposition see: R. Holzhacker, *The Power of Opposition Parliamentary Party Groups in European Scrutiny,* "Journal of Legislative Studies" 3–4 (2005), 428–445; See also: K. Auel, *Democratic Accountability and National Parliaments: Redefining the Impact of Parliamentary Scrutiny in EU Affairs*, "European Law Journal" 4 (2007), 500.

[33] Many reasons are discussed in the literature, e.g. dynamics of decision-making in the Council, collegiality between ministers responsible for certain portfolios, ethos of expertise that prevails in the work of national administrations (V. Röben, *Constitutionalism of Inverse Hierarchy: The Case of the European Union*, "Jean Monnet Working Paper" 8 2003, 9, the tension resulting from the fact that the majority political parties may be willing to support the government actions at the EU level but at the same time they must be careful for essential national interests in order not to lose electors to the opposition parties, the informal policy-making in EU (A. Benz, *Compounded Representation in EU Multi-level Governance*, in B. Kohler-Koch (ed.), *Linking EU and National Governance*, (Oxford: Oxford University Press, 2003), 89, 101), lack of resources and expertise of national parliaments to engage in the EU agenda that presents only one part, although an important one, in their general legislative, supervisory and other competences.

institutions) might not be regarded as sufficient.[34] The threat that some constitutional court might consider an act of EU institutions unconstitutional on the basis of an insufficient involvement of the national parliament seems to be an efficient, if somewhat extreme, motivation for the governments not to circumvent their parliaments.

Although the Central European constitutional courts, already proven to be tough players,[35] did not subject the ratification of the Lisbon Treaty to the enactment of rules ensuring the exercise of the new rights of the national parliaments,[36] they did not rule out the possibility of reviewing these new regulations on cooperation in EU matters either. While the EU law created a gap between the national parliaments and their respective governments, and now leads to the separation and introduction of some autonomous rights of the national parliaments, the constitutional courts can strengthen the influence of the parliaments over the governments.

Conclusion

We can reasonably question the claim of whether the Lisbon Treaty brought about the empowerment of national parliaments to the extent that would weaken the objection regarding a democratic deficit. However, the Treaty clearly brought about the preconditions for a significant change in the relationship between the governments and their national parliaments regarding EU issues, changes that challenge the existing theories on their relationship. In the future, to grasp these new aspects, the general assessment of the dyadic (government–parliament) or triadic (government–governing party–opposition party) relationship will not suffice. Not only the distinction between the direct or indirect involvement of the national parliaments by the EU Treaties needs to be taken into account, but special attention should also be given to the jurisprudence of the national constitutional courts that focuses on identification of the issues for which the national parliaments must have the final word. And so, the relevant relationship multiplies to four (government–governing party–opposition

[34] See COSAC Biannual Reports and especially the replies from the national parliaments: *Bi-annual Reports of COSAC*, http://www.cosac.eu/en/documents/biannual/ (accessed March 1, 2012).

[35] See: W. Sadurski, *"Solange, chapter 3": Constitutional Courts in Central Europe—Democracy—European Union*, "EUI Working Paper LAW", No. 40, 2006, http://cadmus.eui.eu/bitstream/handle/1814/6420/LAW-2006-40.pdf?sequence=1 (accessed March 1, 2012).

[36] Contrary to the German Federal Constitutional Court, see: M. Wendel, *Lisbon Before the Courts: Comparative Perspectives*, "ECL Review" 1 2011, 115 and foll.

party–constitutional court) or even more relevant players, if we consider the role of the national banks and other independent agencies that have become visible in the current financial crisis.

The author is PhD of Jurisprudence at the Charles University School of Law in Prague. She specializes in EU law and constitutional law.

CHAPTER EIGHTEEN

SMALL(EST) PARTIES IN CENTRAL EUROPE: THE PIRATE PARTY AS A SWEDISH EXPORT

CHRISTIAN NESTLER

Introduction: Land Ahoy—Pirates in Central Europe

Like a modern-day Jim Hawkins, one may want to explore a rather exciting story about a political upstart called the "pirate party". In comparison to the kind Robert Louis Stevenson depicted—"that filthy, heavy, bleared scarecrow of a pirate of ours, sitting far gone in rum"[1]—the modern day phenomenon does not favour suits like the average political animal, but is a good bit removed from the grisly type the nineteenth-century novelist had in mind. Their emblem does not feature the Jolly Roger but still contains the "black flag of piracy"[2], in a black circle on white ground.

Historically, pirates roamed the Baltic Sea, a famous example being Klaus Störtebeker. It can be seen as ironic that the first pirate party was founded in Sweden in 2006. Since then, similar parties, naming the same main goals and sporting the same insignia, have been founded almost everywhere in Central Europe. Due to the surprising electoral success, for example in Germany, this paper focuses on the distribution of pirate parties in the region, the first election campaigns in the aforementioned country, and the results, voters and membership.

The epistemological interest is reflected in the following question: Is the rise of the pirate party in Sweden and Germany and the spread around the world the birthmark of a new worldwide party movement, or will it not reach established party systems? An initial observation is that the pirate party has right now a registered or soon to be registered offshoot in sixty-

[1] R. L. Stevenson, *Treasure Island*, (London: Penguin, 1994), 6.
[2] Ibid., 116.

one independent countries around the world,[3] the fastest and farthest spread since the rise of communism in the 1920s.[4]

To start from the beginning, one needs a valid demarcation of Central Europe. Geographically[5], Central Europe is situated from the Baltic Sea to the North and the tip of the Adriatic Sea to the South. As a southern border, the river Danube would be adequate. The Elbe is the western border, but Germany as a whole can be counted. How far the region reaches into the East is hard to say, but the river Dnjepr is probably the most eastern border.[6] The concept of Central Europe beyond geography is best described with the words of Milan Kundera:

> As a result, three fundamental situations developed in Europe after the war: that of Western Europe, that of Eastern Europe, and, most complicated, that of the part of Europe situated geographically in the center– culturally in the West and politically in the East.[7]

The Central Europe Kundera is talking about is by all means an old concept, but he points to the fact that in the aftermath of World War II it is no longer used. With the fall of the Iron Curtain in 1989–90 and the recent EU enlargements, most notably on May 1, 2004, the region is back as a concept in the social sciences.

Context: the Pirate Party Movement

The first intellectual cornerstone[8] for the pirate party movement came from a somewhat cranky American. John Perry Barlow is an American poet and essayist, a retired Wyoming cattle rancher, and a cyberlibertarian political activist. On February 8, 1996, contemporaneous to the World

---

[3] PPI, *Member Country's PPI,* http://www.pp-international.net/ (accessed February 20, 2012).

[4] A. Brown, *The Rise and Fall of Communism*, (London: Vintage, 2009), 78–100.

[5] Therefore this paper concentrates on the following states (alphabetic order): Austria, Belarus, Czech Republic, Estonia, Germany, Hungary, Latvia, Lithuania, Poland, Romania, Slovakia and Ukraine.

[6] L. R. Johnson, *Central Europe: Enemies, Neighbors, Friends*, (Oxford: Oxford University Press, 1996), 3–12, 267.

[7] M. Kundera, *The Tragedy of Central Europe*, "New York Review of Books" 7 (1984), 33–38.

[8] The notion of Barlow being an intellectual founding father for the pirate party was taken from: M. Häusler, *Die Piraten Partei—Freiheit, die wir meinen*, (Berlin-München: Scorpio, 2011), 19–23.

Economic Forum in Davos, he published his *A Declaration of the Independence of Cyberspace*. The catchphrases of the text are:

> Governments of the Industrial World, you weary giants of flesh and steel, I come from Cyberspace, the new home of Mind. On behalf of the future, I ask you of the past to leave us alone. You are not welcome among us. You have no sovereignty where we gather ... You claim there are problems among us that you need to solve. You use this claim as an excuse to invade our precincts. Many of these problems don't exist. Where there are real conflicts, where there are wrongs, we will identify them and address them by our means. We are forming our own Social Contract. This governance will arise according to the conditions of our world, not yours ... You are terrified of your own children, since they are natives in a world where you will always be immigrants. Because you fear them, you entrust your bureaucracies with the parental responsibilities you are too cowardly to confront yourselves ... We will create a civilization of the Mind in Cyberspace. May it be more humane and fair than the world your governments have made before.[9]

Despite the similarities of Barlow‘s thoughts and the agenda of the pirate parties, they do not mention him as one of their forebearers. However his thoughts are pretty straightforward as to the nucleus of the conflict; the internet community and governments of the world, and the cleavage between free knowledge and control of populations/capitalist marketing of knowledge.

From Piratbyrån and Pirate Bay to Piratpartiet of Sweden

The infringement of copyright laws dates as far back as the sixth century C.E., and became a real factor with the invention of the printing press by Johannes Gutenberg around 1440. This is an early indication that the development of new technologies drives the need or will to protect written/printed/recorded knowledge.[10]

In the perception of the entertainment industry, radio was going to destroy the record industry, television was supposed to be the end of cinema, home taping should have killed music, and video would be the death of Hollywood. The latest link in the chain or the newest specter for

---

[9] J. P. Barlow, *A Declaration of the Independence of Cyberspace*, https://projects.eff.org/~barlow/Declaration-Final.html (accessed January 18, 2012).

[10] M. Li, *The Pirate Party and the Pirate Bay—How the Pirate Bay Influences Sweden and International Copyright Relations*, "Pace International Law Review" 1 (2009), 281–307.

the industry is the internet.[11] But as the above quoted *A Declaration of the Independence of Cyberspace* shows, the problem goes beyond the previous cases.

Sweden became one of the forerunners in the process of expanding the availability of the internet for its citizens, with forty percent of homes having access in 2000. Eight years later, the number had risen to eighty-four percent. Due to this and the inability of law enforcement, users were able to download content that was theoretically protected by copyright laws. As a reaction, the big media companies[12] founded the lobbying organization Antipiratbyrån [Anti-Piracy Bureau] in 2001.[13] Just two years later, the file sharing community established the Piratbyrån [Piracy Bureau], and in 2004 the infamous Pirate Bay emerged from the ranks of this self-proclaimed think-tank of free copy culture.[14]

The battle between Bittorent[15] sites like the Pirate Bay and the copyright holders reached "a cold-war-like escalation" at this point.[16] This standoff is not the only thing to have driven the development of new technologies; with the involvement of the USA on behalf of their own industry and the founding of the Piratpartiet the conflict has attained a political dimension. The former used the World Trade Organisation (WTO) to bully the Swedish government into action against the Pirate Bay.[17] The latter was founded on January 1, 2006 by Rickard Falkvinge. He had been asked if "privacy policy" takes the place of "environmental

---

[11] D. Horrocks, *Remember when*, http://upload.wikimedia.org/wikipedia/commons/d/d7/The.Pirate.Bay.Cartoon-small.png (accessed February 21, 2012).

[12] Disney, Fox, Sony Pictures, Universal, Viacom and Warner.

[13] T. Neumann, *Die Piratenpartei Deutschland—Entwicklung und Selbstverständnis*, (Berlin: Contumax, 2011), 13–14.

[14] H. Bartels, *Die Piratenpartei—Entstehung, Forderungen und Perspektiven der Bewegung*, (Berlin: Contumax, 2009), 30; 287.

[15] Bittorrent operates through a fairly simple process. The initial file sharer generates a metainfo file (usually a file with a .torrent extension) from the file to be served and the central server's web address. The central server, also known as a tracker, identifies computers which are downloading or have a complete copy of the file (known as the swarm). The central tracker allows computers running the client software and using the metainfo file to trade bits and pieces of the original file with other computers in the swarm. C. Carnack, *How BitTorrents Works*, http://computer.howstuffworks.com/bittorrent2.htm (accessed February 21, 2012).

[16] Li, *The Pirate Party and the Pirate Bay*, 282.

[17] N. A., *USA nutzen WTO als Druckmittel beim "Problem Pirate Bay"*, http://www.heise.de/newsticker/meldung/USA-nutzten-WTO-als-Druckmittel-beim-Problem-PirateBay-134649.html (accessed February 20, 2012).

protection" as an issue in the twenty-first century. In his opinion, "yes or no" was not for him to decide, but "criminalization of a whole stratum of the population" was not acceptable. That was the reason for his political activism.[18] The Pirate Bay and Piratpartiet are an offspring of the original Piratbyrån, but otherwise they are only connected through their name.[19] As far as the Piratpartiet is concerned, the name derives from an attempt to get an ironic connection to the Antipiratbyrån and the media industry that denounces file sharer as "Pirates"[20]. The second chairman of the German pirate party, Jens Seipenbusch, narrows the issue: "Above anything else we are concerned with freedom."[21]

The Swedish Piratpartiet needed 2,000 support signatures until February 29, 2006 to run for the election in September of the same year. Falkvinge later admitted that he had doubts that he would receive that many clicks on his website, not to speak of real pen and paper signatures. But within twenty-four hours he had accumulated 2,268. Despite this early success, the party needed more publicity and "fortunately" the Swedish police raided the offices of Piratbyrån and the Pirate Bay with the aim of shutting down their servers. Part of the legend that constitutes the myth of the Pirate Bay for the hacker society is the fact that within three days the homepage was running again.[22]

The publicity for the issue correlates with the first hike in membership for the party (Fig. 18.1 below). The last couple of weeks before the election, the main campaigning phase, have triggered the second jump in membership to 10,000.

The Piratpartiet had success in the election; they harvested 34,918 votes, which amounts to 0.63 percentage points. In order to get a seat in the national Parliament they would have needed 225,000 votes or four percentage points. There are two obvious reasons for the relatively low number of votes. The first is the short time span between the founding of the party and the election. Even more important is the fact that the established parties (apart from the Social Democrats) recognized the issue and liberalized their point of view during the campaign.[23]

---

[18] M. Moorstedt, *Die Piraten organisieren sich*, http://jetzt.sueddeutsche.de/texte/anzeigen/251718 (accessed January 18, 2012).
[19] Neumann, *Die Piratenpartei Deutschland*, 15–17.
[20] Bartels, *Die Piratenpartei—Entstehung*, 30–31.
[21] J. Seipenbusch, *Es geht um die Freiheit*, http://www.freitag.de/alltag/0917-piratenpartei-urheberrecht-interview (accessed February 23, 2012).
[22] Bartels, *Die Piratenpartei—Entstehung*, 30.
[23] Ibid., 38.

The biggest rise in membership came with the start of the Pirate Bay trial in February 2009. Again, it was timely for the party because the election to the European Parliament was scheduled for June the same year. At that point, the party had about 45,000 members. On this wave of prominence, they received 225,915 votes in the election, 7.13 percentage points.[24]

Membership peaked slightly above 50,000 and then dropped sharply during the year 2010. At the time of the election for the Riksdag in September there were only around 17,000 members left. The number of received votes amounted to 38,491. It was a slight rise to 0.65 percentage points[25] but by no means what Falkvinge and others had expected. The party and its founder had to decide how to proceed from that point on. Falkvinge answered with two quotes from the pop culture: "There's no fate but what we make for ourselves", and: "So what do we do now? Same thing we always do. We fight until we can't." The first quotation is from Terminator 2, the second from Battelstar Galactica.[26]

In February 2012, membership dropped all the way to 7,700.[27] Right now the light at the end of tunnel is the fact that the next time the Swedes vote, they will do so for their national assembly and the European Parliament, with an interval of only three months.[28] Therefore, a second order election could push the cause of the Piratpartiet.

The founder of the Swedish pirate party has given some thought on "movements". In his opinion, every major social shift follows a three-stage pattern. First, light is shed on the issue by activists on the street or, in this case, on the net. Secondly, academics research the context and the implications.[29] Thirdly, the topic is picked up by political parties and incorporated into their agendas. Falkvinge points out, however, that to this day almost no other party has seized the issue.[30]

---

[24] N. A, *Results by country – Sweden*, http://www.europarl.europa.eu/about parliament /en/00082fcd21/Results-by-country-(2009).html?tab=26 (accessed February 20, 2012).

[25] N. A., *Election results Riksdag* 2010, http://www.val.se/val/val2010/slutresultat/R/rike/index.html (accessed February 23, 2012).

[26] R. Falkvinge, *Dagen efter valet*, http://falkvinge.net/2010/09/20/dagen-efter-valet/ (accessed February 23, 2012].

[27] Piratpartiet, *Medlemsstatistik*, http://piratpartiet.se/partiet/medlemsstatistik (accessed February 23, 2012).

[28] Falkvinge, *Dagen efter valet.*

[29] Body of research needs to be highlighted in this regard: M. Castells, *The Information Age—Economy, Society, and Culture*, Vol. I-III, (West Sussex: Wiley, 2010).

[30] N. Anderson, *Political Pirates—A History of Sweden's Piratpartiet*,

Fig. 18.1. Piratpartiet of Sweden. Membership development 2006–2012.

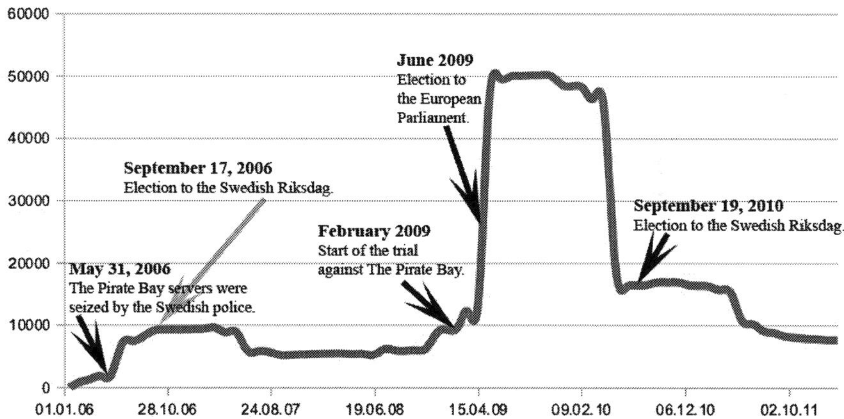

Source: Piratpartiet, Membership development, Pirate Party International (PPI)

In light of this, it should be no surprise that within a year there were up to a dozen parties around the world. For the sake of their cause, this group founded an umbrella organization—the Pirate Parties International (PPI). Up to 2010, it was a loose group.[31] Regular conferences were held to organize for the upcoming election for the European Parliament in 2009. An important step in the process of becoming a movement was passing of the Uppsala-Declaration in 2008 (see below).[32]

Since October 2009, the group has held the status of an NGO, with its headquarters in Brussels. From April 16–18, 2010, the PPI held a conference in the city and officially constituted the organization.[33] Specified in the statute, the tasks and aims are the following:[34]

- to act according to the major interests and goals of its members,

http://arstechnica.com/tech-policy/news/2009/02/rick-falkvinge-is-the-face.ars (accessed February 23, 2012).

[31] Neumann, *Die Piratenpartei Deutschland*, 57–58.

[32] Ibid., 57–58.

[33] PPI, *Conferences PPI*, http://int.piratenpartei.de/Conferences (accessed February 23, 2012).

[34] The statute of the PPI can be downloaded from the following link: http://int.piratenpartei.de/wiki/images/a/a6/Statutes_of_the_Pirate_Parties_International.pdf.

- to raise awareness and widen the spread of the pirate movement, and
- to unify the pirate movement and strengthen its bonds internally and externally.

Membership is possible for all parties and organizations as long as they recognize the statute of the PPI. Members are split into "ordinary members" and "observer members". The first group has to be named "pirate". There can only be one ordinary member per country.[35]

Apart from the positive fact that the Pirate Parties have an umbrella organization, this tool for "the spread of the pirate movement" has remained relatively pale. Furthermore, communication in the national forums has not yet been in an universally accessible language for the movement. Therefore, the reciprocity among the multitude of working groups on the national level is rather small. The PPI online forums cannot compensate this deficiency.[36]

The main goals/agenda of the Pirate Party

Due to the development of the Swedish Piratpartiet, the agenda was centered around the freedom of universal copyrights and, after a potential election success, its legalization. An eye-opening fact is that this first election manifesto had a "fun" aspect: "The election programme of the Pirate Party consists of various nautical charts, describing what we want to do in each of the areas within the Pirate Party policies."[37] This was manifested through a non-conventional clothing style and a relaxed attitude in the political arena.

Meanwhile, as mentioned above, the standardization of the party principles were achieved during the third international conference in Uppsala in 2008. This step had taken almost two years and was taken to attain a common approach for the election to the European Parliament in 2009.[38] From this point on, the agenda contained three major topics: "The

---

[35] Neumann, *Die Piratenpartei Deutschland*, 61.

[36] Ibid., 62.

[37] B. Jones, *The Swedish Pirate Party presents their election manifesto*, http://torrentfreak.com/the-swedish-pirate-party-presents-their-election-manifesto/ (accessed February 29, 2012).

[38] PPI, *Uppsala-Declaration*, http://wiki.piratenpartei.de/Uppsala-Deklaration (accessed February 29, 2012).

Pirate Party wants to fundamentally reform copyright law, get rid of the patent system, and ensure that citizens' rights to privacy are respected."[39]

The German Pirate Party developed the basic principles from summer 2009. Starting with "education", they added "direct democracy", "environment", "gender and family" and "transparency of the state" to their *Grundsatzprogramm*[40], amongst others.

Foundings in Central Europe

After the founding of the Swedish Piratpartiet in January 2006, it took only half a year for the first pirate parties to emerge in Central Europe. The easiest way to track the distribution of the party in the region is to use the homepage of the PPI. The typical interface gives the user access to a wiki-page where the relevant information can be found. The problem with this wiki is that the information can be outdated or incomplete. Nevertheless, short of a survey taking account of all the parties in the region, it is a useful tool to gather an impression. Especially when the researcher would need more than ten different languages to compile the data.

In Austria, the Piratenpartei Österreichs (PPÖ) was originally founded in July 2006. At the end of 2010 they had 580 members.[41] Due to internal conflicts the party broke up in early 2011 but was founded anew on July 9, 2011[42].

The Piratenpartei Deutschland (PIRATEN) was founded on September 10, 2006.[43] The development has so far been steady, with no big losses in membership or drop in voter confidence in elections (more on this below).

---

[39] Piratpartiet, *International*, http://www.piratpartiet.se/international/english (accessed February 29, 2012).

[40] Piratenpartei Deutschland, *Grundsatzprogramm der Piratenpartei Deutschland*, http://wiki.piratenpartei.de/wiki/images/0/04/Grundsatzprogramm-Piratenpartei.pdf (accessed February 29, 2012).

[41] PPI, *Membercount*, http://int.piratenpartei.de/Global_Pirate_Party_memberscount (access February 25, 2012).

[42] N. A., *Ehemaliges Mitglied über den IST-Zustand der österreichischen Piratenpartei*, http://derstandard.at/1304551991283/Kommentar-Ex-Mitglied-Piraten partei-Oesterreich-ist-handlungsunfaehig (accessed February 26, 2012); N. A., *PPÖ*, http://int.piratenpartei.de/Austria (accessed February 25, 2012).

[43] PPI, *PIRATEN*, http://int.piratenpartei.de/Germany (accessed February 25, 2012).

Founded on July 27, 2006, the Polish Partia Piratów (P) was officially registered in November 2007. Up to the time of writing, they have not participated in elections.[44] In Poland, the first hint can be seen that the pirate party cannot become a factor when another, most likely more established, party represents the issue. The Ruch Palikota [Palikot's Movement] was able to get 10.2 percentage points in the parliamentary election in 2011. The party is young and their fame stems from the persona of their founder.[45] Right now, Janusz Palikot takes up every issue that is bound to get publicity and voter support and thus far he is successful especially with young voters: "But the proof in the pudding will not be whether he gains the spotlight (he will), but rather whether he can actually influence how Poland is governed."[46]

In the Czech Republic, the Česká pirátská strana (ČPS) was founded on April 20, 2009. Under the slogan "The Internet is our Sea" and with fewer than 200 members, they embarked shortly after their founding on election campaigns (see below).[47]

The Romanian Partidul Piraţilor (PP) started its life with the launch of their website on June 9, 2009. At the time of writing, they are gathering the 25,000 signatures to become officially registered.[48]

The Baltic states Estonia, Latvia and Lithuania are planning to found a pirate party but are currently only active in the PPI in the cases of Estonia and Lithuania, at least since the election to the European Parliament in 2009. The same can be said about the parties in Slovakia and Ukraine.[49]

Belarus, Hungary and Moldova do not have a pirate party. In the case of Belarus, this is of no surprise because of the Lukashenko regime. For Moldova, the reasons for the non-existence are undisclosed. In Hungary there is a non-political organization called Kalózpárt that represents the ideals of the Uppsala Declaration, a name translating to "pirate party". It is associated with the Lehet Más a Politika (LMP), the Hungarian green liberal party which holds fifteen seats in the national assembly.[50]

---

[44] PPI, *P*, http://int.piratenpartei.de/Poland (accessed February 25, 2012).

[45] P. Sadura, *A Post-Election Analysis of Palikot's Movement*, http://www.boell.eu/web/270-779.html (accessed February 26, 2012).

[46] A. Kureth, *What does Palikot's big win mean for Poland*, http://www.wbj.pl/blog/From_the_editor/post-312-what-does-palikots-big-win-mean-for-poland.html (accessed February 26, 2012).

[47] N. A., *ČPS*, http://int.piratenpartei.de/Czech_Republic (accessed February 25, 2012).

[48] N. A., *PP*, http://int.piratenpartei.de/Romania (accessed February 26, 2012).

[49] A. Platon, *Pirate Parties Map*, http://commons.wikimedia.org/wiki/File:PiratePartiesMap12.svg (accessed February 25, 2012).

[50] A. Platon, *Pirates in Hungary*, http://en.wikipedia.org/wiki/User_talk:M2Ys4U_/Pirate_Parties_International#Hu

This list shows the state of affairs for the pirate party ideal in the region. To sum up, there are five possible situations, with three stages and two likely inhibitory factors. The first stage is the founding process. A base activity is, for example, launching a homepage, and an integral part of this stage are demonstrations or other actions to get publicity. This should lead to the second stage—registering with the authorities. Support signatures are easier to get if the activities have successfully generated attention in the media and the public. The third stage is activity in the PPI. In some cases, the stages are not chronological. To give an example, talk via the PPI is possible before the party is registered. The two factors that influence this process negatively are the non-existence of typical pirate party issues in the country. This factor again has two dimensions. One is an authoritarian regime such as in Belarus that suppresses the issue. Another would be the absence of the issue in the political arena due to the modernization deficit. The first factor leads to the non-existence of a pirate party. The second one are the parties that, beside other topics, have incorporated the pirate party issues into their own agendas. What happens in this setting (which implicates that parties with broader agendas are more successful) is that, as Hungary shows, there will be no pirate party.

Table 18.1. State of affairs for the pirate parties in Central Europe

No party	Party founded	Talk over PPI	Party registered	Other party with same issue
3	6	10	4	2
Hungary Belarus Moldova	Estonia Latvia Lithuania Romania Slovakia Ukraine	Austria Czech Republic Estonia Germany Latvia Lithuania Poland Romania Slovakia Ukraine	Austria Czech Republic Germany Poland	Hungary Poland

Source: Own representation.

ngary (accessed February 25, 2012).

Participation in Elections in Central Europe

Thus far, the participation in elections at least on a middle level (comparable to the German *Länder*) or the national level is rather low in Central Europe.

Austria voted on March 14, 2010 in a local election in the city of Bregenz. The pirate party of Austria got 1.62 percentage points of the vote but they were not able to get a sufficient amount of support signatures for the election to the national Parliament in 2006 and 2008.[51] On May 28–29, 2010, the pirate party of the Czech Republic got 0.8 percent of the votes for the national Parliament and therefore no seats due to the five percent hurdle.[52]

Table 18.2 below shows the exception from the above-mentioned abstinence. The German pirate party has been able to raise their percentage of the vote step-by-step over the last four years. Important for them is that since the Hesse election in 2009 they have been receiving a share of state campaign financing. The threshold for this is 0.5 percentage points in *Länder* elections and 1.0 percentage points in state-elections.[53]

Without long-term surveys on the grounds of the existing data, it is impossible to make a statement about party affiliation. For now, the party generates support for issues rather than their candidates. Therefore, their campaigns are centered around copyrights, file sharing, education etc.[54]

Who votes for the pirate party? With their special worldview and their focus on the (digital) topic of "knowledge society", the party is not an element of mainstream politics. The different approach helps them motivate young voters. Two thirds of their voters in Germany are male, under thirty-five and above-average educated.[55] Therefore, the party gets the most support in urban centres from previously unpolitical people.[56]

---

[51] N. A., *History PPÖ,* http://www.piratenpartei.at/ (accessed February 23, 2012).

[52] N. A., *PPI Overview*, http://int.piratenpartei.de/Main_Page (accessed February 23, 2012).

[53] N. A., *Parteienfinanzierung*, http://www.bundestagswahlbw.de/parteienfinanzierung.html (accessed February 29, 2012).

[54] E. Stern, J. Garner, *It`s the Candidate, Stupid? Personalisierung der bundesdeutschen Wahlkämpfe*, in T. Berg (ed.), *Moderner Wahlkampf—Blick hinter die Kulissen*, (Opladen: VS Verlag für Sozialwissenschaften, 2002), 145–167.

[55] S. Krätzig, *Die Piratenpartei als ein Puzzlestück in der neuen Konfiguration der Mehrparteienrepublik*, „Forschungsjournal Neue Soziale Bewegungen" 4 (2010), 91–97.

[56] U. Zolleis, S. Prokopf, F. Strauch, *Die Piratenpartei—Hype oder Herausforderung für die deutsche Parteienlandschaft?*, (München: Hans-Seidel-Stiftung, 2010), 31.

Table 18.2. Election results of the Pirate Party of Germany

Election	Election results by number of votes	Election results by percentage points
Hesse 2008	6955	0.3
Hamburg 2008	1373	0.2
Hesse 2009	13,796	0.5
European Parliament 2009	229,117	0.9
Saxony 2009	34,651	1.9
Schleswig-Holstein 2009	847,870	2.0
Bundestag 2009	28,837	1.8
North Rhine-Westphalia 2010	121,046	1.6
Hamburg 2011	73,126	2.1
Saxony-Anhalt 2011	13,828	1.4
Baden-Württemberg	103,618	2.1
Rhineland-Palatinate	29,319	1.6
Bremen	21,080	2.7
Mecklenburg-W. Pomerania 2011	12,513	1.9
Berlin 2011	130,105	8.9

Source: A. Wilde, *Piraten Ahoi!*, Berlin 2011, 12.

Conclusion—the Rising Tide?

The pirate flag flies in ten out of thirteen Central European countries and in others under the disguise of a non-political association. Membership is on the rise as is participation in elections on every level. Thus far, the German Pirate Party accounts almost exclusively for the success later on. The scarce participation can be attributed to the short timespan the parties have had to build a country-wide infrastructure

For the state of the research, it can be said that the Swedish party is only viewed as the origin of the movement. The negative development since the European Parliament election in 2009 is excluded from recent publications. Concerning this, it can be said that the development in Germany is more sustainable than in Sweden. Testimony to this is the different trend in membership as shown in figures. 18.1 and 18.2.[57]

Fig. 18.2. Piratenpartei Deutschland membership development 2006–2012

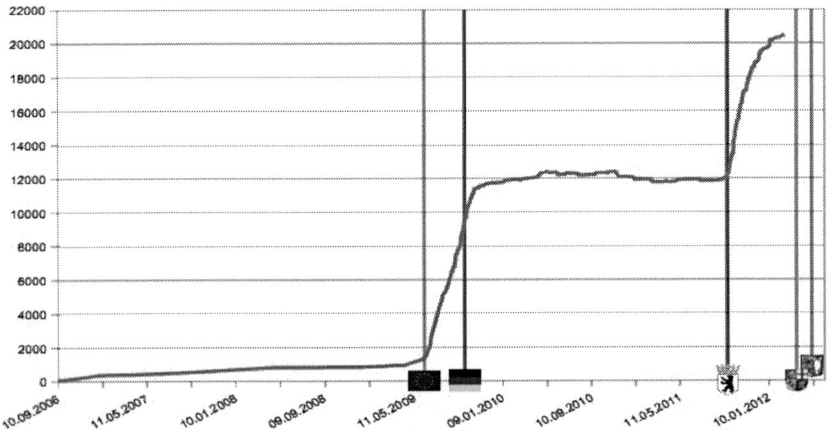

Source: Shinta, *Membership development.*

The second factor is that, in Sweden, the Piratpartiet is still a single issue party. Therefore, they only had support when their issue was important to the media and to public discourse. In Germany, the party had a boost from the issue but used the public support to widen their agenda. This led to success in the Berlin election and a solid position in recent polls for the upcoming elections. In Saarland, they are currently valued at five percentage points.[58] A poll for the Schleswig-Holstein election on

[57] Shinta, *Membership development*, http://wiki.piratenpartei.de/Datei:Mitgliederentwicklung.png (accessed February 22, 2012).

[58] *Politbarometer-Extra Saarland*, Forschungsgruppe Wahlen, http://www.forschungsgruppe.de/Aktuelles/Politbarometer-Extra/ (accessed February 29, 2012).

May 6 put them at the same level.[59] The so called "Sonntagsfrage"[60] [Sunday question] places them at six percentage points.[61]

Concerning the epistemological interest of this chapter, it can be conclusively said that the pirate party has become an actual movement through launching the PPI as an umbrella organization and establishing itself in over sixty countries in the last six years. The German and Czech cases show that the party is taken seriously by the media and established parties. Ultimately, the party will be measured by their successes at the ballot boxes. In this field, Berlin is the silver lining on the horizon in Central Europe, but nothing more. The other countries have to catch up to that success, otherwise Germany will be an exception rather than a starting point.

Still, despite the gloomy summary, the outlook for the pirate party in Central Europe is otherwise very good. Their issue is a hot topic around the world. Legislation such as the Stop Online Piracy Act (SOPA) and the Anti-Counterfeiting Trade Agreement (ACTA) will help to keep it that way. The latter in particular has forced European politicians to change their approach to the topic due to a public uproar.[62] So the pirate party will maximize their success if they are able to raise attention to their issues and themselves.[63]

The author is a Research Assistant at the University of Rostock, Department of Comparative Politics at the Institute for Political Science.

---

[59] *LänderTREND Schleswig-Holstein 2012*, Infratest dimap, http://www.infratest-dimap.de/umfragen-analysen/bundeslaender/schleswig-holstein/laendertrend/2012/februar/ (accessed February 29, 2012).

[60] *Wen würden sie wählen, wenn am nächsten Sonntag Bundestagswahl wäre?* [Who would you vote for, if the Bundestag election was next Sunday?].

[61] *Politbarometer Februar 2012*, Forschungsgruppe Wahlen, http://www.forschungsgruppe.de/Aktuelles/Politbarometer/ (accessed February 29, 2012.)

[62] N. A., *ACTA up*, "The Economist" June 2012, 55.

[63] Wilde, *Piraten Ahoi!,* 52.

CHAPTER NINETEEN

THE MOLDOVAN POLITICAL SYSTEM IN CRISIS SINCE 2009: CONSTITUTIONAL OR POLITICAL CRISIS?

MARCIN ŁUKASZEWSKI

Moldova is one of the least-known countries in Europe. In 2009, this post-Soviet republic had to deal with a crisis of authority. Its sources cannot be found, however, in 2009 or even in 2000, when an amendment to the Moldovan constitution was adopted. It seems that the roots of this crisis lay in the political and social system resulting from the declaration of independence in the early 1990s. The present chapter answers the following question: is this crisis political or only constitutional, and what are its possible solutions?

Establishing the Presidential Office and Direct Presidential Elections

In 1990, when the communist regime had become a thing of the past, a shift in the Moldovan legislature (Supreme Soviet) introduced the institution of the President of the Republic. A presidential form of government was proclaimed, and the head of state had to be chosen in a direct election. The ex-chairman of the Presidium of the Supreme Soviet Mircea Snegur ran as an independent candidate. Having no opponents, he won after the Popular Front's efforts to organize a voter boycott had failed.[1]

A new constitution adopted in 1994 retained the direct presidential election formula[2]. In May 1996, the Parliament adopted a new law on the

[1] He received 98 % of the votes. W. Crowther, *Ethnic politics and the post-communist transition in Moldova*, "Nationalities Papers" 26 (2007), 9.

[2] According to art. 78: "The president is elected by freely expressed, universal,

election of the President of Moldova.[3] In the same year, there was a second general presidential election with three important actors involved: President Mircea Snegur seeking a second term, Speaker of the Parliament Petru Lucinschi and the ex-First Secretary of the Party of Communists of the Republic of Moldova Vladimir Voronin. In the first round in November 1996 Mircea Snegur won (see Table 19.1.). Surprisingly, two weeks later in the second round, Lucinschi registered more votes and became new President.

Table 19.1. The results of the presidential elections in 1991 and 1996

DIRECT PRESIDENTIAL ELECTION IN 1991		
	1st round	2nd round
Mircea Snegur (independent)	98 %	-
DIRECT PRESIDENTIAL ELECTION IN 1996		
	1st round	2nd round
Mircea Snegur (Party of Rebirth and Conciliation of Moldova)	38.8 %	46 %
Petru Lucinschi (independent)	27.7 %	54 %
Vladimir Voronin (Party of Communists of the Republic of Moldova)	10.2 %	-
Andrei Sangheli (Democratic Agrarian Party of Moldova)	9.5 %	
Valeriu Matei (Party of Democratic Forces)	8.9 %	
Others (independent: Veronica Abramciuc, Iuliana Gorea-Costin, Anatol Plugaru, Marina Leviţchi)	5 %	

Source: Munteanu, *Political Parties Legislation in Moldova: Review and Recommendations for Reform*, OSCE/ODIHR 2010, 27.

The Amendment to the Constitution in 2000

On May 23, 1999, a national referendum was held at the initiative of President Lucinschi: Do you support amending the constitution in order to introduce a presidential form of government in the Republic of Moldova, in which the President of the Republic shall be responsible for forming and leading the government, as well as for the results of the country's

---

equal, direct and secret suffrage". *Constitution of the Republic of Moldova* (1994), art. 78.

[3] *Law regarding the election of the President of the Republic of Moldova*, No. 833-XII, May 16, 1996.

governance? Due to a low turnout of about 58 % (below the minimum turnout of 60 %), the referendum was invalid.[4] President Lucinschi decided to form a special commission supposed to prepare amendments to the constitution that would change the political system into a presidential one.[5] Lucinschi proposed a system similar to the Russian one, i.e. super-presidentialism.[6] Nonetheless, rather than to strengthen the position of the head of state, parliamentarians weakened its role giving more prerogatives to the Parliament. Thus, the Moldovan semi-presidential system changed into semi-parlamentarism.

In 2000, the Parliament passed an amendment to the constitution which abolished the direct election of the President. According to the new article 78, the President of the Republic of Moldova "shall be elected by the Parliament based on secret suffrage".[7] Further, the choice would be considered valid if the nomination were to opt for at least 3/5 of the Parliament members.[8] Therefore, a candidate must gain the support of at least 61 of 101 deputies to be nominated. This amendment transformed the state from a semi-presidential (or *quasi*-presidential) to a parliamentary regime overnight.[9]

---

[4] I. Munteanu, *Political Parties Legislation in Moldova: Review and Recommendations for Reform*, OSCE/ODIHR 2010, 32–33.

[5] S. Lipcean, *Free and Fair election*, in V. Berbeca, C. Ciurea, M. Gurin (eds.), *The audit of the democratic system of Republic of Moldova: Anthology of Analysis on Governance*, (Chişinău: IDIS Viitorul, 2011), 93.; E. McDonagh, *Is Democracy Promotion Effective in Moldova? The Impact of European Institutions on Development of Civil and Political Rights in Moldova*, "Democratization" 15 (1) (2008), 151.

[6] Moldova's political system provided a strong role for the President to play. It also created, in addition to the presidency and the Parliament, a premiership subject to parliamentary confidence. The position of the Prime Minister is weaker because he needs support of only a half of MPs and the President. As Thomas Baylis has explained, in post-communist systems the executive authority had to be shared, although it could potentially result in a conflict. However, it can also lead to a system of mutual checks and balances between the President and the Parliament. E. Mazo, *Post-Communist Paradox: How the Rise of Parliamentarism Coincided with the Demise of Pluralism in Moldova*, "Working papers of Center on Democracy, Development, and the Rule of Law Stanford Institute for International Studies" 17 2004, 22.

[7] *Constitution of the Republic of Moldova*, 1994, art. 78.

[8] Ibid.

[9] However, as rightly observed by Eugene Mazo, Moldova did not become a pure parliamentary republic. Rather, it now resembled a new and rare regime typology that should, for analytical reasons, instead be termed *semi-parliamentary*. Although the President was now to be elected indirectly, he still served for a fixed term in

The Political System of Moldova after the Adoption of Amendments to the Constitution—Voronin Presidency (2001–2009)

The new parliamentary election in February 2001 resulted in a victory of the Communist Party of the Republic of Moldova (PCRM). With seventy-one seats in the Parliament[10], it gained a monopoly that, as Krzysztof Brzechczyn pointed out, meant a slowdown of the democratization process[11]. The Communists had the unfettered right to form the government and to elect the new head of state.

On April 4, 2001 Voronin was elected by the Parliament as President of the Republic. Out of eighty-nine deputies participating in the vote, seventy-one voted for him, fifteen votes were given in favour of Dumitru Braghiş (Electoral Bloc Braghiş Alliance), and only three deputies voted for Valerian Cristea (PCRM) (see Table 19.2.)[12]. Voronin was sworn in the office on April 7, 2001 and became the first Communist to be democratically elected in the former Soviet Union.

---

office. He also "retained the power to nominate the prime minister, who served alongside him and who was still the head of government. By retaining a fixed term after his parliamentary selection, the new president could not all of a sudden, like a prime minister, be brought down by parliament's vote of no confidence. In short, the two branches, executive and legislative, still held on to their fixed term of office, but they did not have separate sources of popular legitimacy anymore". E. Mazo, *Post-Communist Paradox*, 29–30.

[10] The Office for Democratic Institutions and Human Rights of the Organization for Security and Cooperation in Europe (OSCE/ODIHR) which had deployed an Election Observation Mission to Moldova, has concluded that parliamentary election on February 25, 2001 met the international standards for democratic elections. C. Neukirch, *Moldovan Headaches: The Republic of Moldova 120 days after the 2001 Parliamentary Elections*, "Working Papers of Institute for Peace Research and Security Policy at the University of Hamburg" 3 (2001), 5.

[11] K. Brzechczyn, *Paths to Democracy of the Post-Soviet Republics: Attempt at Conceptualization*, in E. Czerwińska-Schupp (ed.), *Values and Norms in the Age of Globalization*, (Berlin: Peter Lang, 2007), 562.

[12] To make sure that these elections were in conformity with the idea of "democratic choice", even if Braghiş had withdrawn at the last moment, the Communists would have proposed a second candidate, Valerian Cristea. Cristea was backed by three deputies, who most probably came from the Braghiş Alliance as the PPCD had decided not to take part in the presidential election. C. Neukirch, *Moldovan Headaches*, 10.

Table 19.2. The results of the presidential and parliamentary elections in 2001

PARLIAMENTARY ELECTION IN 2001		
PARTIES AND BLOCKS	%	MPs
Party of Communists of the Republic of Moldova	50 %	71
Braghiş Alliance	13.3%	19
Christian Democratic People's Party	8.2 %	11
Others (Party for Rebirth and Conciliation of Moldova, Democratic Party of Moldova, National Liberal Party, Social Democratic Party, National Christian Democratic Peasants' Party of Moldova, Electoral Bloc Motherland, Social-Political Movement For Order and Justice, Democratic Agrarian Party of Moldova, Independents)	28.5%	-
PRESIDENTIAL INDIRECT ELECTION IN 2001		
CANDIDATES	VOTES	
Valerian Cristea (Party of Communists of the Republic of Moldova)	3	
Dumitru Braghiş (Electoral Bloc "Braghis Alliance")	15	
Vladimir Voronin (Party of Communists of the Republic of Moldova)	71	

Source: Munteanu, *Political Parties Legislation*, 2010, 28.

When the Constitutional Court decided that one is allowed to be President of the Republic and leader of a political party at the same time, Voronin was free to be at the forefront of the state and to monitor the policies of communist activists. Thus, by combining the highest office in the country with leadership of the largest party in the Parliament[13], Voronin strenghtened both his political position and the significance of the the presidential office. The process of building of a parliamentary system in place of a semi-presidential one stalled.

In the subsequent parliamentary election in 2005, the Communists had lost the support of nearly 80,000 voters, which allowed them to occupy

[13] C. Neukirch said: "Voronin might control the Parliament in a way neither Snegur nor Lucinschi could have ever dreamed of". He has also noticed the increasing power of Voronin: "Thus, less than a year after the introduction of a 'parliamentary' system, the new President has emerged as the most powerful political player in Moldova. Voronin`s strong position was indirectly confirmed by (then nominated) Prime Minister Tarlev, who stated that the list of ministers had to be agreed upon with the President. The Moldovan Constitution does not foresee anything like this, however, it also does not rule it out". Ibid.

only fifty-six seats in the Moldovan Parliament. They were able to establish a new government[14] but the election of Voronin for another term became impossible. The germ of the first constitutional and political crisis could be solved with the agreement concluded between the Communists and the opposition MPs. President Voronin received the necessary support from the Christian Democratic People's Party and the Democratic and Social Liberal factions after he had promised to deliver the needed reforms and Euro-Atlantic integration for the country. He was re-elected with seventy-five votes. Another candidate, Gheorghe Duca (independent, academic, former Environment Minister of Moldova) received one vote.

Table 19.3. The results of the presidential and parliamentary elections in 2005

PARLIAMENTARY ELECTION IN 2005		
PARTIES AND BLOCKS	%	MPs
Party of Communists of the Republic of Moldova	46 %	56
Electoral Bloc Democratic Moldova	28.5%	34
Christian Democratic People's Party	9.1 %	11
Others (Electoral Bloc Fatherland, Social Democratic Party, Social-Political Movement "Equality in Rights", Party of the Socio-Economic Justice of Moldova, Christian Democratic Peasants' Party of Moldova, Labour Union Party "Fatherland", Centrist Union of Moldova, Republican Party of Moldova, Independents)	16.4%	-
PRESIDENTIAL INDIRECT ELECTION IN 2005		
CANDIDATES	VOTES	
Gheorghe Duca (independent)	1	
Vladimir Voronin (Party of Communists of the Republic of Moldova)	75	

Source: Munteanu, *Political Parties*, 2010, 28;

Moldovan Political System after the Election in 2009

In 2009, according to the constitution, after the expiry of two terms of Voronin`s presidency, the new head of state should have been elected. In the parliamentary election, the Communists gained four seats more than in the previous one. Having sixty seats, they lacked only one mandate to elect a new President. Moreover, riots broke out due to allegations of an

[14] For the Moldovan political system the number of required votes, by a decision of the Court, is 52. Ibid., 3.

electoral fraud[15] and the date of the presidential election was postponed. The Constitutional Court decided that the presidential election would have to take place on July 7, 2009, otherwise the Parliament would be dissolved and a premature election would be held. The opposition parties announced they would boycott the Parliament because of the electoral fraud. They feared that the Communists would use the re-count to obtain the single seat they needed. The presidential election was finally set for May 20.[16]

Before the election, in early May 2009, Vladimir Voronin was elected Speaker of the Parliament and became President *ad interim*.[17] Voronin proposed to support the Communist candidate for the office of the head of state. Three opposition parties which had just entered the Parliament (Liberal Democratic Party, Liberal Party and Our Moldova Alliance) decided to refuse the proposal of one vote to "preserve" the stability claimed by the Communists after the election.[18] In the first round, Zinaida Greceanîi (the then Prime Minister) got sixty votes, so the second round needed to be conducted.

---

[15] A wave of protests by many young people in Chisinau and in other towns was known as the "Twitter Revolution". F. Parmentier, *Moldova, a Major European Success for the Eastern Partnership?*, "European Issue" 186 2010, 2.
[16] I. Munteanu, *Political Parties Legislation*, 49.
[17] According to article 91, when the office of the President of the Republic of Moldova becomes vacant, the responsibility of the office shall devolve *ad interim* on the President of Parliament or the Prime Minister, in that priority order. *Constitution of the Republic of Moldova* (1994), art. 91.
[18] I. Munteanu, *Political Parties Legislation*, 49.

Table 19.4. The results of the presidential and parliamentary elections in 2009 (April to June)

PARLIAMENTARY ELECTION IN 2009 (April)		
PARTIES AND BLOCKS	%	MPs
Party of Communists of the Republic of Moldova	49.4%	60
Liberal Party	13.1%	15
Liberal Democratic Party of Moldova	12.4%	15
Party Alliance Our Moldova	9.7 %	11
Others (Social Democratic Party, Christian Democratic People's Party, Democratic Party of Moldova, Centrist Union of Moldova, European Action Social-Political Movement, Party of Spiritual Development United Moldova, Conservative Party, Alexandr Lomakin, Republican Party of Moldova, Tatiana Ţîmbalist, independents)	15.4%	-
PRESIDENTIAL INDIRECT ELECTION IN 2009 (May)		
CANDIDATES	VOTES	
Stanislav Groppa (Party of Communists of the Republic of Moldova)	0	
Zinaida Greceanîi (formally independent, *de facto* PCRM)	60	
PRESIDENTIAL INDIRECT ELECTION IN 2009 (June)		
CANDIDATES	VOTES	
Andrei Neguţă (Party of Communists of the Republic of Moldova)	0	
Zinaida Greceanîi (formally independent, *de facto* PCRM)	60	

Source: Munteanu, *Political Parties*, 2010, 28.

On June 2, 2009, the former parliamentary speaker Marian Lupu (PCRM) announced that the Communist Party was undemocratic and therefore unable to reform the country. He joined the opposition. The next day, Zinaida Greceanîi got sixty votes in the second round of indirect presidential election, as expected. In view of the failure to obtain the sixty-one votes needed, President *ad interim* Voronin had to announce new parliamentary election.

Table 19.5. The results of the presidential and parliamentary elections in 2009 (July to December)

PARLIAMENTARY ELECTION IN 2009 (July)		
PARTIES AND BLOCKS	%	MPs
Party of Communists of the Republic of Moldova	44.6%	48
Liberal Party	14.6%	15
Liberal Democratic Party of Moldova	16.5%	18
Democratic Party of Moldova	12.5%	13
Party Alliance Our Moldova	7.3 %	7
Others (Ecologist Party of Moldova Green Alliance, Social Democratic Party, Christian Democratic People's Party)	4.5 %	-
PRESIDENTIAL INDIRECT ELECTION IN 2009 (November)		
CANDIDATES	VOTES	
Marian Lupu (Alliance For European Integration)	53	
PRESIDENTIAL INDIRECT ELECTION IN 2009 (December)		
CANDIDATES	VOTES	
Marian Lupu (Alliance For European Integration)	53	

Source: Munteanu, *Political Parties*, 2010, 29.

In the new general election, the Communists won only forty-eight seats. The leaders of the main non-communist parties Vlad Filat, Mihai Ghimpu, Serafim Urechean and Marian Lupu (the ex-minister from PCRM) signed the Alliance for European Integration on August 8, 2009. They wanted to create a governing coalition that could finally push the Communist Party into opposition. Main posts of the state were supposed to be taken up as follows:

- Mihai Ghimpu, leader of the Liberal Party, candidate for the post of Speaker of the Parliament;
- Vlad Filat, leader of the Liberal Democratic Party of Moldova, candidate for the post of Prime Minister;
- Marian Lupu, leader of the Democratic Party of Moldova, candidate for the presidential office.

In August 2009, Mihai Ghimpu was elected Speaker of the Parliament. In September, Voronin resigned from the presidency *ad interim*, and Ghimpu became the Moldovan President *pro tempore.*[19] The Constitutional Court of Moldova confirmed the legitimacy of Mihai

[19] *Voronin files resignation*, http://www.azi.md/en/story/5678 (accessed January 1, 2012).

Ghimpu's position as acting President of Moldova, which gave him the right to nominate the Prime Minister, and on the same day, Ghimpu signed a decree nominating Filat for that office.

One of the main demands of the coalition was to change the constitution. On December 1, 2009, a presidential decree instituted a special commission for constitutional reform (*Comisia pentru reforma constituţională*).[20] It was supported by the Venice Commission, which advised the Moldovan commission to introduce first an amendment on parliamentary and then on presidential election.[21]

In early October, Voronin announced that the Communists would not open up to vote for their own candidate and would not participate in the parliamentary vote. Two days later the Alliance announced that Marian Lupu would be the first official candidate for the head of state. The deadline for applications was established on October 17. Due to a Communist boycott, the special election committee cancelled the accepted date and asked the Parliament to appoint a new one. The Constitutional Court ordered a nomination of the President from between two candidates reported earlier. Therefore, the Parliament adopted a new presidential election law which allowed the election of the President even if there is only one candidate.[22]

In the first round of the election held on November 10, the only candidate received fifty-three votes. The second round was set for December 7 and it also failed, with the same result. According to the new law, the President *ad interim* was entitled to dissolve the Parliament as early as one year after the last dissolution.

Referendum and the Parliamentary Election in 2010

Due to the failure to choose the head of state, a new election needed to be held before the beginning of December 2010. A remedy for the constitutional impasse was found by the presidential commission, that

[20] *Preşedintele interimar al Republicii Moldova, Mihai Ghimpu a semnat un decret privind constituirea Comisiei pentru reforma constituţională în următoarea componenţă*, http://www.president.md/press.php?p=1&s=7375&la ng=rom (accessed January 1, 2012).

[21] *European Commission for Democracy Through Law (Venice Commission), Amicus Curiae Brief on three questions related to article 78 of the Constitution of the Republic of Moldova Adopted by the Venice Commission at its 87th Plenary Session*, (Venice, June 17–18, 2011), Opinion 627/2011, CDL-AD (2011) 014.

[22] *MPs adopt new procedure for electing head of state*, http://www.azi.md/en/story/6633 (accessed January 13, 2012).

suggested a change in the constitution. The procedure for amending the constitution requires a 2/3 majority of the Parliament or a referendum. For obvious reasons, the coalition decided to use the second procedure. The referendum was held on September 5, 2010.

Table 19.7. The results of the referendum in 2010

Question: "Would you agree with the Constitutional amendment, which would allow the election of the President of the Republic of Moldova by the entire population?"		
POSITION OF MOLDOVAN POLITICAL PARTIES		
GROUPS IN FAVOUR	Democratic Party of Moldova; Our Moldova Alliance; Liberal Party; Liberal Democratic Party of Moldova; European Action Social-Political Movement; Popular Republican Party; National Liberal Party; Republican Party of Moldova; Ecological Party of Moldova Green Alliance; For Nation and Country; Humanist Party of Moldova; Roma Social-Political Movement of the Republic of Moldova; National Romanian Party; Labour Party; Party United Moldova; Socialist Party of Moldova; Centrist Union of Moldova	
GROUPS AGAINST	Christian Democratic People's Party; Conservative Party; New Force Social-Political Movement; Party "Patriots of Moldova"	
GROUPS CALLING FOR A BOYCOTT	Party of Communists of the Republic of Moldova; Social-Political Movement Equality; Party of Socialists of Moldova Motherland ; Social Democratic Party	
RESULTS OF REFERENDUM		
IN FAVOUR	87.83 %	
AGAINST	12.17 %	
TURNOUT	30.29 % (the official voter turnout announced by the Central Electoral Commission)	30.07 % (results after carrying out mathematical calculations on detailed data on voter participation provided by CEC)
TURNOUT REQUIRED	33.33 %	

Source: *Republican Constitutional Referendum of September 5, 2010*, http://www.e-democracy.md/en/elections/referendum/2010.

The voters were asked the following question: Would you agree with the Constitutional amendment, which would allow the election of the President of the Republic of Moldova by the entire population?[23] The referendum resulted in failure due to an insufficient turnout: 30 % as opposed to 33 % necessary to be considered valid. After the constitutional referendum aimed to approve the reform failed in September 2010, the Parliament was again dissolved and a new parliamentary election was scheduled for November 28, 2010.

The new winner turned out to be the Communists. However, they did not have an absolute majority in the Parliament. Leaders of the three parties of the Alliance came to a new coalition agreement on December 30, 2010. Their new cabinet was installed on January 14, 2011. It was obvious that once again there would be no election of a new President.

Table 19.8. The results of the parliamentary election in 2010

PARTIES AND BLOCKS	%	MPs
Party of Communists of the Republic of Moldova	39.3%	42
Liberal Party	9.9 %	12
Liberal Democratic Party of Moldova	29.4%	32
Democratic Party of Moldova	12.7%	15
Party Alliance Our Moldova	2.0 %	0
Others (Ecologist Party of Moldova Green Alliance, European Action Movement, Humanist Party of Moldova, Humanist Party of Moldova, Social Democratic Party, Christian Democratic People's Party, Roma Movement of the Republic of Moldova, United Moldova, For Nation and Country, Equality, Labour Party, Popular Republican Party, Republican Party of Moldova, Patriots of Moldova, independent)	6.7 %	-

Source: *Parliamentary Election 2010*, http://www.e-democracy.md/en/elections/parliamentary/2010.

In 2010, the Constitutional Court stated that the coalition did not have to perform a quick election of the President, giving them the same opportunity to develop a long-term strategy for a way out of the political impasse. The court declined to decide whether the current situation was applicable to a constitutional requirement for election of the President within two months after the beginning of the vacancy, preferring to press a

[23] From the referendum campaign three positions emerged: for, against and calling party to boycott the referendum.

legislative duty to clarify this requirement. There was a conflict within the coalition about the final position of the office of President in the political system. Vlad Filat wanted direct presidential election, but his coalition partners wanted to lower the requirement of the majority needed to choose the head of state (from 3/5 to absolute majority).[24]

Table 19.9. The results of the indirect presidential elections in 2011-2012

PRESIDENTIAL INDIRECT ELECTION IN 2011 (December)—annulled	
CANDIDATES	VOTES
Marian Lupu (Alliance For European Integration)	58
PRESIDENTIAL INDIRECT ELECTION IN 2012 (January)—cancelled	

Source: *Moldova fails to choose a new president*, http://www.dw.de/dw/article/0,,15606728,00.html; *Socialists voted against Marian Lupu*, http://www.allmoldova.md/en/moldova-news/politics/1249052029.html

On November 15, the deadline for candidates' applications expired with none provided, and so the election had to be postponed. Finally, on December 16, the only candidate Marian Lupu received fifty-eight votes. Before the 2nd round on January 11, 2012, after Marian Lupu resigned and the Communists proposed Leonid Talmach,[25] the Moldovan Constitutional Court annulled the December presidential election which produced no winner. The court said that some MPs broke the law by showing how they had voted[26], and so a second round was cancelled. The next presidential election term was to be announced by the Parliament.

[24] *Mołdawia: Brak konsensusu w sprawie rozwiązania problemu wyboru prezydenta*, "Tydzień na Wschodzie" 7 (167) (2011), 10.

[25] The communist candidate, former President of the National Bank of Moldova Leonid Tălmaci, does not belong to any party. According to the PCRM, his authority, professional and moral qualities can lead to national reconciliation. *Mołdawia: na razie tylko jeden kandydat na prezydenta*, http://wiadomosci.onet.pl/swia t/moldawia-na-razie-tylko-jeden-kandydat-na-prezyden,1,4995365,wiadomosc.html (accessed January 13, 2012).

[26] *Mołdawia: unieważniono wybory. Nie były tajne*, http://www.wprost.pl/ar/287826/Moldawia-uniewazniono-wybory-Nie-byly-tajne/ (accessed January 20, 2012); *Nie będzie prezydenta w Mołdawii*, http://www.rp.pl/artykul/6998 7,790784.html (accessed January 20, 2012).

Summary—Constitutional or Political Crisis?

The first reason of the political and constitutional crisis is the desire to weaken the political position of the head of state after Voronin`s presidency. What cannot be forgotten is his still strong position both in the Party of Communists of the Republic of Moldova and in the Moldovan political system as a whole.

Another reason is more social than political, and concerns the stable electorates of both sides (pro-European young people and pro-communist elders who remember the Soviet regime). It seems that the Moldovan society is torn. People do not know if they want to strive for a deeper cooperation with Russia or with Romania and the European structures.[27] What cannot be overlooked is the behaviour of the Constitutional Court. According to the Venice Commission, it is the only authority which can interpret the Moldovan Constitution. However, the court seems to be going far beyond this competence, a perfect example being its violation of the principle of secrecy in voting.

The third reason is the general attitude of the Communists who aimed at solving the problem by boycotting the referendum and refusing to work on a revision of the constitution in the Parliament.

Given more than two and a half years vacancy in the post of the head of state, it should be noted that the constitutional system fulfils only its primary role: to maintain the continuity of power. It cannot assure the election of the President. The only solution considered at this point is his nomination by an absolute majority. However, it seems to be highly undesirable by each legislator. The most important office in the country would then be elected by the same majority as is required in a vote of confidence or passing ordinary laws. Such a solution is possible anyway.[28]

The crisis in Moldova is more political than constitutional. It seems that as long as a few members of the Communist Party are able to support a compromise candidate, then the next general election will not imprint its mark on the finances of the country.

Few other possible solutions to the crisis remain. The first one is a referendum on a change of the Moldovan constitution.[29] The problem may

---

[27] M. Rojansky, *Moldova: the growing pains of democracy*, US Commission on Security and Cooperation in Europe Washington, D.C. January 31, 2012, 1.

[28] One can see such solutions in the procedure of the election of head of state in the constitutions of Greece (from two-thirds to three-fifths), Germany (from absolute majority to simple majority) and, in 2007, also in the Vatican (from two-thirds to absolute majority).

[29] In the middle of January 2012, the Alliance announced that they wanted to hold

be a low turnout that can lead to another failure of the referendum.[30] The Communists play a key role at this point. Instead of calling for a boycott of the referendum, they could call to vote against the amendment to the constitution. The boycott, although in accordance with the law, is highly undesirable in the perspective of building of a civil society. Moreover, it is possible to change the constitution through the Parliament, but it is almost impossible to get a 2/3 majority. In both cases, without the cooperation of the ruling coalition with the Communists, the change is unlikely.

Another way might be a split in the coalition (the Liberal Democratic Party of Moldova seems to be the splinter party) that would lead to a strengthening of the position of the Communists in the Parliament and the election of a new head of state could be possible. A somewhat less realistic scenario appears to be a split within the Communist camp, that would result in a support to elect a new President. Nonetheless, one should not forget that such a split had already occurred when Marian Lupu left the Communist Party.

The author is a PhD candidate at the Adam Mickiewicz University in Poznań. He specializes in modern political systems, the role of small European states in the integration processes, microstates, party systems of European states, Polish constitutional law and the problem of continuity of power.

---

a referendum on changing the majority which is necessary to elect the head of state from three fifths to an absolute majority. *Moldovan ruling alliance wants to amend constitution via referendum*, http://emoldova.net/ (accessed January 29, 2012).

[30] As rightly observed by W. Rodkiewicz, even if the current government wins the referendum, it is possible that the constitutional court will deem that the new procedure of election of the President cannot be used by the current Parliament, thus forcing its dissolution and, once again, early elections. W. Rodkiewicz, *Ryzykowna próba przełamania politycznego impasu w Mołdawii*, „Tydzień na Wschodzie" 3 (204) (2012), 1.

CHAPTER TWENTY

TWENTY YEARS OF THE CZECH PARTY SYSTEM: 1992–2011

MACIEJ STOBIŃSKI

Introduction and Definitions to Determine

More than twenty years after the fall of communist regimes, it is still too soon for Central and Eastern Europe to create stable party systems similar to those in Western Europe. However, in each country of the region one can already see some patterns of party behaviour and relationship of the main parties. On this basis, some conclusions or generalizations can be drawn. The Czech Republic is regarded by researchers as a country with a relatively stable (as for the region) political scene, and as such it is a very interesting example to analyse.

The party system can be defined as:

> a system of interactions, which is the result of rivalry between parties … It is based on dependence of parties, the fact that every party is a function (in the mathematical sense) of another party and reacts in a more or less competitive way to the behaviour of other political parties.[1]

Douglas W. Rae states that "the party system is not a mere sum of the political parties, people, institutions and forms of activity. It's rather a rivalry between two parties within a particular political regime, giving democratic political parties a unique meaning".[2] Thus, one cannot limit the category of party system only to a static shot of its component groups. To

---

[1] R. Herbut, *Systemy partyjne w Europie Zachodniej—ciągłość* i *zmiana*, (Wrocław: Wydawnictwo Uniwersytetu Wrocławskiego 1996), 136.
[2] Ibid.

create a system, some interactions between them are crucial. This is especially problematic because the same post-communist parties in Europe are currently under development and are definitely far from stability, both when in terms of their size (membership base), resources and ideological concepts. The need for rapid action during the democratic transition and the homogeneity of the population (and hence the openness of the electoral constituency) also impedes the institutionalization of political parties.[3] Against this background, the Czech Republic is still an exception. From the very beginning of transition, there have been at least three parliamentary groups able to maintain their seats throughout the time, and since 1998 the number of parliamentary parties have consistently remained at five.

In the years since the beginning of transition, the most suitable approach to analyse the relationship between the parties seems to be taking into account the concept of "family" of political parties, with one caveat. In Europe, the post-communist political party system is not as developed as in Western Europe, so it is better to use the conception of main poles of the competition instead of party families. A political pole can be defined as:

> a concentration of support for a party (bloc of parties), dealing with alternative positions on issues that deeply and permanently divide voters—whether due to different values or because of different group interests, leading to the creation of a real or symbolic alternative to the ruling ones or opposition.[4]

The basis for this approach is given by the attitude of political parties, that passed through the early 1990s evolution from the amorphous social movements of "forum" to the "classical" parties, such as those operating in Western Europe. A similar direction of change also emphasizes the desire to enter the transnational structures of political parties (as well as party groups in the European Parliament), where membership is based on the criterion of programme. The definition of political poles of competition can be complemented by the recognition of visible and distinct formations, separated from each other, both ideologically and when it comes to electoral base.[5] The description of the party system using this concept

---

[3] P. Mair, *Party System Change,* (Oxford: Oxford University Press, 2002), 175.

[4] A. Antoszewski, *Wzorce rywalizacji politycznej we współczesnych demokracjach europejskich,* (Wrocław: Wydawnictwo Uniwersytetu Wrocławskiego, 2005), 29.

[5] P. Fiala, M. Strimska, *Ideove-Politicke rodiny a politicke strany v postkomunistickych zemic stredni a vychodni Evropy,* in P. Fiala, J. Holzer, M. Strimska (eds.), *Politicke strany ve Stredni Evrope*, (Brno: Mezinárodní

perfectly complements the categories referred to above, regarding the format and mechanism of the system. In other words, each of the poles of competition must have a distinct identity that occurs at the level of political elites and voters. At the same time, it should be intuitively easy to note each of them separately because of their ideological boundaries. Therefore, the number of poles will be determined by the number of relevant political parties in the country.[6]

As far as the size of electoral support and the time needed to create a pole of competition is concerned, it is worth to recognize and qualify a party or a coalition as a political pole. Moreover, the factor of size may be insufficient, so the impact and interactions between the pole and the environment should be also taken into account. If the pole is perceived by other parties and they adjust to it when creating and implementing their electoral and coalition strategies, one can therefore speak of its appearance. It must be also noted that the existence or emergence of new poles of competition is limited because of space and the possibility of expansion among the electorate of other parties or poles. In other words, political competition takes place not only among parties under the same pole, but also among the poles—while some increase, others must decrease. Sometimes, it is difficult to clearly include one political party in a specific pole or to place it at a particular point of the political spectrum. Moreover, in the past twenty years, parties have changed positions held in the political space, moving left or right. This supports the hypothesis of this chapter, that the Czech party system has had a relatively low level of stability over the past twenty years.

It is worth noting that Czech voters base their political decisions on the criterion of programme concerning the economy. According to studies, at least two-thirds of them do so. This facilitates structuring of the political market and forces newly formed groups to define themselves on the left-right economic axis.

The Evolution of the Czech Party System

The description of changes in the Czech party system in the last two decades is limited to relevant and parliamentary parties.

---

politologický ústav Masarykovy univerzity, 2002), 21–24.

[6] M. Strimska, *Parties, Poles, and the Post-Communist Party Arrangements: A Study on Conceptualization of Poles and Polarity*, "Středoevropské politické studie", 4 (1) (2002), 1.

Table 20.1. Support for the political parties 1992–2010[7]

Elections	1992	1996	1998	2002	2006	2010
KSČM	14.1*	10.3	11	18.5	12.8	11.3
ČSSD	6.5	26.4	32.1	30.2	32.3	22.1
SZ	6.5**		1.1	2.4	6.3	2.4
VV						10.9
KDU-ČSL	6.3	8.08	9	14.3****	7.2	4.4
DEU		2.8	1.5		0.3****	
US			8.6	14.3****	0.3****	
TOP 09						16.7
ODS	29.7***	29.6	27.8	24.5	35.4	20.2
ODA	5.9	6.36		0.5		
SPR-RSČ	6	8.01	3.9	1.0		
HSD-SMS	5,87					

Source: *Výsledky koleb*, http://volby.cz.

Table 20.2. Number of seats won by parties[8]

Elections	1992	1996	1998	2002	2006	2010
KSČM	35	22	24	41	26	26
ČSSD	16	61	74	70	74	56
SZ (LSU)	16				6	-
VV						24
KDU-ČSL	15	18	20	31*	13	
US			19	31*		
TOP 09						41
ODS	76	68	63	58	81	53
ODA	14	13				
SPR-RSČ	14	18				
HSD-SMS	14					

Source: *Výsledky koleb*, 1992–1997—the domination of the centre-right http://volby.cz/

[7] * Left Bloc coalition (LB); ** LSU coalition; *** with KDS; **** as Quad-coalition; ***** US-DEU.

[8] * Quad-coalition.

The first years of transition can be described by a few dominant factors. Firstly, by 1996, Václav Klaus' ODS remained the only big party, regularly collecting almost 30 percent of votes. It was impossible to form a coalition cabinet without its participation. The system remained highly polarized. Beyond the pro-system parties (up to 1996 ČSSD, HSD-SMS and LSU), in the Parliament there were also two extreme groups—leftist Communists and far-right Republicans. Their coalition potential was equal to zero but they were able to impede significantly the cooperation among other political actors. Those two isolated parties (supported by about 20 % of voters) created a bargaining "dead zone" as they had no chance to get into the coalition. Thus, the government had to seek the support of 101 among 160 rather than 200 MPs. which was obviously more difficult.

In 1996, there emerged another large pole of competition—the Social Democrats on the left. The dominant party at this time was the conservative ODS, which initiated coalition negotiations twice and finally nominated its leader for the Prime Minister. Both the first cabinet of Václav Klaus (1992-1996), having a narrow majority, and his second minority government (1996-1997) can be defined as ideologically and programmatically convergent centre-right coalitions. They were comprised of the ODS, ODA, KDU-ČSL and KDS (which in 1995 was absorbed by the ODS).[9] After the next election, smaller coalition parties remained rather small (gaining about 10 percent of votes), but the KDU-ČSL (Christian Democrats) was able to establish a stable position in the centre-right, between the Liberals, Conservatives and Social Democrats. At the end of this period, due to unpaid campaign debts dating back to 1992, the ODA dramatically lost its popularity and decided not to take part in the parliamentary election in 1998.

1998-2002—the "Opposition Agreement"

The 1998 election brought a concentration of the party system. The Republicans and the ODA failed to maintain their parliamentary seats. The latter was succeded by the UD (*Unie Svobody* – Freedom Union), founded in 1998 together with a group that had split from the ODS. The other four parliamentary parties were ODS, ČSSD (approximately one-third of MPs each), KDU-ČSL and the isolated KSČM. Again, none was able to set a majority government on their own.

[9] W. Sokół, *Partie polityczne i systemy partyjne krajów postkomunistycznych w okresie transformacji systemowej*, in J. Rybczyńska (ed.), *Europa Środkowo-Wschodnia. Region, państwa i społeczeństwa w okresie transformacji*, (Lublin: Wydawnictwo Uniwersytetu Marii Curie-Skłodowskiej, 2000), 101.

The years of the so-called “opposition agreement” were an exception in a rather clear case of coalition cabinets initiated by the ODS or ČSSD. It is worth noting that the agreement itself was a continuation. A reversed situation occured in 1996, when Miloš Zeman allowed Klaus to create a minority government along with the ODA and KDU-ČSL in exchange for the post of President of the Chamber of Deputies and other concessions for his party members. The agreement of 1998 itself was signed as a reaction to the stalemate following the election. Centrist parties did not want to cooperate with the ČSSD (mainly for ideological reasons) or respectively with the ODS (due to their concerns with the role of Klaus in future governments), while the Communists were still consistently isolated and it was not possible to build any other majority coalition.

In this case, a confidence vote was abandoned. That meant that the new cabinet had to receive only 68 out of 137 votes rather that 101 out of 200. The ODS committed itself not to support any vote of no confidence for the new ČSSD-led government, which meant that it could not be overthrown by the rest of the parties. In exchange, the party of Klaus received a number of parliamentary posts, such as the chairmen of both chambers, the commission for special services and the budget commission.

The “opposition agreement” may be assessed variously. Some deny it as an attempt to eliminate the other political parties. It is also claimed to be the fullest expression of cartelization and the appropriation of the state. It was often criticized for its lack of democracy by the centre-right (for allegedly breaking the spirit of constitution) and President Havel, who called it “wicked”. It led to the creation of a strange political environment, in which cooperation is based on specific rules without a coalition agreement and the principle of effective opposition is eliminated. On the other hand, it seems that this peculiar arrangement worked very well as the formation of a stable majority government was not possible due to the existence of:

(1) an isolated communist party;
(2) two reluctant centre-right parties with low coalition potential (especially the US) due to large expectations (office seeking), personal conflicts and programmatic differences with large parties.

The “opposition agreement” managed to stabilize the Czech political scene for four years and led to the first alternation of power since the beginning of transition.

2002–2006—Centre-Left Governments

At the end of the "oppositon agreement" term, polarization of the political scene increased. As a result, the ČSSD left the agreement. The outcome of the new election brought a victory of the left (seventy seats) but it did not allow any of the parties to form a cabinet on their own. The Quad-coalition, a unitary project of small centre-right parties, failed to win the election and fell apart. Between the ODS and ČSSD, there appeared again two small parties— KDU-ČSL and US-DEU. They eventually joined the social democrat-led coalition and did not leave it until the end of the term.

In that period, the Czech Republic had three governments with three Prime Ministers, united mostly by pro-European policy. Since 2005, there have been two parallel coalitions—a cabinet and a parliamentary one. The latter means a cooperation between the ČSSD and KSČM in enforcing some laws (e.g. labour code) against the votes of other coalition members. Nonetheless, the last cabinet of Jiří Paroubek was able to remain in power until the end of the Parliament's term.

2006–2011—Centre-Right Governments

The title of this section may be a bit misleading. Two sub-periods can be distinguished here. The first one 2006-2010 and the second one 2010-2011.

A strange example of stalemate after the 2006 election. Both the left and the right had one hundred MPs and no coalition could acquire the majority of seats. The ODS struggled for months to form a cabinet. Finally, its coalition with the KDU-ČSL and SZ had only one hundred parliamentary votes at its disposal. Thanks to the support of two independent MPs, it gained a narrow majority of 102 out of 200 votes. In 2009, the coalition lost some of its MPs, so that the government did not have a majority any more and it was overthrown by the left opposition. Eventually, that led to a new election in 2010 and the failure of smaller coalition partners to achieve parliamentary status.

At this time, the ČSSD remained the main party of the left and won the 2010 election. However, it was a Pyrrhic victory. The party moved to the left, preparing itself to cooperation with the Communists, but it lost the capability of cooperating with the centre parties. The ČSSD and KSČM had only eighty-two seats together, clearly not enough to even start a coalition bargaining.

The next government was formed by the centre-right ODS, a very strong liberal TOP 09 (a split from the Christian Democrats) and the anti-establishment party of VV. This new coalition pattern has served for two years, despite a few serious crises.

Conclusions

To summarize and analyse the relationship between parties in the Czech political system, it should be noted that twenty years from its inception to the present day are a relatively short time. In a changing and challenging political environment, it was definitely not easy to create stable patterns of behaviour and relationships. However, it is sufficient to make a summary and to attempt to generalize some processes and phenomena.

The first and most important variable is the number of parties in the Parliament. Since the beginning of transition it has consistently declined, and in 1998 it stabilized at five. Firstly, it shows a partial closure of the party system. There appeared a practical need for elimination of rivals in order to obtain the parliamentary status. Secondly, it substantially closes the number of actors participating in coalition bargaining. This diagnosis is confirmed by the effective number of parties index value. For the Czech Republic it amounts to respectively 5.0 (constituency level) and 3.9 (parliamentary level), which clearly outlines the downward trend of the index.

From this data, one can identify a slow concentration of the Czech party system, especially after the 1996 election. It may be said, with some reservations, that the inter-party rivalry began to take on a centripetal nature, especially in the case of two largest parties. The ČSSD managed to dominate the left side of the political scene thanks to its location in the proximity of the political centre. The ODS, dominant in the first part of 1990s, then spent eight years in the opposition. Afterwards, in 2006 it was able to go beyond its stable electoral base. It expanded the number of its electorate by getting "centrist" voters. Thus, the ODS achieved the best result in its history.

The large parties dominate their competition poles, and thanks to situational (e.g. leaders` charisma) or institutional factors (5 percent electoral threshold), they managed to permanently occupy a significant place in the Czech party system. Any attempts to compete with them using similar political programmes were doomed to fail because voters consistently supported the stronger party on each wing of the political scene.[10] Gradually a bipolar system of competition has been formed, thus becoming a system of balance. The main poles are occupied by the ODS and the ČSSD, which have been winning regularly 20–35 % of the votes each since 1996. They remain the most important parties in the Czech Republic, representing the dominant socioeconomic conflict of the left-right.

This means that there are no other such relevant conservative-liberal parties, except the TOP 09, which gained considerable success in the election in 2010 (however, this is a case of just one election). At the same time the potential of a coalition of these two groups is large, as they initiate coalition bargaining. Except the temporary, half-bureaucratic cabinets of Tosovski and Fischer, the ODS and the ČSSD have initiated the negotiations and nominated the Prime Ministers of all governments since 1992. As one of these parties takes office, the other smoothly becomes opposition.[11] The other parties remain rather small. KDU-ČSL, US-DEU, ZS, VV and perhaps TOP 09 may be called hinge parties, as they operate "in between", moving left or right depending on the political situation. They can cooperate in government creation with the conservative ODS or the social liberal ČSSD. It means that if there are no other factors (such as after the 1998 election, with the personal reluctance between the ODS and the US), the coalition potential of these parties is the greatest. This is definitely the case of the Christian Democrats, who have participated in governments in 1990–1998, 2002–2006 and 2007–2009.

On the left side of the political scene, one should regard the continuous and fierce competition between the Socialists and Communists. This is the result of a centrifugal movement of Zeman's ČSSD in the first half of 1990s and the "squeezing out" of the Communists into the extreme left. The ČSSD consistently denied cooperation with the KSČM to create a "left" government, although it could have been a majority government in the 2002–2006 term. Only the cabinet of Paroubek (2005–2006), despite the official coalition support of the KDU-ČSL and the US-DEU, passed a few important laws with support of the extreme left against the opposition of the centre-right coalition parties.[12]

---

[10] L. Brokl, Z. Mansfeldova, *How the Voters Respond in the Czech Republic*, in K. Lawson, A. Rommele, G. Karasimeonov (eds.), *Cleveages, Parties and Voters*, (London: Greenwood Publishing Group, 1999), 210.

[11] P. Kopecky, C. Mudde, *Explaining Different Paths of Democratization*, "Journal of Communist Studies and Transition Politics" 16 (3) (2000), 75.

[12] P. Fiala, V. Hlousek, *System partyjny Republiki Czeskiej*, in A. Antoszewski, P. Fiala, R. Herbut, J. Sroka (eds.), *Partie i systemy partyjne Europy Środkowej*, (Wrocław: Wydawnictwo Uniwersytetu Wrocławskiego, 2003), 60.

In 1990s, the Czech right was dominated by the conflict over the personality of Václav Klaus. The ODS supported him, while other smaller conservative and liberal parties such as the ODA, KDU-ČSL and US-DEU opposed him. After Klaus was elected President in 2003, the competition focused more on programmatic issues, but the Czech right still remains more divided than the left. Nowadays, the ODS still dominates the right pole and holds the Prime Minister office (Petr Nečas since 2010). Its coalition partner is the liberal-conservative TOP 09. Another new parliamentary group is the VV.

Until 2010, every new parliamentary party was the weakest force in the Chamber of Deputies, which confirms the stability of the system and the difficulties of new entrants to obtain a relevant political position. Moreover, the above-mentioned lack of inter-party cooperation schemes and patterns shows that the Czech party system is still in the development stage, although some of the fixed and immutable foundations in recent years are noticeable, determining the level of competition in the cabinet. The nature of competition and a relatively strong and stable position of the big parties strengthen the emerging dominant axis of political division, which lasts despite changes in the party system (appearance of new and disappearance of the previous parties).[13]

In the Czech Republic, only pro-system parties can be regarded as relevant and recognised as a potential coalition partner. The Communists and the Republicans had only the potential for political blackmail. They have been gaining a significant number of votes but it does not translate into the relevance of government. Their presence in the Parliament, to some extent, has been determining the behaviour of other political parties (especially in the relation KSČM– ČSSD), but the real impact of extreme poles on the policies and government negotiations remained low and played only a negative blocking role.[14] KSČM and SPR-RSČ are marginal parties, acting outside the mainstream of the left-right axis, which leads to their isolation and reduction of the potential coalition to virtually zero.

The total isolation of the Communists (and the Republicans earlier on) has had a very strong and negative impact on the government formation process. The KSČM has consistently been isolated by other parties on the parliamentary level.[15] Of course, in many issues it was the position taken

[13] N. Sitter, *Cleavages, Party Strategy and Party System Change in Europe*, "East and West Perspectives on European Politics and Society" 3 (3) (2002), 443.

[14] M. Strimska, *The Communist Party of Bohemia and Moravia: A Post-Communist Socialist or a Neo-communist Party?*, "German Policy Studies" 2 (2) (2002), 236.

[15] J. J. Wiatr, *Europa postkomunistyczna: przemiany państw i społeczeństw po*

by the Communists that contributed to the isolation. However, they dominated the extreme left and regularly won at least 10 % of votes (in 1992–1998 along with the right-wing Republicans). Thus, they significantly reduced the possibility of forming a colaliton by others. The continous isolation of the KSČM by the ČSSD (despite some attempts to open up on both sides) prevented the rise of a two-bloc competition model based on the dividing lines of left–right, forcing both major parties to move to the centre of the political scene and find allies among the centrist parties. However, assessing the role of the anti-system Communists, it is worth noting the fact that in practice they do not constitute a real threat to the consolidation of democracy. Their greatest influence on the functioning of Czech cabinets, therefore, consists in the mere presence of a regular anti-system opposition, depriving other parties of votes of the electorate and limiting the possible configurations of government coalitions.[16]

Despite the relatively stable position of each party on the socio-economic axis, one still cannot speak of the stability of links and relations between political parties. An example would be the US, reluctant to enter the government along with the ČSSD or with the ODS in 1998.

One should also pay attention to the phenomenon of bilateral opposition.[17] It involves the confrontational behaviour of the parties appearing to the left or to the right of the government. The governments of the centre-right coalition of the ODS, ODA and KDU-ČSL were criticized by the left (ČSSD and KSČM) and the nationalist (SPR-RSČ until 1998). The cabinets dominated by Socialists were subject to attacks from the right (ODS) and the left (Communists). Only in 2006–2010, when ODS (alone or with coalition allies) occupied the entire right-wing of the parliamentary spectrum, this phenomenon disappeared and the successive governments of Topolanek and Nečas met only with an opposition from the left.

An inherent feature of the Czech party system seems to be, paradoxically, the lack of "being a system". One cannot talk about the creation of lasting and stable interactions among the parties. For the latter, due to the open political market and risk of disappearance, the main electoral goal is to survive by building structures and preventing fractionalization. Of course, against the background of Central and Eastern Europe, the Czech party system can be described as one of the most stable,

---

1989 roku, (Warszawa: Wydawnictwo Naukowe Scholar, 2006), 122.

[16] G. Pridham, *Democratic Consolidation in the Czech Republic: Comparative Perspectives after Twenty Years of Political Change*, "Politologický časopis" 4 (2009), 282.

[17] J. Wojnicki, *Kształtowanie się systemów wielopartyjnych Europy Środkowo-Wschodniej,* (Pułtusk: Akademia Humanistyczna im. A. Gieysztora, 2004), 172.

but one can still note the creation of certain patterns of behaviour rather than a stable system.[18] The context of the 2010 election (two new parties in the lower chamber) shows that even the parties seemed to have a stable position within the political system (like the Christian Democrats) can be deprived of parliamentary positions.

In coalition politics one can indeed see certain foundations of stable patterns (e.g. stability of parties initiating bargaining), but there is no consequence in the process of the alternation of power, which in turn leads to instability of the cabinets themselves. The role of the centrist parties, whether they are Liberals, Christian Democrats or Greens, is to complete the government. These parties have never managed to get the post of Prime Minister, limiting their aspirations to ministeries. Thus, their role and influence in the cabinet will certainly be smaller than the significance of the initiating party. However there is no alternative to their presence in the government, which strongly increases their bargaining power. Otherwise, the *force majeure* parties (such as the ODS and the ČSSD) need to seek alternative solutions, such as the "opposition agreement" of 1998.[19] As a result, the high level of stability of the party system may not be reflected and translated into the stability of cabinet patterns. The format and mechanism of the party system seem to be the most important factors determining the creation and functioning of Czech governments and coalitions.

Maxmilián Strmiska, characterizing the Czech multipartism, stated that the current coalition formula, frequent crises and instability may in the long term prove to be a threat to the political system.[20] The thesis of this author was confirmed more than ten years later (in 2010), when the party system, previously considered as relatively stable, experienced significant changes, such as the loss of parliamentary status of two groups while two new parties gained it. This forced the ODS to invite those new parties to the cabinet without any earlier experience, what was the seed of future crises and conflict situations in the coalition. However, the maturity of a party system does not exclude change. Otherwise, it would mean a

---

[18] R. Chytilek, J. Sedo, *Party System Stability and Territorial Patterns of Electoral Competition in the Czech Republic*, in V. Hlousek, R. Chytilek (eds.), *Parliamentary Elections and Party Landscape in the Visegrad Countries*, (Brno: Centrum pro studium demokracie a kultury, 2007), 23.

[19] R. Y. Hazan, *Centre Parties, Polarization and Competition in European Parliamentary Democracies,* (London: Continuum International Publishing Group, 2000), 158–167.

[20] M. Strimska, *The Czech Multipartism in the Late 1990s. Some Remarks*, "Středoevropské politické studie" 2 (2000), 4.

stagnation. A mature system possesses appropriate patterns of change, reproduction or recovery by ensuring the stability of the government majority. The above-mentioned elements could be seen in the Czech party system since its beginning in the early 1990s.

The main axis of the allocation and structuring of the political scene in the Czech Republic remains the economic left-right axis. A much smaller role is played by other factors, like cultural or religious issues, as well as the quickly overwhelmed division between post-communists and the anti-communist opposition, which disappeared with the disintegration of the OF (*Občanské Fórum*, Civic Forum) and the marginalization of Communists in the KSČM.[21] This means that for both voters and politicians, the view on the role of the state in the economy is the most important point of reference on whether to cooperate, support or exclude.[22] It seems that the similar constitution of the political spectrum facilitates the stability of the party system, providing the centripetal competition and reducing polarization.

One of the most important factors affecting the durability of cabinets is the polarization of the party system and the strength of extreme parties in the Parliament. Studies clearly show a correlation between the occurrence of the extremists and the instability of cabinets and the entire political system. And vice versa, support for the extremists should be for each cabinet a sign that their actions (along with the political system) may meet with complete rejection by a larger part of the society. According to G. Bingham Powell[23], strong ("smoothly functioning") party systems marginalize extremism, which makes their cabinets stronger. On the other hand, weak party systems, in which radical parties regularly win at least ten percent of the vote, are not institutionally capable of establishing a strong stable cabinet. Comments by this author referring to Western Europe seem to be confirmed at least partly in post-communist countries. In the Czech Republic, seizure of power by extreme parties should be seen as purely theoretical, but the level of electoral support achieved by them makes the creation of cabinets difficult.[24] The radical right has been

---

[21] H. Kitschelt, Z. Mansfeldova, R. Markowski, T. Gabor, *Post-commuist Party Systems: Competition, Representation and Inter-party Cooperation*, (Cambridge: Cambridge University Press, 1999), 288.

[22] G. Evans, S. Whitefield, *The Structuring of Political Cleveages in Post-Communist Societies: the Case of the Czech Republic and Slovakia*, "Political Studies" 46 (1998), 115–129.

[23] G. B. Powell, *Extreme Parties and Political Turmoil: Two Puzzles*, "American Journal of Political Science" 30 (1986).

[24] V. Hlousek, P. Pseja, *Europeanization of Political Parties and the Party System*

deprived of the parliamentary status in the 1990s, and despite several attempts, it has failed to return.

In 2006, the upward trend in the results of the KSČM election was interrupted and the Communists have remained a small party with a limited electoral base. This seems to have prevented the possibility of the creation of a third (Communist) large-pole competition. In the next election, this possibility has returned, with a difference. The newly created TOP 09 won the votes of those losing parliamentary status (KDU-ČSL and SZ) and gathered over 16 %. Whether this party (with a still lower level of institutionalization) will maintain a high level of support and a strong position in the party system, remains an open question. Nevertheless, the relative weakness of the Czech central parties allowed the ODS and the ČSSD to move towards the centre of the political scene, creating a competing centripetal situation and reducing the polarization of the political scene.

The Czech party system in the period in question could by compared to systems in Western Europe. It was characterized by a fixed number of political parties (five, except the parliaments formed in 1992 and 1998, in which there were more factions) and a stable political division between the left and the right. Large parties occupied two main poles of the competition, while the centre of the political scene allowed the operation of smaller, complementary pivotal parties.[25]

To summarize the impact of factors resulting from these characteristics, several important observations can be made. First, since 1996 two major parties have dominated the coalition bargaining process, reserving the status of the initiating party. Smaller groups only completed the coalitions. Second, the moderate polarization of the political scene and the dominant one-dimensional axis of political divisions created stable patterns of competition. Third, the consequent isolation of the extreme parties has become a rule. On the one hand, it limits the amount of post-election possibilities, but on the other hand, it forces pro-system parties to work together and find (sometimes extraordinary) solutions. Fourth, the model of opposition is characterized by opposition in minor issues and at the same time readiness to compromise or even cooperate and fully accept the rules of the political game. This obviously concerns the relationship

---

in the Czech Republic, "Journal of Communist Studies and Transition Politics" 25 (4) (2009), 513–539.

[25] S. Hanley, *The New Right in Europe: Czech Transformation and Right-wing Politics 1989-2006,* (London: Routledge, 2007); S. Saxonberg, *The Czech Republic Before the New Millennium: Politics, Parties and Gender,* (New York: East European Monographs, 2003), 43.

between the pro-system parties. Fifth, each of the cabinets after a shorter or longer period of time is exposed to the so called "effect of being in power", what seems to be the rule also in established party systems. It means that the support for all governments and their parties is steadily decreasing, which may cause additional influence on parties' actions.

To sum up, the Czech party system can be considered as moderately stable. There are some foundations and patterns of relationship and coalition bargaining. It is a system between—according to Giovanni Sartori's typology—moderate and polarized pluralism. This fact is confirmed by political scientists studying democracy, according to which the Czech party system at the moment is in a position to guarantee the stability of governments or smooth alternation of power, which also provides the consolidation of democracy.

Prospects for the Evolution of the Czech Party System

The next few elections will show if the above described patterns will easily transform into a stable party system or rather new political actors will change it totally. It seems that in the coming years, the ODS and the ČSSD will maintain their positions as the strongest parties, alternating in cabinet. The dominance of the two major parties seems to be unchallenged in the near term. The unknown answer concerns smaller centre parties, which include TOP 09, VV, KDU-ČSL and SZ and their ability to secure or retake parliamentary status and use this pivotal position to gain influence on country policy and offices. For the KSČM the most important issue is how to convince the Social Democrats towards government collaboration.

Abbreviations used

ČSSD	Czech Social Democratic Party
KDU-ČSL	Christian Democratic Union – Czechoslovak Peoples Party
KSČM	Communist Party of Bohemia and Moravia
ODA	Civic Democratic Alliance
ODS	Civic Democratic Party
OF	Civic Forum
SPR-RSČ	Republicans of Miroslav Sladek
SZ	The Green Party
TOP 09	Tradition, Responsibility, Prosperity 09
US-DEU	Freedom Union – Democratic Union
VV	Public Affairs

The author is a PhD student at the University of Wroclaw. He specializes in cabinets, coalitions and political parties.

PART SIX

ECONOMIC AND SOCIAL PROBLEMS

CHAPTER TWENTY-ONE

STRUCTURAL BARRIERS TO ECONOMIC GROWTH IN THE EUROPEAN UNION

ŁUKASZ GOCZEK

Introduction

Europe's current economic problems have manifested themselves in the unsustainable debt of some of the EU member states, the continuing depreciation of the euro against other major currencies and the lack of ability of the EU leaders to establish a common political stand. These issues are collectively labelled as the "euro crisis" in the current public socioeconomical debate and are accompanied by forecasted reduction of economic growth over 2012 to 2013 in the euro area, with significant recessions in many countries, which could be potentially deep in some of the more pessimistic scenarios (see Table 21.1 below).

A point could be made that the measures taken in response to the earlier financial crisis of 2007 to 2010 have generally provided good results as to the short-term demand and income losses from the recession, and that these measures were fully exercised up to the point, in which they are no longer working. Furthermore, it could be argued that Europe's debt problems are not transitory, and it is therefore difficult to describe them using the concept of crisis, which assumes the temporality of the adverse situation. Thus, the aim of the chapter is to present some of the structural barriers to long-term growth, such as an ageing population and lagging innovation, and (partly resulting from these problems) productivity stagnation and Balance of Payments imbalances. The first part of this chapter presents the failure of short-run macroeconomic policies in managing the crisis. The second part presents four structural barriers to growth in the European Union. The third part concludes, providing guidelines for policy.

Table 21.1. Gross domestic product, volume (percentage change on preceding year)

	2006	2007	2008	2009	2010	2011	2012
Belgium	2.7	2.9	1.0	-2.8	2.3	1.9	-0.1
Germany	3.7	3.3	1.1	-5.1	3.7	3.0	0.6
Estonia	10.1	7.5	-3.7	-14.3	2.3	7.5	1.2
Ireland	5.3	5.2	-3.0	-7.0	-0.4	0.9	0.5
Greece	5.5	3.0	-0.2	-3.2	-3.5	-6.8	-4.4
Spain	4.1	3.5	0.9	-3.7	-0.1	0.7	-1.0
France	2.5	2.3	-0.1	-2.7	1.5	1.7	0.4
Italy	2.2	1.7	-1.2	-5.1	1.5	0.2	-1.3
Cyprus	4.1	5.1	3.6	-1.9	1.1	0.5	-0.5
Luxembourg	5.0	6.6	0.8	-5.3	2.7	1.1	0.7
Malta	2.8	4.3	4.3	-2.6	2.9	2.1	1.0
Netherlands	3.4	3.9	1.8	-3.5	1.7	1.2	-0.9
Austria	3.7	3.7	1.4	-3.8	2.3	3.1	0.7
Portugal	1.4	2.4	0.0	-2.9	1.4	-1.5	-3.3
Slovenia	5.8	6.9	3.6	-8.0	1.4	0.3	-0.1
Slovakia	8.3	10.5	5.9	-4.9	4.2	3.3	1.2
Finland	4.4	5.3	0.3	-8.4	3.7	2.7	0.8
Euro	3.3	3.0	0.4	-4.3	1.9	1.4	-0.3
Bulgaria	6.5	6.4	6.2	-5.5	0.2	1.8	1.4
Czech Republic	7.0	5.7	3.1	-4.7	2.7	1.7	0.0
Denmark	3.4	1.6	-0.8	-5.8	1.3	1.0	1.1
Latvia	11.2	9.6	-3.3	-17.7	-0.3	5.3	2.1
Lithuania	7.8	9.8	2.9	-14.8	1.4	5.8	2.3
Hungary	3.9	0.1	0.9	-6.8	1.3	1.7	-0.1
Poland	6.2	6.8	5.1	1.6	3.9	4.3	2.5
Romania	7.9	6.3	7.3	-6.6	-1.6	2.5	1.6
Sweden	4.3	3.3	-0.6	-5.2	5.6	4.2	0.7
United K.	2.6	3.5	-1.1	-4.4	2.1	0.9	0.6
EU	3.3	3.2	0.3	-4.3	2.0	1.5	0.0

Source: *Interim Forecast. February 2012* (http://ec.europa.eu/).

Failure of Short-Run Macroeconomic Policies

Most economists support the abandoning of discretionary fiscal policy, considered as a tool for managing aggregate demand in favour of a much more effective monetary policy. There are several reasons for his view.

The first is that there are significant delays associated with the introduction of fiscal policy in the real economy. Second, the nature of the sizes of the disturbance associated with booms and busts is unknown and, therefore, lack of knowledge of the necessary size of changes in fiscal policy is prevalent. Third, fiscal stimulus crowds out the private sector. Fourth, there is the long running argument of incompetence or unwillingness of policy makers to manage the economy accordingly. Fifth, regardless of the effect of crowding out, fiscal policies require large budget deficit financing in the long term, which brings about a need to bear a greater burden of taxation.[1]

For these reasons, in modern developed economies the managing of crises is mainly focused on monetary policy. Although its ultimate goal is to ensure price stability, GDP growth goals occupy monetary policy makers just as often as inflation concerns do. However, in the recent financial crisis, monetary policy has been fully exercised up to a point where there is no more room for further macroeconomic stimulation. Therefore, the euro area is now in a situation in which the short-term nominal interest rates cannot be further reduced because they are near or close enough to the zero bound so that it becomes binding and ECB is not able to further reduce them. The liquidity trap concept introduced by Keynes that deals with this phenomenon indicates that if the interest rate falls to such a low level, the increase in money supply may not be effective in accelerating production growth, because of the lack of sensitivity of investment to the interest rates. This means that monetary policy becomes ineffective. When this situation occurs in conjunction with the nominal price and wage rigidity, the financial system cannot fulfill its role of effectively managing the allocation of consumption and investment, resulting in a prolonged economic depression.

Until now, the traditional response of economists to this problem was to recommend the use of aggressive monetary and fiscal policies. In this case, the aggressiveness amounts to the central bank's commitment to a temporary or permanent increase in inflation or lump-sum cash transfers to the financial institutions. These actions may cause an increase in prices, which lowers the real interest rate, even if the nominal interest rate is still equal to zero (or slightly positive). Similarly, fiscal policy can neutralize the lower limit of interest rates, even in the case of the liquidity trap, but only if debt remains sustainable.[2]

---

[1] Ł. Goczek, *Długookresowe skutki stabilności polityki fiskalnej*, „Zeszyty Naukowe UE we Wrocławiu", 2010.

[2] Ł. Goczek, *Policy Response to the 2007–2009 Financial Crisis*, "Equilibirum" 6 (3) 2011.

Today, however, is seems that the possibilities of pursuing an effective macroeconomic policy aimed at stimulating economic activity have come to a breakdown and this is particularly evident in the European Union. The instruments of this policy were from the beginning either impossible to use in a monetary union and fixed exchange rates against the euro (in the case of many smaller countries outside the zone), or they have already been used until exhaustion of their effectiveness.

First, in order to stabilize the European financial system, linked to the US financial system, the European Central Bank (ECB) used an aggressive expansionary monetary policy, and when it reached the limit of zero or near zero interest rates, the countries applied unprecedented fiscal stimulation. This amounted to increased government borrowing to replace the missing private sector borrowing. The ECB, in particular, has implemented large liquidity injections into the credit markets in order to restore lending. While at the outset this should have a direct effect on lending, this was not the case as banks engaged in precautionary hoarding of liquidity or purchased assets at prices well below the level at which new lending becomes attractive. At the same time, however, the financial crisis transformed into a global crisis that caused a sharp drop in economic activity in the United States with the unemployment rate remaining persistently high even after the world economy started to recover. The worldwide recession that resulted from the financial crisis turned out to be the most severe economic contraction since the depression of the 1930s.

This resulted in the nationalization of private debt which was transferred to the budgets of states. Soon, the fiscal expansion has encountered resistance from the debt sustainability constraints. At this point, the ECB entered an unprecedented era of macroeconomic policy.[3] It consisted of the expansion of the European Central Bank balance sheets against debt instruments issued by states and risky instruments from private companies. This amounted to the widening scope of the intervention in order to provide missing liquidity in the interbank market. The effect of such a broad-based intervention was to destabilize the common currency, exacerbating the growing Balance of Payments imbalances which was at this time covered by the lack of balance from the contributions of individual member countries in the ECB. Although it must be emphasized that the severity of these problems is not the same in different countries, and some of them deviate to some extent from this pattern, the overall trend is common to all member states.

---

[3] Ibid., 4.

Nevertheless, it can be argued that until the financial crisis, worsening problems of European Union countries were not seen as fully manifested. The actual level of intervention and imbalances is covered by foreign transfers of the ECB in the eurozone[4] and uncontrolled indebtedness of countries that do not yet have the possibility to recover a competitive advantage through the depreciation of their currencies,[5] such as the so-called PIIGS countries (Portugal, Italy, Ireland, Greece, Spain). These imbalances could be traced back to the lack of integration of fiscal policy across members of the euro area. The adoption of euro was accompanied first by imposing convergence criteria on budget deficits and public debt, and then by the Stability and Growth Pact (SGP) which established some rules about deficits. For some high-debt countries (e.g. Italy, Belgium, and Greece), the threat of being left out served as an incentive to initiate fiscal adjustments. However, once the euro was introduced, the threat of exclusion vanished, large deficits reappeared in several member countries, and the SGP was widely violated.[6] This has caused a growing debt crisis in most of the European Union's peripheral countries.[7]

All actions aimed at a short-run stabilization to maintain the present high standard of living in Europe, but it may be that these actions were short-sighted. They have increased the level of debt and current debt levels of many EU countries that have exceeded their repayment capabilities. In view of the results of empirical studies[8] which show a negative relationship between economic growth and the level of debt, countries with large deficits on current accounts can have serious consequences for the further growth of the EU's economy. The need to repay debts resulting from the crisis, together with interest, reduces future growth, and in turn it reduces the chances of repayment of debts in a vicious circle. Therefore, the reasons for the lack of effectiveness of a short-run stimulation could potentially be the problems associated with a long-term decline of Europe as the economic centre of the world. These problems can be thought of as

[4] H-W. Sinn, T. Wollmershäuser, *Target Loans, Current Account Balances and Capital Flows: The ECB's Rescue Facility*, "CESifo Working Paper Series 3500", CESifo Group Munich 2011.

[5] M. Feldstein, *The Euro and European Economic Conditions*, "NBER Working Paper Series", Vol. 17617 (2011).

[6] Ł. Goczek, *Przyczyny kryzysu fiskalnego w Unii Europejskiej*, in *Bilans polskiej prezydencji w Unii Europejskiej*, ISP PAN (2012).

[7] Peripheral in the economic sense, which differs from the political sense, as the author was informed during discussion.

[8] Ł. Goczek, *Dług, wzrost gospodarczy i kryzys finansowy*, „Prace i materiały Instytutu Handlu Zagranicznego Uniwersytetu Gdańskiego" 28 (1) (2010):

structural barriers to growth and the next part of the chapter covers these barriers in detail.

Structural Barriers to Economic Growth in the European Union

Four potential sources of long-term economic stagnation in Europe can be identified. The first one are the demographic problems in the labour market. The second one is an insufficient aggregate demand caused by the lower purchasing power of pensioners held by unsustainable pension systems. The third source is weak innovation and resulting stagnation of productivity in Europe. The fourth is regional imbalances that manifest themselves in adverse terms of trade conditions and worsening Balance of Payments imbalances of peripheral countries against the economic core of Europe.

The economically most important effect seems to be the impact on the decrease in productivity through the labour market. Currently, most of Europe's population lives in regions where fertility has fallen below the level of simple renewability for generations. This is due to the so-called second demographic transition from high mortality and high fertility to low mortality and low fertility. Partly in response to these changes, fertility declines because parents can now afford to give birth to fewer children, expecting that the greater number of them survive. Declining fertility results in slower population growth, reducing the number of children and causing the structure of the population to age. Over time, reduced fertility also leads to a reduction in the number of young people, and eventually to a reduction in the fraction of people working.[9] Moreover, the same advances in medicine that caused the decline in infant mortality also resulted in the lengthening of life expectancy. These combined phenomena result in the further ageing of the population. Europe has become the leader of these negative trends and quickly reached levels of fertility below 1.3 children per woman.

This situation has dramatic consequences: if fertility persists at such a level, it will result in a decrease in the number of births in a given year by 50 % and a reduction of the population by half in just 45 years. The average rate of fertility in Europe is only 1.31, i.e. slightly above the level of 1.30. What's more, the improvement is unlikely. After the fertility rates

---

[9] Ł. Goczek, *Bariera demograficzna w marketingu nowych technologii*, „Biuletyn Polskiej Akademii Nauk Komitet Przestrzennego Zagospodarowania Kraju" 235 (2007), 182–193.

decline below this level, this will set off demographic processes that seek to perpetuate the low fertility. This will mean that in several years, Europe will be an old, almost childless society. In 2050, there will be as much as 19 % less children aged up to fourteen years, as compared to the current level. Meanwhile, the number of people older than sixty-five will increase up to fifty-eight million, an increase of 77 % (see Fig. 21.1 below). The number of people over eighty will increase by 174 %.

These changes will bring serious economic consequences. Because of the demographic collapse, Europe's productivity per person will fall, as economic activity falls with the increasing ratio of people of retirement age for the entire population. Moreover, older workers, although more experienced which is valued in many professions, become, in the case of professions which are accompanied by physical activity, less productive with age. In addition, training them for another type of activity may not be possible at this age. The result of these demographic events may be increasing structural unemployment and a barrier to growth.

Fig. 21.1. European population by age group

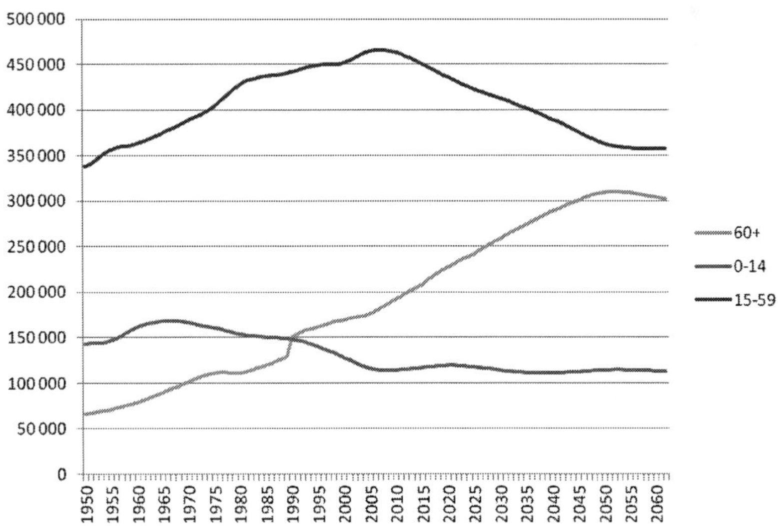

Source: Own research based on data from the United Nations, Department of Economic and Social Affairs, Population Division: *World Population Prospects DEMOBASE*, 2010.

Second, the countries with ageing populations will have trouble keeping up with countries with younger populations. This may be coupled with a drop in aggregate demand due to general impoverishment, associated with the transition of the growing percentage of the population to retirement. This is even more important, given the fact that current pay-as-you-go (PAYG) pension systems are already unbalanced and require additional budget transfers.[10] At the same time, modification of these systems is difficult because of obligations to current retirees having the legal nature of acquired rights. It is worth noting that with the ever-smaller generations entering the labour market it is not possible to balance the system even with additional state aid, because there is some kind of interchangeability between contributions from the employed and subsidies financed by taxes levied largely on the working population. Therefore, the end of the PAYG system seems inevitable. The need to increase the tax wedge in order to finance the deficit of the system in the future will be a serious barrier through which legal employment will become more expensive. As a result, the official unemployment rate may rise because people will try to escape the grey area and avoid paying taxes, registering at labour offices, and will receive benefits and force the state to pay for health insurance, generating high costs for the budget.

Capital funded schemes based on individual contributions are only a partial solution to the problem of smaller generations on the labour market. Moreover, the system requires work of young people, so that they can buy consumption goods produced by diminishing population. Otherwise, savings will be either worthless due to inflation or a fall in share prices due to a fall in productivity. Of course, this system outperforms the PAYG system in terms of debt obligations, but it should be emphasized that there is no easy way out of demographic problems in the labour market.

---

[10] In these systems, the payment of benefits is financed from current contributions of workers and subsidies to the system from the state budget if the current contributions are less than the pay-outs to existing pensioners.

Fig. 21.2. EU's total factor productivity as a fraction of the US total factor productivity

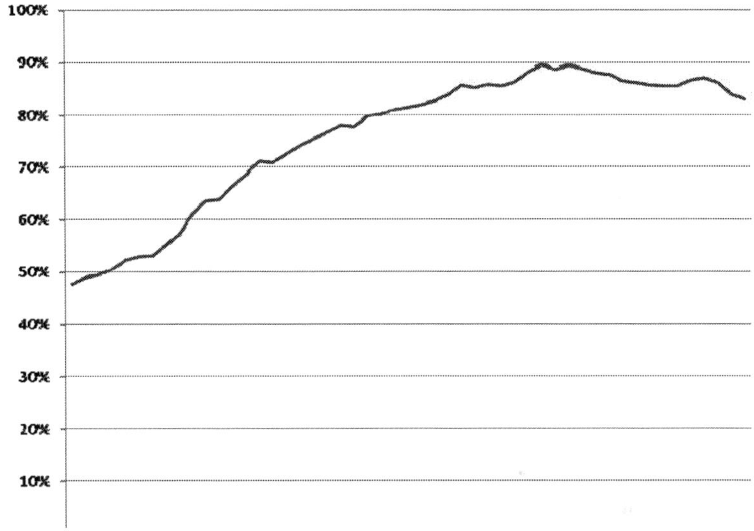

Source: Own research based on data from *The Conference Board Total Economy Database, September 2011.*

Third, technological innovation is low in the European Union and this causes a stagnation in total factor productivity. Back in 2004, the Lisbon strategy was devised to make the single market of the European Union the most competitive and dynamic knowledge-based economy in the world. The aim was to challenge the economic supremacy of the United States in the field of productivity. Today, it is easy to see that the distance between the European economy and the US did not decrease, but in fact it is increasing alarmingly (Fig. 21.2 below). This is particularly worrisome given the fact that the technological leaders in the race, the United States and Japan, seem to be widening the gap between themselves and Europe.[11]

The reasons for the strong resurgence of productivity in the United States are widely discussed in academic literature.[12] Firstly, these changes were driven by the rapid pace of innovation in information and

---

[11] Ł. Goczek, *Wyrosnąć z długów – polityka podażowa i regulacje w Unii Europejskiej*, in M. Guzek (ed.), *Ekonomia i polityka w kryzysie—kierunki zmian w teoriach*, (Warszawa: Uczelnia Łazarskiego, 2012).

[12] A. Aizcorbe, S. Oliner, Daniel E. Sichel, *Shifting Trends in Semiconductor Prices and the Pace of Technological Progress*, "Business Economics" 43 (3) (2008), 23–39.

communication technologies, which was in turn driven by the rapid and steady decline in semiconductor prices. With some delay, probably due to the necessary changes in production processes and organizational practices in the United States, there has been an increased factor of productivity in industries using new information and communication technologies, especially in services. Therefore, productivity growth in the United States seems to be a combination of a high level of investment in the rapidly progressing revolution of information and communication technologies in the late 1990s, and then the rapid productivity growth in the market services sector in the first half of 2000. On the other side of the Atlantic, the slowdown in productivity growth in European countries is largely the result of delayed investment in the telecommunications sector, a sector that Europe has not been able to create, despite protectionist attempts and an active industrial policy in this area. This was the reason for slower growth of productivity in market services, particularly in trade, finance, and business services.[13]

The problem of the European Union as a single market lies in the fact that borders of the member countries still have great importance for both businesses and consumers of services. The reason is a different kind of problem in the field of trade in services, in contrast to trade in goods—it is easier to produce goods in one country and sell them in another than to provide services across borders. In the case of services, trade problems arise because there are significant cultural, linguistic and regulatory barriers (individual member countries still differ to a great extent in regulating the market), which the entrepreneurs from the European Union are not able to overcome. Given the fact that the number of hours worked in market services is now more than 2.5 times larger than in manufacturing, these barriers are a significant impediment to economic growth in the EU, because low competitive pressure in the services sector holds back productivity. Competition in network industries is especially hindered by the incompleteness of the single market and regulatory barriers, and this prevents the EU countries from benefiting from large positive network externalities. Moreover, trade and allocation are distorted due to agricultural support under the Common Agricultural Policy (CAP), since it removes the economic incentive to concentrate economic activity, move to cities, and is thereby harmful to overall productivity by taking away resources from productive sectors and promoting global Balance of Payments imbalances.

---

[13] B. Van Ark, M. O'Mahony, M. Timmer, *The Productivity Gap Between Europe and the United States: Trends and Causes*, "Journal of Economic Perspectives" 22 (1) (2008), 25–44.

Fig. 21.3. Regulation level across the world

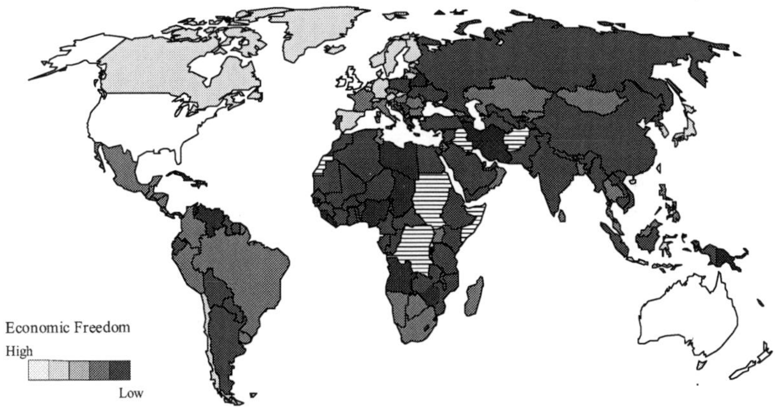

Source: Own research based on data from the Heritage Foundation

Furthermore, a relatively high level of regulation relative to productivity leaders (see Fig. 21.3 above) causes the EU's structural unemployment to be high and hours worked and labour force participation relatively low. This can be seen from the Fig. 21.4 below, in which the relation between regulation and productivity is portrayed (EU countries are on the decreasing right hand side of the figure which means that they exhibit an inefficiently high level of regulation). This allows us to conclude that right now in Europe there is no sign of a return to acceleration of the growth rate of total factor productivity, which highlights the urgent need to accelerate the pace of technological change and innovation, combined with continuing regulatory reform of labor and product markets.

Fig. 21.4. Regulation and productivity

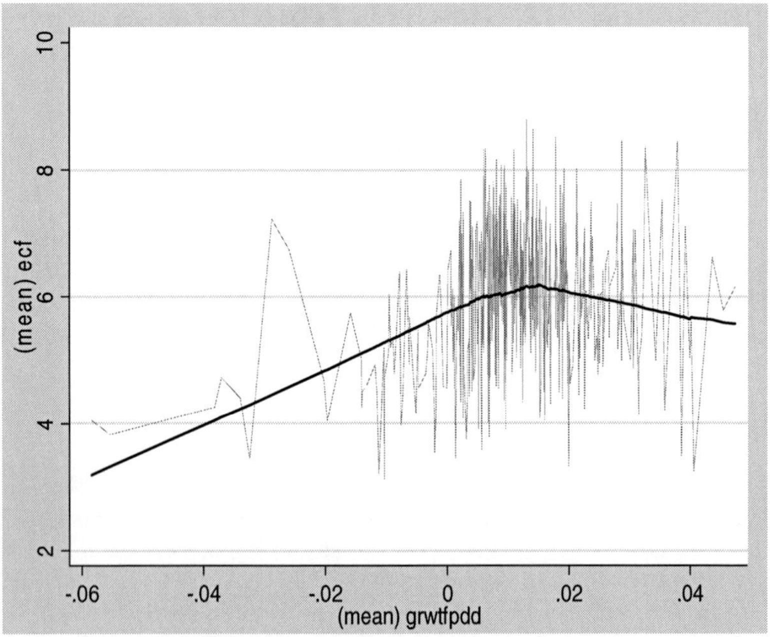

Source: Own research based on data from Goczek, *Analiza empiryczna regulacji gospodarki w kontekście innowacyjności i produktywności*, in *Rola informatyki w naukach ekonomicznych i społecznych*, edited by Z. Zieliński, (Kielce, 2011).

The fourth barrier is the Balance of Payments imbalances caused by the lack of ability of some countries to face an adverse aggregate shock, combined with an adverse shock to productivity. This can be particularly seen by comparing Germany's and the Netherland's current account surpluses with PIIGS countries current account deficits (see Fig. 21.5 below). As can be seen, this barrier becomes more pressing over time. What is worse is that the problems seem to be persistent, since the countries that face those shocks are continuingly not able to push socially costly reforms or devalue their currency under the monetary union regime. These imbalances will continue in the future, becoming apparent during numerous debt crises, unless there is some form of integrated approach to failing productivity growth in the peripheral countries of the European Union.

Fig. 21.5. European current account imbalances

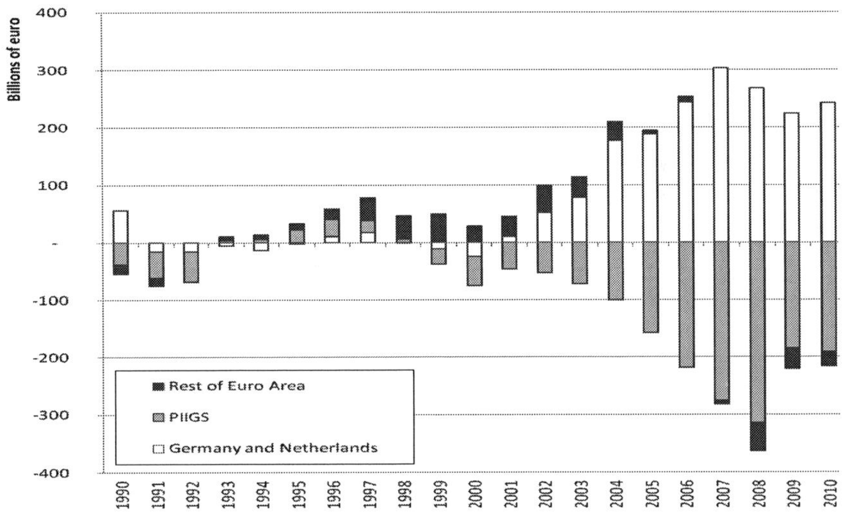

Source: Own research based on the International Monetary Fund, *Balance of Payments Statistics Yearbook* (2012).

Conclusions

The unprecedented response to the economic and financial crisis in terms of short-term stabilization and necessarily temporary measures taken to avert its effects for the euro currency stability have reduced the emphasis on the EU's and individual countries' economic reforms. This chapter has presented the case for the current crisis of the euro currency to be considered in the long-term context. It argues that, in fact, the reasons for the crisis are permanent and structural, focusing on problems associated with demographics and stagnation in productivity. While it is debatable as to whether the measures taken in response to the crisis have generally supported short-term demand and avoided worsening of the recession, it is crucial that the EU's politicians now turn their interest to economic policy reforms that will remove long-run barriers to growth. It could be pointed out that despite the fact that these problems are structural, their effects can be mitigated by supply side policies.[14] In particular, the

[14] J. Fernández-Villaverde, D. Guerrón-Quintana, J. Rubio-Ramírez, *Supply-Side*

productivity and employment effects associated with the removal of various anti-competitive barriers to competition can be large even in the short run. In most cases, pushing through reforms will require overcoming political obstacles to reform.[15] The outlook is optimistic, though, as economic crises often make structural weaknesses more visible, and thus may provide incentives for pursuing difficult reforms, for example in regulating the labour and product market.[16]

The author has a Ph.D. in Economic Sciences from the University of Warsaw. He specializes in macroeconomics and macroeconomic policy.

Policies and the Zero Lower Bound, "CEPR Discussion Paper" No. 8642, November 2011.

[15] *Economic Policy Reforms: Going for Growth 2010*, OECD, Paris 2010.

[16] A. Bassanini, L. Nunziata, D. Venn, *Job protection legislation and productivity growth in OECD countries*, "Economic Policy" 24 (2009): 349–402.

Chapter Twenty-Two

Poland's Mass Privatization Programme: Institutions and the Market

Chris O'Neill

Who remembers John Cleese, from the British comedy group Monty Python? After the well-known 1970s show *Monty Python's Flying Circus*, Cleese created *Fawlty Towers* in which he played the owner and operator of the small hotel of the title. Fawlty is a play on the word Faulty, as in deficient. As a hotel owner, Cleese is in a customer service intensive business, but hates people—an inherent contradiction that makes for good comedy but undermines the sense of his business. And so it went with Poland's mass privatization programme, built on an inherent contradiction: institutions that the state created but then neglected. It was true that these institutions were flawed, but most importantly they were poorly overseen and controlled by the state, with the end result being an institutional and economic failure.

Overview

The mass privatization programmes in the former Soviet sphere were economic experiments fueled by ideology and the perceived need to privatize large numbers of state-owned enterprises (SOEs). The negative economic outcomes of these programmes have been attributed to their occurrence in institutional voids that led to market imperfections. Poland's MP programme, on the other hand, enjoyed a robust institutional framework both in terms of the structure of the programme itself and in the capacity of the state to effect and enforce a rule of law. In Poland's case, this institutional capacity facilitated the economic failure of the programme. The programme created "institutional enrichment platforms" for insiders from NIF funds and management firms to prey on common goods, and provided the legal sanction of their operational control of equity that facilitated their actions. This sanction was strengthened by Poland's adherence to the rule of law. In addition, the Polish state adopted a policy of passivity that tolerated mismanagement by these state-created market institutions responsible for secondary privatization. This process of privatization was not effective in protecting and developing the economic potential of the common goods entrusted to the programme, but instead led to their dissolution or decrease. The key ingredients of this institutional failure were the deficient design and particularly the deficient application of the programme. The state, in spite of its legal right to control the course of the programme, remained passive and allowed market forces to utilize state-created institutional infrastructure of the programme to its short-term advantage.

Mass Privatization: a Product of its Times

Mass privatization (MP) was one of the more innovative approaches to privatization that took place in the former countries of the Soviet bloc. It entailed the issuance to the general public of vouchers or certificates for free or at nominal charge that would allow them to participate in the privatization of a significant amount of pre-selected state-owned enterprises (SOEs). Seventeen out of the twenty-two nations that arose from the former Soviet bloc introduced MP programmes and of these, twelve were large, encompassing at least 25 % of medium and large SOEs and taking place over several years.[1] These programmes emphasized market forces over institutional frameworks.

The negative economic and social effects of rapid and massive MP has been the subject of numerous studies.[2] Even the World Bank, an early

[1] L. King, P. Hamm, *The Governance Grenade: Mass Privatization, State Capacity and Economic Development in Postcommunist and Reforming Communist Societies*, "Technology Governance Working Papers in Technology Governance and Economic Dynamics" 40, Tallinn, 2008. See Appendix C for breakdown of program size. Note, Slovenia and Bulgaria also had MP programs.

[2] See: K. Pistor, A. Spicer, *Investment Funds in Mass Privatization and Beyond Evidence from the Czech Republic and Russia*, Center for International Development (web archive), paper 565, 1996, http://www.cid.harvard.edu/hiid/565.pdf (accessed March 5, 2102); A. Spicer, G.A. McDermott, B. Kogut, *Entrepreneurship and Privatization in Central Europe: The Tenuous Balance Between Destruction and Creation*, "The Academy of Management Review" 25 (3) (2000), 630–649; B. Black, R. Kraakman, A. Tarassova, *Russian Privatization and Corporate Governance: What Went*

proponent and financier of mass privatization that also participated in creating the political climate that made mass privatization possible[3] issued a report critical of mass privatization.[4] One of the major conclusions of most of these studies was that the lack of proper institutions and excessive speed were the main causes of mass privatization's negative outcomes. Even Russian MP programme advisors and architects such as Dmitry Vasilev, David Pitt-Watson, Ira Lieberman, Vladmir Mau and Anders Aslund, cite the institutional void as key to the negative economic impact of that country's mass privatization programme.[5]

The National Investment Fund Programme

Poland's programme was unique. It was limited in scale, occurred over a prolonged transitional period and took place within a structured institutional context that tried to channel the power of the market to the benefit of participating companies.

Wrong?, "Stanford Law Review" 52 (2000), 1731–1808; Z. Sid Blaha, *Czech Capital Markets: a View from Abroad*, http://samba.fsv.cuni.cz/~blahaz/ (accessed March 5, 2012); B. Kogut, A. Spicer, *Institutional Technology and the Chains of Trust: Capital Markets and Privatization in Russia and the Czech Republic*, W. Davidson Institute [University of Michigan], "Working Paper" 291, March 1999; L. King, *Shock Privatization: The Effects of Rapid Large-Scale Privatization on Enterprise Restructuring*, "Politics & Society" 31 (1) (2003), 3–30; J. Miller, *Evaluation of Mass Privatization in Bulgaria*,W. Davidson Institute, "Working Paper" 814, 2006; L. King, P. Hamm, *The Governance Grenade: Mass Privatization, State Capacity and Economic Development in Postcommunist and Reforming Communist Societies, Technology and Governance*, "Working Papers in Technology Governance and Economic Dynamics", Tallinn, 2008, 40; D. Stuckler, L. King, M. McKee, *Mass Privatisation and the Post Communist Mortality Crisis: A Cross-National Analysis*, "Lancet" 373 (9661) (2009), 399–407.

3 J. Nellis, *The World Bank, Privatization and Enterprise Reform in Transition Economies: A Retrospective Approach*, The World Bank, Washington DC, 2002, 50. According to Polish ministerial workers, World Bank consultants working on Poland's mass privatization programme in the Polish ministry of ownership transformation in the early 1990s were "enthusiastic believers": ministry of treasury interviews MSP–2, Jan. 5, 2012, MSP–1, April 2011.

4 Ibid., 50.

5 C. O'Neill, *Transcript from the CEELBAS conference: Privatization in Russia: Decisions and Outcomes 1991-1997*, St. Anthony's College, Oxford November 12–13, 2010 [unpublished notes]. For the most part, however, except for David Pitt-Watson, they see the economic outcome as secondary in importance to the political goal of removal economic property from state control. Ibid.

Poland's MP programme differed from the region's other MP programmes in that institutions had the opportunity to play a significant role in the programme's realization. In terms of strength of institutions and the dynamics of institution building, Poland post-1989 was relatively robust in the context of the countries of the former Soviet bloc. Poland emerged from the Soviet period with both strong trade unionism and a large and articulate political class, instruments that helped to channel popular sentiment into the political process. Poland's institutional foundation was strengthened in the early 1990s by the creation of financial institutions such as the Warsaw Stock Exchange (1991) and numerous other entities and statutory acts meant to regulate economic activity and to make it transparent. In a study on the institutional characteristics of nation states, the French Ministry of Economy placed Poland in a category with France, Japan, Norway, Germany and Korea, countries that it classified as: "mildly liberal" and which "ensure ... security and protection of citizens through proper application of the law ... [and where] ... security and transactions and property rights go hand in hand with an efficient administration".[6]

According to the Worldwide Governance index, Poland in 1996 scored much higher than almost all other post-Soviet mass privatizers in areas such as government effectiveness, regulatory quality and rule of law. Under the indicators of "rule of law", "regulatory quality" and "government effectiveness", Poland scored 79, 70 and 80 compared to Russia's 30, 31 and 28. Only the Czech Republic had similar results.[7] Scholars, however, that specifically compared Poland's regulatory climate to that of Czech, found that Poland's financial regulation and company law to be of higher quality and more stringently enforced then that of its southern neighbour.[8]

---

[6] P. Berthelier, A. Desdoigts, J. Ould Aoudia, *Institutionnal* [sic] *Profiles Presentation and Analysis of an Original Database of the Institutional Caracteristics* [sic] *of Developing, in Transition and Developed Countries*, [French] Ministry of the Economy, Finance and Industry, Paris 2003, 35–36.

[7] Worldwide Governance Indicators,
http://info.worldbank.org/governance/wgi/pdf/c177.pdf [Poland],
http://info.worldbank.org/governance/wgi/pdf/c187.pdf [Russia],
http://info.worldbank.org/governance/wgi/pdf/c57.pdf [Czech],
http://info.worldbank.org/governance/wgi/pdf_country.asp (accessed May 5, 2012).

[8] See: S. Johnson, A. Shleifer, *Coase V. The Coasians*, National Bureau of Economic Research, "Working Paper" 7447, Cambridge (MA) 1999; I. Grosfeld, I. Hashi, *Changes in Ownership Concentration in Mass Privatised Firms: Evidence from Poland and the Czech Republic*, "Corporate Governance-an International Review" 15 (4) (2007).

It was upon this platform of a relatively successful rule of law, and institutionalized instruments of societal control over the political process, that Poland constructed its mass privatization programme, utilizing institutions that were newly created for the NIF programme as well as adapted institutions. We can categorize the specific-purpose entities, the laws and contracts that made up these institutions into three subcategories or groups: custom-built and program-specific institutions; adapted institutions and, lastly; instruments. The first two groups will be characterized.

The first group consisted of three types of actors: the fifteen National Investment Funds (NIFs), modelled on private equity funds, into which the 512 portfolio companies were evenly divided; the private management firms that were hired by the individual funds (first vetted by the ministry) to restructure and successfully privatize NIF participant companies, and; the NIF department at the Ministry of Treasury, meant to oversee the interest of the state.

The second group, adapted institutions, consisted of the NIF supervisory boards and the portfolio firm supervisory boards. In Polish commercial law, supervisory boards constitute the highest authority (except for shareholder meetings) of economic entities. It is the supervisory board that puts into place decisions that affect entity operational activity and thus, for example, management board appointments and approving company investment and restructuring activities. During the first stage of the MP programme that lasted from 1995 to 1999, the state had a controlling equity in the NIFs, and thus, through its representatives, had direct and indirect control over both levels of supervisory boards.

It is important to emphasize that the legal structure of this gradual MP programme retained for the state direct and indirect ownership of 85 % of equity of each participant company and 100 % equity of each fund for roughly the first four years of the programme—that is until mid 1999 with the privatization of the funds themselves.

Concerning the size and make-up of the programme, in its final form it encompassed 512 companies, which constituted about 11 % of total state assets and employed 426,000 people.[9]

---

[9] Figure of state assets from M. Bojańczyk, *Program Narodowych Funduszy Inwestycyjnych* [National Investment Fund Programme], (Warszawa: Szkoła Główna Handlowa Oficyna Wydawnicza, 2002), 8; The amount of employees (for 1993) from A. Suwalski, *Uwłaszczenie* obywateli *jako element polskiej prywatyzacji* [TheTransferal of Ownership to Citizens as an Element of Polish Privatization], (Poznań: AE Poznań, 2004), 154.

Table 22.1. Portfolio companies based on branch

Transport	2 %
Trade	3 %
Construction	12.5 %
Other industry	3 %
Metal working industry	2 %
Wood and paper industry	5.5 %
Chemical industry	7.5 %
Mineral industry	8.5 %
Food processing	11.5 %
Light manufacturing	12.5 %
Electro machinery	28.5 %

Source: Kostrz-Kostecka, *Narodowe Fundusze Inwestycyjne na giełdzie* [National Investment Funds on the Exchange], (Warsaw 1997), 50.

Table 22.2. Portfolio companies based on employee amount

To 50 persons	1 %
51-100	2.8 %
101-200	8.4 %
201-500	33.6 %
501-1000	33.8 %
over 1000	20.4 %

Source: *Prywatyzacja przesiębiorstw państwowych według stanu na 30.06.1998* [Privatization of State Enterprises as of June 30, 1998], GUS [Central Statistical Office], (Warsaw, 1998).

Outcomes

What were the economic outcomes of this programme?

Based on a longitudinal (1995–2005) and cross-sectional study of a sample of seventy-four companies that participated in the programme (out of a total 512) and about thirty elite interviews of management firm personnel, portfolio company management and ministry personnel:

(1) The NIF programme did not contribute to Poland's economic growth.
(2) Most of the firms that participated in the programme had poorer economic results in 2005 than when they entered the programme in 1995.

Data from the National Commercial Court Registry[10] (herein known as KRS) from an ongoing research project reveal a negative trajectory of economic outcomes for NIF portfolio companies. In 2005, ten years after the commencement of the National Investment Fund programme, most of its participating portfolio companies were worse off than they were in 1995. Out of a sample of seventy-four NIF participant firms, forty-eight were still in existence in 2005 and of these only sixteen experienced real sales growth, and six of this sixteen grew at a rate that exceeded Poland's economic growth over 1995–2005, thus making themselves more significant in size in 2005, relative to the country's economy, than they were in 1995.[11] Thus, only sixteen of the seventy-four NIF companies

[10] [KRS] Krajowy Rejestr Sądowy [National Commercial Court Registry], Warsaw, Poznań, Bydgoszcz, Wrocław, Toruń, Łódź and Kraków offices, most visits made in first eight months of 2010. Through the KRS were accessed: **RHB** [Rejestr Handlowych – Registry of Commercial Companies] and **RPP** [Rejestr Przedsiębiorstw Państwowych – Registry of State-Owned Enterprises]. The citation "KRS", used in this chapter, includes RHB and RPP records. It would be onerous to cite all the specific KRS, RHB and RPP sources on the basis of which the data was created, particularly since citations are often based on composite data from numerous pages and documents of an act. The paperwork I created that I used to create my datasets, however, are all documented. I can provide specific references upon request. The following is the list of the act call nos. utilized in this paper (each number refers to documentation pertaining to a single entity, from one to multiple tomes). In many instances, the given KRS act call no. would also include RHB and sometimes RPP files. If that was not the case, and such files had to be ordered separately, the appropriate RHB no. is given below as well: **KRS:** 140844, 91927, 97716, 32536, 55763, 60928, 66883, 118325, 49603, 92108 165031, 179749, 208171, 130985, 67499, 46947, 25719, 35107, 169421, 223978, 163619, 203801, 130684, 34606, 75484, 175977, 248534, 19179, 41640, 150908, 128107, 155422, 11012, 113517, 92567, 96722, 206222, 24955, 64700, 58346, 64168, 103903, 49446, 66231, 130375, 220076, 59023, 13604, 13132, 24833, 33561, 48943, 6916, 133335, 42354, 142419, 11226, 29544, 86450, 125384, 71250, 91584, 46593, 134374, 20350, 22653, 123339, 84266, 60950, 24389; **RHB:** 931, 1007, 1289, 1013 Siedlce; 1460, 1553, 1571, 1447, 1520 Radom; 5816, 8365, 3806, 5984, 8246 Krakow; 2204 Kielce; 30655, 42546 Warszawa; 585 Ciechanów; 367 Tarnów; 915 Płock; 1943 Torun.

[11] Annual inflation data from *Miesięczne wskaźniki cen towarów i usług konsumpcyjnych w latach 1989-2012* (Monthly price indices of consumer goods and services from 1989 till 2012), Główny Urząd Statystyczny (Central Statistical Office), http://www.stat.gov.pl/gus/5840_1638_PLK_HTML.htm (accessed March 5, 2012]. GDP growth based on data from *Historical Real GDP Values*, excel worksheet, http://www.ers.usda.gov/Search/?qt=historical+real+gdp+values (US Dep't of Agriculture Economic Research Service: Real Historical GDPs for baseline Countries and Regions) (accessed March 5, 2012).

examined did not shrink or disappear. The number of profitable companies dropped from 51 % (thirty-eight out of seventy-eight) in 1995 to 40 % (thirty out of the original seventy-four) in 2005. Sales revenue for this sample of seventy-four NIF firms came to 2,337,658,296 złoty in 1995 while sales revenue for those of this group still in existence in 2005 came to 2,552,274,222 złoty. When adjusted for inflation (calculated annually 1995–2005[12]), however, this 1995 sales revenue of 2,337,568,296 złoty would need to have grown to a level of 4,529,506,087 złoty in 2005 to equal the 1995 figure in real terms. If we include annual economic growth in this equation, the 1995 sales figure for these seventy-four NIF participant firms would need to have grown to 6,754,871,105 złoty in 2005 to correspond to its equivalent weight in Poland's 1995 economy.

We also see a drop of about 73 % in employment.[13] A sample of seventy-six NIF participant firms employed 48,520 persons in 1995.[14] In 2005, 13,399 persons were employed in the fifty-one firms from this sample that were still in existence.

These outcomes do not really constitute news; more interesting is why these outcomes occurred.

Role of Management

The role of management was key in determining the success or failure of individual firms and, by extension, of the success or failure of the programme itself. Defenders of the economic results of the programme will probably cite the poor state that many companies were in when they entered the programme. It is true that many companies were in a difficult economic situation and that many would not have survived in any case, and the great majority needed restructuring. However, many more would probably have survived and prospered under proper management, which the management firms generally did not provide. A study of KRS records[15] in the form of market and company reports and analyses contained

---

[12] *Miesięczne wskaźniki cen.*

[13] One author sees a drop from 426,000 in 1993 to about 125,000 in 2003. A. Suwalski, *Uwłaszczenie* Obywateli, 154.

[14] This includes nineteen firms for which only 1996 employment information was available, and one firm for which only 1994 employment information was available, thus the 1995 employment amount was undoubtedly higher. If we use a rate of 12 % personnel reduction from 1995 to 1996 (in keeping with examples of other NIF firms), we would have a 1995 amount of 49,786 employees for this sample of seventy-six firms.

[15] See footnote no. 11.

information on modernization and investment in technology, the search for cooperating/strategic partners or investors, personnel polices at management board and director levels, and asset and personnel rationalization, and showed a general correlation between the level (in terms of quality and quantity) of management factor data reported to the KRS, and their economic success. Research undertaken up to this point has identified what management companies could have done, and sometimes did, to help ensure the economic growth of their charges. In their striving for short-term returns, however, the management firms generally hindered rather then fostered the development of their charges.

Role of Institutions

The negative outcome of the NIF programme can be summed up in one equation: "Passive state + opportunistic management firms/funds = economic failure." The Polish state had a policy of passivity towards the operational aspect of the programme—that is, the secondary privatization to be carried out by the NIFs. The state created the programme, endowed it with the institutions of funds and management firms and brought these institutions to life by inviting the spirit of market forces to inhabit them. Then, on the seventh day, the state stood back and looked upon what it had wrought and ... did nothing. As Minister Emil Wąsacz wrote in response to a parliamentary interpellation concerning irregularities in the NIF management of FASTY, a large textile factory: "The Universal Privatization Programme is based on the principle that up until the complete disposal of NIF shares (and thus no later than 2005) held by the Ministry of Treasury, its role as an NIF shareholder will be passive."[16]

Issues of Institutional Size, Quality and Control

This approach is reflected in the tools the state used to oversee the programme. An indicator of the lack of emphasis that the state placed upon programme oversight and control are the numbers of employees dedicated to that purpose. The Ministry of the State Treasury was created in 1996 on the basis of the former Ministry of Ownership Transformation. During the period in question (1995–2005), roughly 800 people were employed in the Ministry. The amount of ministerial personnel, on the

[16] [Letter to parlamentary deputy Józef Mozelewski from Minister of Treasury Emil Wąsacz], December 5, 1997, Ministry of State Treasury archives, act call no. 2425/12, 100.

other hand, working on the NIF programme ranged from about sixty during the programme's conceptual and preparatory phase (1991–1995) to an average of twenty persons during the programme's operational period from 1996 onwards. By 2005, only eight employees were expressly dedicated to NIF affairs.[17]

The state's basic tools for exercising oversight and control were through the supervisory boards of the NIF funds and the NIF portfolio companies. Since, as mentioned before, for the first three to four years of the programme, most of the equity in direct or indirect form was in the hands of the state, specifically the Ministry of the Treasury, the state had the power to exercise effective oversight and control. To do so, however, it would have had to cross the border between the mechanical exercise of its legal rights and an interventional policy of pro-active control. It did not do so—its passivity manifested itself in the **small size** of its NIF department, the **dubious quality** of fund and portfolio company supervisory board members representing the state and the tenuous and **problematic control** that the NIF department often had over these state appointees.

In the opinion of a longtime former NIF department director:

> … in the great majority of cases, representatives [fund SP members] were appointed who should not have been there. They did not have the experience and knowledge enough to exercise control in a correct manner. Usually they were appointees from a "political key". So even if something was going on in the fund, before members of the supervisory board found out, it was too late; rather most of them did not even discern these things and we would find out ourselves that something was not right only when looking through the paperwork. They were weak representatives.[18]

One former VP of a management firm, and later president of an NIF fund, described these first appointees as passive, afraid to take pro-active positions: "They accepted the management firm fees; they accepted the sales of portfolio companies; but they were afraid to accept bankruptcies and liquidations."[19]

In addition to the quality of fund supervisory board members, there was the issue of control. The NIF department, as the operational arm of the Ministry in exercising oversight and control over the funds, had three instruments of "mechanical" oversight and control: quarterly reports, lengthy documents detailing the economic condition of the entity; voting instructions for SP representatives at shareholder meetings, and; post-

---

[17] Interview – MSP -1.
[18] Ibid.
[19] Interview FM-4, October 27, 2010.

meeting reports on votes taken.[20] According to the former NIF department director:

> These were professors, very important people, they felt the prestige of their position as fund supervisory board members, and thus the influence of the NIF department on these supervisory boards was zero. We were not partners for discussion with them. The department was simply not "at their level". They contacted with the ministers, not with departments. Sometimes I did have someone from the supervisory board who would come every quarter and provide feedback, but that was a rarity.[21]

The issues of quality and control also appear in reference to the representatives of the state treasury that sat on the portfolio company supervisory boards. These representatives of the state could be employees of the Ministry, the preference of the director of the NIF department:

> A ministry employee is better at controlling the companies, he/she knows the policies of the ministry and as an employee, I have contact with him, I have influence over him, regardless of whether he is in my department or another. I call him to report and please give me this and that information and he does.[22]

Most of the SP representatives on the supervisory boards of NIF portfolio companies were not, however, employees of the Ministry. Between 1995 and 2005, the amount ranged from 10–30 %, depending on the political party in power. The rest were chosen from outside the Ministry (from a pool of several thousand persons that had passed the standardized supervisory board member exam), a process imbued with

---

[20] From a review of documents concerning the Ministry of Treasury oversight concerning fourteen selected NIF companies (various funds and branches and with weak, middling and strong economic status) from 1995–2005. Archiwum Ministerstwa Skarbu Państwa [Archives of Ministry of Treasury]. These companies are: Krakowska Fabryka Aparatów Pomiarowych KFAP S.A.; Mera Pnefal S.A.; Warszawskie Przedsiębiorstwo Budownictwa Przemysłowego Kablobeton S.A.; Bydgoska Fabryka Urządzeń Chłodniczych Byfuch S.A.; Zakłady Tworzyw Sztucznych 'ERG' Wąbrzeźno; Białostockie Zakłady Przemysłu Bawełnianego „Fasty" SA; Fabryka maszyn „Fadroma" w Wrocławiu SA; Zakłady Chemiczne Jelchem SA; Warszawskie Zakłady Fotochemiczne Foton SA; Zakłady Graficzne im. Komisji Edukacji Narodowej; Bydgoszcz Bawełna Silesiana SA; Szydłowieckie Kopalnie Kamienia Budowlanego „Skalbud" SA; Zakłady drzewiarskie 'Mewa' SA, and Polmo-Łódź SA.

[21] MSP-1.

[22] Ibid.

political pressures as all appointments required the signature of the minister, a politician.

The quality of these appointees was often an issue:

> They were political appointees, not chosen for competence, and thus often lacking knowledge and experience. We had supervisory boards, where there was no lawyer member, or nobody from the company's particular branch of industry, but with three economists or three financial analysts.[23]

This was compounded by the profile of the representatives from the management companies. According to the former president of a management firm: "The two or three supervisory board members from the management firm tended to be economists or financial analysts that were often not prepared for the particular company's needs."[24]

The matter of control over these external appointees to SP seats on company supervisory boards was also an issue:

> I had SP representatives that I, director of the NIF department, never saw face to face. Such representatives went to confess to the minister, not to me. How was the department to conduct oversight? I had one guy, now a parliamentary deputy, who was SP representative back then. He was a politician all along. And I had zero information from him about a company where there was a strike or something hot was going on. I phoned to say that this cannot continue, and I was told directly: "Regardless of what happens, we will not remove this guy." That is how it was, from the beginning of the programme.[25]

The struggle for information also had a logistical aspect. The companies had a month in which to prepare and submit their quarterly report, which meant that the SP had information post factum.

Institutional Deficiencies

Thus, for one part of the equation we have sanctioned passivity and a limited and ineffectual bureaucracy responsible for oversight and control. The next crucial element constituted the national investment funds, and particular their operational arms, the management firms. These firms were primarily populated with private equity/venture capital type people that

---

[23] Ibid.

[24] FM-6, series of interviews spring and summer 2011.

[25] MSP-1. About half were removed through the initiative of the department and half from the minister. Ibid.

were used to gaining returns from investments with three to five years and not industrial restructurers aiming to increase long-term potential, say, over a period of ten years. In terms of personnel, the management firms were heavy on the financial analysts and light with the restructuring specialists.

The management firms were not prepared to development long-term potential. They were interested in quicker returns. Although there were "stars" NIF companies of immediate market value—like the cement factories—for which strategic investors could be found quickly, or other companies in various sectors, such as ERG Wąbrzeźno (chemicals, plastic films) and PZZ Lublin (macaroni), the potential of which encouraged funds to take a nurturing approach to development. In most cases, it appears that the fund management firms did not adequately develop the economic potential of companies in their custody. In fact, it can be said that the proxy owners that were the management firms took an approach of managing assets, not potential.

This management of assets instead of potential, this search for short-term gain, and the fact that the management firms/funds, as proxy owners, enjoyed a very strong institutional position created for them by the state, a position reinforced by the relatively strong position of Poland's commercial law, which effectively sanctioned shareholder equity, facilitated various practices, evident from interviews, archive data and press reports, that I classify as dubious, borderline and illegal. Dubious practices were legal and consisted of focusing on the value of real estate and not the development of a company, which happened with many companies that held valuable property in cities. A good example is the process control company KWAP in Cracow. Another dubious practice was a quick sale to a buyer not interested or capable of developing long-term potential, such as the veterinary medicine producer Biowet Drwalew. The result was often asset stripping and company decline or destruction.[26]

The next category of "borderline" includes practices on the border of morality and legality, consisting of cross-investment, forcing companies to employ insider consultant companies at high prices. This created debt that was exchanged later for ownership shares, as in the case of Fabryka Urządzeń Dźwigowych in Mińsk Mazowiecki. In this example, management boards were reduced from, say, five to two hand-picked persons, to better facilitate management firm plans focused on liquidation and real estate sales. This exerted employment pressure on protesting

[26] Biowet escaped this predicament thanks to the proactive stance of its longtime director – and a lot of luck. Interview PC-2, Aug. 25, 2010; KRS records, Warszawa, act call no. 55763.

union representatives, (documented management firm practices at both KWAP and POLMO-Łódź, the latter a manufacturer of auto parts), resulting in the selling of companies to management firm insiders (as in the case of the commercial cooler producer Byfuch, located in Bydgoszcz). This illegal category consists of much of the above if the "acting against the economic interest of the company" can be proven, as well as cross-investment, which was outlawed in time.

The NIF programme created what can be called "institutional enrichment platforms". These are inhabited by insiders, mainly associated with the management firms and funds, that utilize their position and knowledge to embed themselves in NIF programme participant firms and to consequently enrich themselves from property entrusted to the mass privatization programme by the Polish state. An analysis of these institutional enrichment platforms is forthcoming.

Conclusions

A major goal of Poland's mass privatization programme was to prepare a significant portion of its industrial economy for privatization through the utilization of the assumed Western management expertise of the fund management firms. Despite the fact that the Polish programme was characterized by significantly more structure and probably more oversight than other mass privatization programmes in the region, this control and structure were insufficient to overcome deficiencies in good management practice towards NIF portfolio firms. In most cases it appears that the fund management firms did not adequately develop the economic potential of companies in their custody, and consequently did not provide their charges with effective long-term internal restructuring nor effective management.

The NIF programme might have been an example of how state involvement and foresight, through the creation of innovative economic institutions, could have had a beneficial effect on economic development, particularly in a period of transition of unequal players, increasing competition and institutions that were still being developed. Instead, it seems to be an example of the practical pitfalls of the inadequate preparation and inadequate application of such institutions. Mismanagement and negligent management of NIF participating companies had adverse effects on the Polish economy and caused the economic and societal dislocation of portfolio company employees. Fund management firms, instead of discharging their role of being the good shepherds of the portfolio companies and leading them through their period of transition, became one more factor of uncertainty in the portfolio companies' struggle of survival. They were not leaders but administrators, exhibiting an uneven mix of management practice and presiding over the economic decline of the majority of NIF programme participants.

The author is a PhD Candidate in Sociology at the Cambridge University. He specializes in economic transformation, its processes and societal outcomes.

CHAPTER TWENTY-THREE

THE CULTURE OF POVERTY IN POST-COMMUNIST COUNTRIES: THE CASE OF MOLDOVA

ALEKSANDRA JANUS

The process of transition has brought a lot of new phenomena to post-Soviet countries. Some of them are positive, but the young democracies also have to cope with certain problems and challenges. One of them is the problem of poverty. This is not only an economic phenomenon, but also a social and cultural one. In this chapter, the non-economic aspects of poverty in the Republic of Moldova are stressed.

To start, it is worth to present one of the most famous theories that shows the relations between culture and poverty—Oscar Lewis' conception of culture of poverty. Lewis (1914–1970), an American anthropologist, created his idea after much research in different parts of the world. Finally, he came to the conclusion:

> The culture of poverty is not just a matter of deprivation or disorganization, a term signifying the absence of something. It is the culture in the traditional anthropological sense in that it provides human beings with a design for living, with a ready-made set of solutions for human problems, and so serves a significant adaptive function.[1]

Lewis also specified some characteristic features of the culture of poverty, amongst them:

- the tendency to create non-formal relationships,

[1] O. Lewis, *The culture of poverty*, "Scientific American" 215 (4) (1966), 19, http://lchc.ucsd.edu/MCA/Mail/xmcamail.2010_11.dir/pdfKPNFlustp6.pdf (accessed December 10, 2011).

- special economy: buying small quantities of food at higher prices, the lack of food supplies, informal credit arrangement between neighbours, and use of secondhand clothing and furniture,
- disengagement from larger society, hostility to basic institutions, and mistrust of government and people on higher positions,
- poor housing and overcrowding,
- the family not cherishing childhood as a prolonged and protected stage in the life cycle,
- early initiation into sex,
- a strong feeling of fatalism, helplessness, dependence and inferiority.[2]

It is also important that Lewis noticed that being poor not necessarily means belonging to the culture of poverty. He also points out that this phenomenon is characteristic for Western societies, and mentioned the conditions that have let it develop:

> The setting is cash economy, with wage labor and production for profit and with persistent rate of unemployment and underemployment, at low wages, for an unskilled labor. The society fails to provide social, political and economical organization, on either a voluntary basis or by government imposition, for the low-income population.[3]

This chapter is an attempt to see the Moldovan society from this point of view and to show some important non-economical aspects of poverty. It is hard to compare the poor people of Moldova with those from Mexico City or Puerto Rico, who were the subject of Lewis' researching. The anthropologist mentioned that communist countries are a special case of culture of poverty and require special treatment. Moreover, there has to be taken into consideration the fact that, for Lewis, the culture of poverty was transmitted from one generation to another, and the process of transition is too short to talk about the existence of intergenerational phenomenon. Here the non-economical aspects of poverty in Moldova are presented, and the need for the non-economic research in the area of poverty is stressed.

Moldova is considered to be one of Europe's poorest countries. According to the National Human Development Report of the Republic of Moldova, absolute poverty has fallen from 67.8 % in 2000 to 26.3 % in 2009, but the character of this reduction is unsustainable, what can be noticed in the employment rate (it has declined from 54.8 % in 2000 to

---

[2] Ibid., 19–25.

[3] Ibid., 21.

40.0 % in 2009).[4] For many people in Moldova the process of transition was particularly hard. Some who once had a normal life suddenly found themselves in very poor conditions. As Charles King describes it:

> Soviet propaganda portrayed MSSR as a flourishing orchard, a region nestled in the rolling hills along the Dnester, where happy peasants collected the bountiful harvest for delivery to the other fraternal people of the Soviet Union.[5]

Rural areas were parts of the country that suffered most during the transition. A lot of people lost their positions and became poor, although in the previous system they had had a normal life. Now poor housing, overcrowding and sometimes even the lack of food became their everyday reality leading them to desperation. Subsistence hardship was followed by a feeling of shame. Hermine de Soto and Nora Dudwick in their work quote a lot of poor people's opinions. Here are some examples:

> For a poor person everything is terrible—illness, humiliation, shame. We are cripples. We are afraid of everything. We depend on everyone. No one needs us—we are like garbage that everyone wants to get rid of.[6]

> Poverty is pain; it feels like disease. It attacks a person not only materially but also morally. It eats away one's dignity and drives one into total despair. A person feels poverty every moment without even noticing it.[7]

Earning money has become one of the most problematic things. Moldovans don't trust their government to help them. The Labor Force Survey conducted by the National Bureau of Statistics shows that in 2009 over 23 % of the total active population worked abroad, mainly due to the lack of work in Moldova, or because of low salaries. The majority were men from rural areas. Over three quarters were 25–54 years old. They

---

[4] *National Human Development Report 2010/2011,* Chisinau 2011, 3, www.undp.md/presscentre/2011/NHDR2010_2011/NHDReaport_2010_ENG_26-04-11_web.pdf (accessed January 13, 2012).

[5] Ch. King, *The Moldovans. Romania, Russia and the politics of culture*, (Stanford: Hoover Press, 1999), 99.

[6] H. De Soto, N. Dudwick, *Eating from One Pot: Survival Strategies in Moldova's Collapsing Rural Economy*, in N. Dudwick, E. Gomart, A. Marc (eds.), *When Things Fall Apart. Qualitative Studies of Poverty on the Former Soviet Union*, (Washington: World Bank, 2002), 341.

[7] Ibid., 335.

found employment in construction (53.0 %), private households (19.6 %), and trade (11.4 %).[8]

Migrations influence not only the people who are leaving the country, but also their families who are staying home, especially children. The oldest ones very often have to cope with the things that their parents should be held responsible for. It is proved that the children whose parents work abroad achieve worse results in education than their peers growing up in full families (UNICEF)[9], frequently caused by relatives who take care of children during their parents' absence. They think mainly about providing material things like clothes, food, etc. Sometimes it can also happen that educational help in a family is impossible because of the language barrier. Moldova is a bilingual country. Although the official language is Moldovan (Romanian), Russian is still very popular. It is also possible to meet people among older generations who do not even know the Latin alphabet. So if the child is brought up by their grandparents, educational help is simply impossible. Furthermore, the excess of duties can disturb the process of education.

Problems at school are not the only negative result of parents' migrations—another is the impediment to the development of family bonds. Sometimes, after a long absence, children do not recognize their parents. The stressful feeling of being abandoned by a mother or a father (or both) also causes misunderstandings between these members of the family who are staying in the country and have to cope with everyday life problems. Poverty has an effect on social and family life not only because of migrations. De Soto and Dudwick point to other consequences such as alcoholism and shifting gender expectations.[10] Men who used to bring money home have become helpless and can no longer fulfill the expectations of their wives and children. Sometimes, women take over responsibilities that are considered traditionally male.

Although the biggest migration group is male, women are particularly in danger. According to different sources, a few thousand Moldovan women are victims of human trafficking. So far, they have been sold to more than forty countries such as Albania, Austria, Belgium, Czech Republic, Egypt, France, Georgia, Germany, Greece, Italy, Portugal, Romania, Syria, Angola, Saudi Arabia, Bahrain, Switzerland, Lebanon, Libya, Great Britain, Slovakia, Spain, the USA, Tajikistan, Tunisia,

---

[8] *National Human Development Report 2010/2011*, 58.

[9] *The impact of migration on children in Moldova*, www.unicef.org/The_Impacts_of_Migration_on_Children_in_Moldova%281%29.pdf (access January 2, 2012).

[10] H. de Soto, N. Dudwick, *Eating from One Pot*, 371.

Turkmenistan, and Hungary. The Moldovan foundation La Strada created a social profile of a victim: an unmarried woman, between eighteen and twenty-five years old, from a rural area, unemployed, without any income or with income so low that it does not even cover the costs of nutrition, with complicated family relations.[11]

One of the most dangerous ways to earn money is to sell organs, especially kidneys. According to Susanne Lundin, the most endangered group are men from villages. The price of a kidney—approx. 2500-3000 US dollars — is not enough to ensure prosperity for a long time. Instead of the promised wealth, men receive a lifetime injury. It causes not only physical and material damages, but also psychological ones—the feeling of being ashamed, aversion to speak about what happened, and even the sense of an attack on their gender identity.[12]

Migrations are not the only way to earn money—informal employment is also popular. Hermine de Soto and Nora Dudwick point to most common forms of this phenomenon:[13]

- buying and selling,
- small-scale retail vending,
- petty enterprises,
- renting out rooms,
- bribes,
- begging,
- theft.

Another very important problem connected with poverty in Moldova is social exclusion. The National Human Development Report identifies some factors that have allowed it to develop:

- a weak institutional support mechanism,
- a legal framework that is discriminatory or inadequate in its implementation,
- political and institutional obstacles,
- discriminatory social values and cultural practices,
- exclusion caused by geographical factors.[14]

---

[11] *55+1 Questions to La Strada Molodova*, www.lastrada.md/publicatii/ebook/55_q.pdf (accessed January 10, 2012).
[12] S. Lundin, *The valuable body. Organ trafficking in Eastern Europe*, http://balticworlds.com/the-valuable-body-organ-trafficking-in-eastern-europe/ (accessed January 5, 2012).
[13] H. de Soto, N. Dudwick, *Eating from one Pot*, 366–369.

This also indicates socially excluded groups in Moldova, such as disabled persons, immigrants and ethnic minorities (including Roma), persons without a fixed residence, former prisoners, drug and alcohol addicts, old people, and children.[15]

During my three-months stay in Vadul lui Vodă in Moldova in the summer of 2010 I worked in the centre for children and teenagers with physical disabilities (*Asociaţia Motivaţie din Moldova*). I had the opportunity to meet young people who could not read or write. A twenty-four-year-old girl said that she had never received any formal education. She could hardly write and read in Russian and did not know the Romanian language. Her knowledge about the world was very narrow. Only very few young people in the centre had the possibility to continue their education after they became disabled. According to the NHD Report, disabled people are one of the groups particularly endangered by poverty and social exclusion: "In the households with people with disabilities in 2009, the incidence of poverty was 28.6 %. Poverty risk is higher among men with disabilities (27.5 %), which is higher than in the overall population."[16]

Values and attitudes within the Moldovan society have changed due to the poverty. Events like weddings or christenings used to be celebrated with a huge amount of people, sometimes with a whole village or a neighborhood. Now they are limited to a small circle of relatives, and it can happen that even the closest ones are absent because they're working abroad. People are afraid to participate in social life. Visits, revisits, gifts and guests require some money which can be a big problem. As Dudwick and De Soto note:

> Social institutions were no longer funded by municipalities, and people could no longer afford to go. In many villages, clubs and movie theaters were open only a few times a year. Pensioners who used to seek solace in the local church could not afford to buy candles yet found it shameful to go without lightning a candle.[17]

It is hard to say that in post-Soviet countries a process called the culture of poverty can be seen at this time, but only twenty years have passed since the moment of transition, and only one generation born after the collapse of communism have became adults. Still, there is the risk that poverty and social exclusion will develop and there may be a great need to

---

[14] *National Human Development Report 2010/2011*, 2.

[15] Ibid., 39.

[16] Ibid., 56.

[17] H. de Soto, N. Dudwick, *Eating from One Pot*, 373.

apply a cultural point of view in the poverty studies. If some patterns of behaviour, values and attitudes that can emerge among poor people are known, it can be easier to prevent their exclusion and marginalization. Despite many controversies and quarrels connected with the culture of poverty, this idea may allow poor people to speak and be heard by others.

The author is a PhD candidate at the Institute of Cultural Studies at the University of Wrocław. She specializes in the problem of international migration and its cultural aspects.

CHAPTER TWENTY-FOUR

BUFFER ZONE: SOCIO-CULTURAL CHANGES IN THE FIELD OF MIGRATION AND RELIGIOUS GROUPS IN THE CZECH REPUBLIC

DANIEL TOPINKA AND DUŠAN LUŽNÝ

Introduction

Two decades after the beginning of the socio-economical transformation in the Czech Republic one can judge the progress from at least a partial distance. Fundamental changes have led to the creation of a free, democratic, capitalistic and consumer society, having all the basic features of a common Western society. It is worth evaluating that progress over a relatively short period in which the intensive changes came about.

This chapter focuses on spheres adverting to the rareness and particularity of the transformation processes. It discusses two aspects: contemporary religious life and the presence of immigration groups in the Czech Republic. The country has become a buffer zone, gradually filled with different religious and immigration groups.

Buffer Zone

In the past, beyond certain exceptions, the Czech society was ethnically homogenous. The population resided on the state territory and the idea of a nation almost completely fused with the idea of state. The Czech state was mostly populated by ethnic Czechs. Moreover, the country was one of the most secular in the world. Here, from a sociological point of view, one can analyse and compare the transformation of the Czech society from a homogenous into a more heterogeneous one, on the ethnical and religious level. The Czech society has become exceptional in the both fields.

After 1989, the state territory was opened up to external influence. As the economicy transformed, attractive jobs were offered to foreigners. As various immigrant and religious groups have come into the country, internal transformation processes have proceeded coincidentally. The originally homogenous and monolithic Czech society has met the category of "Others", and its homogeneity has started to erode. As a moral and spiritual revival has been required, religion was supposed to play a significant role. Thus, the state territory has been an ideal goal, a mission territory with many opportunities and perspectives.

The metaphor "buffer zone" is used to explain the processes and changes in question. Czechoslovakia was a largely secularised country before 1989. According to Marxist interpretations, religion was considered as an ideological rival or enemy, regarded as a menace to the development of a socialist society. Religion was openly denounced and became a symbol of reaction and resistance to progress. From the point of view of the ideologically biased Hussitism, religion was an obscurantism.

The population of Czechoslovakia was largely homogenous with only minor exceptions. Czechs stayed in one part of the country and Slovaks in the other. This division was strengthened by the split of Czechoslovakia in 1993.

As a secular country, the Czech Republic is a challenge for missionary religious groups.[1] While the society, craving for freedom and moral renewal, seems to be open to religions, its ethnical homogeneity starts to dissolve. Although at the beginning it was rather a transit country for migrants, the Czech Republic has now become a sought-after immigration destination with an attractive job market, a liberal approach and a sense of freedom. The influx of immigrants, religious groups and ideas has been continuing since the early 1990s. It coincides with an intensive internal socio-economical transformation. Therefore, the metaphor "buffer zone" can be realised.

Specifics of a Secular Country

According to sociological surveys, the Czech Republic, along with Estonia and the former East Germany, is the most secular country in Europe. In the 2001 Population and Housing Census, more than six

---

[1] D. Lužný, *Nová náboženská hnutí,* (Brno: Masarykova univerzita, 1997), 156–158.

million people (59 % of the population) declared themselves to be "non-believers". According to the survey of the International Social Survey Programme in 2005, more than 60 % respondents mentioned they didn't profess any religion. As the Czech Statistical Office informs, the number of atheists grew from 519,962 in 1950 to 6,039,991 in 2001, an almost twelvefold increase.

It is often considered to be a consequence of the communist regime, but this is only partially true. The somewhat lukewarm attitude of Czechs toward traditional, institutionalized religions has deeper roots. Thus, the Czech form of secularization is determined by certain factors:

- First, anti-Catholic attitudes in the Czech society. The origins of the Czech nation in the nineteenth century and the establishment of the Czech state after World War I were closely related to the refusal of the Catholic Habsburg monarchy. Catholicism was seen as an embodiment of the "old regime", and for this reason was regarded as problematic and hostile.
- Second, secularisation tendencies caused by structural differentiation of all modern societies. On the one hand, there have been processes resulting from urbanisation. On the other, there have been processes purposefully leading to a weakening of religion and especially church power.
- Third, atheistic propaganda and the brutal actions of the communist regime, which waged a brutal war against religion. A number of priests were imprisoned or executed, church orders were abolished, church property was confiscated and religious life was submitted to state surveillance. Religion was pushed out of the public sphere into the private sphere of individual citizens or illegal structures.
- Fourth, the removal of Germans at the end of World War II and the evacuation of large regions meant not only a "national purification" and the formation of a nationally homogenous and mono-cultural society, but also a decrease in the number of Catholics. Above all, it caused the successive destruction of local communities and degradation of the significance of tradition.
- Fifth, following 1989, great expectations concerning religions, particularly Christianity, have been disappointed. At the beginning, religion seemed to be an important component of the new identity and became a substantial part of public life.

Nonetheless, Czech society is not atheistic. It is secularized in the manner that the number of people belonging to large traditional churches has been declining. Not many people believe in God, and few people attend Holy Mass but it does not mean that religion is coming to an end. It means that a large part of religious life has adopted a form of non-church attendance, with strongly individual religiosity, which often manifests itself in the belief in impersonal transcendental forces.[2]

The recent Population and Housing Census (2011) shows that 3,612,804 (34.2 %) people do not have religious beliefs. Almost five million people (45.2 %) used the possibility not to answer the question, while ten years earlier it was less than a million inhabitants. 13,9 % inhabitants belong to a church. Most of them (1,083,899) declared their links with the Roman Catholic Church, followed by the Evangelical Church of Czech Brethren (51,936) and the Czechoslovak Hussite Church (39,276). Unlike in the previous census, 707,649 people (6.7 %) were reported to be believers, but do not belong to any of the registered Churches.

Apart from the regular census, several representative sociological surveys focused on the religious issue were conducted after the Velvet Revolution in 1989, such as the international European Value Survey (1991, 1999, 2009) and ISSP (1998, 2008). Besides, the Aufbruch International Comparative Survey (Religiosity in the reformed East- and Middle-European countries) was conducted in 1999, and the original Czech survey DIN (Detraditionalisation and Individualisation of Religiosity) was conducted in 2006.[3]

Those surveys show a long-term decrease in the numbers of people who declare affiliation to a church (respectively institutionalised religiosity). From 1991 to 2001, the number of people belonging to any particular religious group decreased by more than 10 % (to 32.2 %). On the other hand, the number of those declaring themselves as churchless grew by nearly 20 % (to 59 %). In absolute figures, religious groups lost 1.2 million people out of a total 10.2 million Czech population. The number of people professing any religion, including Catholicism, decreased.

Furthermore, there is a strong distrust of churches. According to the DIN 2006 survey, only 13.3 % of respondents declared their utter or partial confidence in churches, and 56.2 % of respondents declared their utter or partial distrust. The data needs to be perceived in connection with a thoroughly low distrust in institutions in the Czech Republic. Attendance

---

[2] As in many other countries of the world, many people in the Czech Republic reported to professing the moral values of the Knights of Jedi from the Star Wars film saga in the Population and Housing Census (2011). In the Czech Republic, 15 070 inhabitants filled in Jedi as their religion.

[3] Z. Nešpor, D. Lužný, *Sociologie náboženství,* (Praha: Portál, 2012), 196–202.

of a divine service is very low. According to the DIN 2006, 41.7 % of respondents had never attended a divine service. 7.6 % of people had been attending a divine service at least once a week and 7 % once a month. 8.8 % of respondents had been attending a divine service several times a year and 37.3 % less often.

What is more, believers are aging. The 2001 census showed a higher number of believers among elderly people. In the age groups over forty-nine the rate of religiosity is significantly higher in comparison with the average (32.2 %). Among people over seventy, the rate of believers exceeded 65 %.

The DIN 2006 survey revealed that more than 50 % of respondents believed in a certain form of transcendence represented by a higher power, a spirit or a natural force, but individual ideas were very diverse. Approximately one tenth of respondents identified the transcendence with the Christian God. Such a privatised, individualised and non-traditionalised type of religiosity is very common within the Czech society. Czechs compensate their weak interest in traditional religiosity with their inclination to non-church forms of religiosity. Traditional forms of religiosity and trust in church authorities are connected with the respondent ages. The younger generation inclines more to traditional religiosity than the middle generation, but it is not followed by an active consultation with church authorities. A low interest in traditional religiosity can be seen among the youth who incline towards non-traditional (alternative) forms of religiosity. They seek non-traditional religious authorities, and more often believe in the existence of a transcendental force, in the influence of amulets and horoscopes and in fortune-tellers' abilities.

On average, women are more religious than men. According to the 2001 census, 37.8 % men and 44 % women professed a religion. According to the DIN 2006 survey, 17 % women and 9 % men attended a church once a month at least. Women also believed more than men in a life after death, in the existence of a certain supernatural force, and in amulets and horoscopes. A reproduction of religion closely relates to socialisation, and religious surroundings influence the form of faith. Those who attended a divine service in their childhood more often believe in a supernatural existence which is not, however, automatically connected to Christianity. The Christian faith is confessed by those who attended a divine service frequently. Education and place of residence influence religiosity but the most important factor for maintenance of religiosity is practising of religion and the frequent attendance of ceremonies.[4]

Another characteristic is the difference between cities and the countryside. A higher rate of religiosity is to be seen in smaller villages whereas the least number of believers live in cities.[5]

The main change after 1989 has been the regaining of freedom and democratisation of the society which has led to a plurality of religious life. Not only the existing churches but also new religious groups have been given an opportunity to act. Amongst others, groups that had been active in Czechoslovakia before the communist regime seized power, as well as those persecuted by the Communists, were able to rebuild their position in the society. The role of religion has been a particular one, and innovative institutionalized and non-institutionalized forms of religion have developed in the Czech Republic.

Specifics of an Ethnically Homogeneous Country

The ethnic composition of the Czech Republic has been determined by history. According to the census of 1921, there was a minority of 3,124 thousand German-speaking people in the Republic of Czechoslovakia—6,570 thousand Czechs and two million Slovaks. The Germans were the largest ethnic minority in Europe. Other minorities were Hungarians, Ruthenians, Poles and Jews. Today's homogeneity of the Czech Republic is a result of the irrevocable disappearance of Jews and Roma during World War II, the displacement of Germans (more than three million people) and Hungarians after 1945, the loss of the Carpathian Ruthenia as well as the division of Czechoslovakia into two independent states in 1993.

The situation has changed in the last two decades. In 2001, only 173 thousand people did not answer the question about their nationality. Ten years later, according to the Population and Housing Census in 2011, 2,740 thousand respondents chose not to answer the question. 6,732,104 people claimed to be Czechs, while 522,474 respondents declared themselves Moravians whereas 149,140 said that they were Slovaks.

The number of people claiming Moravian nationality has significantly increased. In 2001, this was reported by 380,474 respondents (3.8 %). In

[4] D. Hamplová, Čemu Češi věří: dimenze soudobé české religiozity, "Sociologický časopis" 44 (4) (2008), 703–723.

[5] D. Hamplová. *Religiozita a demografické charakteristiky*, in Z. R. Nešpor (ed.), *Příručka sociologie náboženství*, (Praha: Sociologické nakladatelství, 2008), 198.

2011 the rate increased to 6.7 %. The Roma nationality was reported by the total of 13,150 inhabitants but only 5,199 of them declared to be exclusively Roma. Most of them (7,951) stated the Roma nationality in combination with another, for example Roma and Czech or Roma and Moravian.

Since the 1990s, the number of foreigners in the Czech Republic has increased tenfold. Between 1994 and 1999, it more than doubled to around two hundred thousand, and increased in the last ten years by 260.5 %. The country has become a buffer zone, which has been gradually filled. According to the Ministry of Interior, on May 31, 2010 there were 426,749 foreigners, including 184,724 with permanent residence and 242,025 with a residence permit for over ninety days. At the end of 2011 there were 424,291 foreigners in the Czech Republic, and 188,952 of them were entitled to a permanent residence

Fig. 24.1. Foreigners by type of residence 1990–2010

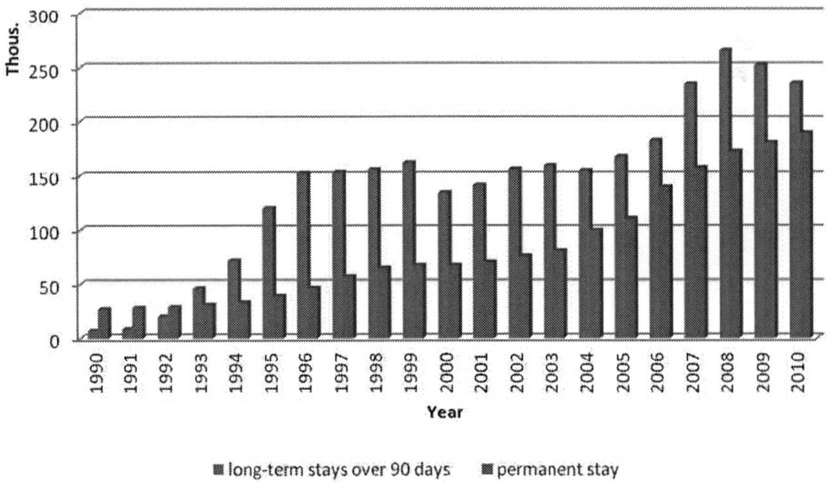

Source: Czech Statistical Office, Ministry of the Interior of the Czech Republic

The most numerous group of foreigners are people with the citizenship of Ukraine (117,810), followed by Slovaks (84,380), Vietnamese (53,110), Russians (36,055), Germans (20,780) and Poles (17,856). In total, people from 182 countries have been noted. In comparison to 2001, the biggest increment concerned Germans, Ukrainians, Russians and Slovaks.

Fig. 24.2. Five most frequent citizenships 2012

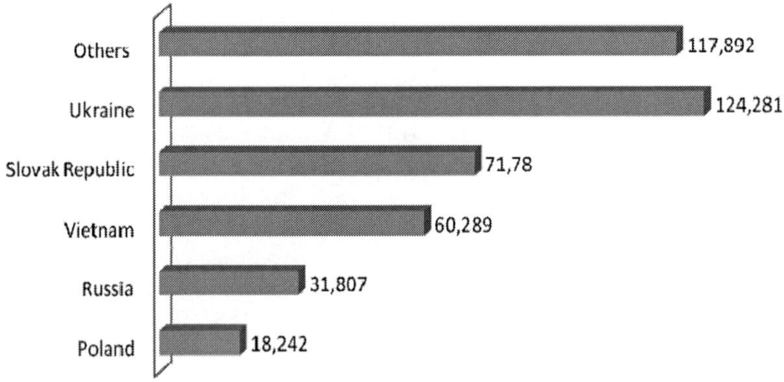

Source: Czech Statistical Office, 2011.

In the first years after 1989, a rapid growth of the number of asylum seekers took place. After the Czech Republic joined the European Union in 2004, the number of applicants has significantly fallen. The rate of applicants as well as the real possibilities to apply for asylum have declined.

Fig. 24.3. Number of Applicants for International Protection

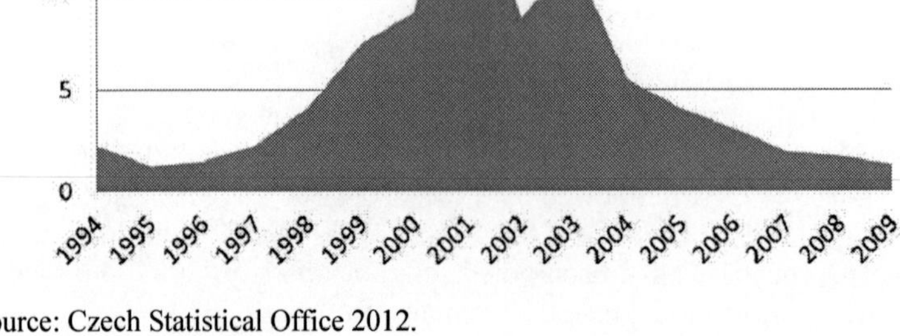

Source: Czech Statistical Office 2012.

As can be observed, the Czech Republic's migration profile has fundamentally changed during the last twenty years. First, a stage of a transit migration took place. Subsequently, tens of thousands of immigrants started to settle in the country. Since the early 1990s, the number of persons with permanent residence has tripled. For a certain time, the country was attractive for applicants for international protection but nowadays the interest is rather orientated to gaining a permanent residence. The Czech Republic has become an immigration country attracting certain groups of migrants. The homogenous character of the society has disintegrated in two decades.

Three Phases of Transformation of Attitudes to Religiosity and Migration

Three phases of development of attitudes to religiosity and migration in the Czech Republic can be distinguished: liberalisation, stabilisation and specialisation according to their main attributes. The first phase took over roughly six to eight years. The second lasted until around 2000 and the third covers the period from the early 2000 until now.[6]

Liberalisation

As far as religion is concerned, openness, search and a religious revival can be observed. This phase was characterized by an effort to fill the empty space created by the communist regime, that systematically liquidated religious life by means of persecution, from intimidation to physical liquidation. After the collapse of the atheistic communist regime, expectations were aroused, directed towards traditional as well as non-traditional, non-Christian religions. The former were, in particular, the Roman-Catholic Church and the "national" churches—the Czechoslovak Church (founded in 1920, in 1971 renamed as the Czechoslovak Hussite Church) and the Czech Brethren Evangelical Church (founded in 1918). The latter were among others Buddhism and Hinduism (including yoga).

The first phase was marked by the atmosphere of the Velvet Revolution and was characterized by openness and the search for alternatives being a result of frustration and loss of confidence in everything associated with the former regime. Religion (not a specific content) was viewed as a source for building the foundations for a new

---

[6] A. Baršová, P. Barša, *Přistěhovalectví a liberální stát,* (Brno: Masarykova univerzita, 2005), 221.

arrangement, and all religions were welcome. Liberal principles were introduced that paved the way to a religious pluralism.

In religious life, efforts were made to restore the dominant tradition. The disposal of communist heritage and collaborators, controversy over the legitimacy of the "hidden church", and making use of the moral authority of existing churches were the topics. New forms of Christianity appeared, such as Pentecostal Christianity, the American model (prosperity gospel, large popular gatherings in stadiums and halls), Jehovah's Witnesses, the Church of Jesus Christ of Latter-day Saints or the Unification Church (founded in Czechoslovakia in the 1960s and dispersed by the secret police in the 1970s). Moreover, groups developed that had previously existed but had been hidden and not persecuted by the communist regime, e.g. Yoga in Daily Life, Hare Krishna, and Theravada Buddhism. Entirely new religious groups from abroad, such as Scientology and Tibetan Buddhism, gained ground in the country and new original religious groups like Cosmic people were founded.

As far as migration is concerned, a significantly liberal approach could be seen. A new Alien Act was applied in 1992, which was the first effort to control migration, and foundations of the migration policy and legal regulations of foreigners' stay in the country were laid. An infrastructure providing care for asylum seekers and an administration concerning permission of foreigners' stay was built. Apart from the immigrants, many Czechs who had found themselves outside the country in the past returned. The Czech Republic also experienced the first influxes of migrants going West.

Stabilisation

In the second phase, the situation of religion in the Czech Republic was stabilised. Religious organisations developed their activities and focused on their organisation. Two trends could be observed.

The first was a diminishing of the public space. Ideologies of individual success and wealth became more and more important, whereas solidarity and morality lost their significance. This coincided with the government of Václav Klaus.

The second trend balanced the first one. It consisted of numerous initiatives, such as the activities of Václav Havel and his Forum 2000, interreligious dialogue, the visit of the Dalai Lama, and presenting religion as a *force majeure* and morality. At the same time, a multicultural approach was launched and grant programmes were created to promote ethnic (national) minorities and the immigration policy. This coincided with the government of ČSSD.

In the field of migration, regulations and practices were tightened up. However, most important was the harmonisation with European Union laws that directly involved migration.[7] The reactive migration policy was formed under the influence and pressure from the EU.

Specialisation

In the third phase, religion lost its importance in the society. As the disenchantment with religion grew, economic issues became a priority and the neoliberal ideology and right-wing conservatism dominated. The manifestation of privatised and individualised beliefs became a permanent part of religious life.

Migration became a specific issue and was not present in public discourse.[8] Migration policy was aimed at the conceptualisation of partial issues, and efforts were made to find comprehensive solutions and to follow the EU migration policy. The Czech Republic definitely became an immigration country, and the integration of foreigners and securitisation of migration were new issues. Even so, religion and migration were not considered to be important aspects in Czech society.

Conclusions

Religion and migration have not become common topics in the Czech society. The last two decades have been marked by liberality and openness, and various religious and migratory groups have entered the country, while the religious groups that survived the communist regime have been revived. Religion has been associated especially with a moral regeneration and a return to the roots in the Czech society. The influx of immigrants has been considered to be a part of the country's opening to the world. Nowadays, after a liberal period, the situation of both religion and migration has been subsequently stabilised. An administrative and legal base has been built to manage the migration.

---

[7] D. Drbohlav, *Migrace a (i)migranti v Česku,* (Praha: Sociologické nakladatelství, 2010), 77.

[8] Y. Leontiyeva, L. Novotný, *Je česká společnost tolerantní?*, in H. Maříková, T. Kostelecký, T. Lebeda, M. Škodová (eds.), *Jaká je naše česká společnost?*, (Praha: Sociologické nakladatelství, 2010), 227.

The Czech society has moved towards a higher tolerance. In comparison with institutionalised religions, privatised, individualised and de-traditionalised forms of religiosity have been pursued in the society, while distrust in churches has persisted. Migration has remained closed by the barrier of expert knowledge and there is a low awareness of it in public. It is surprising, especially when the permanent growth of the number of foreigners is taken into consideration. The issues are outside of the interest of politics except for several interconnected questions, for example church financial reparations, economic crisis and foreigners in the job market or security questions. The laws were adopted during the liberal period but practical questions regarding religious education and foreigners′ education are beyond public interest. Media reports on religion and migration especially concern terrorism, various scandals and extraordinary phenomena. The day-to-day life of migrants and believers is covered by specialised programmes of public media. Attempts to establish contacts with the public meet with unconcern and constraint or evoke disapproval from the public. The religion does not play a social-integrative role and does not unite the society. On the other hand, migration issues do not divide it for now.

Daniel Topinka works as an expert assistant at the Department of Sociology and Andragogy of the Philosophical Faculty at the Palacký University in Olomouc. His research focuses on the problem of social inclusion of minorities, sociology of migration, integration of the migrating and ethnical groups and sociology of religion.

Dušan Lužný is head of the Department of Sociology and Andragogy of the Philosophical Faculty at the Palacký University in Olomouc. He is the author of several books on the sociology of religion. The topic of his research is the theory of sociology of religion, new religious movements, the contemporary religious situation and globalization.

PART SEVEN

RELIGIOUS AND ETHICAL ISSUES

CHAPTER TWENTY-FIVE

BIOETHICAL QUESTIONS IN DOCTRINES OF POLISH CALVINIST AND LUTHERAN DENOMINATIONS AFTER 1989

PIOTR BUKOWCZYK

Preface

The attitude of the Polish Roman Catholic bishops towards bioethical problems is widely described in Polish media and scientific literature[1]. It does not differ from the papal doctrine.[2] Polish scientists rarely write about the point of view of Protestant denominations on those questions. This chapter focuses on bioethical questions in the doctrines of the Evangelical Church of the Augsburg Confession in Poland (*Kościół Ewangelicko-Augsburski w Rzeczpospolitej Polskiej*), the Evangelical-Reformed Church in Poland (*Kościół Ewangelicko-Reformowany w Rzeczpospolitej Polskiej*), the Evangelical Reformed Church in Gdańsk (*Ewangeliczny Kościół Reformowany w Gdańsku*), and the Evangelical Reformed Church of Poznań (*Ewangeliczny Zbór Reformowany w Poznaniu*). The analysis is therefore wider than the reflections of Polish evangelical theologian, Marcin Hintz, and political scientist, Tomasz Dębowski.[3]

Bioethical problems, as a matter of legislation and arguments among political parties[4], are also relevant political and legal questions. For those

---

[1] See: J. Gowin, *Kościół w czasach wolności 1989–1999*, (Kraków: Znak, 1999), especially 160–166.

[2] See: John Paul II, *Evangelium vitae*, http://www.vatican.va/edocs/ENG0141/_INDEX.HTM (accessed December 30, 2011]. The quoted texts are in Polish.

[3] See: T. Dębowski, *Zarys myśli społecznej Kościołów protestanckich w Polsce w latach 1945–1995*, (Wrocław: Arboretum, 2002); M. Hintz, *Etyka ewangelicka i jej wymiar eklezjalny. Studium historyczno-systematyczne*, (Warszawa: Chrześcijańska Akademia Teologiczna, 2007).

[4] See: *Nowoczesna, bezpieczna, solidarna Polska. Program Prawa i Sprawiedliwości,*

reasons, it could be interesting not only for a theologian but also for a political scientist. The notion "bioethical questions" refers to abortion (artificially interrupted pregnancy), contraception (all means and methods aiming at avoiding conception during a sexual intercourse), the death penalty (capital punishment—depriving a criminal of live by public institutions), euthanasia (either coercive or voluntary shortening of lives of incurably ill people) and war (a military struggle between states, nations or social strata and classes). "Doctrine" refers to public pronouncements of official organs of denominations and religious leaders. This chapter contains statements issued in Poland after 1989. The sources of information are books and the internet as well as, above all, the official statements of the denominations.

First the community and then its attitude to bioethical questions and its justification are briefly described, and potential errors in analysed texts are pointed out. Eventually, the influence of social and cultural context (tradition, including the religious one, public opinion, law etc.) on presented points of view is assessed. For further analyses, it is important for all communities to accept the principles of the *sola Scriptura*.

The Evangelical Church of the Augsburg Confession in Poland

The first Lutherans appeared in the Kingdom of Poland in the sixteenth century among the German bourgeoisie. Soon, Polish priests and noblemen converted into Lutheranism. The Piast dukes, Frederick of Legnica and Vaclav Adam of Cieszyn, dependent on the Roman Emperor, as well as the Prussian duke Albrecht von Hohenzollern, who was a vassal of the King of Poland, converted to Lutheranism. From around 1540, Calvinism became more popular than Lutheranism among the Polish and Lithuanian gentry. The democratic structure and independency from the state proposed by the reformers from Geneva was seen as a basis for the so called "golden freedom".

The Evangelical Church of the Augsburg Confession in Poland was established after World War I. In 1936, a special act regulated its relations

---

176,
http://www.pis.org.pl/download.php?g=mmedia&f=program_ pis_2009 (accessed December 29, 2011);
Sojusz Lewicy Demokratycznej. Jutro bez obaw. Program dla Polski, 118, http://www.sld.org.pl/program/jutro_bez_obaw_-_program_sld.htm
(accessed December 29, 2011).

with the Polish state. The first bishop was Juliusz Bursche, later murdered by Germans in the concentration camp in Oranienburg. Since January 2010, the post has been held by Jerzy Samiec.[5]

One can read in the Pronouncement of the Evangelical Church of the Augsburg Confession concerning the protection of human life from 1991[6] that "the Evangelical Church of the Augsburg Confession in Poland stands for protection of human life since its conception ... A discussion on 'admissible' and 'inadmissible' preventive measures and methods is considered to be empty due to the lack of its justification in the Bible." Pastor Marcin Hintz finds it chaotic because it mixes the protection of human life with "sexual ethics, ecology and social policy".[7] Abortion could only be admissible in the case of a serious threat to the woman's life, but "the Church is not authorized to make a list of threats to life in case of pathology of pregnancy". Some paragraphs of the Bible may be used as a justification.[8]

In 2009, the Pronouncement of the Evangelical Church of the Augsburg Confession in Poland concerning admissibility of application of the *in vitro* fertilisation was created. Polish Lutherans accept that method as a measure to heal infertility. However, they reject it in case embryos are created and kept without a clear intention to be implemented into the mother's organism. They also oppose the application of foreign gametes and surrogate mothers.[9]

The church raises an objection to the death penalty: "A serious treatment of the issue of protection of human life requires the abolishment of the death penalty."[10] However, a statement on the website of the Evangelical Military Pastoral Office may be regarded as contradictory: "There are no biblical arguments against the death penalty ... It seems that the ban of sentencing and applying capital punishment accepted in Europe nowadays has much to do with a characteristic ideology and aesthetics of

---

[5] *Dzieje Kościoła Ewangelicko-Augsburskiego*, http://www.luteranie.pl/pl/?D=7 (accessed January 11, 2012).

[6] *Oświadczenie Kościoła Ewangelicko-Augsburskiego w sprawie ochrony życia 1991*, http://www.luteranie.pl/pl/index.php?D=3353 (accessed January 10, 2012).

[7] M. Hintz, *Etyka ewangelicka i jej wymiar*, 383.

[8] Jeremiah 1:5; Psalms 139:13-18; Galathians 1:5.

[9] *Oświadczenie Kościoła Ewangelicko-Augsburskiego w RP w sprawie dopuszczalności stosowania metody in vitro*, http://www.luteranie.pl/pl/index.php?D=3354 (accessed January 1, 2012).

[10] *Oświadczenie Kościoła Ewangelicko-Augsburskiego w sprawie ochrony życia 1991.*

Western leftist thinking rather than with Christian ethics and appreciation of human life."[11]

The Evangelical Church of the Augsburg Confession in Poland, along with the Evangelical Methodist Church in Poland and the Evangelical Reformed Church in Poland, opposed the war against Iraq in 2003. In a statement, heads of the churches wrote that "war is irreconcilable with the teaching and life example of Christ". They argued that "self-defence, for example against terrorism, cannot be equated with an aggression against any state until all means justified by law are used up". They stood for "voluntary, universal and complete disarmament under a strict and effective international control", and opposed production, possession and use of the ABC weapons.[12] However, the denomination has its chaplains in the Polish Army, which may be seen as a contradiction. Hintz points out that a pacifist Methodist tradition, different from the Lutheran one, prevailed in this case.[13]

As far as euthanasia is concerned, the church considers it a trespass of the Fifth Commandment both by the person demanding his or her own death and those who kill.[14]

The Evangelical Reformed Church in Poland

The Evangelical Reformed Church in Poland was established after World War II. Before this, there had never been one Calvinist community. In the sixteenth century, there were three Brethren in the Polish-Lithuanian Commonwealth: one in Lesser Poland (*Małopolska*), one in Greater Poland (*Wielkopolska*) and one in Lithuania. They had separate structures and their representatives met rarely in General Synods. The first synod of Polish Calvinists took place in Słomniki near Cracow in 1554. Many

---

[11] *Etyka wojskowa. Piąte przykazanie*, http://www.edw.wp.mil.pl/pl/5_3.html (accessed January 10, 2012).
The orginal text: *„Nie ma biblijnych argumentów przeciw karze śmierci ... Wydaje się, że przyjęty obecnie w Europie zakaz orzekania i stosowania kary śmierci ma więcej wspólnego ze swoistą ideologią i estetyką lewicującego zachodniego myślenia niż z chrześcijańską etyką i chrześcijańskim szacunkiem dla ludzkiego życia."*

[12] *Irak. Oświadczenie*, http://www.reformowani.pl/index.php?option=com_content&task=view&id=134&Itemid=47 (accessed January 10, 2012).

[13] M. Hintz, *Etyka ewangelicka i jej wymiar*, 407.

[14] *Etyka wojskowa. Piąte przykazanie*, http://www.edw.wp.mil.pl/pl/5_3.html (accessed January 10, 2012).

members of famous noble families, such as Filipowski, Rey, Szafraniec, Stadnicki and Ossoliński acceded to Reformed-Evangelic communities. Due to the activity of the Society of Jesus and invasions of Protestant countries—Sweden and Transylvania—in the seventeenth century, the popularity of Protestantism in the Polish-Lithuanian society decreased. The partitions of the Polish-Lithuanian state by Prussia, Russia and Austria in the eighteenth century caused a further disintegration of Polish Calvinism. After World War I, two Brethren with seats in Warsaw and Vilnius existed. In 1995, an act regulated the relations between the denomination and the Polish state. Since 2002, the head of the denomination has been Marek Izdebski.[15]

The church opposes abortion. In the pronouncement of its synod concerning protection of human life, one can read: "Since the junction of gametes nobody can interfere with its development in order to annihilate the life arising in the womb of mother, experiment on it or manipulatively utilize it to reach side effects."[16] According to the text, the most appropriate methods of family planning are those requiring periodical abstinence, but "they can be applied by healthy women with untroubled monthly cycle and whose husbands respect their needs and rights". Moreover, the community accepts artificial contraception, except abortifacients.[17]

No other statements of the denomination on bioethical problems can be found.

---

[15] For further information see: *The History of the Polish Evangelical Reformed Church*, http://www.reformowani.pl/index.php?option=com_content&task=view&id=12&Itemid=9 (accessed January 11, 2012); R. Lipiński, *Kościół Ewangelicko-Reformowany w RP – historia i współczesność*, in J. Budniak, P. Jaskóła, R. Porada (eds.), *W nurcie myśli Jana Kalwina*, (Opole: Redakcja Wydawnictw Wydziału Teologicznego Uniwersytetu Opolskiego, 2009), 123–141.

[16] *O ochronie życia poczętego. Oświadczenie Synodu Koscioła Ewangelicko-Reformowanego w RP w sprawie ochrony życia*, http://www.reformowani.pl/index.php?option=com_content&task=view&id=140&Itemid=47 (accessed January 10, 2012). *"Od chwili połączenia się komórek nikt nie ma prawa ingerować w ich rozwój w celu przerwania powstałego w łonie matki życia ludzkiego, dokonywania na nich eksperymentów ani instrumentalnego posługiwania się nimi dla osiągnięcia ubocznych skutków".*

[17] Ibid. The original text: *"Za najbardziej wskazane środki uważa się metody naturalne wymagające okresowej wstrzemięźliwości. Ponieważ korzystać z nich mogą jednak tylko kobiety zdrowe, o niezakłóconym rytmie miesięcznym, których mężowie szanują prawa i potrzeby swych żon, konieczne się staje stosowanie innych środków antykoncepcyjnych, męskich i żeńskich, z wykluczeniem tak zwanych wczesnoporonnych."*

The Confederation of Reformed Evangelical Churches in Poland

In 2004, the Confederation of Reformed Evangelical Churches in Poland (CREC Poland) was founded. It includes the Reformed Evangelical Church in Gdańsk, the Reformed Evangelical Church in Poznań, and the Evangelical Reformed Church in Wrocław (the oldest), as well as parishes in Legnica and Leszno. Since 2006, the CREC Poland has been a member of the Communion of Reformed Evangelical Churches (CREC), an international organisation of Calvinist communities. CREC Poland is independent from the Reformed Evangelical Church in Poland.[18] The positions of the confederation on bioethical questions can be derived from the pronouncements of its pastors.

Andrzej Polaszek from the Poznań community calls abortion a "statutory lawlessness".[19] Paweł Bartosik from Gdańsk writes: "The Holy Scripture speaks many times about sanctity and inviolability of human unborn life and its existence since conception."[20] In support of that opinion, he quotes paragraphs of the Bible[21] and analyses more exactly the Exodus (II Moses 21:22–23):

> When men have a fight and hurt a pregnant woman, so that she suffers a miscarriage, but no further injury, the guilty one shall be fined as much as the woman's husband demands of him, and he shall pay in the presence of the judges. But if injury ensues, you shall give life for life.[22]

Bartosik points out differences among translations in some versions of the Bible. According to the Gdańsk Bible, a man that hits a pregnant

---

[18] See: *Welcome to the Evangelical Reformed Church website*, http://www.kalwini.pl/English.php (accessed January 10, 2011]; Historia, http://wroclaw.reformacja.pl/historia/ historia.html. There are some contradictions between pieces of information presented in these websites.

[19] A. Polaszek, *Sprawiedliwośc i prawo*, http://www.kalwini.pl/sprawiedliwosc.php (accessed January 10, 2012).

[20] P. Bartosik, *Aborcja*, in *Czytelnia. Rodzina i wychowanie*, http://www.gdansk.reformacja.pl/ (accessed January 10, 2012). The original text: "*Pismo Św. wiele razy mówi o wartości i nienaruszalności nienarodzonego życia oraz o jego istnieniu od samego poczęcia.*"

[21] Genesis (I Moses) 25:22; Judges 13:5; Job 3:3, 13:9; Psalms 51:7 and 139:13-16; Isaiah 49:1; Jeremiah 1:5; Luke 1:15; 1:44.

[22] The quotation after: *The New American Bible*, http://www.vatican.va/archive/ENG0839/_INDEX.HTM (accessed January 12, 2012).

woman causing a miscarriage has to be killed. According to the Warsaw Bible, he must only pay a compensation to the woman's husband if he kills her too. In Bartosik's opinion, that is a proof of recognition of the humanity of an embryo by the author of the quoted text.

Bartosik writes that "a just repayment is a remedium for criminality according to the Bible".[23] From that principle, the acceptance of the death penalty for a murderer is derived: "If we murder somebody, we must render our life ..."[24] Bartosik refers to I Moses 9:56:

> For your own lifeblood, too, I will demand an accounting: from every animal I will demand it, and from man in regard to his fellow man I will demand an accounting for human life. If anyone sheds the blood of man, by man shall his blood be shed; For in the image of God has man been made.

Pastor Bogumił Jarmulak from Poznań asserts the same.[25]

Bartosik states that "in the Bible there is no direct commandment forbidding birth control".[26] In I Moses 38:8–10, God punishes Onan to death for pouring out his sperm onto the ground in order to avoid impregnating his brother's widow. According to Bartosik, in this case, rather than the application of contraception, it is the motivations and the context in which Onan committed his act that are condemned.[27] In his opinion, the Bible does not give a direct answer as to whehter birth control is forbidden or not. Therefore, he regards the approach of the Roman Catholic Church as faulty and casuistic in recognising "artificial" contraception (for example preservative) as a sin and a "natural" one (the method of natural conception control) as acceptable.[28]

---

[23] P. Bartosik, *Aktualność Bożego Prawa*, in *Czytelnia. Życie chrześcijańskie*, http://www.gdansk.reformacja.pl/ accessed January 10, 2012). The original text: "*... sprawiedliwa odpłata jest lekarstwem na przestępczość wg Biblii.*"

[24] Ibid. The original text: "*Jeśli kogoś zamordujemy, musimy oddać swoje życie* (1Mj. 9:5-6)"

[25] B. Jarmulak, *Odpłata*, http://jarmulak.com/2008/09/odplata/ (accessed January 10, 2012).

[26] P. Bartosik, *Kontrola urodzin - grzech czy odpowiedzialność*, in *Czytelnia. Rodzina i wychowanie*, http://www.gdansk. reformacja.pl/ (accessed January 10, 2012). The original text: *"... nie ma w Biblii bezpośredniego przykazania zakazującego kontrolę narodzin."*

[27] Ibid. The original text: "*Sam tekst jednakże nie sugeruje, że jego przewinieniem było stosowanie antykoncepcji, lecz motywacje i kontekst, w jakim dopuścił się swego czynu.*"

[28] Ibid. The original text: "*Czy kontrola narodzin jest zabroniona czy nie? W moim przekonaniu Biblia nie daje bezpośredniej odpowiedzi na to pytanie, stąd za błędne*

As far as the issue of war is concerned, Jarmulak writes that Christian pacifist Tolstoy:

> in an unjustified way sets Jesus against Moses, the Gospel against the Old Testament and even Jesus against Paul and the Gospel against Letters of Paul … It is hard to call a good father or a president somebody who does nothing but prays when a ruffian or an enemy murders his children, rapes his wife or murders citizens of his country.[29]

Military service is therefore justified.

Conclusions

It is to assume that in order to understand positions of the above-mentioned religious communities on bioethical issues, one must pay attention to their cultural and social context.

All of them oppose abortion. The attitude of Poles toward this has changed rapidly in the last forty years. In 1977, 620 thousand pregnancies in Poland were interrupted. Up to 1995, that number had decreased to around 100 thousand.[30] A government report from 2011 shows that most Polish youngsters reject abortion.[31] The Polish law has also changed—article 4a of the "Law on family planning, protection of human embryo and conditions of permission for abortion" from 1993 allows interruption of pregnancy only in three cases: crime, a serious and irreversible impairment or a threat to the mother's health or life.[32]

All of the communities accept artificial contraception. Sociologist Marek Okólski writes: "In the mid 1990s the impact of abortion on the

---

uważam kazuistyczne podejście Kościoła Rzymskokatolickiego uważającego 'sztuczną' antykoncepcję (np. prezerwatywa) za grzeszną, zaś 'naturalną' (metoda naturalnej regulacji poczęć) za dopuszczalną."

[29] B. Jarmulak, *Tołstoj, Królestwo Boże i pacyfizm*, http://jarmulak.com/2010/11/tolstoj-krolestwo-boze-i-pacyfizm/ (accessed January 10, 2012).

[30] M. Okólski, *Przemiany ludnościowe w Polsce w perspektywie minionego stulecia*, in M. Marody (ed.), *Wymiary życia społecznego. Polska na przełomie XX i XIX wieku. Wydanie nowe*, (Warszawa: Wydawnictwo Naukowe Scholar, 2007), 37, 55.

[31] *Raport "Młodzi 2011"*, 55, 380, http://zds.kprm.gov.pl/mlodzi-2011 (accessed March 1, 2012).

[32] *Ustawa z dnia 7 stycznia 1993 r. o planowaniu rodziny, ochronie płodu ludzkiego i warunkach dopuszczalności przerywania ciąży*, (Dz. U. z 1993 r., nr 17, poz. 98), http://isap.sejm.gov.pl/DetailsServlet?id=WDU19930170078 (accessed December 29, 2011).

level of fertility became irrelevant in the West and the impact of contraception relevant."[33] According to Bartosik, it happend in spite of Roman Catholic Church opposition.

The Evangelical Church of the Augsburg Confession in Poland has an incoherent opinion about the death penalty. The CREC Poland is in favour whereas the Evangelical-Reformed Church in Poland remains silent on this issue. The position articulated in the "Pronouncement the Evangelical Church of the Augsburg Confession on prevention of human life" is contradictory to the view of Martin Luther, expressed in the "Large Catechism"[34] but conforms with the position of Western Evangelic communities, for instance the Evangelical Church in Germany.[35] The point of view on capital punishment presented by CREC Poland is coherent with the contents of Calvin's "The Institutes of Christian Religion".[36] Moreover, it conforms with Polish public opinion on the death penalty,[37] although the present Polish penal code does not foresee the death penalty,[38] contrary to the one from 1969[39], What is more, Poland has even ratified international pacts prohibiting its application.[40]

---

[33] *Wymiary zycia społecznego,* 55.
[34] M. Luter, *Duży katechizm*, in *Mały katechizm. Duży katechizm*, Andrzej Wantuła (transl.), (Bielsko-Biała: Wydawnictwo Augustana, 2000), 74, http://www.luteranie.pl/ (accessed January 10, 2012).
[35] See: *Todesstrafe - ein Schwerpunkt der Menschenrechtsarbeit der EKD*, http://www.ekd.de/ international/menschenrechte/aktuell/2000/4400.html (accessed January 24, 2010).
[36] See: J. Kalwin, *O zwierzchności świeckiej, porządnie według sznuru Pisma Świętego opisanie. Zaraz o pożytkach i powinnościach urzędu jej. Z łacińskiego na polskie wiernie przetłumaczone. Anonimowy przekład polski dwudziestego rozdziału czwartej księgi Institutio Christianae religionis nunc uere demum suo titulo respondens Jana Kalwina wydany w 1559 r.*, (Warszawa: Wydawnictwo Naukowe "Semper", 2009), 79.
[37] See: M. Wentzel, *Polacy, Czesi, Węgrzy, Litwini i Rosjanie o poczuciu bezpieczeństwa, pracy policji i stosowaniu kary śmierci,* http://badanie.cbos.pl/details.asp?q=a1&id=2535 (accessed January 11, 2012); R. Boguszewski, *Opinie o karze śmierci,* http://badanie.cbos.pl/details.asp?q=a1&id=3706 (accessed January 11, 2012).
[38] See: *Kodeks karny z 6 czerwca 1997 r.*, Dz. U. z 1997 r., nr 88, poz. 553, z późn. zm., www.sejm.gov.pl [accessed March 1, 2010).
[39] See: *Kodeks karny z 19 kwietnia 1969 r.*, Dz. U. Z 1969 r., nr 13, poz. 94., www.sejm.gov.pl (accessed March 1, 2010).
[40] See: *Protokół nr 6 do Konwencji o ochronie praw człowieka i podstawowych wolności z 23 kwietnia 1983 r.*, Dz. U. z 2001, nr 23, poz. 266, http://isap.sejm.gov.pl (accessed March 1, 2010); *Protokół 13 do Konwencji o ochronie praw człowieka i podstawowych wolności z 3*

Attitudes of the Evangelical Reformed Church in Poland and the Evangelical Church of the Augsburg Confession in Poland towards the war against Iraq is unclear. The CREC Poland accepted it as a kind of ultimate defence act. A survey conducted by the Centre for Public Opinion Research in September 2002 showed that 46 % of respondents did not accept the intervention of the USA and its allies in Iraq.[41]

The author graduated in Political Science at the University of Wrocław. His scientific interests concentrate on the history of political thought.

maja 2002, European Treaty Series/Serie des traites europeens (STE) nr 187, www.mswia.gov.pl/download.php?s=1&id=658 (accessed March 1, 2010).

[41] *M. Strzeszewski, Polacy wobec ewentualnej akcji przeciw Irakowi. Komunikat z badań*, http://badanie.cbos.pl/details.asp?q=a1&id=2785 (accessed January 12, 2012).

Chapter Twenty-Six

Ethical Dilemmas in Romanian and German Police

Aurelia Iana

Purpose of the Study

The purpose of this comparative study is mainly to answer the question of how groups in the police force and individuals formulate their judgments on what is moral and what is immoral in their activities. Helping to determine the attitude of policemen while on duty, this chapter focuses on obtaining basic demographic and police information, determining ethical positions (ideologies) of police personnel, and the relationship between demographic/police information and ethical ideology. Establishing the police's responses to hypothetical ethical dilemmas was accomplished by administering an extensive questionnaire to police officers in a middle to large police department.

This research summarizes a study that measured methods in solving ethical dilemmas in police agencies across Romania and Germany. The study was based on an organizational/occupational approach to moral values. Researchers asked officers for their opinions about five hypothetical cases of police behaviour and measured how seriously policemen regarded moral values, how willing they were to support punishment, and how willing they were to report misconduct.

The target audience was criminal justice researchers, legislators, police administrators, police officers and police trainers in Romania and Germany.

Literature Review

Police personnel today broadly agree that citizens' support for the police is important for ethical behaviour and successful policing. Not only is public support fundamental to the legitimacy of the police, but it is also important for enlisting moral values in efforts to fight against crime. Moreover, there is growing evidence that public support depends on the public's perception that police treat people according to ethical ideology.

Literature has shown that most people generally support the police and are satisfied with the way the police perform their duties. The reason for this is that police-public contacts indirectly impact, as well as directly affect, police behaviour. It seems plausible that police behavior in routine encounters could affect public opinions of the police through a ripple effect, as persons who encounter police retell their stories to families, friends and neighbours. A second possibility is that police-public contacts or examples of police corruption or misconduct that receive media attention assume an amplified and disproportionate effect on public opinion, compared with the large number of routine police-public interactions that do not receive media attention. While both theories are plausible, neither has received much empirical attention. This comparative research specifically addressed the relative importance of these two factors alongside the direct effect of encounters with the police among those who seek police services or those identified as neighborhood community leaders by police commanders.

The study began with an effort to take advantage of a questionnaire conducted by the Romanian Police and the Federal German Police in some of their departments. This chapter is a part of a doctoral thesis and the opinions or points of view expressed are those of the author. They do not reflect the official position of the Police Departments in Romania and Germany.

Many people are aware of the stereotype of the "dirty cop", perpetuated by television, books and movies. This stereotype assumes that policemen are oblivious to ethics and incapable of making the right decision when faced with an ethical dilemma. However, researchers have failed to correlate the ethical ideologies of the police with their responses to actual ethical dilemmas. There has been no attempt to analyse the most effective elements of an ethical code in the critical perspective of police ethics. Some police trainers asserted that it is impossible to teach ethics; it is a facet of the job that police personnel must learn on the street. Citing Habermas,[1] they posit that the most effective type of ethics code for law enforcement is a symbolic-interactive system. Codes of ethics for police personnel rest on a framework of basic principles. Generally speaking,

[1] J. Habermas, *Moralbewußtsein und kommunikatives Handeln*, (Frankfurt am Main: Suhrkamp Verlag, 1983), 124

these are: respect for autonomy (ensuring that the citizen is free from external constraints and promoting their capacity to make voluntary informed decisions); non-maleficence (avoiding harm to the citizen); beneficence (the welfare of the citizen is the primary goal of the police activity); and justice (ensuring that the citizen is treated fairly, equitably, and in accordance with his or her rights and entitlements). When these principles conflict (as they invariably must), the norms and rules that they produce should be suitably applied to cover the particular dilemma which demands specific research.

In order to establish these types of principles, communication between police personnel and police management or administration must be direct, without the intervention of an arbitrator or any other third parties. There must also be role reciprocity, the opposite of the current hierarchical system in most police departments. Officers and management must be on the same level. Finally, both sides—police officers and administration—must agree to the same ethical norms. The optimal ethics code will be reached by a consensus of all law enforcement officials, not simply handed down by administration or management.

Milan Pagon, Dean of the College of Police and Security Studies in Slovenia, in an article in support of establishing a law enforcement code of ethics, asserts that "law enforcement officials need an ethical code of conduct in order to become fully professionalized like the fields of law, psychology, and medicine".[2] He believes that other "methods of professionalization, such as education, training, better pay, and proper equipment, are not effective in promoting ethical norms".[3] Another opinion also asserts that police officers need their own code of ethics. However, while Pagon believes that a police code of ethics will lead to the greater professionalization of law enforcement, the present opinion in Romania is that the nature of the job requires an ethical code. In order to deal with violent criminals and also ensure that the public feels safe, some standards must be established for police to follow.

The Romanian ideal code of ethics for law enforcement includes moral rules, not moral principles or ideals, as many ethical codes today include. It defines moral rules as "requirements (or prohibitions) one is supposed to obey all the time"[4], as opposed to moral principles or ideals which become

---

[2] M. Pagon, *Police Ethics and Integrity*, http://agu.academia.edu/MilanPagon/Papers/420253/Police_Ethics_and_Integrity (accessed January 1, 2012).

[3] Ibid.

[4] *Code of Ethical Conduct for Police Personnel*, Romanian Government, Decision Number 991 from 25 August 2005.

progressively vaguer, harder to follow and harder to enforce. Its ideal ethical code of conduct is to be enforced by convention "in order to explain the evolution of punishment strategies"[5], which is defined as "a practice in which the participation of each is valuable only insofar as others participate as well".[6] This means that the primary reason Romanian police officers will follow the ethical code is because they, as a group, have decided that it is to their benefit to adhere to the code. In accordance with older researchers, the present opinion says that the ideal ethical code would be one agreed upon by the police officers who have to follow it.

In a prior study addressing police officers' ethical orientations, Romanian police trainers examined the effect of the police subculture on the ethical orientations of police officers. They hypothesized that there is an interaction between the value placed by other police officers on ethical conduct, other officers' attitudes about the general unethical conduct of their peers, and officers' attitudes about questionable ethical practices that lead to morally acceptable ends.

Romanian Police researchers found that an officer's comparative value of ethical conduct was not related to either an officer's tolerance of the misconduct of other officers or the viewpoint that the ends justify the means. They also found that an officer's scores on the "suspicion of the public"[7] and "subcultural alienation from the public"[8] scales were positively and significantly correlated to both the officer's tolerance of the misconduct of other officers and the view that the ends justify the means but not to the comparative value that the officer placed on ethical conduct.

Methodology

The objectives of this study point out the collection of data and the evaluation of the current situation in applying the Code of Ethical Conduct in Romania and the European Code of Police Ethics. These data could not be gathered from official statistics in Romania and Germany or at the European level. There is currently a lack of information regarding the ethical ideologies and decision making strategies of police personnel in Romania, an the literature review in Romania is based on the European theoretical studies only, without analysing the Romanian Police Force cases.

---

[5] R. Joyce, *Evolution of Morality,* (Cambridge: MIT Press, 2006), 90.
[6] *Code of Ethical Conduct for Police Personnel, art. 4.*
[7] J. Habermas, *Moralbewußtsein und kommunikatives Handeln,* 113.
[8] Ibid., 115.

The comparison to the German Federal Police emphasizes the main principles and moral values that emerge all over the law enforcement officials.

The sample size was 227 policemen, which represent a 90.8 % response rate in Romania and 178 policemen in Germany, which represents a 98.88 % response rate in Germany.

Demographic variables measures included age, gender, number of years of service, race and disciplinary action taken against the officer. Officer ethical ideology was measured by the questionnaire and officer responses to hypothetical ethical dilemmas.

Hypotheses

For the purposes of this research, the following hypotheses were tested:

Hypothesis 1:
H0 = amount of disciplinary actions does not impact the ethical dilemma decision making
H1 = amount of disciplinary actions does impact the ethical dilemma decision making

Hypothesis 2:
H0 = policeman's age does not impact the ethical dilemma decision making
H1 = policeman's age does impact the ethical dilemma decision making

Hypothesis 3:
H0 = policeman's rank does not impact the ethical dilemma decision making
H1 = policeman's rank does impact the ethical dilemma decision making

Hypothesis 4:
H0 = policeman's education level does not impact the ethical dilemma decision making
H1 = policeman's education level does impact the ethical dilemma decision making

Data Analysis

Data analysis was conducted by using SPSS. First, descriptive statistics for subjects were computed. Second, the analysis centered on determining the Ethical Position of the subject, as measured by the questionnaire. Third, analyses were conducted by testing hypotheses concerning the relationships between selected independent variables and subject questionnaire.

Before a formal analysis could be conducted, additional work needed to be completed on the data set. First, one descriptive variable, race, could not be used in the analysis given that there were too few minorities in the data pool. Second, certain subjects did not answer all questions which resulted in having to count five subjects as missing data for the questionnaire results and analysis. Therefore, the descriptive results and findings from analyses using the questionnaire resulted in four hundred total subjects. Third, certain independent variables were recoded in order to make these variables more manageable for purposes of analysis. For instance, age was recoded to create interval level grouped categories. The length of time in the service was recoded to create two categories: twelve or fewer years and thirteen years or more. The length of time in the subject's current position was recoded similarly: five or fewer years and more than five years.

Findings

This section is divided into descriptive subject data, descriptive results, and hypothesis testing. Each of these areas are addressed in turn.

The following data, shown in Table 26.1, shows the categorical breakdown of questionnaire scores among four possibilities. In order to obtain this information, additional analyses of the data had to be made in order to construct scores on the questionnaire. Depending on how a subject responded to the questionnaire scale items, responses were recoded in order to categorize each subject into one of the four "Ethical Ideologies".[9]

[9] The four categories in Ethical Position are Exceptionist, Absolutist, Pragmatist and Relativist. Moral behaviour has been identified in the main philosophical fields, movements and orientations across the ages (Plato, Kant, Nietzsche, Hume, Spinoza, Wright, Fiske, Peirce).

Table 23.1. Questionnaire results Romania

Pragmatist	25.1 %
Relativist	21.4 %
Absolutist	21.4 %
Exceptionist	32.1 %
Total	100.0 %

The majority of subjects in Romania are included in the category of exceptionists, followed by the opportunists. The relativists and the absolutists are equal in scores. The majority of the subjects in Germany are included in the category of absolutists, followed by the relativists. The pragmatists and the exceptionists are at the last places.

Table 23.2. Questionnaire results Germany

Pragmatist	14.8 %
Relativist	27.4 %
Absolutist	37.2 %
Exceptionist	20.6 %
Total	100.0 %

Based on the strong preference for the exceptionist category, most of the respondents believed that conformity is desirable, exceptions are often possible, they do not maintain that harm to others can be avoided, that innocent people can always be protected, and that risking the welfare of others is not always wrong or possible. While the exceptionist would prefer to rely on moral principles to guide behaviour and outcomes, judgments must often be made to balance the positive outcomes of a situation against any negative consequences. Relativists hold that "good and bad is relative and the importance and value we place on them should also be relative".[10]

It should not be surprising that most respondents in two countries fell into the absolutists and exceptionists categories. Absolutists adhere strictly to moral principles. However, as officers know, it is desirable, yet unrealistic, to always adhere to universal principles of morality as codified in criminal law due to the tremendous "grey area" of police interpretation of law and morality and the inevitable presence of police discretion.

---

[10] F. Nietzsche, *On the Genealogy of Morals: A Polemic*, (Oxford: Oxford Paperbacks, 2008), 362–363.

Summary of Overall Results

From the descriptive questionnaire results we can conclude that most of the policemen surveyed tended to follow the ethical ideology of exceptionist, although the three other ethical ideologies were also strongly represented. The analyses allow us to conclude that discipline and age do not have an impact on an officer's ethical ideology, while an officer's rank, the amount of time an officer has been at the department, and the amount of time an officer has been in his or her position do influence the policemen's ethical ideology.

The study on strength of the ethical ideologies is a new aspect of police ethics and psychology. Although it has been studied extensively in the general population, it has not been investigated in police prior to this study. Therefore, although exploratory in nature, this study sheds light on a subject that many researchers have failed to examine: police ethical ideology. This new comparative aspect of police ethics and police psychology emphasises that the study gives new insight into the cognitive and behavioural worlds of police personnel. These results show that the situational demands in the questionnaire had no effect on the attributions of the observers when people in the responses of the questionnaire behaved immorally. The researchers found that people who are immoral in one aspect of their lives are more likely to be perceived as immoral in other situations as well. Researchers have also investigated whether the attribution of morality or immorality can change or if the perceived morality of another remains constant.

The study limitations consist in the fact that there is merely an explanatory study, meant to open the field to further research on the ethical ideology of police personnel. The questionnaire results do not reflect whether respondents answered the questionnaire with a civilian or a law enforcement official mindset.

Finally, an interesting approach to measuring police officer's ethical ideologies would be to examine them cross-culturally. There are bound to be differences between the findings in Romania and those in Germany. New and innovative ethics policy and training issues might be discovered in a cross-cultural comparison.

The author has graduated in German and Romanian language at the University of Bucharest. She is a PhD candidate in Journalism and Mass Communication. She is also the Head of the Department for International Missions Training at the Institute of Studies for Public Order in Bucharest.

CHAPTER TWENTY-SEVEN

PROTESTANT AND ORTHODOX MEDIA IN ROMANIA: A COMPARATIVE APPROACH

CHRISTIAN APOSTU

Introduction

Religious actors are important players in the public sphere of most Eastern European countries, marked both by the collapse of communism and the tribulations of the post-communist period. Attempting to offer a sense of identity and security that state institutions have often failed to provide, all churches are influential in this part of Europe, with a remarkable record of recent success in assuring that their voices are heard in the political, ideological, economical and media turmoil of post-communism.

In order to increase and maintain their influence in the public realm, most religious entities entered the media landscape with their own church-owned mass-communication channels. From the multitude of such endeavours, two are representative due to their convergence as fully-fledged media centres. Opposites as regards to their size, two religious actors have initiated and are sustaining intense broadcasting organizations: the Romanian Orthodox Church and the Seventh-day Adventists Church.

Although their impact on the public opinion is still to be measured, both in terms of audience and influence, analysing such media is important to understanding radically different positioning in society, religious discourse and construction of broadcast evangelical journalism.

As a working hypothesis, it can be assumed that the addressability of religious media is in inverse proportionality to the amount of believers of the respective church.

Thus, although the Orthodox media theoretically address almost 90 % of the Romanian population and is trusted by many people who express their adhesion to its tenets and rituals, there are numerous people who do not participate in the life of the church. Its position as a central institution of the Romanian society assured, the strategy employed by the Orthodox church is to carve out an audience of elites, both internal and external.

On the other hand, the Seventh-day Adventist Church, with a little more than a hundred thousand believers nationwide, cannot but assume an entirely different strategy. Reinforcing a comprising term as "Christian", which is supposed to be friendly in the traditional Romanian environment, as opposed to denominational stress, the Adventist media promotes an integrative strategy under the sign of dialogue on various themes as health, youth culture, and so on.

The corpus for this research has been represented by products of the media of the Orthodox and Seventh-day Adventist churches in 2011.

Religion in Post-Communist Romania

The inevitable[1] fall of communism in Central and Eastern Europe represented the equivalent of an ideological vacuum. After half a century of repression backed by the Red Army, of a top-to-bottom imposed official communist doctrine, generating generalized anomie[2], these societies had to cope with the new and often difficult experiences of transition toward liberal political regimes and market economy, the very paradigms of change being multifaceted.

Religiosity has thrived on this shifting situation in all of Eastern Europe, Romania being a clear example of the increase of popularity of religion. The failure of other state institutions to meet the needs and expectations of population has resulted in a respective rise of demand in religious compensations.

Thus, whereas all across Western Europe religion was considered to be slowly but irreversibly dying[3], secularization theory considered religion to be a social practice doomed to be cast away by the increasing capacity of human institutions to offer existential security. Classical sociology described this direction from the nineteenth century:

---

[1] G. Schopflin, *The End of Communism*, in "International Affairs" 66 (1) (1990), www.jstor.org (accessed February 19, 2012).
[2] M. Tomka, M. Imhoff, G. Imhoff, *Les transformations religieuses en Europe centrale et orientale*, "Revue d'études comparatives Est-Ouest" 35 (4) (2004), Religions, identités et territoires, 11–35, www.persee.fr (accessed March 1, 2012).
[3] B. Wilson, *Religia din perspectivă sociologică*, (Bucureşti: Editura Trei, 2003).

> Weber argued that the increased rationalization of society—bureaucratic, scientific and technical progress, and the expanding pervasiveness of instrumental reasons in all domains of everyday life would substantively attenuate the scope of religion, both through the increased specialization of institutional spheres (of family, economy, law, politics,) and as a result of disenchantment in the face of competing rationalized value spheres.[4]

However, in former communist countries reality contradicted this direction, escalating a vigorous rise in religion in the last part of the twentieth century and the first decade of the next. In this part of Europe, there was not such a success in offering this sense of ontological security as Anthony Giddens put it.[5] In direct relation to it, religion developed and gained an important place in the emergent public spheres, capitalizing on its former opposition to communist regimes. This tendency can be observed on a larger global level, making the case of the societies in Western Europe rather an exception than a model, a prime example which would consequently be followed by other cases.

A serious challenge of one of the main tenets of sociology of religion is posed, which requires important adjustments and clarifications, if not complete rejection. As Peter L. Berger, one of the former most prominent theorists of secularization theory, puts it:

> The assumption that we live in a secularized world is false. The world today, with some exceptions, is as furiously religious as it ever was. This means that a whole body of literature by historians and social scientists loosely labeled secularization theory is essentially mistaken.[6]

An important difference in the experience of these (Western) societies, formerly the free part of Europe, and those formerly occupied by the Red Army, is communism as an ideological canopy. If in Western societies rationalization has been a polymorphous process, allowed by the peaceful conditions of economic and social life, in the East communism has artificially tried to re-enchant the world by means of a process of sacralization of politics.

Contrary to more optimistic perspectives, which sought to present this transition as an instant process, in Romania, the sui-generis form of

---

[4] B. S. Turner (ed.), *The Cambridge Dictionary of Sociology*, (Cambridge: Cambridge University Press, 2006), 507.

[5] A. Giddens, *The Consequences of Modernity*, (Cambridge: Polity, 1990).

[6] J. Proctor, *Introduction: Theorizing and Studying Religion*, "Annals of the Association of American Geographers" 96 (1) (2006), 166, www.jstor.org (accessed February 19, 2012).

communism of the late years of North-Korean-style dictator Nicolae Ceauşescu, national-communism, although rejected on the official level after the collapse of his regime, did not disappear altogether from the public language or imagination. Elements of it survived in different discourses of the newly-born public sphere.

Ernest Troeltsch's[7] famous analysis of religious entities is very useful to understand not only the features of Romanian religious life, but the relation of diverse entities to mass-communication, to its possible uses, strengths and stakes. According to the German sociologist, a church is a general type of formal religious organization that is well integrated into the larger society. We must stress the fact that this organizational dimension is common both to a church and to mass-communication, which reveals the necessity of rationalization of both in order to preserve their privileged status within a given society.

In this category, we can identify an ecclesia, which is a church-like organization formally allied to the state. Although in Romania, at least according to its constitution, there is no state religion, the state declaring itself as being secular, there are important advantages and privileges the Romanian Orthodox Church, as a majority Church and a historical religion, is granted, from religious education in schools to public subsidies to clergy.

Denomination, according to Troeltsch, "is a church-like organization that recognizes religious pluralism but denominations do not form alliances with state. They usually exist in societies where Church and state are separate".

If we goes further in this direction, one can find sects which are "distinct from churches (not well integrated), as a general type of informal religious organization that is not well integrated into the larger society".

According to this taxonomy, denomination is a religious group which recognizes religious pluralism, this view of society usually being in its direct interest, as denominations tend to be minorities. An ecclesia is the dominant religious group which tends to identify itself with the entire nation, trying, more or less vigorously, to eliminate other religious competitors from the public sphere or even from the society altogether.

In the case in question, it must be pointed out that even before communism the state encouraged nationalism as represented by the two historical Romanian Churches, namely the Romanian Orthodox Church and the Greek-Catholic Church, excluding other denominations as rightful

[7] J. Macionis, *Sociology*, (New York: Prentice Hall, 1989), 433.

representatives of the Romanian nation, though not completely banning them.

The Orthodox Media

As far as media are concerned, they follow the positioning in the public sphere. The channels of the Romanian Patriarchate are dedicated to sustain a national stance, identifying themselves with the entire nation, expressing the religious discourse of Romanian Patriarchate as the main religion of the Romanian nation. Borrowing from national communism, as well as from the previous nationalist tradition of the Interbellum, the Orthodox discourse has been, and still is, characterized by nationalist overtones, with relatively little support to democratic change.[8]

In order to better understand a religiously-based nationalism, it is necessary to have an insight into the theological underlying ideology of Eastern Orthodox Christianity. Nationalism is a common trait of all Orthodox churches, their very organization being based on national churches with specific organization, and being mutually autonomous. Distinct from Roman-Catholicism, where the Pope is the supreme head of the church, the Patriarch of Constantinople, though recognized as superior, does not have direct hierarchical jurisdiction over different national churches. Moreover, the power and number of churches like those in Russia or Romania largely overwhelms the tiny minority of the Greek speaking church in Turkey, the present basis of Ecumenical Patriarchate.

Currently, as an important imagological direction, the most important project of the Romanian Patriarchate is the building of the cathedral for the Salvation of the Nation, under construction near the very centre of communist power, the House of the People. This controversial project implies important financial resources and is one of the main communication efforts of the Orthodox Church, including the church-owned broadcasting channels. Meeting with criticism within the society in the context of the present economic crisis, it is therefore more important to defend the project on every communication channel available.

Symbolically, the communist architecture is reinterpreted and recreated as an architecture of post-communism. The Parliament seats in the House of the People, near the headquarters of the Ministry of Defense and the future building of the cathedral, the latter being the most trusted

---

[8] D. Philpott, *Explaining the Political Ambivalence of Religion*, "The American Political Science Review" 101 (3) (2007), 505–525, www.jstor.org (accessed February 19, 2012).

institutions in the country lending legitimacy to the former, is one of the most mistrusted institutions of post-communist Romania.

The Orthodox media-trust comprises the daily *Ziarul Lumina*, a tv and radio-station with national coverage. It was initiated by the present Patriarch of the Romanian Orthodox Church, Daniel, during his term as the Metropolitan Chair of Moldavia, and developed after his election as Patriarch in 2007.

All of these channels feature an elite-oriented discourse. Both media products, as well as interviews made by the author of this chapter with producers of *Radio Trinitas* and *Ziarul LuminaI*, show that this direction is clearly stated and applied. For instance, although one did not admit a high-brow ideal audience for *Radio Trinitas*, he admitted:

> I would not say elitist nor high, but I would say verified or tested. Now, being a radio station or a media center that has a certain standard, you must have some value to be based on … Because that is how I see it: the task is not a media channel to comply with the wishes of listeners which are swinging. So, not as an elitist, but as culture of education, of instruction.

Discussing culture, the director of *Radio Trinitas* Ciprian Olinici adds:

> The cultural area is very important for us because we have found that we are among few radio stations in Romania, not to mention the public radio, which is obliged by law, we are about the only radio that gives a lot of cultural information. A lot of cultural information not found even at the *Radio România Actualităţi* (Radio Romania News). As for the cultural information that *Trinitas* broadcasts, partly we get it from websites, but we have correspondents in the country.

Another trait of Orthodox broadcasting comes from its ecclesiology, which represents an important difference to the Protestant one. According to the Orthodox Church, similar to that of the Catholic Church, the mystical body of Christ, as the church was named by the Apostle Paul, is divided into two ontological, but not functional categories (as in Protestantism): the clergy and the laymen.

Thus, the bishop is a consecrated person, the source of divine grace in his bishopric. He represents the link between the specific community and the larger community of believers but, most importantly, the link with Christ and, through Apostolic Succession, the Apostles themselves. This syntagm, important in both the Roman-Catholic and the Eastern Orthodox churches, assumes an uninterrupted link through the centuries. By means of this link, successive generations of bishops have passed down the very power bestowed on the Twelve Apostles at the Pentecost.

Due to his most prominent role in the religious community, the bishop is the person most entitled to explain the contents of the faith, having a quasi-monopol for the spiritual interpretation of a given time or space.

For instance, *Tv Trinitas* features a daily informative broadcast, *Jurnalul Trinitas*, in which, usually at the beginning, a bishop is shown celebrating the Holy Mass in a church whose patron saint is celebrated on the given day. The place may be a cathedral, an ordinary parish church or, quite often, a church under construction. The bishop explains the sense of that particular day or feast from a theological point of view. Thus, his explanation defines the meaning of that specific situation.

The priest, the second figure in Orthodox broadcasting, is also a member of the clergy. He is not a detainer of the plenary Holy Grace but a simple delegate empowered by the Bishop. He usually repeats, in a lower register, what the Bishop already said, often citing the adept management and the generous help that his superior had shown in relation to that specific community.

As a stark difference from secular, ordinary media, all members of clergy do not indulge in profane activities like laughing, eating, drinking or even playing with children, not even when the subject of the story is an act of philanthropy towards children. They appear in hieratic postures, the media projecting a sense of super-humane persons, whose life is entirely dedicated to their work.

An image and an archetype of this stance is the byzantine iconography. What orthodox media try to construct is a similarity to the saints in byzantine icons, who depict idealized, ascetic pictures of the world. Contrary to the Western, mainly Roman-Catholic tradition of a certain realism in icons, the Orthodox Church has preserved and currently even explicitly encourages an Oriental view on the icons as highly hieratic, other-worldly illustration, whose living illustrations are implicitly promoted by the clergy.

This imagological parallel is based on a theological perspective. The Orthodox media relates the two bodies of the church. The visible one, namely the living people, especially the clergy, is engaged in a permanent battle against the evil. The invisible body, the church, the community of saints and Jesus Christ, overcame the sin and entered the Kingdom of Heaven.

The link between the two worlds is permanently constructed by the Orthodox media, using both an audio-visual and a verbal language, for example the depiction of bishops in their preaching attire. In the background, icons of ordained bishops like St. John Chrysostom or Basil the Great, also painted in their sacramental attire, can be seen with identical postures. When in church the clergy never sits, as the saints in the icons are upright.

Another important focus of orthodox media are rituals. In the so-called Apostolic Churches, the doctrine of ritual is entirely different from the one in Protestantism, including Neo-protestant denominations. According to the former, rituals are able to sanctify matter and thus people. The doctrine of Sacraments (or Mysteries) focuses on the presentation of the activities of the church as a mediator.

Closely related to this aspect is the promotion of cultural heritage. Both image (when the camera focuses on certain icons, or, on the contrary, it reveals some historical architecture of representative buildings) and sound (when byzantine hymns can be heard in the background) confronts the spectator's eyes and ears with the liturgical and artistic past of the Orthodoxy. It also becomes a form of legitimacy. The whole thesaurus is both a link to the invisible Church, the community of the saints, and a link to the past of the Romanian people, with the history of its art and architecture.

There is also another aspect of presenting the artistic heritage in its multiple musical, architectural and artistic forms. The Church strives to gain support for building new churches and monasteries. Throughout the post-communist transition, building has been and still is one of the priorities of the Romanian Patriarchate:

> The construction of Orthodox churches in post-communist Romania is a large-scale phenomenon, partly attributable to the restrictions imposed by the communist authorities on religious life, partly motivated by the social expansion of the majority denomination. According to our estimates, the Orthodox Church erected around 2,200 churches between 1990 and the end of 2004. Generated at first by the sheer need of places of worship in the communist neighborhoods, where there were none, this impetus evolved towards a symbolic appropriation of spaces, including public spaces.[9]

The Seventh-day Adventist Church media

Contrary to the broadcasts of hierarchical structures, the Seventh-day Adventist Church uses its mass-media channels in order to participate in the public sphere as a legitimate and recognized minority.

---

[9] L. Andreescu, *The Construction of Orthodox Churches in Post-Communist Romania*, "Europe-Asia Studies", May 2007, 167, www.jstor.org (accessed March 3, 2012).

One of the themes of the discourse of such a church is change, both at an individual and a society level. The individual change is based on the whole tradition of Protestantism, inspired by revivalism, which considers the perpetual need for a religious person to continuously improve one's spiritual life, trying to overcome the tradition one was born into in order to get to a superior moral and spiritual level. Inspired by the American experience, marked by both individualism and the presence of religious pluralism understood as a religious market, which encourages religious participation[10], the Protestant tradition reinforces the need and the duty of an individual to seek and find their own spiritual path, irrespective of the given situation or to the religion received at birth:

> Let everyone who knows himself to be a Christian, be assured of this and apply it to himself—that we are all priests, and there is no difference between us, that is to say, we all have the same power in respect to the Word and all the sacraments. However, no on can make use of this power, except by the consent of community or the call of a superior. For what is the common property of all, no individual may arrogate for himself, unless he be called.[11]

Such vision is much more important if one comes down to a minority and relatively new religious group, that must attract people in order to counterbalance the immense majority of traditional religious groups in a rather traditional society like Romania.

Thus, the main communicative strategy of this media is to address a greater audience than its followers. On the one hand, this seems quite natural for a church that has little more than 100,000 believers, for whom evidently could not have been rationally justified the existence of a dedicated media. On the other hand, the presence on the media landscape of an Adventist media centre legitimizes the presence of such an entity, giving it a more powerful and wider acceptance than the sheer protection of the law would give. Supporting religious pluralism may be seen as a strategy to be accepted in a society widely dominated by the Orthodox Church.

Moreover, the fall of communism produced a need for re-learning the free-speech, re-interpreting the relation between the private and public. Alongside the Orthodox discourse, religious discourses, formerly persecuted by the communist regime, at times even more than their

---

[10] R. Finke, R. Stark, *Religious Choice and Competition*, "American Sociological Review" 63 (5) (1998) 761–766, www.jstor.org (accessed February19, 2012).

[11] H.T. Kerr (ed.), *A Compend of Luther's Theology*, (Whitefish: Kessinger Publishing, 2008).

Orthodox counterpart, have entered the public sphere. The Neo-protestant churches, though a minority, have capitalized from the opportunity thus created and have tried to express themselves publicly. Mass media, especially electronic ones, has become one of the main leverages of challenging the quasi-monopole of Orthodoxy.

As a consequence, there are now important religious channels of various Christian denominations. As an example, the Seventh-day Adventists are fully integrated and they are similar to their Orthodox counterparts as far as the convergence of electronic channels and national coverage is concerned.

Following specific focuses as health or general moral points, these channels have an integrative approach under the umbrella of Christian doctrines. Relatively few media products are focused on specific doctrinal difference like the Sabbath or the state of dead, with many other broadcasts with themes as individual conversion or surpassing of difficulties.

The tone of this media, as opposite to the Orthodox, is more mass-oriented, with the individual as the protagonist. There are rubrics in which middle-class proselytes or the Adventist-born narrate their experience, their change towards Christ and the subsequent benefiting of it.

If Orthodoxy relates to nationalism as an idealized, abstract identity, in Protestantism the focus is on the difficult state of affairs in Romanian economy and society. Romania is not a different, specific or even less unique case for Adventists. They apply universal rules to the Romanian case as well as to Latin America, for instance.

Nonetheless, most productions are made in Romania. In an interview given to the author of this chapter, the director of the Adventist media-centre, Valeriu Petrescu, is proud to stress the fact that most programmes are home-produced, not imported from abroad.

Conclusions

Both churches use their media as vectors of communication in order to sustain and reinforce their relative positions in the religious landscape.[12]

On the one hand, the Romanian Orthodox Church, as a majority and a traditional entity, promotes the conservative direction of persuasion. It identifies itself with reference to nation and state, to which it offers an anchor of legitimization and cohesion.

On the other hand, the Seventh-day Adventist Church, as a minority and relatively new religious community, is committed to change, both at individual and societal level.

Consequently, their media channels have different focuses and stakes. One concentrates on the mobilization of elites, internal personnel or cultural elites in order to maintain its present advantage in the public sphere. The other diversifies its addressability in order to increase its acceptance in the same public realm.

The author holds a BA degree in Theology as well as an MA degree in Canadian Studies at the University of Bucharest. In his research he deals with the issues of religion and mass media in post-communist Romania.

[12] Additional literature to this chapter: R. J. Harris, *A Cognitive Psychology of Mass-communication*, (London: Routledge, 2009).

P. Michel, *Religion, nation et pluralisme. Une reflexion fin-de-siecle*, "Critique Internationale", 3, printemps 1999, www.persee.fr (accessed February 15, 2012).

L. Ray, *Post-Communism—Postmodernity or Modernity Revisited?*, "The British Journal of Sociology" 48 (4) (1997), www.jstor.org (accessed February 19, 2012).

L. Stan, L. Turcescu, *Religie şi politică în România post-communistă*, (Bucureşti: Editura Curtea Veche, 2010).

L. Turcescu and L. Stan, *Religion, Politics and Sexuality in Romania*, "Europe-Asia Studies" 57 (2) (2005).

CHAPTER TWENTY-EIGHT

TV SERIES AS AN INSTRUMENT OF DEMOCRACY: THE CASE STUDY OF *GŁĘBOKA WODA*

KAMIL ŁUCZAJ

Introduction

The idea placement strategy in Poland was used in popular TV series in the late 1990s. Therefore, some political concepts, such as EU-integration, were promoted by TV series scenarios. Nevertheless, up to 2011, the idea placement was not a common strategy. It has changed since the TVP1 produced *Głęboka Woda* [Deep Water]. This TV series was financed from public funds and had a purely political aim—promoting the profession of social worker.

This chapter presents a content analysis of the series and the results of a large quantitative audience measurement research. Moreover, a quantitative research on the reception of the new TV series among Polish viewers is presented in reference to the data collected in interviews conducted among socially excluded women from Polish post-PGR (State Agricultural Farm) communities from December 2011 to January 2012. This could be a voice in a debate for the "mission" of public broadcasting channels. A similar research had been conducted in other cultural contexts and had serious implications.[1]

[1] See: L. Abu-Lughod, *Dramas of Nationhood: The Politics of Television in Egypt*, (Chicago-London: University Of Chicago Press, 2005); L. Abu-Lughod, *Egyptian Melodrama—Technology of the Modern Subject?*, in F. D. Ginsburg, L. Abu-Lughod, B. Larkin (eds.), *Media Worlds. Anthropology on New Terrain*, (Berkeley-Los Angeles-London: University of California Press, 2002), 115–133;
J. Tulloch, *Watching Television Audiences: Cultural Theories and Methods*, (London: Arnold, 2000).

Product Placement in Polish TV Series

Idea placement must be understood as a specific form of the product placement concept. According to Carrie La Ferle and Steven M. Edwards, product placement is defined as an "intentional inclusion of brands through audio and/or visual means, within entertainment, educational, or informational content".[2] A definition coined by Pola B. Gupta and Stephen J. Gould emphasizes another important aspect: the broadcaster's benefits. According to that definition, product placement "involves incorporating brands in movies in return for money or for some promotional or other consideration".[3] It means that an advertiser may pay for the placement or provide necessary resources (e.g. Home Depot provided lumber to the reality show *Survivor*, and Dominos Pizza their products to *The Apprentice*).[4]

The history of product placement starts with days of radio because this medium seemed to be perfect for marketing purposes. Producers helped broadcasters in exchange for advertisement of their products. For example, during World War II news from the front contained information that US soldiers smoke only Camel cigarettes.[5] This strategy was adopted in a very short time by the moovie industry and various television channels. The first documented example of product placement in a movie was *Mildred Pierce* (1945) where the bourbon Jack Daniels is frequently presented.

The product placement market steadily increased in the next decades. In the 1970s in the USA, more than three hundred professional agencies dealt with product placement. The premiere of *E.T.—The Extra-Terrestrial* (1982) is recognized as a turning point in this branch of marketing, after which the "industry" of product placement started to develop much faster. Today it is very easy to underestimate this market. Product placement is considered to be both a cheap and effective means of promotion in comparison to a typical commercial.[6]

---

[2] C. La Ferle, S.M. Edwards, *Product Placement. How Brands Appear on Television*, "Journal of Advertising" 35 (4) (2006), 66.

[3] S. J. Gould, P. B. Gupta, S. Grabner-Kräuter, *Product Placements in Movies: A Cross-Cultural Analysis of Austrian, French and American Consumers' Attitudes Toward This Emerging, International Promotional Medium*, "Journal of Advertising" XXIX (4) (2000), 41.

[4] S. La Ferle, S.M. Edwards, *Product Placement*, 81.

[5] R. Niczewski, J. Potrzebowski, *Product placement jako skuteczne narzędzie komunikacji marketingowej*, (Warszawa: Bellini Capital, 2011), 19–22. Some say that an earlier example was Jack's Nortworth song *Take me out to the Ball Game* (1908), in which the mascot Cracker Jack was mentioned many times (Ibid., 64).

[6] Ibid., 91.

According to Stephen Gould, Pola Gupta and Sonja Grabner-Kräuter, one may explain differences in the acceptance of product placement using three main hypotheses:

- the cross-national difference hypothesis (acceptance of product placement depends on the particular country's culture)
- the product difference hypothesis (various categories of products are perceived differently as well as they are accepted to various degrees)
- the individual difference hypothesis.[7]

According to research on classic product placement, people usually recognize the brand placed in a movie but they do not really mind if such placement occurred or not.[8] There are two major arguments explaining why product placement is universally accepted. The first says that movies are better owing to advertisers support (it is estimated that product placement can lower the total production cost by 25 %). The second emphasizes that product placement makes every movie more realistic.[9]

In Poland, due to the communist rule lasting from the 1940s, product placement was absent until the 1990s.[10] Nevertheless, the present Polish product placement market is recognized as one of the most dynamically developing markets in Europe. Poland, along with Italy (the biggest product placement market in Europe) and Russia, is said to have the greatest market increase until 2014.[11] The legal system is a crucial factor here because in many European countries product placement is completely prohibited (Denmark, Finland, Norway, Ireland) or restricted, especially in domestic productions (Austria, UK, Germany, France, Greece).[12] In Poland, every product placement must be properly labelled but there are no further restrictions, except for EU standards, such as the rule of "no product placement in programmes addressed to children or information programmes".

There is only a little scientific data concerning the incidence of product placement in Poland. However, it can be assumed that this phenomenon has a global nature and is similar all over the world. Moreover, according

[7] S. J. Gould, P. B. Gupta, S. Grabner-Kräuter, *Product Placements in Movies*, 52–53.

[8] S. La Ferle, S.M. Edwards, *Product Placement*, 66.

[9] See: R. Niczewski, J. Potrzebowski, *Product placement*, 30.

[10] Ibid., 82, 118.

[11] Ibid., 50.

[12] Ibid., 115–117.

to social evolutionary hypothesis, less developed societies will adopt most of the market strategies from the more developed ones. For this reason, American data from 2002 can be used. According to La Ferle and Edwards, in 2002 product placement was a widespread strategy in the USA: during 105 hours of analysed programming they found 1,992 placements in 98 different programmes. One brand appeared almost every three minutes.[13] Moreover, placements in storied programming are the most popular (49.5 %), ahead of the non-storied programming (38.7 %) and plugs (11.8 %).[14]

Polish data suggest that product placement is widely recognized by Polish consumers. In their opinion, it is visible on all major TV channels (TVP, TVN, Polsat; see Fig. 28.1). Moreover, all of the most popular TV series contain this type of advertisement (see Fig. 28.2).

Fig. 28.1. "In which TV stations do you notice product placement most frequently?" Study conducted in November 2011 by GG Network among users of the communicator Gadu-Gadu.[15]

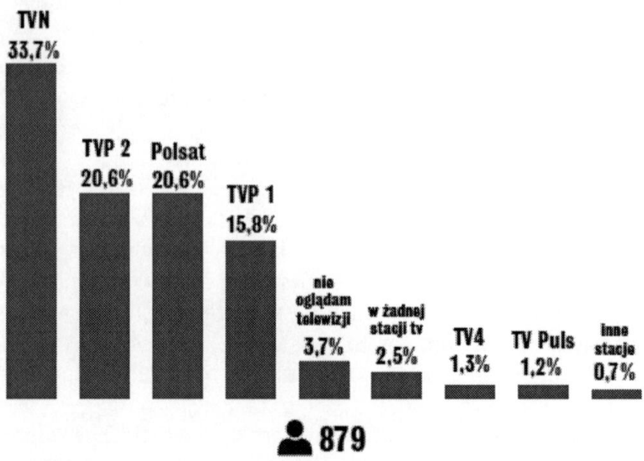

[13] C. La Ferle, S. M. Edwards, *Product Placement*, 68.

[14] Plugs are defined as "a nonscripted verbal mention of a brand delivered by an on-camera personality" (Ibid., 78–81).

[15] Source: http://www.brief.p l/baza-wiedzy/badania/art280,product-placement-czyli-tvn.html (accessed March 1, 2012).

Fig. 28.2. TV series which contain product placement (by respondents)[16]

Idea Placement in Poland

A classic product placement, defined as an intentional marketing method which has to promote a particular brand, should be clearly distinguished from the idea placement. The main difference lies in the object of promotion: selling the product (brand) is completely different form selling an abstract social idea. Thus, idea placements are usually more sophisticated.[17] It is easier to change consumer behaviour than to change someone's worldview.

Idea placement is a relatively new problem in the Polish context. It is worth noting that, contrary to product placement, there are no regulations in the Polish law concerning the issue of idea placement. As has already been mentioned, all programmes containing product placement must be clearly labelled as such. The information must appear at the beginning and at the end of the programme as well as after every commercial break.[18]

---

[16] Source: http://www.brief.pl/baza-wiedzy/badania/art280,product-placement-czyli-tvn.html (accessed March 1, 2012).

[17] R. Ropska, *Ludzie ufają serialom bardziej niż ministrowi*, Homepage of the journal „Rzeczpospolita", http://www.rp.pl/artykul/434522.html?p=2 (accessed January 17, 2012). It is not about the intangibility of the content because product placement can also promote an abstract idea (e.g. music artists, television show title, radio station), see: C. La Ferle, S. M. Edwards, 78.

[18] See: *Rozporządzenie KRRiT z 30 czerwca 2011 r.*,
http://www.krrit.gov.pl/Data/Files/_public/Portals/0/regulacje-

For the first time, idea placement was broadly discussed in 2010 because the Ministry of Education wanted to include dialogue about the benefits of placing five-year-old children in kindergarten (which was one of the most serious political issues at that time) into the most popular Polish TV series like *M jak miłość* [L as Love], *Plebania* [The Presbytery] and *Barwy szczęścia* [Colours of Happiness].[19] One might say that this campaign was expensive (e.g. 250,000 PLN for five episodes of *M jak miłość*, 440,000 for sixteen episodes of *Plebania* and 61,000 for two episodes of *Barwy szczęścia*).[20] Some marketing experts pointed out that traditional advertisements on TV or leaflets would cost even more.[21] Moreover, it is usually difficult to get to the rural societies which this campaign first and foremost addressed. Therefore, promotion via a TV series seemed to be a reasonable solution. Product placements were also used by various humanitarian and charity organizations such as the Polish Humanitarian Action and the Great Orchestra of Christmas Charity (WOŚP).

The concept of idea placement has been also adopted by some commercial institutions. This was a case of KRUK S.A., the leader in the Polish debt collection market. It ran a huge campaign consisting of multiple elements (traditional commercials, press articles) reinforced by a hybrid of product and idea placement, and characters from *M jak miłość* were indebted and co-operated with KRUK. This may be understood as promotion of a particular brand as well as promotion of a more general behaviour ("repaying debts").

Głęboka Woda and its implications

The appearance of *Głęboka Woda* has changed the context presented above because it was the first TV series financed by the state. The Centre for Development of Human Resources (*Centrum Rozwoju Zasobów Ludzkich*), an agency created by the Polish Ministry of Labour and Social

prawne/polska/kontrola-nadawcow/roz110630_lokowanie.pdf (accessed March 1, 2012).

[19] There have been idea placements earlier, e.g. *Plebania* (2008, advertiser: NBP, goal: promotion of entrepreneurship) but they were not so controversial (see: A. Kyzioł, *Zobacz, co masz myśleć*, "Polityka" 2836 (2011), 90–92.

[20] In the USA, the cost of product placement in a movie varies between 5,000 USD (visual or verbal PP) to 300,000 USD (celebrity placement). Moreover, the salary of an agent or the agency's commission (20,000 USD) must be added to this price (R. Niczewski i J. Potrzebowski, *Product Placement*, 80).

[21] See: R. Ropska, *Ludzie ufają serialom bardziej niż ministrowi.*

Policy in 2007, and the Polish public broadcaster *Telewizja Polska* produced this series together. According to the website of the Ministry, "each episode tells a distinct story of families at risk or already socially excluded and shows how social workers help these families, doing their difficult profession".[22] What is interesting is that when the pilot episode was about to be aired on June 2011, the Secretary of State Jarosław Duda wrote a letter addressed to Polish social workers and tried to encourage them to watch the series.[23]

It is worth emphasizing that the series had a widely known cast and high quality production. The main director Magdalena Łazarkiewicz, as well as the supporting directors Katarzyna Adamik and Olga Chajdas, are already known and appreciated for their previous work. Among the actors are both young generation stars like Marcin Dorociński and Katarzyna Maciąg and older, well-known TV personalities, such as Teresa Budzisz-Krzyżanowska.

Głęboka Woda was financed from the funds of Project 1.18, "Creating and developing standards of social assistance and integration", launched by the Ministry of Labour and Social Policy. The project itself is based on the Human Capital Operational Programme, Action 1.2: "System support to institutions of social assistance and social integration." According to the rules of the project published on the website of the Ministry, the main objective was "to raise professionalism and increase efficiency of social assistance and social integration in solving the problem of social exclusion by means of development, testing and implementation of the standards for institutions, assistance services and social integration".[24]

It is worth finding out if this objective has been achieved starting with a content analysis of all the *Głęboka Woda* episodes and then examining audience measurement data. Finally, the results of the author's qualitative research are presented.

---

[22] See: *"Głęboka Woda"—serial z misją*, http://www.mpips.gov.pl/aktualnosci-wszystkie/pomoc-spoleczna/art,5595,gleboka-woda-serial-z-misja.html (accessed January 22, 2012).

[23] The storyline of "Głęboka woda" is concentrated on ordinary work of social assistance workers. See: J. Duda, *List Sekretarza Stanu Jarosława Dudy do Pracowników Socjalnych*, http://www.mpips.gov.pl/gfx/mpips/userfiles/File/Aktualnosci/Pomoc%20spoleczna/Gleboka_woda_03.06.11.pdf (accessed January 24, 2012).

[24] See: http://standardypomocy.pl/portal/strona/pid/2386.html (accessed March 1, 2012).

Content Analysis

The series contains thirteen episodes. The first one was aired on December 4, 2011 and the last one on February 26, 2012. Here the focus is only on the important social topics presented. As a unit of analysis, a "thread" is used. It is meant as a part of the story which is clearly distinguishable and contains at least one social problem. It is possible to distinguish between the main threads, which appear in almost every episode, and other threads, which are usually developed in one episode only.

The storyline is composed of six main threads:

(1) The everyday life of a social assistance centre (financial support, problems etc.).
(2) Family relations (broken families, young couples etc.).
(3) Poverty.
(4) Addictions.
(5) People with physical or mental disabilities.
(6) An internet-based civic TV station.

In Table 28.1 below, all particular threads that were important parts of the storyline are noted. All parts of the storyline which were not related to any social problem (e.g. irrelevant interpersonal relations) are skipped. The table does not contain every social problem mentioned in the series but only those which were broadly discussed (e.g. not every addiction is mentioned, and particular appearances of a civic TV station reporter are skipped).

Table 28.1. Threads (social problems) in episodes 1–13

E1: "Big water" (pilot)	E2: "Return"	E3: "Cult teacher"	E4: "Buddies"	E5: "Palace of the homeless"	E6: "Blue card"	E7: "The role of life"	E8: "Family secrets"
Flood victims	Euro-orphans	Alcoholism	Drug addiction	Illegal alcohol	Domestic violence	Illegal work	Old Age Problems
Cumbersome bureaucracy standards	Single mothers	School violence	Mental diseases	Homelessness	Alcoholism	Slavery	Relations between parents and their grown-up children
Alcoholism	Ex-prisoners	Unfair image of social work in media	Disablity	Missing people	Marital rape	Rapes	
Love for animals versus low standard of living	Support groups	Support groups	Alimony	Nationalization of assets	Disabled people	Mental diseases	
Disability							
Problematic behavior of social assistance employees							

E9: "Tolerated stay"	E10: "Euro-orphans"	E11: "The professional photographer"	E12: "Dogs"	E13: "It's getting clearer"
Artificial insemination	Euro-orphans	Disability	Poor children in a school	Fire disaster
The Romani and their social problems	Elderly people without assistance	War crimes	Mental diseases	Private charitable foundations
Immigration problems	Forced-labor camps	Artificial insemination	Dog fighting	Disability
Rape	Mental diseases	Relations between parents and their grown-up children		Unemployment and family relations (parent-child, marital)
Diseases of elderly people				
Disability				

The number of social issues in the series in question is overwhelming. On average, an episode contains four different threads. This is too much from at least two points of view. The first is related to a psychological burden which every spectator has to face. *Głęboka Woda* seems to be an extremely serious and difficult programme. Furthermore, this accumulation of different social issues lowers the perceived level of reality in the series. It is highly unlikely that all these events would happen in real life, at once. Moreover, in the series this can be understood as a huge idea placement, there are a lot of "sub-placements" (such as La Strada and ITAKA foundations).

Another remark is related to the political significance of *Głęboka Woda*. Although it promotes social work, it is controversial from the feminist perspective. An attentive spectator can identify a few scenes that should be referred to as reinforcing stereotypes. For example, in the second episode, Wiktor tells his son "not to smoke in presence of girls because they don't like it". Is this a universal truth? How can it be proved? It seems to be a rather unreasonable generalization. In episode seven, in turn, one of the characters is praised with the extremely sexist phrase "you've got balls". It is also noticeable that characters do not use feminine or neutral names of professions (e.g. a "police officer" instead of a "policeman"). What is more, social pathologies such as alcoholism are exclusively male problems.

In this context, one may regard *Głęboka Woda* as an instrument of democracy, but one understood in a very narrow sense. Whereas the work of social assistants is depicted in detail, the producers do not bother themselves with solving fragile gender-related issues.

Audience Measurement

Previous observations have been confirmed by the results of audience measurement. According to the numbers obtained by Nielsen Audience Measurement, the first three episodes have been watched by 2.18 million people. It was 14.38 % of all viewers in the group 4+ and 11.26 % in the group 16–49. In previous year, the same programme strip in the analogical period in TVP2 gathered 2.7 million people and its market share was respectively 17.51 % (4+) and 15.07 % (16–49).[25]

[25] *"Głęboka woda" przegrywa z filmami i serialami zagranicznymi*, Homepage "Wirtualne Media.pl", http://www.wirtualnemedia.pl/artykul/gleboka-woda-przegrywa-z-filmami-i-serialami-zagranicznymi (accessed January 26, 2012).

In 2012, TVP2 lost the competition with commercial channels, despite the fact that they did not air any premiere. Polsat, which leads in this strip (16.33 % in 4+ group), chose "CSI. Miami" and TVN (second, 15.51 %) aired dramas and repeated episodes of their series *Przepis na Życie* [Receipt for Life]. Another public channel, TVP1, got even worse results by broadcasting older TV dramas only.[26]

This data is consistent with the assumption that *Głęboka Woda* is not attractive enough to become a successful production. Nevertheless, the idea of promoting social values using a TV series is not doomed to failure by itself. A recipe for disaster is rather an overwhelming number of social-related threads mixed with a naive didacticism and an uninteresting storyline.

Rural Women's Voice

Within a broader research project conducted by the author, two questions concerning reception of *Głęboka Woda* have been posed to sixteen women who lived in three post-PGR villages: Waliły-Stacja in the Podlaskie Voivodship as well as Jodłownik and Szczyrzyc in the Małopolskie Voivodship. The sample has been rather small and unrepresentative because the whole project was planned as a qualitative case study of socially excluded women. Moreover, this was only an initial phase of the project. The respondents were heterogeneous as far as their age, level of education, confession and current material situation were concerned. The most important connective factor was their social environment as well as, given the subject of this study, the fact that all of them are heavy television viewers.

The first question was: "Have you ever seen an episode of *Głęboka Woda*?" The second one had a strictly quantitative character. It concerned each respondent's impressions of the series.

---

[26] Ibid.

Fig. 28.3. Have you ever seen an episode of *Głęboka Woda* (2011)?

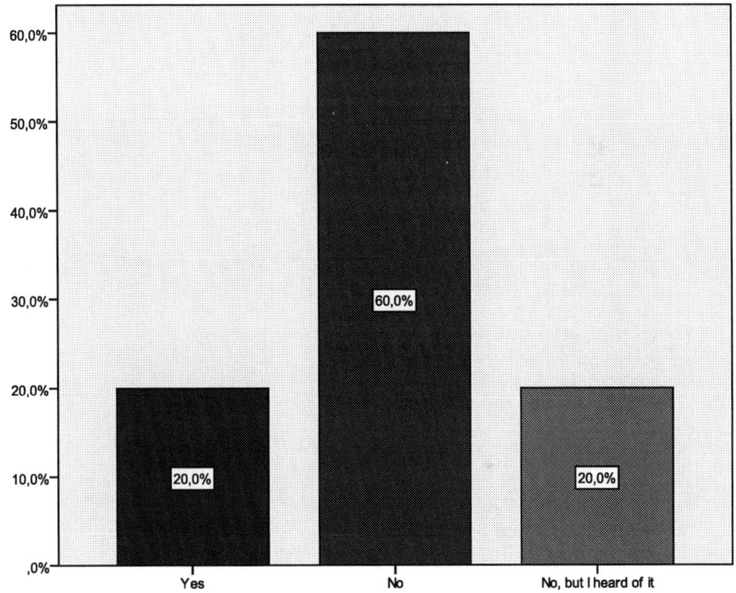

Results from case study of Polish rural women.

The answers to the first question are visualized in the Fig.28.3 above. Only 20 % of the respondents admit to have seen at least one episode. Despite the unrepresentative character of the sample, it is reasonable to say that *Głęboka Woda* is unpopular among the social category in question due to the fact that the interviewed women watch regularly only a few TV series. If they do not know *Głęboka Woda*, then it cannot be a popular series.[27] Moreover, a comparison with the answers presented in Fig. 28.3 with those from Table 28.2 below, which concerns the popularity of major TV series, shows that the most popular one, *M jak miłość*, is regularly watched by almost all respondents (93 %). Other series' popularity is less spectacular. It is crucial that those numbers refer to regular viewers only whereas the data concerning *Głęboka Woda* embraces also incidental spectators.

[27] Maybe an adoption of *Głęboka Woda* must take time (the premiere was in December).

Table 28.2. Audience of major Polish TV series (in sample).

Title	Spectators
M jak miłość	**93.3 %**
Barwy szczęścia	**60.0 %**
Na dobre i na złe	**33.3 %**
Na Wspólnej	20.0 %
Klan	20.0 %
Ojciec Mateusz	20.0 %
Ratownicy	13.3 %

One of the answers to the second question is particularly intriguing. The respondent said that, although the series is "good", it is unrealistic. Focused on alcoholism, she said that they are "up to date with alcoholism", and it was not depicted well in the series.

Many respondents pointed out that they had never seen *Głęboka Woda* but they had heard about it. There have been several trailers which apparently grabbed their attention. Therefore, one can conclude that despite the informational campaign, this particular series has not been an efficient means to promote social values.

Conclusion

This chapter has tried to prove that the idea placement used in the case of the series *Głęboka Woda* has been unsuccessful. The production has fallen into the trap of naivety, and it also seems to be too didactic. Nonetheless, it does not mean that every idea placement is ineffective. Two conditions have to be fulfilled in order to promote socially useful content. First of all, a series (or a movie) must be realistic. Moreover, it must be interesting. It is highly unlikely that such a serious and somber series as *Głęboka Woda* will ever be a real success. Money and good staff are important, but they are not more important than the basic concept of the series.

Previous Polish experiences with idea placement in really popular series such as *M jak miłość* shows that a successful idea placement is feasible. Maybe it is better to put one important issue into an already existing series or movie than to create a new one.

It is also worth noting that some scenes of *Głęboka Woda* are sexist. It is to be believed that any TV series aiming to improve the social world should be aware of all discriminated groups. The producers of *Głęboka Woda* did not take gender relations among their characters into consideration and it is definitely one of the most important drawbacks of this series.

It is not a goal of this chapter to examine the concept of idea placement from an ethical point of view. Perhaps further ethical investigations are needed because it is not clear what the major difference between such placements and propaganda is. For now, it may be regarded as laying in a connotation. Idea placement is usually related to democratic countries, in contrast to propaganda, which has rather undemocratic verbal associations. Nevertheless, one may equal those two mechanisms. This is a perfect topic for social historians, ethicists and political scientists.

The author is sociologist and philosopher, a trainee assistant at the University of Science and Technology in Cracow as well as a Ph.D. student at the Jagiellonian University. He is interested in sociology of culture and visual studies.